THE LABOUR GOVERNMENT
1945-51

THE LABOUR GOVERNMENT
1945-51

by

D. N. PRITT

1963
LAWRENCE & WISHART
LONDON

Printed in Great Britain by
The Camelot Press Ltd., London and Southampton

Preface

THIS book needs little explanation. It speaks for itself, and the tale it has to tell is simple, if pretty disquieting.

Although I lived close to the events I have to relate, as a member of the Parliament of 1945-50, I did not grasp the full tragedy of the story until I came, a decade later, to marshal the facts, look at them as a whole, and put them down on paper.

I could not have marshalled the facts, and got the story before me as a chronological whole, without the continuous help in research of Mrs. Kitty Cornforth. Nor could I have seen the story so clearly without the valuable contributions provided by the writings of my friends Mr. and Mrs. Coates, in Vol. II of their *History of Anglo-Soviet Relations*, and of Palme Dutt, R. Page Arnot, Quaestor, J. R. Campbell and others in the columns of *Labour Monthly*.

D. N. PRITT

The publishers gratefully acknowledge the permission of the following for quotations included in this book:

George Allen & Unwin Ltd.—*Parliamentary Socialism*, by E. Miliband; and *The Cold War and its Origins*, by D. F. Fleming.

Martin Secker & Warburg Ltd.—*The Cautious Revolution*, by E. Watkins.

William Heinemann Ltd. of London and A. S. Barnes and Company of New York—*A Prime Minister Remembers*, by Francis Williams.

The University of California Press—*Crisis in Britain*, by R. A. Brady

Contents

CHAPTER 1

1945: The War Ends

WHAT was the background against which the 1945 General Election was fought, resulting in a great Labour Party victory and the formation of the first Labour Government with an absolute majority?

The Second World War, which had lasted for a little less than six years, was over in Europe; the war in Japan was not over, and was—quite wrongly as it turned out—expected to last for a further year or more. Britain had been greatly impoverished in the war, not only by human losses—which were bad enough, if far lower than in the First World War—but also by financial, economic and industrial exhaustion and the destruction of many houses, factories and other buildings. Mobilisation for war purposes had been carried so far that there were few people, and very few factories, that would not have wholly to change their work in the forthcoming transition from war to peace.

Much of the world outside Britain had undergone similar losses and changes—with in some cases much heavier damage than we had—and there were acute shortages, both local and general, of vital necessities, particularly foodstuffs.

Whatever government was to be elected to rule in Britain was certain to face many formidable tasks of reconstruction, and to have crucial decisions of policy to take, both at home and abroad; among those decisions would be: what was to be done with Germany and the German people, and what relations Britain should develop with the great socialist state, the U.S.S.R., then universally praised (in public) and recognised as having borne the heaviest burden in the war and made the greatest contribution to victory.

Part of the background was, of course, the people of Britain. What was their record in the war? By and large, they had behaved magnificently, both in civilian life and in the armed forces; all their best qualities—courage, patience, endurance, honesty and adaptability—had been well in evidence; and if the army had once again been a "collection of lions led by asses", the lions had at any rate behaved like lions.

THE MOOD OF THE PEOPLE

A more important question was, what was the mood of the British people as the war drew to an end? Were they likely to face their post-war problems with the same partial apathy that before the war had at times allowed governments to get away with worse than murder? This question should perhaps be answered separately for the armed forces and for the civilians, although when the analysis is made I think the moods were essentially the same. (After all, when a whole population is mobilised, those in uniform and those out of it are the same people, as a shrewd young constituent of mine, at a meeting where we were discussing possible conflicts of interest and outlook between men in the forces and men at home, remarked: "This soldier you're all being so puzzled about is in fact the bloke who lives next door.")

Well, what was the mood? Taking the civilian population first—although I had so much to do with the troops that I was at times called "The M.P. for the forces", I was a civilian myself, and saw more of the civilians—I think they formed their mood in the opportunities for discussion which, although they worked long hours under great inconveniences, war-time conditions created for them. In factories, air-raid shelters, air-raid defence and rescue posts, and elsewhere, they did a great deal of thinking and talking, and a good many intelligent and politically conscious people among them helped their thinking very much. Through all the propaganda they saw the horrors and hardships of war; they recollected too the horrors and hardships that peace-time life in the slumps of the 'thirties had given many of them. They had shaken off much of their indifference to politics, and had decided that they wanted no more of these hardships and horrors, and would get themselves a different kind of government to shape their future, so as to avoid such calamities; and a different kind of government in the context of those days meant inevitably a Labour government. I happened to learn, a year or two before the end of the war, that the Home Office "experts" in public morale, who had always seemed to me to be extremely ignorant and foolish, as well as reactionary—they had, for example, taken the public demand for a "Second Front" in Europe in 1943 and 1944 as proof of a panicky collapse in morale!—were greatly alarmed by the opportunities afforded by air-raid arrangements to masses of "ordinary people" to get together and talk; they thought that this was most dangerous, and felt, I was told, that it might lead many people to vote Labour or Communist. They proved to be right for once.

THE MOOD OF THE FORCES

As for the mood of the forces, they had even more experience of the horrors of war, and more opportunity to think and talk. And the pamphlets and discussion classes arranged by the Army Education Corps and the Army Bureau of Current Affairs undoubtedly encouraged them to think and talk politically, in spite of the elaborate efforts of the War Office to ensure that all the education and discussion and reading they should get was "safe". The war was, moreover, both for the forces and civilians, easily seen to be more a political war than most previous wars; it was an anti-fascist war, and the one socialist state had played a tremendous part in it.

If that was the record and mood of the people, what is to be said of those who were destined to form the government? At first sight, it might seem that what they had thought or done between 1939 and 1945, whilst important enough, would not be crucial in its bearing on future events, however much it might incline voters to decide the issue of the election one way or the other. But in truth what the more important leaders had been doing was crucial; for they had been members of the Coalition Government for five years, sharing in its activities, decisions and responsibilities, and to a great extent absorbing its atmosphere.

Whilst the Chamberlain government, which lasted until June, 1940, was largely composed of "men of Munich", by no means anti-fascist or in earnest about the war, and bitterly anti-Soviet, the Coalition Government formed by Churchill was at any rate in the main anti-Nazi and genuinely set on winning the war, in spite of the unsatisfactory elements which survived in it from the days of Chamberlain. But it was nevertheless so anti-Soviet that it was scheming until a very late stage to "slant" the main strategy of the war so as to make the U.S.S.R. emerge from the war as weak as possible, and thus have no effective say in the shaping of the post-war world, which that government hoped to make as capitalist and as anti-socialist as possible. It was with this object in view that Winston Churchill worked so hard and so long both to delay the opening of a Second Front in Western Europe and—if possible—to substitute for such a Front some other large strategic move, either in Africa or in South-Eastern Europe.

It has only gradually become public knowledge—as distinct from intelligent suspicion—how hard Churchill and his government worked against the U.S.S.R. throughout the war. In a memorandum written in October 1942, five months after the signature of the Anglo-Soviet Treaty of Friendship, and at a time when the Red Army was fighting against great odds, with the agony of Stalingrad approaching, he wrote:

> "I must admit that my thoughts rest primarily in Europe—the revival of the glory of Europe, the parent Continent of the modern nations and of civilisation. It would be a measureless disaster if Russian barbarism overlaid the culture and independence of the ancient states of Europe. Hard as it is to say now, I trust that the European family may act united as one under a Council of Europe."

This "Europe", plainly, included Germany, Spain and Mussolini's Italy, but excluded the U.S.S.R. It is curious how he was unconsciously echoing Hitler, who had said in 1936, at the Nuremberg rally:

> "If [Bolshevist] methods succeed . . . European culture . . . would be superseded by the most frightful barbarism of all times."

It would be too long to relate the endless manœuvres by which the Churchill Government sought to defeat the whole Second Front strategy,* and I need only add one other incident, related by Churchill himself:

> "Even before the war had ended and while the Germans were surrendering by hundreds of thousands, I telegraphed to Lord Montgomery directing him to be careful in collecting German arms to stack them so that they could easily be issued again to the German soldiers *whom we should have to work with if the Soviet advance continued.*"

(In other words, the government was ready, if the Soviet forces did no more than advance westwards in their task of destroying the Nazi armies, to reissue arms to surrendered Nazis, and to march with them in war against their Soviet allies.) Point is lent to this disclosure by another (Eisenhower, *Crusade in Europe*, pp. 396-403, quoted by Fleming, op. cit., at p. 214) to the effect that from the 29th March to the 7th April, 1945, Churchill was "fighting a sustained engagement with Eisenhower and the American Chiefs of Staff . . . with the object of throwing General Montgomery forward in a dash to capture Berlin before the nearby Russians could do so".

---

* The story is related in two articles entitled "Diplomatic History of the Second Front", published in *International Affairs* in 1961, and at greater length in *The Cold War and its Origins*, by D. F. Fleming (G. Allen & Unwin, Ltd., 1961).

THE ATTITUDE OF LABOUR LEADERS

Attlee, Bevin, Cripps and other Labour leaders had lived and worked under Churchill all through the war years. Exactly how much of the anti-Soviet atmosphere they absorbed can be gauged by their subsequent conduct. Perhaps they resisted—if in vain—all the anti-Soviet strategy? If they did, they have not told us so; on the contrary Attlee wrote in his autobiography, *As it Happened*:

"I have very pleasant memories of working with my colleagues in the [Coalition] Government. It was very seldom that any Party issue arose to divide us, until the last stage, when I think they were designedly fomented by certain persons. Usually, applying our minds to the actual problems which faced us, we came to an agreement as to what was the best course."

Were Churchill's manœuvres to postpone the opening of the Second Front something that Attlee and his Labour colleagues regarded as "the best course" to deal with the "actual problems", in spite of the strong opposition to them manifested by Roosevelt? One has to wonder even more when Attlee adds:

"Quite naturally, in war, when the public good must take precedence over private interests, the solutions had a strong socialist flavour."

The same "reconciling" operation may have had its effect on Stafford Cripps, who, as his biographer wrote, "had worked with men of other political beliefs than his own; he counted them among his personal friends . . . he appreciated the high principles and personal qualities of his Conservative friends".

It was perhaps one effect of the atmosphere of collaboration just described that, when the war in Europe was over and it became possible to hold a General Election to replace a parliament elected (on a fraudulent pretence of "serving collective security") almost ten years earlier, a number of the Labour leaders in the government were willing and anxious to postpone the election for a period of months, or even a year or so, in order to enable the early stages of post-war transition and reconstruction to be carried on by the Coalition Government (in which the Tories had always been powerful enough to resist any reform that was not clearly and urgently demanded by the mass of the people, on the plea that nothing "controversial"—i.e. unpalatable to the Tory Party—could be undertaken so long as the Coalition Government existed). This attitude is at once revealing and horrifying, for the

Labour Party and its leaders ought surely at that stage to have been thinking and saying: "We want a socialist government at once. We want to replace a government supporting the whole rotten war-breeding system of capitalism by one which will immediately set about laying the foundations of a better, a socialist, system. We want to have all the urgent post-war problems at home and abroad dealt with by ourselves, by a socialist government, on socialist principles, in collaboration with the socialist Soviet Union, which commands the affection, the gratitude, and the admiration of the great majority of people both at home and abroad. We have a splendid opportunity, at this very moment, to capture the imagination, the enthusiasm, and the votes of the millions in and outside the armed forces who equally want an end of the old conditions. The whole capitalist set-up will for some time be so fearful, weak, and unstable that after a general election victory a really vigorous push will topple it over easily and peacefully, making us free to start building socialism at once. We must therefore get swiftly into the election battle, and ride home to victory; then we will tackle both the battle for socialism and all the immense economic and administrative problems that confront us, with the knowledge that we are dealing with them on socialist lines, with the voters behind us."

But this was not the mood of the leaders. Attlee, like Churchill, wanted the Coalition Government to continue until the end of the war with Japan, which was expected to last for a substantial time, perhaps eighteen months. Herbert Morrison and others wanted to let the Coalition run on for another five months, in order to fight the election on the new register which would come into force in October, 1945. The National Executive of the Labour Party was convinced—in my view rightly—that the mass of the Labour Party would not brook much delay—certainly not beyond October. Accordingly Attlee wrote to Churchill urging an October election.

Churchill refused this, and decided to resign at once, which he did on the 23rd May, in the middle of the Labour Party Conference, which was held at Blackpool on the 21st-25th May. (It has become almost a Tory tradition to produce elections or changes of government at the moment of Labour Party Conference, and this move of Churchill's was a sign that the forthcoming election campaign was to be fought—if the Tories had their way—on the old traditional lines of a half-hysterical slanging match.)

A "caretaker" government of mostly undistinguished Tories (with some "Munichite" addition)—still led by Churchill—was formed on the 26th May, 1945, and held office for two months. Parliament was dissolved on the 15th June. Polling-day was the 5th July, but the votes were not counted until the 26th July, as the elaborate (and largely successful) arrangements to take the votes of all the armed forces involved a delay of some weeks whilst their votes were collected and brought to the constituencies.

As we shall see later, when the results were known on the 26th July, Churchill resigned, the caretaker government came to an end, and Attlee was at once invited to form a government, a task which he completed on the following day.

CHAPTER 2

Election Preparations, 1945

AGAINST that background, at that very great moment in history, the British electorate set out to choose itself a government to face all the tremendous problems I have outlined, and shape our political history for a long period. What was to be the outcome?

The election was fought—at any rate in the main, for I shall notice one remarkable difference a little later—on orthodox party political lines, with the Tories and the Labour Party, attacking each other, in the foreground, and the Liberal and Communist Parties also running candidates.

The Labour Party, nearly always an efficient election-fighting machine, went into the campaign in a pretty good state of preparation. The pamphlet *Let us Face the Future*, issued as early as April, 1945 and endorsed by the Labour Party Conference in May, was in effect its election manifesto.

"LET US FACE THE FUTURE"

This was a remarkable manifesto. Millions of electors, with a modest measure of political understanding but a very clear idea that they wanted not only peace, full and secure employment, decent housing, a better standard of living, and friendship with the Soviet Union, but also decisive social changes in a socialist direction, accepted the manifesto as a real response to their aspirations; there was much in it to justify them in doing so.

There were of course many more, with fuller political understanding, who saw that the manifesto failed to present a scientific socialist programme, and was in reality no more than an ambiguous and carefully-drawn reformist document, not socialist at all; and some of them suspected that it was the work of men who aimed at nothing more than reformism but sought the support of those who aimed at much more.

In the first section of the manifesto, "Victory in War must be followed by a prosperous peace", we were told that "after the last war the people lost the peace"—which was true enough—and that the slumps of the inter-war period were the result of too much economic power resting in the hands of too few people. That it did not go on to say that slumps were an inevitable feature of a capitalist economy, and that the war, and particularly the work of the one socialist state both before and during the war, had created a new situation in no way parallel to that of 1918-19, was of the essence of its reformist character; but many of the millions were not repelled by this.

The manifesto went on to give a warning that "anti-controllers, anti-planners" wanted to sweep away the innumerable controls that had been built up during the war (and had indeed created a very good base on which to lay the foundation of a socialist economy) in order to give profiteering interests and the "privileged rich" a free hand to plunder the rest of the nation; this was a justified warning, for the continuance of many controls for an indefinite period was essential, and the Tories were campaigning—under the banner, of course, of "freedom"—for a swift end to controls.

The manifesto went on to "What the election will be about":

"The Labour Party stands for freedom—of worship, speech, of the Press. It will see that we keep and enlarge these freedoms and enjoy again the personal liberties we sacrificed for war. The freedom of Trade Unions, denied by the Trade Disputes Act 1927, must be restored.

"But Labour will not tolerate freedom to exploit others, to pay poor wages, or to push up prices for private profit.

"The Nation needs a tremendous overhaul, a programme of modernisation, and the re-equipment of homes, factories, machinery, schools, social services.

"All parties say so—the Labour Party means it.

"The Labour Party is prepared to achieve it by drastic policies of replanning, keeping a firm constructive hand on the whole productive machinery; putting the community first and the sectional interests of private business after.

"It will plan from the ground up—giving its appropriate place to constructive enterprise and private endeavour but dealing decisively with interests which use talk about economic freedom to cloak a determination to put their wishes above those of the nation."

There was much in this to inspire the millions, however limited it might appear to the more critical and the more politically developed.

B

The only concrete pledge in this section was that the Trade Disputes Act, 1927, would be repealed. This pledge was of course carried out, as we shall see in Chapter 5.

FULL EMPLOYMENT

The pamphlet then turned to the question of full employment, something very much in the minds of everyone old enough to have lived through the 'thirties, although as we know now the problem of securing full employment—after the initial confusion of transition— proved scarcely to be a problem at all for some years to follow:

"Our opponents say 'Full employment? Yes! If we can get it without interfering too much with private industry'. We say—'a firm public hand on industry in order to get jobs for all'.

"What will the Labour Party do?

"1. The whole of our national resources, land, material and labour, must be fully employed. Production must be raised to its highest level and related to purchasing power. The standard of living depends on the ability to produce and organise the fair and generous distribution of the product.

"2. High and constant purchasing power must be maintained through good wages, social services and insurance, and taxation bearing less on lower income groups. But to maintain the value of money and savings, rents and prices of necessities will be controlled.

"3. Planned investment in essential industries and on houses, schools, hospitals and civic centres.

"A National Investment Board to determine social priorities and promote better timing in private investment.

"In suitable cases we would transfer efficient Government factories from war to peace production.

"4. The Bank of England is to be brought under public ownership, and the operations of other banks harmonised with industrial needs.

"But with the policy of full employment must go the policy of economic expansion and efficiency for a higher standard of life as set out in the next section."

Here again, the manifesto struck different readers in different ways, and satisfied millions of the less critical. The most definite pledge given here, to nationalise the Bank of England—and none of the other banks —was carried out, as will be seen in Chapter 5. It could mean much or little, according to the way it was operated.

The manifesto continued:

"4. *Industry in the service of the nation*

"Each industry must have applied to it the test of national service. If it serves the nation, well and good, if it is inefficient, the nation must see things are put right.

"The Labour Party is a Socialist Party—its ultimate purpose at home is a Socialist Commonwealth—free, democratic, efficient, progressive, public spirited—its material resources organised in the service of the people.

"But Socialism cannot come overnight.

"There are basic industries ripe for public ownership, there are many smaller businesses rendering good service which can be left to go on with their useful work.

"There are big industries not yet ripe for public ownership, which must be required by constructive supervision to further the nation's needs, and not to prejudice national interests by restrictive monopoly or cartel agreements.

NATIONALISATION (WITH LIMITS)

"The Labour Party submits the following industrial programme:

"1. *Public ownership of fuel and power industries*

"The Coal industry has been floundering chaotically for a quarter of a century, with many hundreds of independent companies.

"Amalgamation under public ownership will bring economies in operation, make modernisation of production methods possible, and the raising of safety standards.

"Public ownership of gas and electricity will lower charges, prevent competitive waste, open the way for co-ordinated research and development, and lead to the reforming of uneconomic areas of distribution.

"Other industries will benefit.

"2. *Public ownership of inland transport*

"Co-ordination of transport services by rail, road, air, and canal, requires unification. This, without public ownership, means a struggle with sectional interests or the enthronement of a private monopoly which would be a menace to the rest of industry.

"3. *Public ownership of iron and steel*

"Private monopoly has maintained high prices and kept inefficient high-cost plants in existence. Only if public ownership replaces private monopoly can the industry become efficient.

"These socialised industries are to be taken over on the basis of fair compensation, and to be conducted efficiently in the interests of consumers, coupled with proper status and conditions for workers employed in them.

"4. *Public supervision of monopolies and cartels*

"With the aim of advancing industrial efficiency. Prohibition of anti-social restrictive practices.

"5. *Firm and clear cut programme for the export trade*

"State help in any necessary form to get the export trade on its feet and enable it to pay for essential food and raw materials. But State help on condition that industry is efficient.

"6. *Suitable economic and price controls*

"To secure that first things come first in the transition from war to peace and fair play for all, including the demobilised, priorities in use of raw materials, food prices must be held, homes before mansions, necessities before luxuries. No boom followed by collapse as after the last war. It is sound economic controls—or smash.

"7. *Better organisation of Government departments and Civil Service*

"The Government must spur industry forward, not choke it with red tape."

Here, too, many would be inspired, and others disquieted. That "the Labour Party is a Socialist party" was splendid; but its Socialist purpose was "ultimate". That Socialism "cannot come overnight" was perfectly true, but to many that was no reason for not making a quicker and bolder start on the journey. Nationalisation, to many people, is socialist; but in truth the value of any measure depends on its character and conditions, and nationalisation in itself is not either socialism or a guarantee of socialist advance.

There is, moreover, in this section of the manifesto, a hint of something which soon became—indeed, to some extent, had already become—Labour Party policy; namely that efficient industries should be left free to go on running under private management for private profit, whilst inefficient ones should be nationalised, to the concealed delight of their owners and the relative disadvantage of the community, which would gradually become a sort of hospital for sick industries.

As we shall see, a high proportion of the pledges given in this section were carried out—on terms; the details, with such vital points as terms of compensation and the running of the administration of the nationalised industries, will be dealt with later.

AGRICULTURE

The next section of the manifesto covered "Agriculture and the People's Food", and proclaimed the need for "prosperous and efficient agriculture ensuring a fair return for the farmer and the farm worker without excessive prices to the consumer". It foresaw no interference with the elaborate "three-decker" capitalist system of land ownership and cultivation, beyond a threat—or a promise—that if a landlord could not or would not provide "proper facilities" for his tenant farmers the State would take over his land at a fair valuation.

HOUSING

Then came the vital matter of housing, which had been acutely short for the whole of the century and of course had become much worse during the war, by destruction, obsolescence, and arrears of repairs. Housing has probably been the subject of more promises by more governments and aspirants for government than any other human need. What the Labour Party said about it at this vital stage was:

"6. *Houses and the building programme*

"Everybody says we must have houses. But the Labour Party will take the necessary steps—a programme of land planning and drastic action for an efficient building industry which will neither burden the community with a crippling financial load nor impose bad conditions and unemployment on its workers.

"No restrictive price rings.

"Modern methods and materials.

"A due balance between housing, school building and factory modernisation and construction.

"Labour's pledge is firm and direct—it will proceed with a housing programme with the maximum practical speed till every family has a good standard of accommodation.

"This may well mean centralised purchasing and pooling of building materials and components by the State, together with price control.

"Housing should be related to town planning—pleasant surroundings, attractive lay-out, and efficient utility services, including necessary transport facilities.

"There should be a Ministry of Housing and Planning combining the housing powers of the Ministry of Health with the planning powers of the Ministry of Town and Country Planning, and

Government policy to enable the Ministry of Works to act as an efficient instrument in the service of all departments with building needs and of the nation as a whole."

This, although encouraging at first reading, was pretty vague, in the face of the crying need for houses; but, as we shall see, the Government was led from a pretty early date to cut down on housing in order to finance armaments.

LAND

Next came land, out of whose rising values colossal private fortunes were destined to be made in the years and decades to follow.

Here, in this old field of socialist and even of Liberal aspirations, the manifesto said no more than that "Labour believes in land national-isation and will *work towards it*", whilst a "radical solution" was to be sought for the "*crippling problems* of land acquisition and use".

There was also a promise of "revenue for public funds" from "better-ment" (i.e. the increase in land values brought about by improvements to other land, or by developments of public utilities); but in the end nothing was done to achieve this.

EDUCATION

Education was covered by a short paragraph promising that the Education Act of 1944 would be put into practical effect, including the raising of the school-leaving age to 16 at the earliest possible moment, further or adult education, and free secondary education for all.

HEALTH

Health and the social services were dealt with thus:

"9. *Health of the Nation and its Children*

"Good food and homes can prevent avoidable ill health. Also, the best health services should be available for all. Money must no longer be the passport to the best treatment.

"In the new National Health Service there should be health centres providing the best that science can offer, more and better hospitals, proper conditions for doctors and nurses. More research into the causes of disease and the methods of prevention and cure.

"Labour will work specially for the care of mothers and children—children's allowances, school medical and feeding services, better maternity and child welfare services.

SOCIAL INSURANCE

"10. *Social Insurance Against the Rainy Day*

"The Labour Government will press on rapidly with legislation extending social insurance over the necessary wide field to all.

"But great national programmes of education, health and social services are costly. They require full employment and highest industrial efficiency."

This was perhaps the most inspiring declaration, thoroughly responsive to the mood of the people.

Comment can wait for the account of the legislation carried out in these fields.

FOREIGN POLICY

Then came the particularly important matter of foreign policy:

"11. *A world of progress and peace*

"We must make sure that Germany and Japan are deprived of the power to make war again. We must consolidate in peace the great war-time association of the British Commonwealth with the U.S.A. and the U.S.S.R. Let it not be forgotten that in the years leading up to the war the Tories were so scared of Russia that they missed the chance to establish a partnership which might well have prevented the war.

"We must join with France and China and all who have contributed to the common victory in forming an International Organisation capable of keeping the peace. An internationally protected peace should make possible a known expenditure on armaments as our contribution, which should diminish as the world becomes accustomed to the prohibition of war through effective collective security.

"Essentials for prosperity for the world are high production and progressive efficiency, with steady improvement in the standard of life, an increase in effective demand, and fair shares for all who contribute to the wealth of their community. We should build a new United Nations, allies in a new war on hunger, ignorance and want.

"The British must be brave and constructive leaders in international affairs.

"The British Labour Movement has a great asset—its common bond with the working people of all countries who have achieved new influence through the struggle against Nazi tyranny.

"The Labour Party will seek to promote mutual understanding and cordial co-operation between the Dominions of the British Commonwealth, responsible self-government for India, and the planned progress of our Colonial Dependencies."

This was excellent; no one could complain of these passages, however much they had—as we shall see later—to complain of the way in which most of the promises contained in them were broken.

COLONIAL PROBLEMS

The last paragraph of the manifesto, quoted above, dealt with colonial problems in their widest sense. The more socialist among us would certainly have preferred the Labour Party, notwithstanding its earlier acceptance and indeed support of the colonial system, to condemn outright the whole system, which was as we now know destined to die off at incredible speed in the next two decades; it is a vivid illustration of the rapidity of development that even as late as this the Labour Party offered to India no more than "responsible self-government"— with which her people, who were to force complete independence within two years, were not likely to be impressed. "The planned progress of our colonial dependencies", too, was no more than the commonplace of all British governments who have wanted to retain the colonies as dependencies.

The manifesto concluded with an appeal:

"12. *Labour's call to all progressives*
"The effective choice in this election will be between the Conservative Party, standing for the protection of the 'rights' of private economic interest, and the Labour Party, allied with the great Trade Union and Co-operative Movements, standing for wise organisation and use of the economic assets of the nation for the public good.
"This is the fundamental issue.
"We appeal to all of progressive outlook, who believe in constructive change, to support the Labour Party."

LABOUR PARTY CONFERENCE

As I mentioned above, *Let us Face the Future* was adopted by the Annual Conference in May, 1945; but even at that moment, when everyone would want maximum unity in the face of the great opportunity to defeat the Tory enemy, there was plenty in the debates to show that the Left wing wanted to go much further.

Denis Healey, in a speech which would not be easily recognised as his by those who know only his later activities, insisted that "the Labour Party should have a clear foreign policy of its own, which is completely different from that of the Tory Party". He referred to the countries of eastern and southern Europe, which had already been liberated from Nazis and their own fascist ruling-classes, and said that the socialist revolution had already begun in Europe and was already established in those countries. He concluded that "the crucial principle of our foreign policy should be to protect, assist, encourage and aid in every way that socialist revolution wherever it appears. . . . The upper classes in every country are selfish, depraved, dissolute and decadent. These upper classes look to the British Army and the British people to protect them against the just wrath of the people who have been fighting underground against them for the past four years. We must see that that does not happen."

Ernest Bevin, replying to the debate, threw cold water on this proposal. He did not know, of course, that there would soon be a Labour Government, with himself as Foreign Secretary; but he did know that already, many months before, he had been a party to the Government decision to send the British Army to Greece to defend the upper classes there against the just wrath of the people. And, as we shall see, he was destined to carry on that Coalition policy in relation to Greece.

It is worth recalling, in passing, that at this Conference, a motion for unity with the Communist Party was defeated by only 1,219,000 to 1,134,000 votes.

We know now that the Labour Party—or at any rate the leadership that spoke for it—did not stand essentially for socialism. But the manifesto, in spite of its defects, was amply sufficient to encourage the electorate to believe that the Labour Party was offering what it wanted; and it accepted it. It had in fact already largely made up its mind to vote Labour.

CHAPTER 3

The Election Campaign, 1945

LABOUR and Tories alike set out to fight the election campaign on the traditional lines of programmes and promises, but there were two remarkable departures from custom. This first was that all efforts at "scares" failed. The Tories have never fought a General Election without producing one sensational scare—like the famous Zinoviev letter forgery—at some stage (generally too late to give time to expose the falsity of the scare and deprive it of effect). Their object has been to secure, by frightening a sufficient number of electors, a victory which they would not have won three weeks before or three weeks after, and thus to obtain the "consent" of the electorate to their governing the country for the next five years: their methods, if applied to, say, an issue of shares, would have led to the conviction of the ringleaders for obtaining money by false pretences. (This method of electioneering is part of what they call democracy.) On this occasion, not just one but three or four scares were tried one after another, and all failed; the most prominent of them was the story that Professor Laski was going to lead a violent revolution to establish socialism, by means of a Gestapo.

THE QUIET ELECTORATE

The second departure was that the electors, at any rate according to my own experience in my constituency and all the reports I received from others, were extremely quiet; superficially, one might have thought, both at public meetings and elsewhere, that they were simply not interested in this very vital election. The truth was, as I held at the time and many other observers agree, that they were extremely interested, and that they were quiet only because, for the most part, they had already thought things out and made up their minds. This was clearly the reason for their rejection one by one of all the scares.

The Tories sought to build their campaign on the lines that there was a terrible "threat" of socialism, which must be averted at all costs, and thus went far to establish the proposition that the Labour victory that was to come was a victory and a mandate for socialism. One bright side-feature of the election was the vigour and efficiency with which Attlee scored off Churchill in an exchange of correspondence on various acute issues that arose in the course of the campaign.

UNEXPECTED VICTORY

One particularly interesting feature of the election—apart from the result!—was the Labour leaders' misjudgment of the prospects of victory. Several of them told me privately that they expected to lose. Mr. Attlee, as one can see from *A Prime Minister Remembers*, by Francis Williams (Heinemann, 1961) told Molotov at the first stage of the Potsdam Conference that the result would be "a close thing"; privately, he told his friends that he expected the Tories "to pull it off"; and the general view of Tory, Liberal and Labour headquarters was that it would be a very near thing. Winston Churchill himself thought the Tories would win by between 30 and 80.

For myself, with pretty close contacts with the Labour Party, many trade union branches, and the armed forces, not only in London but in many other parts of the country, I never doubted that Labour would win, with a working majority; but I did not expect so large a majority as actually emerged.

The Labour Party had 209 net gains; they only lost two seats, one in Wales where various personal factors influenced the result, and the other in North Hammersmith, which they reckoned as a "loss" because it had been held at the 1935 election by myself as the official Labour Party candidate, and retained by me at this election as an independent; technically it could be counted as a "loss", but in reality all those who voted for me were Labour Party people who preferred me to the official candidate, and the Labour vote as a whole was in fact more than doubled.

The "swing" of votes over the whole country was about 12 per cent. something much larger than it sounds; the Labour Party had 392 seats, and its overall majority was 180. The Tories, in spite of all their efforts to scare the electorate and to cash in on the immense prestige of Winston Churchill (whom they had earlier spent two decades in an almost successful effort to destroy as a political figure), wound up with 189 seats, their smallest number since their great defeat in 1906.

WHY LABOUR WON

The victory was due to a variety of causes; one important one certainly was that the electorate, as I have already said, had made up its mind what it wanted; and the great popularity of the Soviet people, and the recognition of the overwhelming part they had played in the military victory, led many electors to vote Labour in the belief—to be proved tragically to be unfounded—that the Labour Party would abide by the policy of friendship for the U.S.S.R., and thus advance peace and progress in the world.

The electorate was plainly ahead of the Labour leaders in its political thinking, and in its desire for socialism and for friendship with the Soviet Union. I am attracted by the thesis developed by Mr. Ralph Miliband, in his book, *Parliamentary Socialism, a Study in the Politics of Labour* (G. Allen & Unwin, 1961) that one should really regard the new era in British history that was, or ought to have been, associated with the Labour victory as beginning in 1940 rather than in 1945, in that a new popular radicalism developed under war conditions, of which the Labour Party was the "electoral beneficiary", and that the high degree of social and economic planning developed in the war, with pretty remarkable success, helped forward the socialist cause by showing that such planning could work well, and could ensure improvements for the mass of the people. He sums up the encouraging effect, at p. 274 of his book, thus:

"All this is not to suggest that the popular radicalism of war-time Britain was, for the most part, a formed socialist ideology, let alone a revolutionary one. But, in its mixture of bitter memories and positive hopes, in its antagonism to a mean past, in its recoil from Conservative rule, in its impatience of a traditional class structure, in its hostility to the claims of property and privilege, in its determination not to be robbed again of the fruits of victory, in its expectations of social justice, it was a radicalism eager for major, even fundamental, changes in British society after the war."

I would myself have judged that the radicalism was at least a half-formed socialist ideology, but it is difficult to be positive on such matters. It is significant that a substantial number of the new Labour members acknowledged—many to me personally, and some even publicly—that they owed their victories partly to the support given to them in their election campaigns by the Communist Party.

THE ELECTORS BETTER THAN THE LEADERS

Looking back, I think it is clear that the electorate was in truth far ahead of its leaders, far ahead of what anyone—except some shrewd

observers in the Communist Party—imagined, and that if they had
been represented by leaders as good as themselves the country would
have seen sensational changes within a couple of years.

What did the Labour leaders think had brought them this great
victory, which few of them anticipated? In particular, what did Mr.
Attlee think? Did he see it as a great blow for the socialist future of our
country? Apparently not, for his assessment, as given at pp. 8 and 9
of *A Prime Minister Remembers* was:

> "I think, first of all, people wanted a positive new policy, and not
> an attempt to go back to the old. Secondly, there was by that time a
> good deal of feeling among many people against what was felt to
> be the one-man business Churchill was running. And there was a
> good deal of suspicion of the forces behind him—Beaverbrook in
> particular. . . . And even those who would have liked Churchill
> weren't prepared to have him if it meant having the Tories too. They
> remembered Munich and they remembered pre-war unemploy-
> ment. They didn't want the Tories again."

A more positive view is expressed by Palme Dutt, in the August,
1945, issue of *Labour Monthly*:

> "This glorious political leap forward in Britain is the sequel of
> military victory in the people's war of the United Nations against
> fascism. . . .
>
> "The 1945 leap forward is the counterpart of the sweep to the left
> throughout Europe, following victory over fascism, the alliance with
> the Soviet Union, the tremendous role of the Soviet Union and the
> resistance movements in the struggle, the triumph of the Left in the
> French municipal elections, and the formation of new democratic
> Governments with Communist representation in the majority of
> European countries."

CHAPTER 4

The New Parliament and Government, 1945

WHEN the new Parliament met, it was a great pleasure to me personally to meet the many new Labour M.P.s. They seemed to be for the most part just what I expected and hoped—good ordinary rank-and-file political workers, many of whom I had met up and down the country in the previous ten years, mostly well to the left of their leaders in political thought, and to my mind good raw material for the construction of a really progressive Parliamentary Labour Party and the carrying through of socialist legislation. They thought it the most natural thing in the world to sing the Red Flag in the chamber at the end of their first sitting,* and in contrast to the ordinary parliamentary habit of spending only a small part of the working-day actually in the Chamber of the House of Commons—they sat for most of the time in serried ranks in the Chamber. They soon discovered that the Chamber only has seats for about half the members, and they must have been disconcerted by one of Attlee's early answers to questions. The Commons' Chamber had been destroyed by bombing during the war, and the Commons were sitting in the Lords' Chamber whilst their own was being rebuilt; Churchill had already put the work in hand, on the old architectural lines, particularly wasteful of space, so that the rebuilt Chamber was to provide no more seats for members than the old one; many Labour members thought that the rebuilding presented an excellent opportunity to provide a Chamber where every member would have a seat, and thus be able to take a more intelligent part in

---

* The effect of this sort of behaviour on the "establishment" may be measured by the account given by Mr. Ralph Miliband in *Parliamentary Socialism* of the conversation in January, 1924, when King George V received Ramsay MacDonald on the formation of the first Labour Government. The King referred to "'the unfortunate incident at the recent meeting at the Albert Hall, presided over by Mr. Ramsay MacDonald, at which the Marseillaise and the Red Flag were sung". MacDonald replied that he was sure the King would be generous to him and understand the very difficult position he was in *vis-à-vis* his own extremists. Had he attempted to stop them singing the Red Flag, he said, there would have been a riot. There had been a serious possibility a few days before of it being sung in the House of Commons, but he had managed to stop it. "They had got into the way of singing this song, and it will be by degrees that he hopes to break down this habit."

what it was hoped would be more intelligent debates; and a question was accordingly put to Attlee as to whether he would not reconsider the existing plans, and build a Chamber which would accommodate the members. The Question ran: "If he proposes to reconsider the recommendations for rebuilding the House of Commons with a view to providing facilities for Members to carry out their duties more efficiently." (*Hansard*, Vol. 414, Col. 92.) The answer was "No," delivered snappily; Attlee added: "I am advised that the scheme prepared in accordance with the Report of the Select Committee on Rebuilding and approved by the House provides all possible facilities for Members, having regard to the limitations imposed by the site and *to the accepted procedure of this House*." (My italics.)

Thus did the Prime Minister of this new victorious Labour Party take an early opportunity to make it clear to his followers that "the more it changes the more it is the same", that the long-ago "accepted procedure" by which only half the members could sit in the Chamber at a time was sacrosanct; that the Report of a Select Committee appointed by the previous House of Commons (elected ten years earlier, with a Tory majority) and approved by *that* House, was equally sacrosanct, and that the members should accustom themselves to an "accepted procedure" which made it impossible for half of them to attend important debates!

That was an early blow, but we shall see that those of the new members who had come with real socialist principles and hopes were in for much graver shocks; and the gradual reshaping (called by the Nazis *Gleichschaltung* and by more recent pests brain-washing) to which their leaders subjected them in order to turn them into well-disciplined, anti-Soviet, anti-communist, and non-socialist lobby-fodder, was one of the saddest things I watched in the following four and a half years.

A RIGHT–WING GOVERNMENT

If the Parliament was largely left-wing, the Government was overwhelmingly right-wing. Almost the only apparent left-winger who was given a post of any importance was Aneurin Bevan, who found himself in one where the difficulties —particularly in relation to housing —were almost bound to earn him unpopularity. The famous "switch", by which Dalton went to the Treasury and Bevin to the Foreign Office, instead of the other way round, as was originally intended, was probably significant; for Bevin was extremely anti-communist and anti-Soviet, and his appointment was not only bound to create friction between Britain on the one hand and the U.S.S.R. and the new "people's democracies" of Eastern Europe on the other, but was in truth an early and emphatic demonstration of a policy of hostility towards them. The reason why Attlee, who had convinced himself even before the Potsdam Conference was over that "the Russians were going to be difficult", chose Bevin rather than Dalton for the post of Foreign Secretary is discussed in Chapter 6.

TREMENDOUS TASKS

This government and its parliament had, as I have mentioned, tremendous tasks ahead of them. They had a great deal of definitely pledged legislation to carry through, especially in the field of nationalisation and social services, in addition to the Trade Disputes and Trade Unions Bill. They had to face all the economic and social problems of transition, including the movement of multitudes out of uniforms into overalls or jackets. They had to cope with acute shortages of food and other raw materials, including coal, both at home and nearly everywhere else. They had to deal—and deal, one hoped, on the basis of a definite foreign policy—with all the problems of Germany, and of other countries in Europe who had been involved in the war, several of whom were getting rid of fascist rulers and replacing them by governments in which communists predominated, and many of whom were in desperate need of food and other materials, equipment and finance. And they had to rebuild our export trade, under circumstances of confusion, shortages, and other difficulties (even if they had for a time the relief of not being faced by competition from Germany and Japan).

TRADE WITH THE EAST?

All this involved a whole foreign-policy decision as to how export trade should be developed and orientated; was it to aim at a great growth of trade with the U.S.S.R., Eastern Europe, and Asia and Africa, in much of which we could help socialist countries, and in all of which we could find ready markets for our products if we could give reasonable credit, or were we to seek trade with the U.S.A., where our exports would have more difficulty in overcoming customs barriers and would tend to tie us into the anti-socialist camp? And were we to have a military policy which would be modest enough in expenditure to enable us to export effectively, or vice versa? (This was of course all tied up with the broader question: were we to be friends with the socialist world, or not?)

They had, moreover, although they were not yet aware of it, to face in the next few years a series of acute financial crises (due almost entirely, after 1946, to their being led into rearmament expenditure far beyond our economic strength, under the pressure of a foreign policy substantially dictated by the U.S.A., and designed in reality to "contain communism", i.e. to prevent any country in western Europe from becoming socialist). What a task for a Labour Party claiming to be socialist!

The government had, in addition, to have a definite policy on colonial questions and colonialism generally, not least in relation to India.

CHAPTER 5

The First Session, 1945-6

THE legislative programme of the first session of the new Parliament in 1945-6 was necessarily very heavy, and in fact imposed a great strain on the parliamentary draftsmen—skilled workers of whom the public hears little—who have to prepare the drafts of Bills embodying in precise legal language the intentions of governments.

THE KING'S SPEECH

A good general advance view of any year's legislative programme can be obtained from the "King's Speech", the formal speech which the King (or Queen) reads at the State opening of a parliamentary Session; it is drafted by the Cabinet, and states not only various matters of policy but also all the more important legislation which the Government hopes to pass in the course of the session. It is discussed in Parliament for three or four days following its reading, in what is called the "Debate on the Address".

The King's Speech of this very important first Session was delivered on the 15th August, 1945 (see *Hansard*, Vol. 413, Cols. 53-7); by chance, this was the day after the surrender of Japan, which came a week after atomic bombs had been dropped on Hiroshima and Nagasaki; (the bombs did not bring about the surrender, for the Japanese were at the end of their tether, and were urgently preparing to surrender before the bombs were dropped).

The King's Speech contained:

A promise to work with the governments of the Dominions and with all peace-loving peoples for a world of freedom, peace, and social justice;

A welcome to the establishment of the Council of Foreign Ministers to continue the work done in Berlin in preparation for the final peace settlement with Germany;

A promise to work for the orderly demobilisation of the armed forces as speedily as possible, for the full employment of our national resources with the greatest efficiency, and for rising living standards, with special attention to the special problems of Scotland and Wales;

A declaration that the most immediate tasks were the conversion of industry from war to peace, and the expansion of our export trade;

A declaration of the intention to control industry, or to extend public ownership, so as to ensure that industries or services should make the maximum contribution to national well-being;

Promises to set up machinery for planning investment, to bring the Bank of England under public ownership, and to nationalise the coal-mines;

A demand for the necessary legislative powers to ensure during the transition from war to peace, the right use of commercial and industrial resources, and the distribution of essential supplies and services at fair prices.

A promise to organise building and manufacture to meet housing and other building requirements;

A promise of legislation to deal with compensation and betterment in relation to town and country planning, and to improve the procedure for acquisition of land for public purposes;

A promise to introduce a scheme of insurance against industrial injuries, to extend and improve existing social insurance measures, and to establish a national health service;

A promise to repeal the Trade Disputes Act; and

Promises, in rather more general terms, to develop the home production of food by continuing the war-time policies of organised food production, to carry forward educational reforms already approved (i.e. the Education Act, 1944), to work for the early realisation of full self-government in India, and to press on with the development of the Colonial Empire and the welfare of its peoples.

ATTLEE SPEAKS

On the following day, in the Debate on the Address Attlee made his "programmatic" speech as Prime Minister, (see *Hansard*, Vol. 413, Cols. 95-113). There was naturally not a great deal in it that was not foreshadowed in the King's Speech, but one or two points may be noticed. He emphasised the gravity of the economic situation, stated that we still needed to maintain substantial armed forces to meet our "commitments in Europe", the occupation of Japan, and the recovery of our colonial possessions—presumably in Asia—and to help in "restoring order". One sees already from this phrase that the Labour Party leaders were and remained imperialist, and that their reasons for giving up India and Burma were basically the same as would have led the Tories to do so had they been in power, namely that it was no longer possible to hold them.

The "maintenance of substantial armed forces" to which Attlee refers was destined to grow and grow through the following years, in association particularly with the anti-Soviet policy which developed into the Cold War and NATO; more and more we shall see it dominating the whole political and economic scene, ruining all hope of prosperity, increasing the danger of war, and failing to achieve that "security" which the capitalist world always seeks but—however much it spends on armaments—never finds.

Attlee went on to warn of the dangers of inflation and unemployment. Happily the latter never developed, except for a brief period during the terrible winter of 1947; but it was reasonable enough to fear it, in the light of the then expected slump in the U.S.A.

Attlee announced that housing would not be dealt with by a separate Ministry as proposed in *Let Us Face the Future*, but by the Ministry of Health in England and Wales, and by the Secretary of State in Scotland; and he repeated the various pledges of legislation given in the King's Speech.

That was a heavy programme; much of it, as we shall see, was actually carried out, if not always very well; and I now turn to see how it was done.

THE LEGISLATION

I need not deal with every piece of legislation, but I must go into a little detail about the Bank of England Act, passed on the 14th February, 1946; the Act to repeal the Trade Dispute and Trade Unions Act, 1927, passed on the 22nd May, 1946; the Coal Industry Nationalisation Act, 1946, passed on the 12th July, 1946; the National Insurance (Industrial Injuries) Act 1946, passed on the 26th July, 1946; the National Insurance Act, 1946, passed on the 1st August, 1946; the Civil Aviation Act, 1946, passed on the same day; the National Health Service Act, 1946, passed on the 6th November, 1946; and the Cable and Wireless Act, 1946, passed on the same day.

These eight Acts fall into three sections; nationalisation, social services, and trade union law. Taking nationalisation first, there were in this first section four measures, dealing respectively with the Bank of England, Coal, Civil Aviation, and Cable and Wireless.

NATIONALISING THE BANK

Any estimate of the importance of the measures taken to nationalise the Bank of England—the Bank of England Act was the first national-isation measure introduced—depends on three considerations; firstly, a comparison of the control the Government, through the Treasury, had over the Bank of England before nationalisation, and the control it had afterwards; secondly, what persons were put on to the Board (called "The Court") of the Bank after it was nationalised; and thirdly, what compensation was fixed.

On the first of these points, it was well-known that before national-isation all really important matters of policy were decided in consulta-tion between the Bank and the Treasury; few people know who had the last word in such consultations, although most people realised that the banking world as a whole, led by the Bank of England, could always create a crisis that would bring down any government, although it might be reluctant to do so, since crises tend to become uncontrol-lable in modern times. Thus it was not—and is not—easy to determine to what extent, if any, government control over the Bank of England was increased by nationalisation; for problems would still have to be settled in consultation, and the advice of orthodox bankers who were on the Board of the Bank, or otherwise in its service, might have as much weight as they did before. The importance of this first consideration thus really depends on the second consideration, as to who was put in charge of the Bank after nationalisation. Only if one found a number of genuine socialist workers and economists at the head both of the Treasury and of the Bank could any real change be expected.

And the answer is that, after nationalisation, the Treasury was unchanged and the "Court" of the Bank consisted, not just immediately but for the whole period of the Labour Government, of the same Governor (Chairman) as before, of a group of orthodox bankers and "high-ups" from big industry and commerce, and—the solitary exception—one right-wing trade unionist.

The third consideration, that of compensation, was dealt with by giving the stockholders enough government stock to assure them the same income as they had been receiving for a good many years from the Bank, namely 12 per cent. per annum on the Bank's capital. Thus, one group of owners of capital was guaranteed against any lessening of their wealth or power by the new Labour Government.

· The real unimportance of the nationalisation, from a socialist point of view, can be gathered from the comments of the capitalist press and politicians at the time. *The Economist* said on the 1st October, 1935: "It would take a very nervous heart to register a flutter at what is contained in the Bill. Nothing could well be more moderate." And on the 13th October, 1945, the same journal wrote: "From the City point of view . . . this is plainly nationalisation in its most palatable—or least un-palatable—form. The stockholder, certainly, has no legitimate ground for complaint. . . . It is plain that the present government does not contemplate revolutionary changes in personnel, and is certainly not intending to recommend 'political' appointments to the Court. The recommendation of Lord Catto—and his willingness to serve—as the first Crown appointee are sufficient proof of that." (Lord Catto had himself been Governor of the Bank of England, and a director of several other banks and banking companies, as well as of large trading concerns).

Winston Churchill himself, according to Hugh Dalton, who as Chancellor of the Exchequer introduced the Bill and carried it through, said that "the national ownership of the Bank of England does not, in my opinion, raise any matter of principle".

I must make some general comments on the whole nationalisation policy and programme later; of this particular measure I will only say that its modesty—except as to compensation—and limited scope (for it left all other banks untouched) must have made socialist supporters of the government feel that, even if this modesty was not gravely ominous for their future, the nationalisation produced little or no benefit; and it must have made all but the most timid opponents think that they had nothing to worry about. In the years that followed, it has not been possible to notice anything done or left undone by the Bank which would have been dealt with differently if the Act had never been passed. As in the case of the famous curse uttered by the Church against the Jackdaw of Rheims, "nobody seemed one penny the worse", or better.

The late Lord Dalton, as Chancellor of the Exchequer, carried the Bill through the House of Commons, where he asserted that it would "in due course make a streamlined Socialist measure". In his book *High Tide and After* (Frederick Muller, Ltd., 1962) he claimed that it would make a great difference, ensuring that as a result of it "the Chancellor, in disagreements with the Bank, always has the last

THE FIRST SESSION, 1945-6

word". But the way in which he dealt with the crucial office of the Governor, re-appointing, as already mentioned, the old Governor, showed that on the vital consideration mentioned above, that of the personnel of the bank with whom the Treasury might have to argue, he was doing all he could to appease the Bank, and the City generally. And the tribute which he paid to the Governor in his speech in the House showed how "establishment-minded" he and the government, elected to lay the foundations of a socialist state into which the old City would hardly fit, had already become. What he said, as he puts it at p. 43 of his book, is:

"I renewed my tribute to Lord Catto, who 'to my great satisfaction has expressed his willingness to continue to serve as Governor under the new dispensation which this Bill will inaugurate. Lord Catto commands the confidence both of His Majesty's Government and of all thoughtful and knowledgeable persons in the City of London; and I count myself fortunate in being able to rely on the loyal co-operation, on the ripe experience, and on the unfailing public spirit of this remarkable and distinguished man'."

Thus did Dalton prove that "the more it changes, the more it is the same"; thus did he provide for the "socialisation" of the bank, i.e. the transfer of power over our finances from private hands in the City to the hands of a socialist government representing the people to whom finance meant so much. Nor can it be said that he was looking to the appointments of the other members of the Court to secure a socialist orientation, for he adds:

"I did not regard the composition of the Court of the Bank as of the first importance. I thought there were too many of them and, therefore, reduced their numbers by a third. And I thought that there were too many merchant bankers among them. I told Catto that I wanted them to be fewer, younger, and more diversified. I wanted to bring in industry—both employers and trade unionists—as well as finance, and, if I could find suitable specimens, an economist or two, and other men of ability with valuable experience in other fields."

So, as mentioned above, he brought in one trade unionist. One can understand that sort of thing if one has worked with social-democratic leaders; but it takes a little more experience to see how Dalton was able, in the face of all the facts, to say that "the Government has an emphatic mandate, for at least five years, to lay the foundations of an economic plan for this country and of a new social order. That is what this great Labour majority is here for, and this Bill is one of the foundations." It is far easier to understand why the Press and the City were not alarmed.

There were two Communist members in the Parliament, William Gallacher for West Fife and Philip Piratin for Stepney. Within the limits of parliamentary time, which is so restricted in important debates that perhaps one-tenth of the back-bench members who wish to speak succeed in getting "called" by the Speaker to do so, these two took every opportunity to express the socialist point of view. (They were not the only members who did so, for there were a good handful of left-wing Labour members who followed the same course, and I myself, as an independent, also took part.)

The first opportunity that either of them had to speak in an important debate came on this Bill, when Piratin on the 29th October, 1945 (*Hansard*, Vol. 415, Cols. 120 *et seq.*), welcomed the Bill as "not fully a socialist measure" but as "on the road to socialism". He expressed regret that the Bill was not extended to cover the Joint-stock banks and criticised strongly both the excessive compensation terms and the proposed composition of the Court of Directors.

NATIONALISING COAL

The next nationalisation measure introduced (on the 19th December, 1945) was that of coal-mining. This was, and is, a very large industry, of vital importance to the country, with a long history of cruel exploitation of its workers. The demand for its nationalisation was one of the oldest points in Labour Party agitation, but in truth—at this period—the coal-owners themselves, although they would not admit it, must have been as anxious as the miners for it to come about. It had been clear before the war broke out in 1939 that the industry could not run for much longer without very heavy expenditure on major works of mechanisation and reconstruction for which it would have been difficult if not impossible for the owners to borrow the necessary money. By 1945, with all the pits six years older, with expenditure even on maintenance having been cut to the minimum, the industry could plainly not raise the money to rehabilitate itself, and it was doomed to decay—with terrible effects on the national economy—if it were not nationalised.

The measure was therefore beneficial, and indeed absolutely necessary from all points of view; and we have to consider, in order to estimate its merits, what personnel was put in to run the industry, and what compensation was paid to the owners for their decaying assets.

As for the personnel, the first chairman was Lord Hyndley, who had been managing director of the Powell Duffryn coal-mining giant, and a director of other great organisations; and the deputy chairman was a senior civil servant. The full-time members of the Board contained two general secretaries of trade unions (including the great Ebby Edwards of the Mineworkers' Federation of Great Britain), and five people drawn from the upper classes, including one managing director of a colliery company. There was one part-time member, who was a former director of colliery companies and a director of a bank, a railway company, and an insurance company.

For compensation, a global sum of £164,660,000 was fixed by a special tribunal set up to calculate the nett yearly revenue that all the owners might be expected to earn in the future if the industry was left in their hands, and to multiply this figure by a number of years' purchase, also fixed by the tribunal. This global sum was then divided by a Central Valuation Board into district allocations and then into the sums to be paid to each owner. That this compensation was generous can be shown by the fact that the coal-owners in general accepted it as reasonable. Socialists regarded it as much too high. Once again, a section of the property-owning community was guaranteed against any loss of its wealth; and the new national industry was left with the heavy burden of providing in one way or another the £164,660,000.

Of the Civil Aviation Act and the Cable and Wireless Act I need not write. They were necessary and useful measures, and scarcely controversial.

That was all the nationalisation enacted in the 1945-6 Session of the Parliament. No one with knowledge of the difficulties of passing legislation in this country, and of the many other problems facing the government, would complain that this was too little in quantity, on the assumption that the government was not going to carry out the Party's many promises—as it never did—to reform fundamentally the procedure of Parliament. It is of the nature and quality of the legislation that criticism has to be made.

UNSATISFACTORY NATIONALISATION

For years the Labour movement had been demanding nationalisation on a large scale, capable of really beginning the shift of power from the old ruling class to the working class. The movement in general wanted socialism, and regarded nationalisation as almost equivalent to socialism, and certainly as an essential condition of its realisation.

What did it get? To begin with, if one looks over the whole six years of the government, nationalisation covered a much too narrow field; the "commanding heights" and the most profitable sections of industry were left in private ownership.

Next, both in the terms of the legislation and—far more—in the actual staffing of the administration of the nationalised sector, control by personnel of capitalist outlook, training, and conviction survived, with no idea of workers' or of any socialist control, or even of any benefit to the workers. (The bitter and open hostility—and even sabotage—of many people high up in the administrations was brought home to me personally by a long string of detailed complaints of both the words and actions of these people, given to me, at some risk to themselves, by Labour Party members working in the administrations. I investigated these as far as I could, and reported them to the Ministers involved; I was always met with expressions of thanks and a promise to look into the complaints, but I was never told either on the one hand that the complaints had been found to be baseless or on the other hand that the hostile personnel had been removed or otherwise dealt with.) There was really no change of spirit whatever, and in most of the industries employer-worker relations grew, if anything, tougher.

CAPITALISTS TO RUN NATIONALISED INDUSTRY

The practice of staffing the nationalised industries with capitalist-minded personnel was in truth a matter of definite policy; whether it came from a desire to avoid Tory criticism, or from the deep distrust of working-class capabilities and intelligence which is so often revealed among the leaders of the Labour Party, or from both, it is difficult to say, but that the policy is there is clear. The late Philip Snowden, in 1928, had indicated the pattern by speaking of "getting Socialism through a public corporation controlled in the interests of the public by the best experts and businessmen". (He was a victim of the illusion, described by G. B. Shaw, that the best person to prefer the public good to his own selfish interests is the man who has spent his whole working life preferring the latter to the former.) And Herbert Morrison in 1946 said that the State (i.e. the Labour Government) should "go out into the market and buy brains", as if there were no brains available except in the upper regions of private-profit-hunting.

Sir Stafford Cripps, too, said in a speech at Bristol in October, 1946:

> "From my experience, there is not as yet a very large number of workers in Britain capable of taking over large enterprises. . . Until there has been more experience by the workers of the managerial side of industry, it would be almost impossible to have worker-controlled industry in Britain, even if it were on the whole desirable."

(They were not, I suppose, to venture into the water until they had learnt to swim!)

The Labour Party, moreover, defending itself against Tory accusations of "Jobs for the Boys", i.e. of staffing the nationalised industries (in true Tory fashion), with hordes of their own supporters, published formidable lists to show how overwhelmingly they had in fact pursued the policy of "Jobs for the Enemies"—making all good socialists wish that the Tory accusations had had some measure of truth in them.

SUBSIDISING THE ENEMY

Another defect was that the basic industries of coal, gas and electricity, which supply other industries as well as private consumers, consistently under-charged the profitable privately owned industries which were large consumers of the nationalised products. This meant, in effect, that the national industries were run at a loss in order to increase the profits of the owners of private industries, whilst the propagandists against nationalisation used the published figures of the resulting losses to "prove" that nationalisation was a bad thing in itself.

PAYING TOO MUCH

There was, next, the ridiculously generous compensation, which served the treble purpose of securing wealthy owners in their wealth and power, burdening the nationalised industries with heavy capital or debt charges, and providing a superficial case for accusing the nationalised industries of running at a loss. These industries suffered further in that, when they needed to raise more capital, there was no provision enabling them to do so at any rates but the high rates of the open market.

These compensation arrangements went far to ensure that financial power should remain substantially untouched, and gave the "expropriated" owners moneys which they could invest in profitable industries drawing cheap supplies of power from the nationalised industries.

THE "VICTIMS" REJOICE

It is significant that the bulk of the nationalisation carried through by the Labour Government in the whole of its six years, except for iron and steel (and to some extent transport) was substantially non-controversial. Virtually all of it had been recommended in the past by Royal Commissions or similar bodies on which the Labour outlook was represented by a minority (the Bank of England in the Macmillan Report, coal in the Reid Report, gas in the Heyworth Report, and electricity in the McGowan Report). Much of it was the only way out of difficulty or even disaster, even for the owners themselves. All of it was accepted without resistance by the "victims" as soon as they knew the terms of compensation. (As we shall see later, the steel industry resisted nationalisation, and it was in the end carried through on a half-hearted basis that made it easy for the next government to rescind it, and restore the eggs to their shells. The government would have done better to fulfil its promise to nationalise steel in the first session, when its strength and its backing by public opinion were fresh and unchallengeable.)

NATIONALISING THE CRIPPLES

This consideration is linked with the Labour policy of defending nationalisation as something which should not be operated on any socialist principle, but only for the economic good of the country in cases where a particular industry is inefficiently conducted. This was not only a retreat from socialism but a guarantee that relatively well-run industries could continue in their anti-socialist profit-seeking, thus ensuring that the "commanding heights" remained in the hands of the enemies of socialism, which could never be brought any nearer by nationalisation, while the sickly industries could be taken into hospital at the public expense; this tended to divide the country automatically into the healthy and powerful (private) industries, and the poor (public) ones. Mr. Robert A. Brady, in his *Crisis in Britain* (Cambridge University Press, 1950), put the matter thus:

"The goal . . . has shifted from nationalisation to achieve Socialist and workers' control over a basic industry to nationalisation in order better to effect technical rationalisation."

Mr. Miliband, to whose book I have already referred, did not put the position any too strongly, at p. 288 of his book, when he wrote:

"In regard to nationalisation, there was no ambiguity at all. From the beginning, the nationalisation proposals of the Government were designed to achieve the sole purpose of improving the efficiency of a capitalist economy, not as marking the beginning of its wholesale transformation, and this was an aim to which many Tories, whatever they might say in the House of Commons, were easily reconciled, and which some even approved—with the exception of iron and steel."

(This was accurate, but it contradicted a good many election statements by Labour Party leaders.)

So much for the nationalisation legislation. I come next to social legislation, the National Insurance (Industrial Injuries) Act, introduced on the 23rd August, 1945, the National Insurance Act, introduced on the 20th December, 1945, and the National Health Service Act, introduced on the 19th March, 1946.

THE WELFARE STATE

This creation of something which can fairly be described as "the welfare state" (and indeed is reviled under that name by well-to-do Tories who think that no one but themselves should be allowed to fare even moderately well, or to get all or part of their necessities of life from moneys which they do not directly earn) presents a strange mixture of good and bad. On the one side it was a great achievement to establish machinery under which nearly everybody had some measure of financial provision for ill-health, accident, unemployment, and old age, and a largely free medical service; and on the other hand there were defects in what was provided.

Moreover, it could not be claimed that the programme was a socialist programme, or even that it had been planned by the Labour Party, for it had been foreshadowed and advocated in various pre-war reports, and was expressly based on the Beveridge Report on Social Insurance made in 1942* under the Coalition government. (True, it had taken all the efforts of Arthur Greenwood and other Labour men in the years following to keep it in the public eye, and there was no fear of the Labour Government abandoning it.)

* The political parties compete nowadays in claiming that they are the real authors of social services. Mr. R. A. Butler, in a speech made some years ago in a district neighbouring my then constituency of North Hammersmith, asserted that not merely were the Tories entitled to the credit, but these services had been begun by Mr. Pitt. The compositor of the local paper, being more accustomed to setting up my name than those of nineteenth-century statesmen, spoilt Mr. Butler's point by misprinting "Pitt" as "Pritt".

PLANNING SOCIAL SERVICES

The task of planning the services and putting them into legislative form was a heavy one, particularly in relation to the medical service. The government had to deal with private hospitals, local authority hospitals, medical specialists, general practitioners, and local authority medical services. The medical profession, very hard-working and in general not too well rewarded, was for a large part hostile to accepting any form of salaried employment, and indeed too often was opposed to the whole scheme of universal state-provided or state-guided medical service. And the Minister of Health, Aneurin Bevan, vigorous, intelligent and impatient, had never got on well—collectively—with doctors. The result of long controversies was a series of compromises, intended to be made workable by Health Centres, which would bring together the preventive medical services of the local authorities and the curative services of the general practitioners. In actual practice, largely owing to cuts brought about by financial crises, practically no health centre was ever built.

In the other main section of the social services—sickness and disablement benefit, unemployment, and "retirement"—which consist essentially in payments of money, there were also defects in a scheme that was basically good, and could have been made wholly good.

BENEFITS TOO LOW

One great defect was that the scales of benefits were never sufficient for normal needs. From the start, they were fixed at a level below what Beveridge had proposed on the basis of prices prevailing at the time of his Report. His proposal—pretty modest in itself and indeed insufficient for full maintenance—was 24s. per week for a single person and 40s. for a married couple, on the assumption that the price level would be 25 per cent. over pre-war. By the time the Labour Government came to fix the benefits in 1946, the price level was at least 54 per cent. over pre-war, so that, if they had wished to do no more than keep pace with Beveridge, without any allowance for the basic insufficiency of his proposed benefits, or any provision for further rises in the cost of living, they would have had to fix about 30s. for a single person and 49s. for a married couple; they actually fixed 26s. and 42s. The direct result was that many people in receipt of "full" benefit had to resort to the hated "National Assistance", with its means test; and in 1960 Katherine Hood, in her excellent book *Room at the Bottom* (Lawrence and Wishart), showed that by that time one-fifth of those drawing retirement pensions were also receiving supplementary payments from the National Assistance Board because it was demonstrated to be impossible for them to live on their pensions.

DEFECTS OF CONTRIBUTORY SCHEME

Another defect, probably even graver, was that the scheme was made contributory. Until 1937, the Labour movement had stood for a non-contributory scheme, but from then onwards it accepted the contributory basis, and under the scheme brought in in 1946 the workers pay by deduction from their wages a substantial part of the cost of their benefits. This not only means that they are specially and heavily taxed to provide what are now necessities of life, it involves also a regressive form of taxation, burdening those who are already over-burdened or under-paid, whereas a non-contributory service, met out of general taxation, would draw substantial contributions from those who enjoy rents, interest, and profits. It carries with it, too the temptation (or the argument) not to increase benefits, because the weekly contributions would have to go up in proportion. The scheme also enables governments seeking to escape from crises—one of the main occupations of modern governments in this country—an opportunity to help themselves to a few millions by increasing the contributions.

Another defect is that the contributory basis renders workers' title to benefits dependent on a certain number of contributions having been made in a certain number of years. This operates to deprive of benefits just those who most need them, i.e. those whose sickness or unemployment records are high. (From Katherine Hood's book quoted above we learn that, when she was writing, the universality of the system, so much vaunted and so important, was in fact so full of gaps due to "insufficient contribution records", that one-fifth of those who ought to have been drawing retirement pensions were not getting them at all, and nearly two-fifths of those who ought to have had unemployment benefits were in the same position.)

The evils of the contributory basis are indeed much more far-reaching. They alter the whole nature of the scheme. In place of proclaiming the duty of the State to spend out of its vast resources whatever is needed for the maintenance of our greatest human and economic asset, the working population, contributory schemes base everything on a "fund", notional or actual, with all its capitalist implications of solvency, of balancing a budget, of "we can't afford". As a result benefits are kept low, and the bogey of "financial practicability" is allowed to prevail over true economy—just as if it was the duty of all of us to ensure always that no worker should ever for a moment even appear to be getting out of the community more than he puts in. (If one takes Bernard Shaw's famous definition of a gentleman as "one who does not seek to consume more than he produces", then the workman can never for a moment cease to be a gentleman, and become a cad like the Tories who design these social service schemes to postpone the revolution.)

The "flat-rate" basis of the scheme is another defect. It penalises everyone who, quite legitimately, has been living on a rather better than average standard—on the basis, say, of his differentially better earnings; and, worse still, it leaves it open to Tory governments to reduce the real value of the payments by inflation. Inflation is no more a "necessary evil" than war, but is in truth an important secret* weapon whereby the ruling and employing class can secure for a time real wage reductions without negotiation.

One can perhaps express the socialist attitude to this scheme by saying that only under socialism can we get satisfactory social services; and yet under capitalism, what we have in fact got is so much better than nothing that we could not dream of losing it.

It is noticeable in the case of this scheme, as it was for most of the nationalisation, that it met with very little opposition from the Tories. Mr. Butler took the line that "this Bill forms part of a series of Bills . . . which . . . foresaw the pattern of the new society long before this Parliament was ever thought of", and there was no division against the Second Reading of the Bill (which is the traditional method of indicating opposition in principle). This was of course partly due to a Tory desire not to appear too obviously resistant to social services— they had adopted the same attitude to Lloyd George's social legislation in 1911—but it was also an indication that the Labour Government was not hitting the wealthy really as hard as they expected, or as it might easily have done.

TRADE DISPUTES ACT

The remaining piece of important legislation was the Trade Disputes and Trade Unions Act, 1946, introduced on the 23rd January, 1946. This was the redemption of pledges given by the Labour Party over

* Not indeed always secret, for now and then ministers blurt out that they are planning it deliberately.

many years, to reverse the position brought about by the Trade Disputes and Trade Union Act, 1927, which was passed by the Tory government as part of its vengeance against the workers after the General Strike of 1926.

To understand the effect of this repeal of the Act of 1927, one must know what that Act did; and to understand properly what that Act did, one must know the previous state of the law, which had been built up by many years of struggle between workers and their trade unions on the one side and employers and their governments on the other. It is quite a complicated matter, but it is well worth understanding.*

The Act of 1927 had dealt with four main topics: the legality of sympathetic strikes and general strikes, the law relating to picketing, the political funds of trade unions, and the union organisation of civil service and local government employees.

The legality of any strike was itself a matter of a long history of working-class struggle, of legislation grudgingly conceding such legality step by step, and of decisions of Courts whittling away the effect of the legislation; and the sympathetic strike, i.e. a strike in which workers in other sections of an industry affected by an already existing strike, or even in other industries altogether, come out on strike in order to bring to bear in favour of the original strikers much greater pressure than would otherwise be available, had naturally had a harder passage than a direct strike, limited to workers directly involved in the dispute which gave rise to the strike. The famous Trade Disputes Act, 1906, passed in the first year of the Liberal Government which won the great General Election victory of that year—a government which was not only the most progressive that this country had seen up to that time but also highly susceptible to working-class pressure (see, particularly, pp. 61-4 of *The Law versus the Trade Unions*) —went some way towards legalising sympathetic strikes.

GENERAL STRIKES AND THE LAW

The general strike goes a step further than the sympathetic strike (and many thousand of steps further in frightening governments); for the essence of a general strike is that a central body such as the Trades Union Congress General Council calls out all the workers throughout industry. Whether any general strike, or the general strike of 1926, was

* The whole topic is more fully dealt with in *The Law versus the Trade Unions*, by the writer and Richard Freeman (Lawrence & Wishart, 1958).

D

lawful even after the Act of 1906 came into force was a matter of considerable doubt (the controversy over the legality of the 1926 general strike is described in *The Law versus the Trade Unions*, at pp. 76-81).

The Act of 1927 put the matter beyond doubt for the time, by provisions which clearly made both general and sympathetic strikes illegal. (It also used dangerously vague phraseology, giving the Courts the possibility of going very far in condemning strikes which could not even fairly be called sympathetic: see pp. 83-5 of *The Law versus the Trade Unions;* but that does not matter for present purposes, since the Act of 1927 is no longer in force).

PICKETING

The law relating to picketing had also been the topic of both legislation and Court decisions; picketing is in essence the attendance of strikers in and about the places of work or the homes of other workers who might be disposed to weaken the strike by "blacklegging" (i.e. working in defiance of a strike call) in order to persuade those other workers not to blackleg. Acts of Parliament had legalised peaceful picketing under an elaborate variety of conditions and restrictions, and Courts had often treated mere persuasion as threats rendering the picketing unlawful; few people were clear as to what was and what was not lawful in actual practice (see pp. 51-4, 62-3, 82-4 of *The Law versus the Trade Unions*). This uncertainty was disposed of for the time by the Act of 1927, which enacted some very wide provisions, characteristically vague and elastic. Picketing of the most peaceful character became, if not positively illegal, so fraught with danger of prosecution as to be virtually impracticable. The authors of *The Law versus the Trade Unions* wrote of these provisions, at p. 84:

"[The Act] defined intimidation as 'causing in the mind of any person a reasonable apprehension of injury to him or to any member of his family or to any of his dependants, or of violence or damage to any person or property'. And 'injury' was further defined as including, amongst other things, 'any actionable wrong'. Thus, if any householder told a magistrate that he was afraid one of the pickets *might* open his garden gate, which would constitute the 'actionable wrong' of trespass to his property, or *might* call him a '—— blackleg' in the hearing of others, which would constitute the 'actionable wrong' of slander, the picket could be sent to prison for three months, although he had not even touched the garden gate or given any description of the occupant."

POLITICAL FUNDS: CONTRACTING OUT

The matter of "political funds" dealt with in the Act of 1927 was the long-standing problem of "contracting-in or contracting-out". Any expenditure by trade unions on political objects—and as is well-known the Labour Party lives largely on contributions from the trade unions— had been declared to be illegal in the famous Osborne case (Amalgamated Society of Railway Servants v. Osborne, Law Reports (1910), A.C., p. 87), and then legalised in Parliament in 1913 on the basis of "contracting out", i.e. that every union member had to contribute to the political fund unless he had expressly given notice that he would not do so. The Act of 1927 provided that no union member was to contribute to the political fund unless he expressly agreed to do so; i.e. it established "contracting-in". The difference was greater than it seemed, for many union members, unfortunately, are or were sufficiently indifferent to their true interests to make no active decision either way, and would accordingly contribute under a "contracting-out" system and would not do so under "contracting-in".

CIVIL SERVICE UNIONS

The position of civil servants—a large body—before 1927 was that their unions could affiliate to the T.U.C. (Trades Union Congress) and thus take part in the main working-class struggle if they wished; and some of their unions did so. The 1927 Act in effect prevented such affiliation.

The position of local government servants was a little different; what the authors of the Act of 1927 were dealing with in their case was the practice adopted by a good many Labour local authorities of making membership of a union a condition of employment under the Council. The Act of 1927 made this practice illegal; in addition, it laid down certain other provisions making it almost impossible in practice for employees of local authorities to strike.

THEY DID TOO LITTLE

Now, one can well understand that the Labour Party would pledge itself to repeal this retrograde and revengeful Act of 1927, and that the Labour Government would hasten to fulfil this pledge when it had the power to do so. And it duly repealed it. But what is difficult to forgive is that the Government was content to do no more than restore the pre-1927 position, with all its defects and uncertainties; and it must be remembered that uncertainties are almost as bad as prohibitions, for if no one can be sure that some particular activity is lawful many organisations and many individuals will in practice not carry it on, and Courts are moreover only too likely to decide any particular case against the workers.

Among the uncertainties, of course, was the position of any sympathetic or general strike. Before 1927, as I have explained, this position was quite uncertain, and merely to restore the old position was almost as bad as continuing the prohibition, and depriving the workers of the weapons both of the sympathetic strike, a valuable weapon in any particular battle, and of the general strike, a weapon of tremendous and crucial value at any high point in the class struggle. And picketing, a very important tactical weapon, was left in equal confusion.

The Act of 1946, with all its defects, was nevertheless an important step forward; among its advantageous results was the accession to the Trades Union Congress of nearly 350,000 members from the Civil Service unions.

The limitation of the Act to the mere restoration of the pre-1927 position, with all its defects and uncertainties, was not of course an oversight, nor could it be due to any doubt as to the capacity to carry through Parliament any reform of the law that was desired. It was a deliberate decision of the right-wing leadership, due surely to its hostility to the left wing and its fundamental distrust of working-class forces. It is interesting that, whilst the Bill was going through the House, I was asked by a number of trade union M.P.s to help them to draw up amendments, designed to clear up the dangerous ambiguities resurrected by the repeal of the Act of 1927. One thing they wanted was to have the maintenance of parliamentary representation in Parliament and the creation of a parliamentary fund for that maintenance made clearly a legal object of trade unions, so that contracting-out would disappear; and another was to make it clear that general or sympathetic strikes are not illegal. The first of these was outside the scope of the Bill; the second did not suffer in that way, but it made no headway.

So much for legislation; as I have mentioned, there is much more in government than legislation, and I must now turn to other fields of the new Government's activity in 1945-6.

CHAPTER 6

Foreign Policy, 1945-6

In the field of foreign policy, which affected all our history, our domestic politics, and the hopes of peace in the world, the principal problem was that of our relations with the U.S.S.R., and of our attitude to that country in connection with Germany and the many other parts of the world that called for resettlement, such as Greece, the East European countries, and the Italian colonies. Many foreign policy problems were already active and urgent, naturally enough, at the time the new government was formed.

UNITED NATIONS CHARTER

The draft charter of the United Nations was signed at San Francisco on the 26th June, 1945; and from the 17th to the 25th July the first stage of the Potsdam Conference was held, Attlee being present as well as Churchill, since it might turn out—as it did on the 26th July—that Attlee would become Prime Minister before the Conference was over.

In the first stage of the Conference, with Churchill as Prime Minister, and the secret of the Labour victory still hidden in the ballot-boxes, there was for the moment no reason to expect any change in the British attitude, personified by Churchill; his position of outward friendliness and inward bitter hostility to the U.S.S.R. was already pretty well-known, even if it is now far better and more widely realised. Whether any great change was to come when Attlee replaced Churchill, we shall soon see.

After an adjournment from the 25th to the 28th July, for Churchill and Attlee to return to England for the declaration of election results (and, as it proved, for the formation of the Labour Government) the Conference resumed, with Attlee at the head of the British delegation, supported by Bevin as Foreign Secretary, and lasted until the 2nd August. It provided one of the earliest and unhappiest examples of the Labour Government adopting Tory foreign policy, including the hostility to the U.S.S.R.

ALAS! NO CHANGE

Mr. Byrnes, the American Secretary of State, must have been watching to see how great would be the difference in the British attitude and position now that a socialist government had taken power. In his autobiography, *Speaking Frankly*, he wrote:

> "Britain's stand on the issues before the Conference was not altered in the slightest, so far as we could discern, by the replacement of Mr. Churchill and Mr. Eden by Mr. Attlee and Mr. Bevin. This continuity of Britain's foreign policy impressed me."

Professor Fleming, at pp. 291-2 of his book *The Cold War*, already mentioned, was to my mind quite correct when he wrote of the position as follows:

> "Ernest Bevin, new Foreign Secretary, [now] sat in [Churchill's] place and British policy towards Russia did not change an iota. Bevin was a Labour Churchill, still more volcanic and irascible, without Churchill's aristocratic graces. Bevin had long been an inner member of the Churchill coalition cabinet. His opposition to Russia was even greater than Churchill's, since to Sir Winston's defence of Imperial positions vis-à-vis Russia he added the hatred of the democratic socialist for the dictatorial brand. Neither tact or diplomacy would restrain British attitudes toward Russia thereafter, as the Conservative-dominated Foreign and Colonial offices stiffened Bevin for conflict with the Soviets."

Already, only two months after the Labour Party Conference had approved *Let us Face the Future*, the leadership seemed to have travelled a very long way from the assertion in the Manifesto that the British Labour Movement had "a common bond with the working-people of all countries, who had achieved new influence through the struggle against Nazi Germany", and the promise to "consolidate in peace the great war-time association of the British Commonwealth with the U.S.A. *and the U.S.S.R.*" (my italics).

Mr. Byrnes noticed, in the same passage of his book, that Bevin's manner towards "the Russians" was so aggressive that "both the President and I wondered how we would get along with this new Foreign Minister".

Churchill, in intelligent anticipation of this "continuity", had explained to the House of Commons on the 14th June that he and

Attlee had "always thought alike on the foreign situation", and that Attlee's presence at Potsdam would show that, "although governments may change and parties may quarrel, yet on some of the main essentials of foreign affairs we stand together".

Attlee himself, in his autobiography, wrote, as it were in confirmation of Byrnes, that when he returned to Potsdam, "our American friends were surprised to find that there was no change in our official advisers and that I had even taken over, as my Principal Private Secretary, Leslie Rowan, who had been serving Churchill in the same capacity".

ATTLEE BETRAYS ATTLEE

It may be noted that Attlee had at an earlier period been able to see clearly what differences should exist between Tory and Labour foreign policy. In 1938, in his book, *The Labour Party in Perspective*, he said that the main fault of the Labour Party in foreign policy after the First World War was that it had been content to borrow its ideas from the Liberals instead of hammering out a socialist foreign policy of its own. And he added:

"There is a deep difference of opinion between the Labour Party and the Capitalist parties on foreign as well as on home policy, because the two cannot be separated. The foreign policy of a Government is the reflection of its internal policy. Imperialism is the form which capitalism takes in relation to other nations."

But in fact when the time came, the change from a Tory government to a Socialist government, which ought to have been standing as the open and declared friend of the great Socialist ally, passed without any visible change.

THE WORK OF POTSDAM

The main work of the Conference was, firstly, to set up a Council of the Foreign Ministers of Britain, the U.S.A., the U.S.S.R., and China, which was to prepare the drafts of peace treaties with Italy, Rumania, Hungary, Bulgaria and Finland; secondly, to decide that the Allied commanders should exercise supreme authority in the four occupation zones of Germany, and should act together as the Allied Control Council, on the following principles:

All industry usable for war purposes was to be eliminated or strictly controlled. Arms production was to be prohibited. All military or semi-military organisations, including the S.S., the S.A., the general staff, and officers' clubs, were to be broken up. The German people were to be made to understand that they had suffered a crushing defeat and must bear a share of responsibility for the crimes committed by Hitler's Germany. All Nazi institutions, organisations, and propaganda were to be destroyed. And preparations were to be made for the eventual reconstruction of political life on a democratic basis.

All officials of the Nazi Party who had been more than nominal members were to be removed from responsible posts; education was to be controlled so as to get rid of Nazi and militarist teaching; and the judicial system was to be reorganised.

The economic control of Germany was to aim at making her able to maintain herself, without external assistance, after payment of reparations, on an average living standard not above the average European (excluding Britain and U.S.S.R.), and to prevent her developing any war potential. The production of metals, chemicals, etc., was to be rigidly limited to what would suffice for peaceful requirements; and a common economic policy for the whole of Germany was to be worked out by the Control Council.

Reparations were to be met by the removal from Germany of assets surplus to peace-time economy. In the main, Russian and Polish claims were to be met from the Eastern Zone and those of the Western Allies from the Western Zone. The U.S.S.R. was also to receive 1 per cent. of the surplus capital equipment of the Western Zone and a further 15 per cent. in exchange for products of the Russian Zone, i.e. food and raw materials, to be delivered over five years. Capital removals were to be completed within two years.

BEVIN'S FIRST SPEECH

Bevin, now Foreign Secretary and not long returned from Potsdam, made his first foreign policy speech in Parliament on the 20th August, 1945. This was plainly a crucial moment, more crucial indeed than most people realised. Foreign policy, which included above all our whole attitude to the Soviet Union, had now to be explicitly or implicitly declared. Would the new Government show that it was working for socialism, that it was in consequence genuinely friendly to the U.S.S.R. and proposed to put an end to the old direction of our foreign policy by the Tories, i.e. by the narrow monopoly-capitalist forces that ruled the country; to break away from the old story of "continuity of foreign policy", i.e. to withstand the clear-sighted and efficient Foreign Office machine, which had always concentrated on serving ruthlessly what it regarded as the interests of the country—in truth the interests of the capitalist rulers—and to adopt instead a foreign policy that would advance the interests of the working classes of our own country and of the world, and so ensure peace?

The answer was clear; it had alas! never in reality been in doubt; and it was congenial enough to Bevin, who was obsessed with a hatred both of Communism and of the U.S.S.R., a country which, as Professor Laski once said, he looked on as a "breakaway from the Transport and General Workers Union".

CONTINUITY OF FOREIGN POLICY

Bevin's speech proclaimed the continuity of foreign policy quite clearly, if implicitly rather than explicitly; to do him justice, I do not suppose that it ever occurred to him that any new departure was needed. He spoke of Greece (with which I deal further at the end of this Chapter) in terms which must have delighted the Foreign Office, treating the progressive elements of the country as "Communists", and the reactionary forces as "law and order". He criticised the new governments set up in Bulgaria, Rumania and Hungary as "totalitarian" and undemocratic, instead of congratulating them on getting rid of their fascist rulers. And—most indicative symptom of all—he supported the American policy of refusing to give the Soviet Union the secret of the atom bomb. It is not surprising that the permanent officials of the Foreign Office openly and joyously stated that Bevin was the best Foreign Secretary they had ever had—praise which most socialists would feel happy to miss. It is interesting, too, that the fascist Spanish Press welcomed the speech as the first full anti-Soviet statement by a representative of the Western Alliance.

LEND–LEASE CANCELLED

Then, in the fourth week of the life of the new government, on the morrow of this speech of Bevin's, which should have been reassuring to Washington as proof that the Labour Government was following in its foreign policy the principle of "the more it changes, the more it remains the same", there came the cancellation by the U.S.A. at a moment's notice of the "Lend-Lease" arrangements. This was a terrible blow at the British economy; whether it was done under a mistaken (and wholly unjustified) belief that the British Government was likely to take any steps towards socialism or to behave in a friendly spirit towards the U.S.S.R., or whether it was a shrewd step designed to ensure that British economy and the British Government should be securely shackled to the U.S.A. for an indefinite period, it is not easy to decide; all one can say with certainty is, firstly, that the American Government never afterwards showed any outward signs of suspecting the Labour Government of socialist leanings, and secondly that the shackles have remained pretty secure from then onwards. I wonder what our Press would have said if it had been the U.S.S.R. that had behaved in this brutal fashion.

With the economic consequences of this cancellation I will deal in Chapter 8.

FIRST MEETING OF COUNCIL OF FOREIGN MINISTERS

In the following month, September 1945, there were various events of importance in foreign affairs. On the 14th September 1945, the first meeting of the Council of Foreign Ministers, the body set up by the Potsdam Conference, was held in London; it lasted until the 2nd October, and ended without agreement.

The course of the Conference is well-described at pp. 142-3 of Vol. II of *A History of Anglo-Soviet Relations*, by W. P. and Z. K. Coates (Lawrence and Wishart, 1958), an invaluable work which throws a flood of light on many of the topics with which the present book is concerned.

The parties attending were U.S.S.R., U.S.A., France and China; it was one more picture of the pattern of Britain always lining up with the U.S.A. against the Soviet Union, a pattern the exact opposite of what one had a right to expect from a government elected—as it claimed—on a socialist platform, and the opposite, I feel sure, of what the majority of the electorate understood it was voting for in the previous July. It was the opposite, too, of what the Labour leaders had promised during the Election in the way of friendship to the U.S.S.R.— the Tory leaders competing with them in this, for the mood of the country, as I mentioned above, was so warmly favourable to the Soviet Union that no speaker dared to display anti-Soviet bias. Bevin himself had said in a speech in his constituency on the 7th June, 1945, as related at p. 117 of Mr. and Mrs. Coates' book:

> "With a Labour Government in office which would be believed and understood by Russia and other countries, a new atmosphere would be created and the whole international situation would be changed."

One of the first matters which arose in the Conference was a dispute as to the right of France and (Kuomintang) China to take part in the drafting of peace treaties with Italy, Rumania, Bulgaria, Hungary and Finland. It had been clearly agreed at Potsdam that for the purposes of drafting treaties the Council of Foreign Ministers should be composed of the members representing only those States which had signed the terms of surrender imposed on the State concerned. Nothing could well be plainer than that; it excluded—and was intended to exclude— France and China, who had not of course signed the surrender terms of those countries, nor taken part in the hostilities against them. But by now three of these countries, Rumania, Bulgaria and Hungary had set up left-wing governments, and the U.S.A., in their anti-communist obsession, wanted to counter them by getting two extra votes to use against the U.S.S.R. on all questions relating to the treaties. This demand was an act of insolence and bad faith; one might have hoped that the British Labour Government, elected only a couple of months before on a programme of friendship with the U.S.S.R., would support the just resistance of the Soviet representatives to the obviously inadmissible attempt to break the Potsdam agreement. But anti-Soviet bias, or subservience to the Americans, or both, prevailed, and the British supported the U.S.A. point of view, which was insisted on throughout the meeting, and contributed to its breakdown.

A SOVIET NAVAL BASE

One other matter brought up at this meeting was the request of the U.S.S.R. to have a naval base in the Eastern Mediterranean. This proposal provided an important opportunity of relieving the position which had long affected the Soviet Union—and indeed Tsarist Russia before it—namely, the lack of convenient ports in Europe. U.S.S.R. had ports in the Arctic Ocean, ice-bound for many months in the year; others, also ice-bound, in the Baltic, a sea that could easily be sealed off by enemy forces at its Western exit; and others (also affected by ice) in the Black Sea, whose exit to the Mediterranean passed through Turkish territory by the narrow waterways of the Bosphorus and the Dardanelles. The Crimean War had been fought by Britain and France to maintain the "bottling-up" of the Black Sea; one of the secret treaties of the First World War had pledged to Tsarist Russia the control of this exit; and after the 1917 Revolution the Western Powers were naturally unwilling to give anything to the Soviet State. That

State had always refrained from pressing the issue on this matter, although it was economically and strategically hampered by it. And now, at the end of the Second World War, it would have been reasonable for the Western allies to support a demand for, say, joint Soviet-Turkish control of the waterways. Even Bevin himself, in spite of his extreme hostility to the U.S.S.R., had been heard to say: "The Russians 'ave a case about the Dardanelles".

Such a base as was suggested would have gone some way to easing the position of the U.S.S.R., which had at any rate a better claim to be regarded as a Mediterranean power than had Britain or the U.S.A.; and support from the new Labour Government for the claim might have done much to secure better relations between East and West. The attitude which would be taken by the British Government was also likely to be indicative of the general trend of its policy towards its Soviet ally. So one waited to see what it had to say. Enlightenment was not long in coming. Bevin took the lead not in arguing against this request but in flatly refusing even to discuss it.

Bevin did not behave very well at this meeting. At one moment, according to the American representative Byrnes (pp. 105-6 of his book, *Speaking Frankly*), he called Molotov's attitude Hitlerian, and Molotov started to walk out of the room, being only brought back by Bevin withdrawing his remark.

On the 9th October, 1945, Bevin made a statement in the House of Commons on the breakdown of the meeting. On the question of forcing France and China into the drafting of the peace treaties, he said:

> "It seemed to me, as to Mr. Byrnes, that the difference of view with the Soviet delegation, technical though it might appear to be, in reality involved a big question of principle—to what extent are the Big Three to exclude other nations from the discussion of matters of grave concern to them? This principle, I felt, it was incumbent on me to defend."

What concern could a peace treaty with Bulgaria have for the tottering government of Chiang Kai-shek? Even the officials of the Foreign Office might have found it difficult to provide Bevin with a convincing explanation. But the principle of keeping your promise to "exclude" from a negotiation people who have obviously no right to be included did not commend itself to Bevin.

ATTLEE VISITS TRUMAN

In November 1945, Attlee went to America to discuss with President Truman and the Canadian Premier, Mackenzie King, various questions relating to both the atom bomb and atomic energy. The footing on which the whole discussion was carried on was that all information on such matters was to be withheld from the U.S.S.R.; it is difficult to imagine a more deadly insult to the U.S.S.R., or a more unsocialist attitude, and the British Press almost unanimously opposed this policy. Our Government was in effect telling the Soviet Union, and the world, that the one socialist country, which had suffered most in the war, contributed most to victory, and needed peace more than anyone else, ought not either to be trusted with the "secret" of the atom bomb, or helped economically with the "know-how" to develop atomic energy, and that Britain's Labour Government could best serve the peace of the world by co-operating with the leading capitalist State, already bitterly hostile to the U.S.S.R. and growing daily more and more aggressive, and by seeking to get for itself from that capitalist State the know-how which it was agreeing to have withheld from the U.S.S.R. Attlee, in his autobiography, identified himself with the whole American attitude by remarking that "the immense forces of Russia, which threatened to give her complete power in Europe, were held in check by this terrible weapon in the hands of the West".

AMERICA BREAKS ITS WORD

The main topic of discussion was the sharing of technical information, then the monopoly of the U.S.A. (gained by them during the war with the help of many British scientists), with Britain and Canada. Both in the conversations and in a memorandum signed in Washington, it was made quite clear that the U.S.A. was to give to Britain and Canada all its information about atomic know-how; but Attlee had not been long back in Britain before it was known that the U.S.A. was going back on Truman's word, and that no information would be supplied. Attlee protested indignantly, privately, but the position had to be accepted, for the British Government was by now so bound to America by economic strangle-hold—as well as by bonds of hostility to the Soviet Union—that it was powerless to do anything else.

When Attlee returned from the U.S.A., he opened a debate on Foreign Affairs in the House of Commons on the 22nd November,

1945. He said that the three Powers (U.S.A., Britain and Canada) had decided to preserve the secret of the atom bomb until an effective system of control was worked out by a Commission under the United Nations. By emphasising the mutual confidence between Britain, Canada and the U.S.A.—which as we had just seen did not exclude a piece of double-crossing by the last-named power—and by expressly asserting that war between Britain and the U.S.A. was "unthinkable", without any corresponding mention of the U.S.S.R., Attlee made it pretty clear that he was hostile to the U.S.S.R., and did not regard war against that country as impossible.

Bevin also spoke in the debate, and showed the same attitude.

SECOND MEETING OF COUNCIL OF FOREIGN MINISTERS

The next event of importance was the second meeting of the Council of Foreign Ministers, held at Moscow from the 16th to the 26th December, 1945. The atmosphere at this second meeting was much more friendly than at the first, and a number of matters were settled, including a recommendation for the establishment of a U.N. Commission for the control of atomic energy, which was to make "specific proposals for the exchange between all nations of scientific information for peaceful ends, and for eliminating atomic weapons and all other major weapons adaptable to mass destruction".

It was an open secret at the time of this meeting, and it was officially disclosed to Parliament in the following June, that Bevin in a talk with Stalin had said that he would be willing to recommend to the British Government that the Treaty of Friendship between the two countries should be extended to fifty years. As the treaty, then about four years old, was being systematically broken, in letter and spirit, by the British Government, an offer to extend its life was either a poor joke or an insult; but this typical piece of Foreign Office hypocrisy was made into a major "talking-point" for a long time, to support the pretence that the Government was genuinely friendly to the U.S.S.R.

GENERAL ASSEMBLY OF U.N. MEETS IN LONDON

The improvement in the international atmosphere shown at Moscow proved to be short-lived. In the following month, January, 1946, the General Assembly of the United Nations held its first meeting, in London. This offered another opportunity to the government, which Bevin alas! accepted—to line up with the U.S.A. against the socialist countries in connection with the offer of the World Federation of Trade

Unions (then a real World Federation, as the British and others had not yet walked out to found a rival organisation) made through Sir Walter Citrine, to take a full part in the work of the U.N. This proposal was supported by the socialist States, but opposed by the British and American representatives, and the Federation was merely given consultative status. As on other occasions, Bevin's trade union roots were not deep enough to prevent him ganging up with the U.S.A. against the socialist world.

At this meeting, the General Assembly on the 24th January, 1946, adopted a resolution establishing the Atomic Energy Commission.

At the same meeting, the U.S.S.R. asked for the situations in Greece and Indonesia to be brought before the Security Council, and called for the withdrawal of British troops from Greece, where—it alleged—they were being used as a bulwark by Royalist and fascist forces. Bevin, once again adopting the Foreign Office and the American version of events, replied that the danger to peace came from "incessant propaganda from Moscow", and from Communists in every country. (On the Greek position, see more fully later in this chapter.)

Gallacher spoke in a Foreign Affairs debate on the 20th February, 1946 (*Hansard*, Vol. 419, Cols. 1218 *et seq.*), criticising the attitude of the Government towards the Soviet Union, particularly in respect of Greece, India, and Indonesia (in which last-mentioned country British troops were being used to assist the Dutch against the liberation struggle of the Indonesians).

CHURCHILL SPEAKS AT FULTON

The next blow to socialist hopes came on the 5th March, 1946, when Winston Churchill, now a private citizen, but still possessing prestige which made his international utterances of the greatest importance—so much indeed that it would have been wise and helpful from the point of view of the government of his country if he had refrained from such utterances—made his famous speech at Fulton Mo., U.S.A., in the presence of President Truman. The speech was quite clearly an appeal for just that Anglo-American military alliance directed against the U.S.S.R. that the developments of subsequent years, including NATO, have brought into being. The assessment and condemnation of the speech by Professor Fleming in his book *The Cold War*, is not too severe. Dealing with the passage in the speech that hinted at action against the new "People's Democracies" in

Eastern Europe, to which States I refer more fully below, Professor Fleming wrote:

> "The inference was clear that we could not go to war to drive the Communists out of Europe *at this time*, but we must keep the matter in mind, and we must keep on insisting that 'the people of any country have the right and should have the power' to exercise all the rights of Englishmen and to enjoy all of the governmental processes and freedoms of the Anglo-Saxon world."

Then, dealing with a passage in which Churchill had drawn on his great prestige as the man who "saw it all coming and cried aloud" in the years before 1939 (adroitly substituting the U.S.S.R. for the aggressive Nazis against whom he had indeed warned the world), to reinforce his call for an immediate showdown with the U.S.S.R., Fleming wrote:

> "The old warrior and world strategist was off again, and with a terrifying start. He had waged war on the Reds in Russia to the limit of British tolerance"—i.e. to the limits of what the British working-class would tolerate—"during 1919 and 1920. Then throughout the 'twenties he had preached the menace of the Red revolution, never losing an opportunity to refer to the Bolshevik leaders 'as murderers and ministers of hell'.
>
> "Forced to welcome their aid in 1941 to save Britain, he had incessantly attempted the impossible feat of using them to beat Germany while denying them the fruits of victory. Now he would mobilise the might of the United States to achieve what he had never been able to do before.
>
> "If . . . there is a Third World War, Churchill's . . . speech will be the primary document in explaining its origins. . . . [He] pre-conditioned many millions of listeners for a giant new *cordon sanitaire* around Russia, for a developing world crusade to smash world communism in the name of Anglo-Saxon democracy. In print Churchill's battle-cry became the bible of every warmonger in the world. It said all they had wanted to say, and with his great name behind it could be used endlessly with great effect. . . .
>
> "In Churchill's swirling proposals that America and Britain combine all their armed forces against Russia, he had put Russia's nightmare into words. She would have full license to believe that she was encircled, with the world actively discussing mobilisation against her. . .
>
> "In Washington . . . Senators Pepper . . . and Taylor . . . issued

a joint statement saying that the Churchill programme would cut the throat of the U.N. and destroy the unity of the Big Three, without which the war could not have been won and without which the peace could not be saved. They found it 'shocking to see Mr. Churchill, who rose to power on the repudiation of Chamberlain, align himself with the old Chamberlain Tories who strengthened the Nazi as part of their anti-Soviet crusade. . . .'

"Churchill . . . had pulled out all the stops in suggesting that 'the Soviet system, alien, secretive, harsh, implacable, could scarcely exist in the same world with the Western democracies'. He had done his best to stir alarm in every cottage and in every workman's mind, and to stimulate fear of this insatiable power which would destroy them unless something very drastic was done at once. . . .

"Few things could have convinced the Russian people of the reality of great danger ahead so effectively as Churchill's speech did. He could and did do it better and more easily than any other living person, binding the Soviet people to their leaders as nothing else could. . . .

"Churchill's speech also encouraged the Germans to redouble their propaganda efforts to split the victors by spreading anti-Russian stories among the United States troops in Germany. . . .

"Churchill's speech had given the embittered Germans full right to believe that they could successfully divide the Allies and recover their own might in a new and greater war of revenge upon the Russians, who had balked all their plans for world conquest."

A CALL FOR ANTI-SOVIET ALLIANCE

The Press of the Western world was unanimous in interpreting the speech as a call for a military alliance of the U.S.A. and Britain against the U.S.S.R.

The *Daily Herald*, in an editorial article on the 7th March, dealt with the problem raised by such a policy speech being made (in Truman's presence, moreover), in the middle of the foreign policy responsibilities of the Labour Government, by an important politician who was not a member of the Labour Government but in fact the leader of the Opposition to it. It wrote:

"There is speculation all over the world about the origin of Mr. Churchill's speech at Fulton. He declared that he was speaking as a private individual, but clearly there are many who believe that the

E

speech was composed in collaboration with the British Government."

The article went on:

"We can say with authority that its contents were neither known to nor influenced by the Government."

Whilst that may well be the case, the attitude of the Labour Government to the U.S.S.R. (and to the U.S.A.) had by then become such that it was easy for Churchill to make a speech of the greatest hostility to the Soviet Union which would be in harmony with the thoughts and the actions of the Labour Government, even if the latter might not like to see the position so blatantly developed in public.

The matter was raised in the House of Commons, where no less than one hundred and five members put their names to a motion:

"That this House considers that proposals for a military alliance between the British Commonwealth and the United States for the purpose of combating the spread of Communism, such as were put forward in a speech at Fulton, Missouri, United States, by [Mr. Churchill] are calculated to do injury to good relations between Great Britain, the United States, and the U.S.S.R., and are inimical to the cause of world peace; and affirms its view that world peace and security can be maintained not by sectional alliances but by progressively strengthening the power and authority of U.N. to the point where it becomes capable of exercising, in respect to world law, order and justice, the functions of a world government."

ATTLEE DOES NOT DISAGREE

Mr. Attlee now had an opportunity to show whether he disagreed with Churchill's policy. What he did was to refuse to give time for the debating of this motion, (which could not be moved unless he did so), and to tell the House of Commons that the Government had no previous knowledge of the contents of the speech, that it was not called upon to express any opinion of a speech delivered in another country by a private individual, and that the policy of the Government had been laid down perfectly plainly in the House by the Foreign Secretary.

To this "stock" evasive reply, Attlee added at no time and in no place one single word of disagreement with the Fulton speech; and we shall see in Chapter 10, below, that he evaded a further opportunity to reject the policy.

In *A Prime Minister Remembers*, already mentioned, Francis Williams writes:

"It was in this delicate situation that Winston delivered his famous Fulton speech. The immediate reaction of the Foreign Office was one of consternation, *not so much because of the content of the speech* [my italics] as because of its possible effect in America. This anxiety was increased when the first telegrams from Washington reported that the speech had been widely misinterpreted as an expression of British official opinion and that the reference to 'fraternal association' contained in it had been seized upon by a good deal of public opinion as the beginning of an attempt to manœuvre America into an unwanted alliance. This was the more troublesome in that it came at the very moment when the American loan to Britain was before Congress."

Thus, the Foreign Office had apparently no objection to the policy suggested in the speech, any more than Attlee had; but Francis Williams tells us that Churchill informed Attlee by cable on the 7th March that Truman had read the final draft of the speech some hours before it was delivered, and "thought that it was admirable and would do nothing but good, though it would make a stir". Mr. Byrnes, the Secretary of State, had also, Churchill cabled, seen the text in advance, was excited by it and made no suggestion for alterations; so had Admiral Leahy, Truman's chief of staff, who also was enthusiastic.

This was not the only assistance (or interference) by Churchill at that moment in the government of the country by the Labour Government. In the same cable he gave news of a significant move by the Americans in policy towards the Near East. The Turkish Ambassador in Washington having died, Truman told Churchill, and Churchill communicated to Attlee, that it had been decided to send the Ambassador's body back to Turkey in the American battleship "Missouri"—probably the strongest battleship in the world—and that this vessel and a strong "task force" would remain in the Sea of Marmora for an unspecified period. Churchill added, for the enlightenment of Attlee, that "this strikes me as a very important act of state, and one calculated to make Russia understand that she must come to reasonable terms of discussion with the Western democracies", and that he felt sure that the presence of such a powerful American fleet in the Straits must be entirely beneficial; it would reassure Turkey and Greece, and would place a demurrer on what Bevin called "cutting our life line through the Mediterranean by the establishment of a Russian naval base at Tripoli".

That Churchill should approve of thus carrying on the cold war, and increasing the risk of a hot war, by getting strong American forces into the Eastern Mediterranean, is easily understood; that he should "poke his finger in" by informing and advising the Labour Government on the matter can be easily understood by those who know his arrogance and his contempt for Labour politicians; and that he should assume that Attlee would welcome his interference might surprise some people who had not so far grasped the extent of the Labour Government's "continuity of foreign policy". At any event his assumption proved to be correct, for Attlee wrote and thanked him for "the long and interesting telegrams which you sent Bevin and me. . . . I hope we may have a talk on your return. I have shown the telegrams to Eden." (This whole story is well told at pp. 162-4 of *A Prime Minister Remembers.*) One wonders whether Churchill thought that he was still Prime Minister, but there is no sign of resentment of his activities on the part of Attlee, or Bevin, or any other Minister. They must indeed have been thinking on the same lines. (I am reminded of an observation by the then American Ambassador to this country, who was asked, about this time, at a meeting of Members of Parliament, what he had to say about the charge that Britain and the U.S.A. were "ganging up together". He replied gently that he did "not think we were ganging up. It is just that we are naturally walking along the same road".)

ANTI-SOVIET FROM THE START

In retrospect, only the most case-hardened and cynical of observers can follow without incredulous surprise the development of anti-Soviet policy by the Labour leaders from the very moment of their taking office. The explanation must lie in their social-democratic obsession against communism and communists of all kinds. The only defence that I have heard advanced for their conduct is that "it was all Russia's fault", and that "the Russians were impossible". One answer to that is that there is not the slightest evidence of any effort ever having been made by the Labour Ministers to overcome any difficulties; but the truth is that from the first, long before "the Russians" had had time to be awkward, our government had been openly anti-Soviet.★ Books could be written on this topic—indeed much has been written on it already—but it may suffice to recall here that Attlee's reason for

---

★ E.g. at Potsdam, as early as July; see earlier in this chapter.

appointing Bevin to the Foreign Office rather than Dalton (as given in *A Prime Minister Remembers*), was his "conviction, even at this early stage, that now that the war in Europe was ended . . . Soviet Russia would become tough, aggressive and unco-operative, and that Bevin was the more suited of the two by temperament and experience to meet such a situation".

That means that Attlee, having won on the 26th July a General Election campaign in which his whole party was preaching friendship with the U.S.S.R., had already made up his mind on the 27th July that the Soviet Union would be tough, aggressive, and unco-operative, and that he should meet this supposed attitude by appointing as his Foreign Secretary the tough, aggressive, and bitterly anti-Soviet Bevin.

SAN FRANCISCO CONFERENCE WAS ANTI-SOVIET

As early as June, 1945, at San Francisco, when Attlee represented Britain as Deputy Prime Minister, he had "no doubt in his mind that after the war was over the Russians would be difficult friends". The whole atmosphere of this San Francisco Conference was pretty grim, with the anti-Soviet pattern being built up at a gathering designed to create world unity for peace. I can best describe it in the words of the courageous American journalist, Mr. I. F. Stone, who wrote on the 6th May, 1945, just before V.E. Day:

"It is time the American people became aware of what is really going on in San Francisco. On the public plane a Charter is being written for a stable peace. But in private too many members of the American delegation conceive this as a conference for the organisation of an anti-Soviet block under our leadership. And it is no exaggeration to say that not a few of them are reckless enough to think and talk in terms of a third world war—this time against the Soviet Union. That this is the basic pattern of the United Nations Conference is the conviction not of myself alone but of many astute American and foreign correspondents here and of progressive members of the American delegation and its entourage."

The Editor of the *New Statesman and Nation*, Mr. Kingsley Martin, agreed with Mr. Stone. In the issue of the 24th May, he wrote of "propaganda whose object—let us have no illusions in the matter—is to provoke war against the U.S.S.R. The London Poles openly talk about a third world war, which they expect within a very short time."

The Labour Government had not of course yet come into being; but its Prime Minister, Mr. Attlee, representing Britain at San Francisco, is not recorded at having protested, even to the "London Poles", that singular emigré government still maintained by British funds, and representing nothing but an evil and reactionary past.

THIRD MEETING OF COUNCIL OF FOREIGN MINISTERS

The next event was the third meeting of the Council of Foreign Ministers, held in Paris from the 25th April to the 16th May, 1946. It discussed the peace treaties with countries other than Germany, as well as various questions relating to Germany, the future of the Italian colonies, and the problem of Trieste. It produced virtually no results, except revised armistice terms for Italy, but personal relations between the delegates were not unfriendly. One matter that came up there was the Soviet proposal that the trusteeship of Tripolitania (one of the Italian ex-colonies which were being put temporarily into trusteeship until it could be decided how they were to be finally disposed of) should be entrusted to the Soviet Union. This was rejected.

There followed a debate on foreign affairs in the House of Commons, on the 4th and 5th June, 1946, in which Bevin (with whom Churchill expressed his full agreement) made a number of criticisms of the Soviet Union (see *Hansard*, Vol. 423, Cols. 1825 *et seq.*). Not all of these need be discussed here; but I should mention that Bevin rejected the claim by the U.S.S.R. for joint control with Turkey of the Dardanelles, and defended the retention by the U.S.A. of the bases which they had established outside the U.S.A. during the war. He also defended the rejection of the Soviet proposal about Tripolitania, and at the same time maintained that other ex-Italian colonies in Somaliland and part of Ethiopia should be placed in British trusteeship. The speech was interpreted by the Press, as a whole, as a warning to the U.S.S.R. that, if she refused to accept the terms which would be put forward at the next meeting of the Council of Foreign Ministers, the Western Powers would proceed without her, making separate peace treaties with Austria, and disposing separately of Trieste, the Italian colonies, and other questions which had not been settled in Paris. Piratin spoke in the debate (Cols. 2076 *et seq.*) combating some of the anti-Soviet and pro-American remarks of Bevin.

LABOUR PARTY CONFERENCE

Just after this, the Labour Party Conference was held on the 10th June, 1946, and following days; Mr. and Mrs. Coates recall that

Laski, the Chairman of the Labour Party, advocated a more friendly attitude to the U.S.S.R., and was particularly warmly cheered for his statement that "no small part of the responsibility for Russian suspicions must be borne by those who decided upon secrecy in relation to the atomic bomb". Another announcement that was warmly welcomed was that the Labour Party had proposed to send a goodwill mission to the U.S.S.R., and that the Soviet Government had accepted the proposal.

There was a good deal of opposition to our foreign policy, both over Palestine and generally; Bevin, dominating the Conference, was able to defeat the opposition; but he did not of course end their dissatisfaction, and we shall see in the debate on the King's Speech in the following November that nearly sixty Labour Members moved an amendment on Foreign Policy. But, for the time, the Conference was reckoned a "triumph" for Bevin.

Harry Pollitt, in the *Labour Monthly* of July, 1946, commented on this conference as follows:

"At no time during the proceedings was any serious effort made by the leadership to face the Conference up to the grim realities of the acute political and economic questions that will begin to arise with increasing gravity. No effort at all was made to give any analysis of Britain's economic position either in relation to the situation at home or against the background of the international situation as a whole."

THE BARUCH PLAN

On the 14th June, 1946, just as the Labour Party Conference was ending, the famous Baruch Plan for the control of atomic energy was put forward on behalf of the U.S. at the first meeting of the Atomic Energy Commission which—as already mentioned—had been set up under a resolution of the General Assembly of the U.N. The plan envisaged an Atomic Development Authority, which was to have "control or ownership of all atomic energy activities potentially dangerous to world security", with power to control, inspect, and *licence* all other atomic activities; it was also proposed that when, and only when, "an adequate system for control of atomic energy, including the renunciation of the bomb as a weapon, has been agreed upon and put into operation, and condign punishment set up for violations of the rules of control which are to be stigmatised as international crimes", the manufacture of atomic bombs was to stop, existing bombs were to be disposed of under the treaty, and the Atomic Energy Authority was to be put in possession of full information as to the know-how for the production of atomic energy. The U.N. veto provisions were not to apply in the deliberations of the Authority, where the U.S. was bound to have a majority for at any rate an indefinite time, and would thus be in a position to decide that the U.S.S.R., or anyone else, had "violated the rules of control", and to postpone accordingly their abandonment of manufacture of atom bombs and the destruction of existing stocks; it was moreover to have "control or ownership" of all atomic energy activities within the U.S.S.R. (since any such activities anywhere could be ruled to be *potentially* dangerous to world security); and no "atomic activities", i.e. no work on atomic bombs or energy, even research, could be carried on in the U.S.S.R., or anywhere else, without the *licence* of the Authority. Any attempt to act without such a licence would presumably offend against the "rules of control", and the U.S.S.R., or any other country, could then be declared guilty of an international crime.

And meanwhile there was to be no halt in the production of bombs —which at that time meant simply their production by the U.S.A.— nor any destruction of existing bombs, nor any sharing of knowledge of atomic energy production, until this American-dominated and all-overriding Authority was satisfied that the various conditions mentioned had been fulfilled.

It is difficult to believe that the Americans, or any one else, thought that the U.S.S.R. could possibly accept such a proposal; and today, probably, anyone who recalls the Baruch Plan will hold that it never could have been accepted, or could have worked in practice if it had been. But the British supported it, and it was long made a major propaganda point against the U.S.S.R. that it had not accepted it.

U.S.S.R. COUNTER-PROPOSALS

Five days later, the U.S.S.R. put forward its proposal to renounce the use, production, or stockpiling of atomic weapons, and to destroy all finished or semi-finished atomic weapons within three months.

(Some months later, on the 20th December, 1946, the Atomic Energy Commission accepted the Baruch Plan, Britain voting for it with nine other states, and the U.S.S.R. and Poland voting against it. Once again, the Labour Government, in defiance of the merits of the matter, and in disregard of all socialist principles, was ganging up automatically with the U.S.A. against the U.S.S.R.)

COUNCIL OF FOREIGN MINISTERS

The day after the Baruch Plan was put forward, namely on the 15th June, 1946, the Council of Foreign Ministers reassembled in Paris, and sat until the 12th July. Some progress was made, drafts of peace treaties with Italy, Bulgaria, Hungary, Rumania and Finland being drawn up. The Italian colonies were to remain under British administration pending agreement on their final disposal. There was no agreement on Austria, and the difficult Trieste problem was sent to a Commission.

U.S.S.R. REPARATIONS

Germany was discussed at great length, without any progress. The long quarrel began as to whether the U.S.S.R. was entitled to draw reparations from current production in Eastern Germany, and as to the extent to which she was entitled to remove capital assets. She was plainly entitled to do this under the Crimea and Potsdam agreements, and she was in far more urgent need of reparations than the Western Powers, owing to the great economic destruction wrought on her by the Nazis; but once again the British Government lined up with the Americans in resisting her. Bevin even went so far, a few months later, as we shall see in Chapter 10 where the matter is fully discussed, as to describe Soviet reparation measures as a "desire and determination to loot Germany at our expense". It was remarkable how many of our public men, and the Press, could work up tears of sympathy for Germany, only a year after the Nazi débâcle, if they could hamper the recovery of the U.S.S.R. by doing so.

A PEACE CONFERENCE

The Council also decided that a peace Conference should meet on the 29th July, not to attempt to prepare any peace treaty with Germany, but to agree with Italy and the other four countries mentioned above the draft treaties which had been prepared by the Council. The parties to this Conference were, on the one side, the twenty-one nations who had fought with substantial forces against European enemy states, and on the other the five states with whom treaties were to be made. Germany, not directly concerned, was not represented. This Conference concluded on the 15th October, with substantial success.

LABOUR PARTY MISSION TO MOSCOW

Meanwhile, the Labour Party's Goodwill Mission had left for Moscow on the 28th July. It was a small mission, containing no one (unless one excepts Laski) who was even moderately friendly to the U.S.S.R. Nevertheless, when it returned home on the 15th August, its members expressed themselves favourably, reporting that they had found "friendliness everywhere", and a sincere desire to understand the British people and the work of the British Government. They had had every facility, seeing everything they wanted to see whenever they wanted to see it. Morgan Phillips said that he trusted that their visit would be the first of many mutual exchanges. Unfortunately, the Labour Party did not follow up this success by inviting a return delegation from the U.S.S.R.; no explanation for this unfortunate failure has been given, but one can be read out of everything that the Party and the Government said and did in the years that followed.

PARLIAMENT TAKES ITS SUMMER HOLIDAY

The House of Commons rose for the summer recess on the 2nd August, 1946—the Labour Government was as "establishment-minded" as any other government in the matter of parliamentary procedure and long parliamentary vacations. The criticism of government foreign policy, published in the *New Statesman and Nation* on the 10th August, 1946, corresponded closely to the view I had formed myself from inside Parliament, except, of course, that I reject the possibility, which the writer accepts, of domestic policy being unaffected by foreign policy. It ran:

> "Very early in the session the Party came to realise that foreign affairs was going to mean Ernest Bevin first and last. The Foreign Secretary has no very deep feeling either for the House of Commons, or for the Labour Party. . . . He appreciates their applause and resents their criticism. In this session most of the applause has come from the Opposition and the criticism from intellectuals on his own back benches. This has confirmed his identification of intellectuals and Russian agents. . . . So long as the Government's domestic policy is unaffected by Mr. Bevin's foreign policy, he will be supported by that solid phalanx of Labour M.P.s who do not worry about events across the channel. . . .

> "The Bournemouth Conference seemed at the time to be a signal triumph for Mr. Bevin. It may prove in retrospect to have been the

high point of his prestige. The last weeks of the session have been marked by increasing uneasiness among members, who a few months ago supported his policy. Now, even those who used to defend his attitude to Greece, Spain and Palestine, and explain away his passionate hatred of the U.S.S.R., are worried by that streak of egotism which makes him identify himself with Britain and use the first person singular more than any of his predecessors. . . . His dislike of criticism has ensured that none of the three men with departmental duties relating to external affairs are dominant personalities. Increasingly throughout the Session he has come to rely on the advice of his permanent civil servants and of the Chiefs of Staff.

"Never has the Foreign Office had a master with a more monumental power of putting over its policy as his very own both to his own party and to the House of Commons. Instead of reforming the Foreign Office . . . he has identified himself with it whole-heartedly, and repudiated as disloyalty to a devoted body of men any analysis of its failings or proposals for its improvement."

I would add two comments. The first relates to the implication I mentioned above, that the Government's domestic policy could be unaffected by its foreign policy. Many people at that period, basing themselves partly on the pretty high level of efficiency with which the government was facing some appalling economic problems, and partly on the nationalisation and social legislation I have described above, had a good opinion of the domestic policy and at the same time a pretty unfavourable view of the foreign policy. Most of them did not realise, but by now nearly everyone must see, that one cannot have a good domestic policy and a bad foreign policy, any more than one can have a partly good egg. A bad foreign policy is bound in a very short time to infect the domestic policy, not just because it affects the morale and the attitude of ministers who have collectively to carry on both the policies, but also because a bad foreign policy is, in terms of national effort and expenditure, the most expensive of all crimes, and speedily draws away from domestic policy the money needed to make that policy good. I can illustrate this here by recalling such activities of the government, already at this period, as the sending abroad of millions of pounds to maintain a Polish *émigré* army of 200,000 under General Anders (most of whom had never fought against the Nazis, many of whom had fought on the side of the Nazis, and quite a few of whom had not *enlisted* in that Army until after the end of the war), and to meet the costly operations against the popular forces in Greece, which I will discuss in a moment.

"DEFENCE"; CONSCRIPTION

But the Government did worse than this; over and above all that expenditure, incurred at a time when, as we shall see, it was becoming more and more difficult to keep the country's economy anywhere near balance, it decided to slow up the demobilisation of the armed forces, to maintain a minimum of 1,500,000 men in the armed forces (at a time when war must have been almost inconceivable), and to impose peacetime conscription of eighteen months. (There were in fact, at the end of November, 1945, still 4,248,000 in the armed forces).

The Government's foreign policy, moreover, cost us even more millions by its policy of hampering and discouraging trade with the socialist world.

TRUSTING THE CIVIL SERVICE

My other comment relates to the concluding passage quoted above. There we see how Bevin was stoutly defending the permanent officials of the Foreign Office, as he would have defended the staff of his Union; he knew well how to delegate work, readily delegated details to subordinates whom he trusted, and then—naturally—defended them. The vital defect here—worse in the case of the Foreign Office than in that of any other department, since that Office was more specialised and more viciously reactionary than others—and affecting all his fellow ministers, lay in the acceptance of the liberal illusion that civil servants serve loyally the ministers and the policy of the government of the day; and they thus put themselves in the hands of able, experienced and establishment-minded, not to say reactionary, advisers who (no doubt sincerely believing that they were serving the best interests of their country) systematically steered them in all their decisions into non-socialist channels. In the years before the Second World War, in many Labour "shadow-cabinet" talks—at which I was present—several of the people who in 1945 took high office in the Labour Government were constantly insisting that a socialist government ought not to trust higher civil servants to change their approach on the arrival of a Labour Government, and that the Labour Party should make up its mind never to take office unless every major Minister carried into his department with him half a dozen intelligent and trained socialist juniors, who could act as watch-dogs, and help to see that the "permanents" did not control policy. Alas, in July 1945, they all walked into office without any such safeguards, apparently trusting the "permanents" to act according to such socialist principles as they themselves professed. (And, of course, too many of the Ministers had principles which did not conflict clearly enough with those the permanents had for long been serving with loyalty and full understanding.)

The Foreign Office, as I have said, was the worst. Mr. and Mrs. Coates were fully justified in writing in their book:

"Probably no Foreign Secretary of this country was as dependent on his permanent officials as was Bevin, and these officials hated the Soviet Union. . . . The Foreign Office did not know and did not want to know the truth about the U.S.S.R., and Bevin was completely in the hands of its officials. Under these circumstances his policy *vis-à-vis* the U.S.S.R. could not but be disastrous."

At the Trades Union Congress in October, 1946, Attlee, attending as fraternal delegate, made a speech denouncing Communists and strongly attacking the Soviet Government; but a resolution critical of the Government's foreign policy received 2,440,000 votes against 3,557,000. The resolution ran:

"This Congress views with serious concern certain aspects of the Government's foreign policy. We note that the policy pursued in Greece has strengthened the hands of reactionary forces, facilitated favourable conditions for the return of the monarchy, and led to the suppression of the progressive forces.

"In Spain, the continuation of economic and diplomatic relations with General Franco assist in maintaining a fascist state of society.

"In Germany the failure to de-nazify the country and establish democratic institutions and economic control is in opposition to the agreement reached at Potsdam.

"The relationship between the Soviet Union and this country has deteriorated during the past twelve months due to the policy of Anglo-American domination, and the isolation of the Soviet Union, along with the tying of the economy of Britain with that of capitalist America, is in our view extremely dangerous and one that may prejudice the fulfilment of the Government's progressive programme outlined in *Let us Face the Future*."

PARLIAMENT REASSEMBLES

Parliament met again after the recess on the 8th October, 1946, and the session ended on the 6th November. On the 22nd and 23rd October, there was a debate on Foreign Affairs, in which Churchill and some of the Labour Ministers seemed to be competing—or co-operating—in a display of suspicion and hostility towards the Soviet Union. I spoke in this debate (*Hansard*, Vol. 427, Cols. 1690 *et seq.*), criticising our foreign policy as being that of the Foreign Office and the Tories, saying among other things:

> "Whenever one attempts to follow the foreign policy . . . one is greatly shocked by the fact that it is nearly always quite easily explicable on the basis that the main object is to weaken and thwart the Soviet Union, while it is not always easy to explain it on any other footing. . . . The tragedy of it, of course . . . from the socialist point of view, is that this is the policy for which not only the Tories but also the Nazis have been working . . . for years and years . . . Get the working-class parties of Great Britain and Europe and everywhere else divided . . . persuade the Labour parties of the world to pay more attention to fighting the Communists than to fighting the reactionaries, and then there will be a chance for the reactionaries. Our foreign policy just simply amounts to that."

COUNCIL OF FOREIGN MINISTERS

On the 4th November, 1946, the Council of Foreign Ministers met in New York, mainly for the purpose of settling the final versions of the Peace Treaties which the Paris Conference of July-August had negotiated. By the 12th December the texts were agreed, without much satisfaction on any side.

THE TRAGEDY OF GREECE

The problems of Greece were also acute in this period, and I will deal with them separately here. They form part of a larger whole, embracing most of Eastern Europe.

Greece and those countries of Eastern Europe which are now in the socialist camp had been the object of a diplomatic bargain negotiated in the course of 1944 between Churchill and the U.S.S.R. (with the knowledge of the U.S.A.). It will be remembered that these countries, other than Greece herself, had been heavily involved by their fascist governments and ruling classes in active war against the U.S.S.R. on the side of the Nazis. The Soviet Union was naturally determined that, after the war, they should have governments, and political systems, that not only excluded all fascist elements but could also be relied upon to be friendly to the Soviet Union. At the same time, the Western Powers, and above all Britain under Churchill, in their desire to see that the U.S.S.R. came out of the war as weak as possible, and that there should be no extension of socialism to other countries, had been intriguing hard to bring those countries into the Western camp; Churchill's advocacy of attacking the "soft under-belly of Europe", and thus of getting the armed forces of the West into the Balkans before the victorious march of the liberating Soviet forces could arrive there, was part of this policy, which was also tied up with Western desires to protect their large investments in, and their trade with the semi-colonial Balkan countries. By the middle of 1944, it was plain that there was no hope of Western forces getting into the Balkans, and Churchill planned to save what he could for his capitalist and anti-Soviet policies by at any rate securing Greece for the West. The bargain he made, well described at pp. 189-90 of Professor Fleming's book already mentioned, was that the U.S.S.R. should concede to Britain a free hand, or sphere of influence, in Greece, in return for a similar recognition by the West of the Soviet Union's influence over its own Balkan neighbours.

The British Coalition Government, and the Labour Government, often proceeded on the basis of this bargain to work their will in Greece, with tragic results for the progressive forces in that country, whilst the U.S.S.R. stood by the bargain and acquiesced in their doing so; and the accounts that I shall have to give in this book of events in Greece should be read in the light of that bargain. It is equally a part of the story that the U.S.S.R. did, by various efforts, secure friendly governments, which became "People's Democracies", in all the countries on its Western frontier south of the Baltic; and the story of the endless quarrels between the Western Powers and the U.S.S.R. about the terms of the Peace Treaties with those countries, and about those countries generally, which occupied the next few years, must be read in the same light. With that introduction, let me turn to the particular story of Greece. It began in the late autumn of 1944, when the British Government, having secured the bargain I have described, sent troops into Greece—at a time when we could ill spare men from Italy and the Second Front—ostensibly to free Greece from the Nazis, but also, as Bevin explained in his speech at the Labour Party Conference of December, 1944, "because the British Empire cannot abandon its position in the Mediterranean". From the imperialist point of view, which was as welcome to Bevin as it was to the Foreign Office officials, the question of a naval base in the Eastern Mediterranean presented a serious problem for the British. Malta lay too far to the west to be really useful, and too near to Italy to be tenable; the growing national-ism of Egypt made it impossible to hope to retain Alexandria or any other Egyptian base; and the ports of the only remaining possibility, Cyprus, were no more than open roadsteads (except Famagusta, which could receive one or two medium-sized destroyers, but no larger vessel). The dispatch of these troops to Greece might have been reasonable as a military operation if the Nazis had not already been driven out of the whole Greek mainland, remaining only on the islands. The real purpose of the expedition was to do what Mr. Denis Healey, whom I quoted in Chapter 2, described as protecting the upper classes against the just wrath of the people who had been fighting underground against them. With the old convenient label of "communist" and in the name of the equally convenient "law and order" the Coalition Govern-ment carried on a war against the progressive forces who had been fighting both the Nazis and the Greek collaborators, and installed the latter in power.

The Labour Government, when it came in, should have reversed this policy, but Bevin had already in December, 1944, at the Labour Party Conference, defended the Coalition Government's activities in Greece. And in fact the same policy of supporting fascist Right against the progressive masses—in due course called "the mob"—was contin-ued, particularly flagrantly in March, 1946, when elections were forced in Greece under conditions of terror which destroyed any hope whatever of a fair vote, and a reactionary government was installed which—among other things—destroyed within a few months the whole trade union movement and imprisoned most of the elected trade union leaders, replacing them by its own "stooges", all with the approval of Bevin, whose anti-communist and anti-Soviet obsessions blotted out all his trade union training.

The Greek people remained in the grip of reaction, savage oppres-sion, poverty, and misery, with the Labour Government—at a cost which in terms of money alone became impossible in a few years, so that the Americans had to take over—supporting every cruel and undemocratic action of the monarchist and more than half-fascist government, always in the name of anti-communism and with the object of encircling the U.S.S.R. with NATO bases.

CHAPTER 7

Colonial Policy, 1945-6

YEAR by year, as the story develops, colonial problems will become more and more important; in this opening year, they were at any rate limited in number to two, Palestine and India. But both were serious.

PALESTINE

Palestine was at this time administered by the British as a mandated territory formerly under the League of Nations and now under the United Nations. Its main difficulties arose from acute imperialist rivalries between the British and the Americans over the control of the Middle East, with its rich petroleum deposits, in which rivalries the Labour Government behaved just as a Tory government would have done. Superficially, but only superficially, the problem lay in the conflict between Jews and Arabs; their conflict was of course fomented by the imperialist contenders.

Palestine is a small country; for centuries it was mainly inhabited by Arabs, nomadic or peasant people of Muslim religion; but many centuries earlier it had been the home of the Jewish people, and some few Jews had always continued to live there.

In the late nineteenth century, the Jewish movement to establish somewhere a national home for at any rate some of the Jewish people had come into being; and the movement finally centred its hopes in Palestine. During the First World War, the British fought and defeated the Turkish rulers of the territory, and gained control of the whole of it. They had for strategic reasons, in the course of the war, promised Dr. Weitzmann that a Jewish National Home should be established in Palestine, and at the same time had promised the Arabs to protect their interests there.

These conflicting promises provided part of the background against which the Anglo-American conflicts were waged; the ambitions of the Jews to build up a State, and of the Arabs to be left alone to cultivate their scanty lands, provided rich soil for conflicts, with Jews and Arabs

F

to do most of the fighting. The Arabs thought of Palestine as their homeland and the Jews as interlopers; the Jews regarded it as the Promised Land in which they could at last have a home of their own. At this particular period of the story, the Americans were "hotting up" the imperialist conflict by insistently demanding immediate large-scale admission of further Jewish immigrants to the territory; the British had for long limited immigration to 1,500 a month, and any substantially greater flow would cause at least temporary hardship for the Jews and additional friction with the Arabs, the available land being very small in area; but the Americans were pressing for the immediate admission of 100,000 new immigrants.

This was not the only difficulty for the British in administering the territory; any obstacle they might put in the path of the great Arab liberation movement by making concessions to the Jews would weaken their position in the Middle East generally, and would create complications in India as well, where the Muslim population of approximately 90,000,000 would sympathise with the Arabs. Palestine was also of potential value to the British as a possible base for control of the Eastern Mediterranean, and particularly over the Suez Canal, since it was no longer possible to use Alexandria.

EXPENSIVE ADMINISTRATION

The expense of administering this difficult country was also a serious element in British calculations, at a time when finance at home was so difficult; and in the end the British Government was forced to accept defeat, and to give up the Mandate; it actually did so on the 15th May, 1948. I must come back to the Palestine story in Chapters 11 and 16.

INDIA

India was another grave problem. Whilst the Labour Government has frequently demanded, and received, praise for "giving" to India in 1947 the independence which it was in fact impossible to withhold for a moment longer, it started—as we saw in *Let us Face the Future* and in the King's Speech of 1945—by limiting itself to a proposal for "responsible self-government", or "full self-government".

A plan for self-government was outlined by Attlee in a broadcast on the 19th September, 1945, and rejected by the Indian Congress Party. Not long after, the hopelessness of any attempt to withhold complete independence was emphasised by the Indian Naval Mutiny, and the extension of this disaffection to the Indian land forces; and in

March, 1946, the Government hurriedly sent a Mission to India, composed of Lord Pethick-Lawrence, Sir Stafford Cripps, and Mr. A. V. Alexander. This Mission worked out a plan for independence which was accepted by the major political groups in India, but its fulfilment was rendered abortive by disputes between the Indian National Congress and the Muslim League as to its interpretation, and in and after August, 1946, communal riots developed, and the situation grew worse. The further story belongs to the following year, and I will take it up again in Chapter 11.

CHAPTER 8

Economic and Industrial Affairs, 1945-6

I come now to the many difficult economic problems the government had to face, and the work it did in the direction of industrial planning and development, housing, and other fields.

LEND–LEASE CANCELLED

Probably the most serious single economic problem was that created by the sudden ending of Lend-Lease by the Americans, mentioned in Chapter 6. Lend-Lease was an arrangement made during the war under which Britain (and other belligerents) drew their necessary supplies of many commodities from the U.S.A. on credit, the question as to how and when they were to pay for them being left until after the war. The British Government had, reasonably enough, expected that the arrangement would run for some time after the end of hostilities and had made its financial calculations on that basis; and it had been assumed by everyone that it would not in any case be cancelled without some months' notice.

The cancellation was a crushing financial blow at a moment when Britain's position was not equal to any serious shock. The war had distorted the pattern of our trade; the cutting off of many of the normal sources of supply had greatly increased our dependence on imports from America; the economic planning of the war had led to the concentration of our manpower in the armed forces and in war production, cutting exports to a minimum; and we had sold £1,118,000,000 of overseas investments during the war, and incurred overseas debts for a further £3,355,000,000, not to mention what we suffered through the destruction of capital assets, including millions of tons of shipping.

POST–WAR SITUATION AND PROBLEMS

The problems we had to face at the end of the war included procuring essential imports during the great transition of industry from war to peace, trying to get some exports going again, getting our foreign payments back into balance, and arranging the settlement of war debts. All this had to be done whilst the greater part of Europe was suffering from acute shortage of food, and here and there from actual famine, as well as from shortages of fuel, power and raw materials; in addition, the means of transport everywhere in Europe were almost destroyed.

On the 13th September, 1945, Lord Keynes wrote in the *Financial News* that there were two possible ways of dealing with the situation:

"The first is for us to do the best we can with the resources we still command, and aim at emerging slowly from our temporary difficulties with as little outside aid as possible. The other alternative is to work out with the U.S. some means of returning at the earliest possible date to normal trade practices and increased freedom and liberality in commercial and tariff policies, in the belief that the resulting general expansion of world trade will result in the final outcome that the U.S. and other countries as well as us ourselves will be much better off on balance than under the first plan."

THE AMERICAN LOAN

The cancellation confronted Britain with a gap between overseas expenditure and overseas income of at least £1,200,000,000 per annum. The easy and tempting remedy was a large loan, and the only possible lender was the U.S.A. Lord Keynes took the view that it would be reasonable—since our economic difficulties were primarily due to our war efforts—to ask the U.S.A. for a free gift, or at the least an interest-free loan, of £1,500,000,000. The Government sent him to Washington to negotiate this, but he found that the atmosphere there made any such proposal unthinkable, and the best he could do, after hard bargaining, was to secure a loan of $3,750,000,000 (plus a further $650,000,000 restricted to "Lend-Lease" and "Reciprocal Aid" items), repayable over 50 years with interest at 2 per cent. per annum. Moreover, to secure this, Britain had to give guarantees as to the "freedom of trade" (i.e. limitation of British import duties) and an early return to the convertibility of sterling; this latter we obviously could not support, but we had to accept it as part of the terms. When it was later brought into force, it created a new financial crisis at once, as we shall see in Chapter 12, and had to be abandoned.

To make matters worse, the American Government, shortly after granting the loan, removed various price controls in the U.S.A., as a result of which prices shot up and reduced the value of the loan to us, in terms of goods, to about two-thirds of what it had been when it was granted. Parliament approved the loan on the 13th December, 1945.

STRIKES

Another economic—and partly political—problem arose in connection with strikes. The first of many strikes broke out in September, 1945. It was a dock strike, starting in Birkenhead and spreading by the following month to Liverpool, the Tyne, the Tees, the Humber, and some of the London docks; later, it embraced Glasgow, Leith, and Avonmouth. It was typical, both in its development and in the attitude of the Government to it, of a good many other strikes that came in succeeding years.

The reactions of the Government were little short of shocking; it would have been bad enough if it had behaved exactly as a Tory government would have done, without any flavour of having been elected by the working class to further its cause against the employing and ruling class.* But it behaved worse, in two respects; first, that it unhesitatingly (on ten separate occasions) used troops as strike-breakers, whereas the Tories had almost always done no more than employ them to protect civilian strike-breakers; secondly, it resorted frequently and eagerly to declarations of emergency under the Emergency Powers Act, 1920, which had been passed by the "hard-faced" Parliament at the end of the First World War to provide handy dictatorial powers for the suppression of activities which it was feared would develop among the working class, which had just seen what the workers of the Soviet Republic had been able to do in 1917.

AN INTERIM BUDGET

In an economic situation inevitably very grave, and rendered graver by the cancellation of Lend-Lease two months before, the Government's first budget, an interim one, was introduced on the 23rd October, 1945.

No attempt was made in this budget to make any preparation for the financial side of any advance towards a socialist state, and it was mainly confined to providing for some remissions in taxation, operating from the beginning of the next financial year, the 1st April, 1946. By raising

* I noticed year by year in the House of Commons, with interested horror, that all the innumerable answers to questions in Parliament relating to strikes made by the late George Isaacs as Minister of Labour were based on the standpoint that the strikers and not the employers were to blame for the strikes.

the income-tax allowances on the first part of taxable income, the Government removed no less than 2,000,000 people from income-tax liability; the standard rate of tax was reduced from 10s. to 9s.; Excess Profits Tax was lowered from 109 per cent. to 80 per cent.; and Surtax was raised. The large subsidies that were being paid to keep the retail prices of all staple foodstuffs from rising, which were growing heavier as world prices rose, were to be maintained.

This interim budget was well received by all sides. It was perhaps too optimistic; the Chancellor had little to say about the burden of "defence" cost, which was destined later to grow ruinous, in the literal sense of that word.

HOUSING

The immense housing problem was one which the Government was pledged to tackle, and in spite of general economic stringencies it offered an opportunity for a real constructive advance of great social value.

Working-class housing has always been short in supply and mostly poor in quality. The problem was acute even before the First World War, at the end of which Lloyd George made his promise of "a land fit for heroes to live in", which was of course to include houses; but few people—heroes or not—found the promise fulfilled. The years between the wars saw many houses built, but never enough. Private enterprise failed completely to solve the problem, for there was never sufficient profit in building working-class houses at rents which working-class tenants could pay; the gap was filled—as far as it was filled—by local authority building.

At the outbreak of the war, in 1939, there were altogether about 13,000,000 homes in Britain. During the war about one-third of these were damaged, including 475,000 rendered completely uninhabitable. From September 1939 to May 1945, all the homes that survived grew, of course, nearly six years older, and the work of repair and maintenance was virtually at a standstill; only 220,000 new homes were built.

At the end of the war, the demand for housing was enormous; the destroyed homes had to be replaced, the immense lag in building over the war years had to be caught up, and—with the increase in marriage and birth rates—the demand for homes was much greater than any calculation of merely catching-up on destruction and lag in building would suggest. To meet this demand, labour and building-materials were needed; the labour force had been reduced to one-third of its pre-war figure, and the shortage of almost all building materials was acute.

To make any serious inroad on this grim situation, it was necessary to restrict the building of homes for sale—the working-class in general not being at that time equipped to buy houses—to subsidise buildings, to provide money at cheap rates for the financing of house building, and to secure a supply of building materials at reasonable rates.

The Government went a good way in the right direction. It applied a limitation on private building of a maximum of one privately-built dwelling to four built by local authorities; this limitation in fact stood until October, 1949, except for the period from August, 1947 to June, 1948. It provided lump-sum subsidies of £22 per house, with additions in certain cases. It provided cheap finance, some rates being as low as 2½ per cent. (This was equivalent to a reduction of rent of 2s. 5d. per week for a council house costing—as the average such house then did—£1,300.)

The Government also extended the powers of local authority to requisition houses and parts of houses, and made the acquisition of land much easier.

At the same time, higher standards of building were laid down (sadly, in later years, under pressure of rearmament, these standards were reduced bit by bit).

DEFECTS AND DIFFICULTIES

The main defects were that the overall programme was too small to make more than a limited inroad into the vast needs. The target of 400,000 houses a year—in itself too small, although practical difficulties may have made it unwise to set a higher target—was never reached; by the end of 1948, i.e. in three and a half years, only 852,000 were actually built, instead of 1,400,000; and, by the time the Economic Survey for 1947 was published (see Chapter 12), the target for that year had been cut down to 300,000.

But there were other grave defects. The vested interests which were accustomed to make big profits out of housing—the building industry itself, the building materials monopolies, the landlords—were scarcely tackled at all. Further, the powers of requisition, which should have been exercised on a vast scale, were not used with much vigour, and a great deal of housing accommodation stood empty for many months because the owners wanted too high a price for it, or didn't want it "depreciated" by being used to house working-class tenants—just the sort of manœuvre with which even an unsocialist government should have dealt ruthlessly.

"SQUATTERS"

One result of this was that already by August, 1945, a large "squatters" movement developed; at first army hutments, and later blocks of empty flats, especially in the Kensington area of London, were invaded by workers, who set up house in them as best they could; at the peak of the movement, no less than 45,000 people had been rehoused in this way. The Government fought them with all the orthodox "law and order" methods that any Tory could wish, cutting off services, using police to bar access to the buildings, and invoking the criminal law. After some weeks, the squatters were got out in one way or another.

Of the many other practical economic problems which burdened the Government I can probably give a sufficient illustration if I write a little about coal and food.

COAL SHORTAGE

An acute coal shortage was announced in September, 1945, and a national campaign for increased output was launched by the National Union of Mineworkers. Even before that, in July, it was announced that stocks were 5,000,000 tons below what was needed. In October the Minister of Fuel and Power (Shinwell) said that coal, gas and electricity supplies would break down in the coming winter unless consumption was cut by 10 per cent.

FOOD SHORTAGES

Food shortages became apparent a little more slowly, probably because the efficient rationing system prevented any sudden increase in consumption; but by the 5th February, 1946, Sir Ben Smith, the Food Minister, announced that there was a world shortage of wheat and rice; the world as a whole required for the first six months of 1946 imports of over 17,000,000 tons of wheat, and only 12,000,000 tons were available to meet this demand. The position as to rice (the major consumers of which are of course always near famine level) showed a corresponding deficiency of 2,000,000 tons.

On the same 5th February, the weekly fat ration in Britain was reduced by one ounce.

RATIONING OF BREAD

By the 11th April, bread rationing (which had not been imposed during the war) had become so much of a possibility that the British Government offered to introduce it if the U.S.A. would follow suit. In April, the British standard loaf was reduced in weight by $12\frac{1}{2}$ per cent. without any reduction in the price, and the barley made available for brewing was cut by 15 per cent. In May, the output of biscuits was cut by 25 per cent. and bread was made darker. In the same month, Herbert Morrison went to the U.S.A. to discuss the food position with President Truman, and after talks there he announced that Britain would forego 200,000 tons of her wheat supplies in the period up to the end of September.

At the end of May, it was announced that a system of bread and flour rationing was being prepared. In June, the rations for livestock and the soap and milk rations were all reduced. On the 31st July, bread, flour and confectionery rationing was introduced. And in September, things being a little easier, we had a whiter loaf and more feeding stuff for livestock.

CONTROL OF INDUSTRY

Finally, the many promises of control of industry produced no more than a scheme, announced by Sir Stafford Cripps, President of the Board of Trade, to set up, in all industries that were not scheduled for nationalisation, working parties to formulate plans for action. I can illustrate the practical development of these working parties, which met with considerable resistance from the "freedom-loving" industrial bosses, although they were calculated to benefit these people in the long run, by giving some particulars of the working party of the cotton textile industry, one of the most inefficient of our major industries. Four representatives each from the employers and the trade unions, nominated by the Board of Trade from panels put forward by the organisations, four independent experts, and a chairman appointed by the Board of Trade constituted the working party, and its terms of reference were:

> "To examine and enquire into the various schemes and suggestions put forward for improvements or organisation, production and distribution methods and processes in the industry, and to report as to the steps which should be taken in the national interest to strengthen

the industry and render it more stable and more capable of meeting competition in the home and foreign markets."

Such an operation, even if, as Sir Stafford Cripps explained, the Committees were to dissolve when they had made their reports, might well be very useful, for cotton was not the only inefficient industry. If suggestions for improvements were adopted and applied, the industries might well achieve prosperity both in export markets and at home. But here again, in some instances, including cotton, much depended on who were appointed as experts. These experts would often be able to sway the balance of a report, for they were neither employers in the industry nor trade union officials or workers. Unhappily, the Government followed the patterns of much of its other actions—e.g. in appointing the "Court" of the Bank of England and many of the controllers of nationalised industries—and most of the "experts" proved to be thoroughly "safe" persons, not likely to interfere too much with the "freedom" of industry.

It was at this time that Cripps, as I mentioned in Chapter 5, showed his true attitude and that of the Government by answering a demand for workers control in industry with an assertion that the workers were not yet capable of exercising such control.

CHAPTER 9

The Second Session, 1946-7

THE second session of Parliament began on the 12th November, 1946, and ran to the 20th October, 1947.

Following on the first year of the new government, which had seen a good deal of important and progressive legislation, much of the economic transition from war to peace, and the beginning of financial crises and swollen military expenditure, but little sign of any attempt at a transition to socialism, the second year saw still more of the unhappy if inevitable consequences of adopting a Tory foreign policy, with continued heavy military expenditure and a failure to co-operate and trade with the socialist world. These consequences manifested themselves in acute crises, which by unmerited misfortune were aggravated by the terrible "freeze-up" of late January to early March, 1947, and the floods which followed. Hugh Dalton, in *High Tide and After*, (the volume of his memoirs covering the years 1945 to 1960), was partly right when he described 1946 as "the wonderful year" and wholly right when he called 1947 "the terrible year".

THE KING'S SPEECH

I begin with the "King's Speech", to see what the Government was planning.

The first important item in the speech was a statement on the future of Germany, to the effect that meetings would shortly be held with the representatives of U.S.A., U.S.S.R., and France to discuss the future of Germany with the aim of establishing conditions which would foster true democracy, would guarantee the world against future attempts at world domination, and would remove the financial burden of occupation.

Next came the expression of hopes for the early conclusion of a peace treaty with Austria, permitting of the withdrawal of occupation forces from that country.

The control of Japan, and the measures to be taken for a stable and just settlement in the Far East would—in the archaic language of King's Speeches—"remain the concern of my Ministers".

The Government was to participate fully in the General Assembly of the United Nations, which had resumed its sittings in New York. It was to continue to develop close relations with the self-governing members of the British Commonwealth, and to forward by all possible means the policy laid down for the governance of India. A royal visit to the Union of South Africa early in 1947 was also announced!

The Government was to press on with the conversion of the national economy from war to peace, and *to endeavour to ensure*—a very modest phrase—the effective employment of national resources for the common good. The increase in the productivity of industry was an urgent task for the achievement of a higher standard of living and for the expansion of the export trade. Special attention would continue to be given to the needs of "development areas". ("Development areas" was the euphemistic name that had been given some time before to distressed areas, i.e. those industrial areas which normally suffer most quickly, most severely, and for the longest time from capitalist slumps, either because their industries are especially subject to fluctuations, or because they have only one main industry, or for both reasons.)

The Speech then went on to declare the urgent need for an adequate flow of volunteers for the Regular Armed Forces; efforts for recruitment were to be intensified, the Territorial and Reserve forces were to be reconstituted, and "a measure for the continuation of National Service" was to be brought forward (i.e. peace-time conscription was to be reintroduced).

Everything possible was to be done to increase the supply and variety of food, and to see that it should be efficiently and equitably distributed.

The urgent task of providing homes would be prosecuted with the utmost vigour, and those in most need should have the first claim on new accommodation.

The school-leaving age was to be raised by April, 1947, (to fifteen, not sixteen as proposed in *Let us Face the Future*).

Legislation was promised to nationalise inland transport and the supply of electricity, to deal with compensation and betterment in relation to Town and Country Planning, and to cover a number of other matters of substantial importance, especially in the field of industrial organisation and development, which do not call for examination here.

The Speech, when every allowance has been made for the traditions of pomposity and platitude that beset "King's Speeches", gives an impression of coming from a tired government, but in truth the Government was not yet exceptionally tired, and the lack of any great content or promise of progress in the Speech was due above all to the fact that the financial position did not permit of any great expenditure on useful developments at home, unless drastic cuts were made in "defence" expenditure, which, as we shall see, the Government never undertook.

NO MENTION OF STEEL

Perhaps the worst features of the Speech were the absence of any proposals to nationalise the steel industry or to increase trade with the socialist world, and of any move towards the establishment of socialism, unless the proposal to nationalise two important public utilities, on the sort of terms likely to be adopted, could rank as such a move. The King's Speech of a Tory government at that moment would not have been very greatly different.

Passing to the fulfilment of the programmes, legislative and other-wise, stated in the Speech, I will deal at once with legislation, leaving foreign and colonial matters (including India), "defence", and the many economic and industrial problems, for later chapters.

Of all the legislation passed in this session of 1946-7, the only Acts with which I need deal expressly are the National Service Act, 1947, (introduced on the 12th March, 1947, and passed on the 18th July, 1947), the Transport Act, 1947 (introduced on the 27th November, 1946, and passed on the 6th August, 1947), and the Electricity Act, 1947 (introduced on the 20th December, 1946, and passed on the 13th August, 1947).

CONSCRIPTION

The National Service Bill was introduced at a time when the armed forces were still very large; at the end of 1946, they had been 1,427,000, and the White Paper on Defence proposed that in March, 1948, they should still be 1,087,000, more than double the mid-1939 figure of 480,000.

The whole policy of continued heavy "defence" expenditure by the Government was part and parcel of our increasingly close links with the U.S.A. against the U.S.S.R. Palme Dutt, in the Notes of the Month, (*Labour Monthly* for December, 1946), written shortly after the King's Speech, expressed the position thus:

"The openly proclaimed outlook of the most powerful reactionary sections of American Big Capital today is directed towards aggressive world expansion and domination, utilising every weapon, economic, political, and military. This is the menace confronting the world today.

"Hence the alarm which has begun to spread through public opinion in Britain at the prospect of being tied to the chariot wheels of the American Juggernaut. Just as Hitler beat the anti-Communist anti-Soviet big drum to paralyse opposition in every country, facilitate penetration, justify intervention, and secure docile allies within each country, so American reaction beats the anti-Soviet big drum today. Panic-stricken at the crisis of the British Empire, conscious of Britain's weakened economic position, and blind with fury and fear and hatred against the Socialist Soviet Union, the advance of Communism and the rising struggle of the colonial peoples, the leaders of reaction in Britain are prepared to surrender their country to American domination, no matter what the cost. . . .

"This question is no mere question of foreign policy alone. It extends to every field—military, economic, political and domestic policy. How far is Britain already tied by the commitments and secret conversations of the Anglo-American Joint Staffs Committee? How far has Anglo-American military and strategic 'integration' already gone? What lies behind the decision to slow up demobilisation, to maintain the staggering figure of one and a half million armed forces in peace time, after every visible enemy has been destroyed, and to impose peace-time conscription of eighteen months . . . The present decisive question is not the question of the principle of conscription. It is the question of the size of the armed forces and of the purposes for which they are used. Are the young people of Britain, desperately needed for reconstruction at home, to be called on to serve as counter-revolutionary armies to maintain the monarcho-fascist regime in Greece or impose colonial subjection in India, Egypt, Iraq, Burma, and Malaya? . . .

"No less serious are the consequences in the economic sphere. The current deficit on the British balance of payments for 1946, on the basis of the available figures for the first nine months, runs at £425 millions for the year. But according to the estimate presented during the Washington negotiations no less than £300 millions of the total deficit is for 'non-recurrent Government expenditure overseas'. What is this Government expenditure overseas? 'Most of it is for military purposes' (*Economist*, 16th November). . . . Two-thirds of the deficit on the British balance of payments are due to Mr. Bevin's policy. The drafts on the American loan, amounting to £150 million so far, are more than eaten up by Mr. Bevin's policy, and have served nothing to help British reconstruction."

The National Service Bill, when it was introduced, provided for a period of conscription of eighteen months. This provoked something of a revolt; eighty Labour members put their names down to an amendment to reject it and 72 actually voted against it; the Government gave way, and reduced the period to twelve months. (The subsequent history is interesting as showing how the Government moved further and further into the arms race; before the Act was even to come into operation—the 1st January, 1949—there was strong military pressure for an 18-month period, and the Government gave way to this, without much opposition in Parliament. Later still, the eighteen months were extended to two years.)

NATIONALISING TRANSPORT

The Transport Act took into public ownership all the railways (including the already nationalised London Passenger Transport Board), together with their ancillary undertakings, among which were some important docks; the canals; and the bulk of long-distance road haulage. Apart from any question of political principle there was a strong case for this measure, for public transport represented a natural monopoly, the proper organisation and co-ordination of which calls for unification under one authority, and the investment necessary to re-organise transport and to bring the railways into an efficient condition was much greater than private enterprise was willing to provide.

Road transport was a little more complicated than railways, since much road transport operates locally over short distances, and many vehicles are specially constructed or adapted to carry special loads. Accordingly, the Act nationalised long-distance road haulage; i.e. all undertakings whose chief business was the carriage of goods by road for distances over 40 miles; and no private carrier could carry goods "for hire or reward" beyond a 25-mile radius without a permit from the Transport Commission, except for the carriage of liquids in bulk, furniture removal, the carriage of meat and livestock, and the use of vehicles specially constructed to carry abnormal indivisible loads.

Operators carrying their own goods were to be restricted to 40 miles, unless they obtained permits to carry further.

Road passenger transport was left untouched, except of course that the interests held by the railways in such concerns passed to the Transport Commission along with other railway holdings.

COMPENSATION

Compensation was, once again, generous. The railway and canal stockholders were given "British Transport Stock", guaranteed by the Government, equivalent in value to their railway or canal stock at the average Stock Exchange quotations for a number of days in November, 1946 (or the prices ruling prior to the General Election if they were higher). They thus got the security of the Government in place of that of various companies which in any view were less reliable than the government; and they were saved from a precarious future in which they would have had to meet very large expenditure to bring the railways, rolling-stock, etc., up-to-date, and would in addition have had to face severe competition in many fields from road-haulage. The large numbers of very varied privately owned railway wagons were taken over at cost less depreciation.

Compensation for road-haulage undertakings was also based, so far as vehicles were concerned, on cost less depreciation; the rest of the property was taken at market value.

RAILWAYS IN POOR CONDITION

The condition of the railways at the time they were taken over, as described in the Labour Party policy statement, *Public Enterprise*, endorsed by the 1957 Annual Conference, "was deplorable. Most of the rolling-stock, engines, permanent way, and stations were in bad repair and obsolescent. The financial position of the companies was precarious, and two were fast slipping into bankruptcy."

And in fact, in the first year of public ownership, 769 locomotives were broken up, and in the first three years 85,000 mineral wagons suffered the same fate. Indeed, one-third of the engines and passenger coaches and over half the goods wagons which had been taken over were scrapped within a few years.

Everything that the Transport Commission had to spend on re-equipment had to be raised by borrowing at current rates.

The power to license private road hauliers to carry over 40 miles was exercised so generously as to drive a loophole through the Act.

PERSONNEL

The membership of the administrative bodies, which as mentioned in Chapter 5 has a very important bearing on the success of nationalisation in practice, followed the same unsocialist pattern as in the previous year. The Transport Commission had a civil servant as chairman, and as members three railway or transport directors, the general secretary of the Co-operative Union, and a former general secretary of the National Union of Railwaymen. The Railway Executive chairman and all but two of the six full-time members were railway officials; of the two exceptions, one was a retired general and one an ex-general secretary of the Locomotive Union.

ELECTRICITY

The nationalisation of electricity under the Electricity Act, 1947, was similar in essence, but different in many details. Electric supply was a relatively modern industry, extremely profitable to private interests, which had had a good share of it, particularly since the 'twenties. Electricity has to be generated, and then distributed; and under modern conditions transmission, i.e. the carrying of high tension current from generating stations to various distribution points, is an important and in some respects separate operation. A national "grid" system of transmission was already in existence under the Central Electricity Board established in 1926, but distribution was still in the hands of 570 undertakings, of which 370 were municipal. The private companies not only charged, in general, higher prices than the municipal undertakings, but had failed to give supplies to large rural areas under their control.

The technical arguments for nationalisation were strong; the great number of unco-ordinated undertakings was wasteful; larger supply areas were essential to efficiency; and a great expansion of the industry, requiring major technical re-organisation, was urgently needed. There was relatively little opposition to the nationalisation of generation, but there was a good deal of resistance—unsuccessful in the end—to that of distribution, where rich profits were still to be had.

The Act established the British Electricity Authority, to which the Central Electricity Board, with its "grid", was transferred; and the Authority took over generation, transmission, and distribution. Fifteen area boards were set up under the Authority; one of these, the North of Scotland Board, was made responsible for generation, transmission, and distribution, but in the rest of the country the Authority was responsible for generation and bulk supply, whilst the fourteen Boards—under the supervision of the Authority—attended to distribution.

On compensation, the story was much the same as before, and the private owners did not suffer. The loan and share capital of the private companies was replaced by electricity stock, the value being calculated exactly as in the case of the transport nationalisation; and the loan liabilities of the local authority undertakings were transferred to the Authority.

One notable "absentee" from nationalisation was the iron and steel industry. The nationalisation of this powerful industry was one of the main purposes on which the Labour Party had fought the 1945 Election; it was the one item of nationalisation that was likely to be met with really heavy opposition, and should accordingly have been taken up at an early stage of the Government's history, when its popular mandate was fresh, popular support was strong, and the enemy were demoralised, and when, if the House of Lords were bold enough to throw out the Bill, there would be time under the Parliament Act, 1911, for the Bill to be carried through over the Lords' persistence. But the Government was timid, and postponed the measure. The results were serious, since all the heavy industries were continuously hampered by shortage of steel, which a nationalised and technically improved industry could have put right.

CHAPTER 10

Foreign Policy, 1946-7

THE problems of foreign policy were acute in 1946-7.

The first incident of note—for the moment an encouraging one—came as early as the 12th November, 1946, at the opening of the parliamentary session. Between fifty and sixty Labour back-benchers, including many trade unionists, tabled an amendment to the "Address", criticising the Government's foreign policy, particularly in relation to the U.S.S.R. The amendment expressed the "urgent hope" that the government would "so review and recast its conduct of international affairs as to afford the utmost encouragement to, and collaboration with, all Nations and Groups striving to secure full Socialist planning and control of the world's resources, and thus provide a democratic and constructive Socialist alternative to an otherwise inevitable conflict between American capitalism and Soviet Communism, in which all hope of world government would be destroyed."

A REVOLT

Following on the motion of criticism which had commanded substantial minority support at the Trades Union Congress in the previous month, as we have seen in Chapter 6, this revolt was extremely significant. Mr. and Mrs. Coates tell us in their book, at p. 200, that it was discussed on the 13th November at a meeting of the Parliamentary Labour Party, at which supporters and opponents of the motion agreed that it should "remain on the Order Paper, but should not actually be moved", (which in the light of what subsequently happened—I take to mean should not be taken to a vote).

This amendment was moved, and discussed at length, in the House of Commons (see *Hansard*, Vol. 430, Cols. 526 *et seq.*, 18th November, 1946). Mr. Crossman, who moved it, put three questions to the Government: (1) will you disavow the policy propounded by Winston Churchill at Fulton?; (2) have you agreed to standardise the arms of our forces with those of the U.S.A.?; and (3) are you holding staff conversations with the U.S.A. Chiefs of Staff?

Mr. Sydney Silverman in the debate asked in effect; "Do you suggest that the reason why you are always in opposition to the U.S.S.R. is because that country is *always* in the wrong?"

ATTLEE WON'T REJECT FULTON

Bevin was in New York at the time, and Attlee replied to the debate. He rejected the splendid opportunity offered to him by Crossman's first question to show some sign of a positive foreign policy and to repudiate the Fulton policy, he simply repeated what he had said, as mentioned in Chapter 6, at the time of the Fulton speech, that "it is not the business of the Government to get up and make answers about speeches made by individuals, however prominent". (The truth is, of course, that if he had said: "No, we do not agree with the Fulton policy", he would not only not have been telling the truth but would have got into trouble with the Americans.)

To Crossman's other two questions, he answered, in effect: Yes.

To Silverman's question he made a curious answer: "When we have voted against Soviet Russia, although we may have been wrong on one or two occasions, we were generally in the right." This came very near to saying—on behalf of a government returned to power in the cause of socialism, on the basis of an election in which it had claimed to be friendly to the U.S.S.R., and that "Left understand Left"—"Well, yes, we have voted steadily against it"—as if that was their *primary* task in the service of American capitalism—"and we have been wrong to do so at times, but we claim that we were more often right." And all this he said whilst also advancing the cliché which the Government often used and the Labour Party adopted in the pamphlet *Cards on the Table*, to which I will come shortly, that "we don't gang up; we decide on the merits of each question", involving the corollary that the capitalist U.S.A. is always right on the merits, and the socialist U.S.S.R. always wrong. (I comment on this "merits" argument later in this chapter).

Incidentally, Attlee disclosed in this speech that the Government had already agreed to fuse their occupation zone in Germany with the American zone to form "Bizonia", and indeed to go on to Trizonia (the fusion of the British, American and French zones). I will come to this in due course.

When the debate on the amendment concluded, Crossman, who had already stated that the movers did not propose to carry it to a vote, (a piece of parliamentary procedure which is quite normal, however curious it may appear to the general public) asked leave to withdraw it.

This is normally granted without opposition, but two members of the old Independent Labour Party mischievously called "No", thus compelling the Speaker to refuse leave and to put the amendment to the vote. The two mischief-makers gave in their own names as "tellers", but no one went into the lobby on their side. The amendment was defeated by 353 votes to nil; the 353 consisted of all those Labour members who were not in favour of the amendment, plus a number of Tories. Not less than one hundred Labour members who agreed with the amendment openly abstained from voting by the orthodox method of remaining seated in the Chamber whilst the vote was taken.

THE REVOLT ANALYSED

I prepared an analysis of the revolt at the time, which shows that it was not a left-wing, still less a communist, revolt, although the left supported it; it came from a core of conscious social-democrats somewhere in the centre, who pursued social-democratic policy deliberately, and not vaguely or in ignorance. They made this public revolt only after they had done all they could by private representation and argument within the Party, and had failed to get their views accepted. The leaders of the rebellion were mostly in close touch with developments in Europe, and they revolted because in those European countries where the social-democrats were fighting the communists (instead of co-operating with them against their common enemies), the crude anti-Soviet "Bevinism" of the British Government was making social democracy so unpopular with the general public that it was losing ground to the communists.

It was a weakness of the revolt, good as it was on the merits, that it came from the centre, for the leaders of centre revolts are apt to abandon the struggle at an early stage, lest they give too much encouragement or credit to the left.

That was one reason for the failure, but a stronger reason, in all probability, was the cunning of the right wing leadership, which has had long experience in crushing revolts by threats and blandishments. It could use among other arguments, the strong one—under a two-party system—that one must not rock the boat, however badly it may be steered, for fear of helping the Tory enemy. I think that Mr. Ernest Watkins, in *The Cautious Revolution* (Secker and Warburg, 1951), was correct in his view that this revolt

"never seriously threatened the Government, and it had the effect of making two things perfectly clear thereafter . . . that, for the purposes of that government, Mr. Attlee and Mr. Bevin could be considered as twin stars, bound together by forces too strong for any minority movement of revolt to defeat or weaken, [and] that the foreign policy of the government would be the foreign policy of Mr. Bevin, pure and simple, and that any resemblance between that and a 'socialistic' foreign policy would be purely coincidental ...

"It hardened the feeling of the trade unionist elements in the party against the intellectuals to their left. . . . Mr. Bevin established an ascendancy that was never shaken, not even after events in Palestine."

"CARDS ON THE TABLE"

One pretty direct result of the revolt was that the Labour Party shortly afterwards published a pamphlet, *Cards on the Table*, which was at once a defence of its foreign policy and an anti-Soviet diatribe. The authors "grasped the nettle" of the revolt with the remark that "apart from disagreement on particular issues like Palestine, Greece, or Spain (which are not discussed in this pamphlet), some loyal members of the Party are genuinely concerned about the general line of Labour's foreign policy, because it is held to take sides with a capitalist America against a socialist Russia, or to entail a diversion of men and money from home production which this country cannot afford. It is mainly to answer these general criticisms that this pamphlet is directed."

The authors went on to refer to certain positive achievements of the Government, claiming that "we have gone far to abolish *the old type of* imperialism" (my italics) in relation to Transjordan, India, Burma, Ceylon, Egypt and other countries.

ANTI-SOVIET SNEERS

They then embarked on a long indictment of the U.S.S.R., sneering at her alleged weakness resulting from her war efforts, at her "ineptitude", and at the "worse than total failure" of her policy, and accusing her of being the cause of all the troubles and tensions in the world and of being especially hostile to Britain. The Labour Government, they said, had "stood patiently firm against Russian encroachment". (An impartial observer might find it difficult to say what encroachment there had been, but the writers probably regarded the birth of the People's Democracies of Central and Eastern Europe as "encroachment" by the Soviet Union.) And, not unnaturally, they praised the Truman Doctrine, the true anti-Soviet and anti-communist nature of which is explained later in this chapter.

Having thus lined up fully with the American policy of indiscriminate anti-Sovietism, in striking contrast to the professions made during the General Election campaign of two years before, and to what might be expected of a party and a government claiming to be socialist, the authors sought to defend the Government against the accusation which they had surely just made good. They wrote:

"*Bevin and Churchill*: The foregoing analysis of Britain's reaction to Russian policy since 1945 may seem to justify the critics who say Bevin has been pursuing the Fulton policy, and is in this respect indistinguishable from Churchill. But . . . there is a decisive difference.

"The policy of the Conservative Party . . . is to seek an exclusive Anglo-American alliance expressly directed against Soviet Russia. The policy of the Labour Government, however, is to judge all questions on their merits, to seek or accept common action with the United States only where there is a clear common interest, but in no case to be drawn into commitments which exclude the possibility of a similar collaboration with Russia."

This "judging on the merits" was not a very convincing answer, for in the light of everything that the Government had done in relation to the U.S.S.R., and of what was written in the pamphlet, it amounted to an assertion that, judged "on the merits", that country was always in the wrong: "Item, the King, to be tried on the merits, condemned and executed." The "merits" answer, redolent of the Foreign Office with its long experience of finding the most plausible excuse—however threadbare—for any and every piece of wickedness designed to advance the interests or condone the conduct of the British ruling class, was obviously borrowed by the pamphleteer from the broadcast by Bevin to the nation on the 22nd December, 1946, in which he said:

"You have all heard the allegation that we are joined too closely in our policies with the United States, that our relations with Soviet Russia are not as close as they should be, and that this course will retard the pacification of the world and may lead to another world war.

"My first answer to these allegations is that Great Britain brings her mind to bear on every problem on its merits. She does not tie herself to anybody except in regard to her obligations under the Charter . . . My second answer is that we hold out the hand of friendship and co-operation to all."

This broadcast, and the pamphlet, could be made the subject of many comments. The only one that I need give here is that it did not occur to Bevin to make the point that he often made at other times, that the U.S.S.R. had singled out Britain as the target of her special hostility.

"KEEP LEFT"

At about the same time as *Cards on the Table*, a manifesto of a group of M.P.s was published under the title of *Keep Left*. I endorse the comments of Mr. Miliband at p. 296 of *Parliamentary Socialism*:

"This document, though paying tribute to the Government's achievement, urged greater boldness upon it at home, denounced 'the fallacy of collective security against Communism', and repudiated the argument that 'the only way to stop Communism spreading is to organise the world against Russia'. 'It would be a betrayal of British and European Socialism', said the document, 'if we meekly accepted Communist leadership. But it would be equally fatal to accept American leadership in exchange for dollars.'

"However, the *Keep Left* group was never more than a fairly loose group of M.P.s without any hard centre. Never in fact had the Labour Left so entirely lacked coherence and organisation as it did after 1945. Nor did it have any leader of any prominence; its standard-bearer of the war years, Aneurin Bevan, was now safely busy as Minister of Health with the creation of the National Health Service."

OUR EMBASSY IN MOSCOW

The anti-Soviet alignment of the British Embassy in Moscow at this period—dictated by the Foreign Office and the Government in London—is related by Archie Johnstone, an able and experienced British journalist who was appointed in February, 1947, as the editor of *British Ally*, a weekly Russian-language paper published in Moscow by the Embassy with the ostensible purpose of explaining life in Britain to the Soviet public.

Johnstone held the post for two years, and then, in April, 1949, resigned in disgust at the anti-Soviet policy of the Government, compulsorily reflected in the paper, and wrote a letter to *Pravda*, the Soviet daily, explaining his reasons.

The following passages from his letter, which are quoted in Mr. and Mrs. Coates' book at pp. 338-9, are illuminating:

"Shortly after I took over the editorship, I was told in the British Embassy in Moscow, to my astonisment, that a series of anti-Soviet speeches by Attlee, Bevin and Morrison would have to be published. . . .

"One instance, typical of many, that shook me particularly was when the Ambassador, Sir Maurice Peterson, gave specific directions to publish a speech by Attlee in which he referred to 'torrents of Soviet abuse of the British people' . . . .

'I protested to the Ambassador that never at any time has the Soviet Press abused the British people. Everybody agreed that Mr. Attlee's speech was false, but nevertheless Sir Maurice Peterson . . . forced me to publish it . . . .

"It became completely apparent to me that the British Embassy in Moscow has no interest in improving relations between England and the Soviet Union, and that in fact they are doing everything to spoil them. . . .

"During the two years of my life in the U.S.S.R. I have never heard of one single Soviet citizen, even in private talk, advocating war or proclaiming the necessity for it. . . .

"I therefore accuse Attlee, Bevin, McNeil, Morrison, and the other Labour Party leaders of using against the interests of the British people the power which they attained by deceiving the British people."

GERMANY

I turn now to Germany. The first thing to report is the steps taken towards a fusion of the British and American occupation zones into a joint zone under the name of Bizonia, which had been mentioned by Attlee in the speech to which I referred above. Whilst formal negotiations to that end began only in November, 1946, the plan had been mooted for some months, and had indeed been the subject of discussion between Britain and U.S.A. in June, 1946; it clearly envisaged the linking up of Anglo-American monopoly capital with a re-born—or rather never dead but temporarily restricted—German monopoly capitalism. *The New Statesman and Nation* of the 19th October, 1946, had reported:

"The merger of the British and American zones is already taking place, and it has been stressed that one objective of this merger is to reduce our financial commitments. This can only be done on the assumption that American Big Business is encouraged to obtain controlling interests in German industry, and the German trusts are reconstructed on American credit. If, for instance, General Motors buys up the Volkswagen factory, United Steel obtains a controlling interest in the Vereinigte Stahlwerke, and Dupont in I.G. Farben, then, it is thought, a reduction in the costs of a joint Anglo-American control can be secured.

"This, no doubt is what Mr. Byrnes means when he states his determination to 'rebuild democracy' in Germany."

It was of course true that the British Government needed to reduce its financial commitments, and that the occupation of Germany was costing a great deal; but this merger was nevertheless important as one of the first steps in the re-establishment of German power which has immeasurably increased the danger of war by establishing the chauvinist and revenge-seeking government of Adenauer, fortified by immense American investment, at the head of the most powerful armed State in Europe, rebuilt in defiance of the Potsdam Agreement as an American weapon against the U.S.S.R. in the service of the insane U.S. anti-communist and anti-Soviet policies. It is worth noting that Adenauer, "the old fox", who was known to cherish a deep hatred for the British, who had removed him on the ground of alleged incompetence from his office as Mayor of Cologne during the British occupation after the First World War, had put forward this plan as early as the 5th October, 1945, when he said: "the best thing would be to form the three Western zones at once into a federal state, and to link that state as closely as possible economically with France and Belgium".

Thus, within six months of "V.E. Day", he was beginning his role of telling an only too willing British Government, step by step, everything it ought to do to please capitalist Germany and U.S.A., oppose the U.S.S.R., and lay the foundations of a new war.

On the 22nd November, 1946, formal talks were held between Bevin and Byrnes on the fusion, in the absence, of course, of any Soviet representatives, early meetings with whom "to discuss the future of Germany" had been promised in the King's Speech; and by the 2nd December an agreement was actually signed, and the fusion was carried through.

As I have shown, the establishment of Bizonia was far more than a mere administrative arrangement; it meant that the Labour Government, abandoning any idea of making Four-Power government work, was linking itself finally with U.S. policy over Germany. In due course, Bizonia was to become Trizonia, and Trizonia was to become the Federal German Republic of Krupp, Adenauer, and NATO.

GREECE

In Greece developments led, or seemed to lead, up to the proclamation by President Truman of the "Truman doctrine" on the 12th March, 1947. The position was going from bad to worse in the early part of 1947. Over the years, at very great expense and loss of life, the British Government—at first the Coalition and then the Labour Government—had been "saving Greece for democracy", i.e. heading off the otherwise certain establishment of a left government under the Republic, and setting up a monarcho-fascist tyranny, with as many (by September 1947) as 50,000 people exiled to the islands and living under terrible conditions—some of whom are still there as I write— many hundreds executed, the trade union movement suppressed and replaced by a "stooge" organisation—all of which created a vast guerrilla movement in the mountains, described of course by the Greek and British governments as "communist". Their inability to suppress the guerrillas—initially only a few thousands in number—was attributed by those two governments to the alleged arming of the guerrillas by the Soviet Union; but every effort, including an elaborate commission of enquiry, failed completely to produce any evidence whatever of this.*

HANDING GREECE OVER

As will be mentioned in Chapter 12, Britain suffered heavy economic losses as a result of the exceptionally severe spell of winter weather which started in the latter part of January, 1947, and lasted through February. The government, driven by this extra financial stringency to seek to get rid of the continuing drain of the Greek adventure, (and perhaps also using it as a pretext to force the Americans to shoulder the burden), informed the Department of State on the 24th February, 1947, that it was no longer possible for Britain, in her economic position, to "continue as the reservoir of financial and military support for Greece and Turkey". The result was that we slowly got out of

---

* There was one comic incident in the course of the inquiry; a rifle with an inscription in the Cyrillic alphabet was found, and carried in propaganda triumph to Athens as proof of Soviet intervention, only to be established—when it came before some official sufficiently educated to read the inscription—to have been manufactured by the government of Serbia in the seventies of the last century. But this sort of exposure did not prevent Bevin making such observations as "a ruthless attempt, constantly maintained, to bring that country into the Soviet orbit" (*Hansard*, Vol. 446, Col. 385).

Greece, handing over the anti-socialist and fascist cause in that country to the Americans; but the operation took some months; our troops were still there in July, 1947, when there was widespread fighting and 2,500 "communists" were arrested; and even the announcement on the 5th August, 1947, that our troops were "to be withdrawn" gave no date.

TRUMAN DOCTRINE

Another apparent result of the British announcement of withdrawal was the proclamation of the "Truman Doctrine", aimed at drawing Greece and Turkey into the anti-Soviet camp, in a speech by Truman to Congress on the 12th March. Truman, who from the day of his succeeding Roosevelt had displayed a bitter and ill-informed anti-Soviet bias, had been preparing this proclamation for a long time, and he used the British announcement as a peg on which to hang it, although all that the announcement had done was to increase slightly the possibility that the Greek people might follow the example of some of their neighbours, and establish a people's democracy in preference to a brutal fascist tyranny.*

The proclamation of the "doctrine" was very oddly timed, for it came at an early stage of the meeting of the Council of Foreign Ministers in Moscow, as if he were determined to wreck it. (I deal with that meeting a little later.)

Alaric Jacob, a very able British correspondent then stationed in Moscow, cabled on the 13th March, 1947:

"Russian relations with America have never been so grim as today. President Truman's message to Congress, urging men and money for Greece and Turkey, has by its tone and timing eclipsed the agenda of the Big Four Conference on Germany."

And *The Times*, after the Conference had ended largely in failure, wrote on the 26th April: "Mr. Truman's new policy on Greece and Turkey . . . abruptly proclaimed on the third day, overshadowed the Conference and helped to make it sterile."

Truman began his speech to Congress introducing the "Doctrine" by describing—or rather misdescribing—the position in Greece as

---

* Professor Fleming, clear-headed but in no sense pro-communist, quoted the following description of the position from the *New York Herald Tribune*:

"[The Soviet Union] has a great deal more to export than bullets. It has energy and enthusiasm; it has order, full employment, the classless society, the end of grosser forms of social injustice." That the writer thought fit to add: "But the totalitarian subjection and the N.K.V.D. which inevitably go with them" would not be likely to deter Greeks who had suffered totalitarian subjection under the Greek fascist government.

one in which "a militant minority, exploiting human want and misery, was able to create political chaos which . . . has made economic recovery impossible". (He would have been nearer the truth if he had said that there was a militant minority opposing a corrupt and impotent monarcho-fascist government, imposed on the Greek people by British policy, British troops, and British money, which government had increased the ever-present want and misery of the Greek people, and made economic recovery impossible.) He by-passed the United Nations by stating that "we" had considered how the United Nations might help, but the situation was urgent and the United Nations and its related organisations were not in a position to extend "help of the kind that is required". (The truth was, of course, that he could not plausibly have put before the U.N.O., which was designed to embrace the whole world, a scheme for quarantining a large part of that world because he and the ruling-class that controlled him feared and hated its political system.)

He went on to talk of the "terroristic activities of several thousand armed men, led by communists", who had created a situation with which the Greek government could not cope. (He would have done better to say that the Greek government was unable to cope with the situation, which it had itself created by driving all opposition into the mountains, partly because it was too incompetent to cope with any serious situation at all, but more because it had alienated almost all Greek public opinion.)

Truman next said that Turkey also deserved attention; it had been spared the disasters of war but "needed modernisation". Its integrity was essential to the preservation of order in the Middle East. (This was no doubt the most plausible explanation for the apparently sudden introduction of Turkey into the problem of Greece; for he could not openly confess that he was plotting to use Turkey as well as Greece as a cold-war base for the attempted encirclement of the U.S.S.R.)

THE DOCTRINE FORMULATED

Then came the most sinister part of Truman's speech, the actual formulation of the "Doctrine". We would not, he said, "realise our objectives" unless we were "willing to help free people to maintain their free institutions and their national integrity against aggressive movements that seek to impose upon them totalitarian régimes". After references to Poland, Bulgaria, Rumania, and other countries, he said that the time had come when "nearly every nation must choose between alternative ways of life", one distinguished by "free" (American code word for "capitalist") institutions and the other by terror and oppression. And, he said, he believed "that it must be the policy of the United States to support free peoples who are resisting attempted subjugation by armed minorities or by outside pressure".

He concluded by asking Congress to vote $400,000,000 for Greece and Turkey and to give him authority to detail civilian and military personnel to those countries.

This manœuvre was an American not a British crime; but it marked such a step forward in the Cold War, was of such tragic importance, and was so fully accepted by the British Government, that it is necessary to give some details of it here. I take them largely from pp. 439 *et seq.* of Professor Fleming's book. Earlier in his book, at p. 205, he had written shortly of it thus: "President Truman re-declared the Cold War on March 12, 1947, in the Truman Doctrine. . . a year exactly after the Cold War had been announced by Churchill at Fulton, Missouri, in Truman's presence." Now, in his fuller comments, he wrote:

"No pronouncement could have been more sweeping. Wherever a communist rebellion developed, the United States would suppress it. Wherever the Soviet Union attempted to push outward, at any point around its vast circumference, the United States would resist. The United States would become the world's anti-communist, anti-Russian policeman.

"This, too, was not the full extent of the Doctrine, for its all-inclusive language also forbade every kind of revolution, democratic or otherwise. . . . The President went on to say that the status quo was not sacred; but he had made it so. So far as the United States was concerned, the method by which this nation was born was outlawed. There would be no more revolutions thereafter, in spite of the fact that many hundreds of millions of people lived a miserable existence under the misrule of a few. . . .

"Truman spoke for the bulk of American conservatives, and allied himself with reaction around the globe. . . . Truman presented to the communists the entire field of revolutionary activity and condemned his own people"—and the British, with the acquiescence of their government—"to the sterile and hopeless task of trying to prevent all forcible social change everywhere. . . .

"The wheel had come to full circle with a vengeance. The isolationist United States, desiring only to be left alone, had become the world's policeman. Wherever public order was disturbed, we would be there. Wherever the Soviet Government or communism attempted an advance, the United States would combat it. The most gigantic land power on the face of the globe, living on the opposite side of the earth from the United States, was to be fenced in at all points. . . . In the two previous balance of power struggles Germany had complained constantly that she was being encircled, but no one of her opponents ever dreamed of admitting that she was. Now Mr. Truman had proclaimed from one of the world's greatest rostrums the most gigantic encirclement ever conceived in the mind of man.

"When the Truman Doctrine was announced, Winston Churchill was jubilant. He had every right to be, since it was essentially the same doctrine he had enunciated at Fulton, Missouri, by Truman's 'desire', only a year before. Not only was his doctrine accepted; it was applied to the one spot on the globe to which he attached most importance and where he had used the most extreme measures to preserve British control and to reinstate the Greek monarchy.

"In Greece, too, the monarchists were equally triumphant. . . ."

Professor Fleming also quoted the comments of the distinguished American journalist, Walter Lippman, to the effect that the basic fallacy of the Truman Doctrine lay in its assumption that the spread of communism could be checked by subsidising the reactionary forces of the world.

TRUMAN DOCTRINE OPPOSED

There was of course opposition to the Doctrine in Britain, even if it had little success. On the 7th April, the Co-operative Party of Great Britain, one of the major arms of the Labour Party, and representing about 7,500,000 working people, approved by a large majority a resolution condemning Truman's programme of aid to Greece and Turkey as "a menace to world peace and the negation of the democratic principles for the preservation of peace for which the grave sacrifices of the last war were made".

An American correspondent in Athens reported at this time that the Greek Government had "managed to fritter away virtually all its foreign exchange, drive more people into the mountains because they were being treated as outlaws for having dared to express opposition, and to hold a club over the Western powers that unless abundant aid is immediately forthcoming Greece would go communist". He added that, when the aid was forthcoming, the Minister of the Interior publicly opposed any international supervision of an amnesty for Greek guerrillas, on the ground that it would offend Greek pride and infringe on Greek sovereignty.

THE CAT OUT OF THE BAG

The true object of the Truman Doctrine was more frankly stated on the 15th May, 1947, when the American Congress finally approved the Greek-Turkish Assistance Bill, providing the $400,000,000 demanded by Truman. Mr. and Mrs. Coates, at pp. 245-6 of their book, describe it thus:

"During the debates in the House and Senate no secret was made of the fact that the aim of the Bill was to build up outposts directed against the Soviet Union."

They quoted the Washington correspondent of the *Daily Telegraph*, who cabled on the 9th May that the remarks of one Congressman Merrow were "characteristic of the temper of today's debate". Merrow had said:

"I would like to know how much longer we are going to be insulted by those in charge of the Soviet Union before taking a stand.

"I do not think war with Russia is inevitable. But if Russia wants to regard this as an act of war let her make the most of it."

The same correspondent cabled nine days later:

"The Army, Navy, and State Department have selected personnel for their Greek and Turkish missions. They now await the word to leave.

"In Turkey the first task will be to correlate Turkish and American ideas on the country's defence. . . .

"Passage through Congress of the Greek-Turkish Bill and the prospective passage this week of the £87,500,000 Foreign Relief Bill represent the first phase of the new United States policy set out by Mr. Truman."

And Mr. and Mrs. Coates added for themselves:

"The other phases of the Truman programme included the re-establishment of Japan on the eastern frontiers of the U.S.S.R., and

H

of Germany on the western frontiers of the U.S.S.R., as Great
Powers.

"The encirclement of the U.S.S.R. was by this date taking very
concrete form."

FOREIGN MINISTERS' CONFERENCE IN MOSCOW

The Conference of Foreign Ministers met in Moscow from the 10th
March—as already noted, just before the proclamation of the Truman
Doctrine—to the 24th April, 1947, Its agenda covered the future
political structure of Germany, peace treaties with Germany and
Austria, and reparations. The Conference failed in the sense that very
little was agreed, but—as was pointed out by R. P. Dutt in the Notes
of the Month in *Labour Monthly* of June, 1947—it was not a complete
failure:

> "The Moscow Conference registered disagreement of the Powers
> on the major issues of Germany and the peace. But it did not
> register the breakdown and rupture which the Truman Declaration
> had been designed to precipitate (Dulles, Republican Adviser to the
> United States delegation, proposed immediate break-up of the
> Conference, following the Truman Declaration). . . . All the
> unresolved issues were remitted for six months to a fresh confer-
> ence."

The reason for the failure to agree was given with unconscious
candour by Ernest Bevin, who wrote to Attlee from Moscow on the
16th April, 1947, towards the end of the Moscow sessions (see pp.
154-9 of *A Prime Minister Remembers*):

> "I am afraid we are going to break down because the Russians will
> not face it, and that is the fundamental question of . . . the type of
> political principles that must be adopted if we are to get a democratic
> Germany, that is, democracy as we understand it."

In other words, Bevin was demanding that the Soviet Union should
agree to the establishment of a new German State on the British or
American pattern of parliamentary democracy—i.e. a capitalist
democracy in which the industrial ruling class should hold power—
—with the certainty that the country would go through all the stages
of development which have in fact since been seen in Western
Germany; rule by such forces as the Krupps, re-armament, integration
in the anti-Soviet cold-war camp, and suppression of every progressive

organisation, leading to militant neo-Nazism. (The whole letter is interesting; it could have been written by any vigorous Tory or American anti-Soviet politician.)

Thus, no headway was made over a German peace treaty. As for Austria, some progress was made, and the unsolved questions were referred to a Commission.

REPARATIONS

The long-standing dispute over reparations, to which I made a brief reference in Chapter 6, contributed greatly to worsening relations between Britain and the U.S.S.R. The latter country had both right and merit on its side; right, because it had been agreed at Yalta that heavy reparations should be paid, and be partly drawn from current production; and merit because the U.S.S.R. had suffered infinitely more than any other major power in loss of human life and property from the Nazi invasion. Nevertheless, the British Government firmly resisted all Soviet efforts to secure delivery of the agreed reparations. The suspicion naturally arose that they had inherited the Churchill policy—and embraced the Truman policy—of trying to retard the recovery of the U.S.S.R. and to keep her as weak as possible for as long as possible—a suspicion in no way lessened by the vulgar sneers at Soviet "weakness" in the pamphlet *Cards on the Table*, which I have mentioned.

The argument advanced by the Government was that the administration of the British zone of occupation was costing Britain many millions, particularly in having to import food to feed the Germans, and that if they were to permit the recovery of reparations it would cost them more still. This would seem to most people a poor reason for breaking an agreement, particularly one made with the ally who had both suffered and achieved more than any other power in the war; moreover, much of the occupation costs were inflated by inefficiency and corruption, and by leaving Nazis in positions of control in German industry, with opportunities for waste and sabotage. Good administration could have avoided most of the losses.

The attitude of the Government can be gathered from Bevin's letter of the 16th April, 1947, to Attlee, already mentioned; he there described the Soviet demand as a "desire and determination to loot Germany at our expense". He had moreover made matters worse as early as the 8th September, 1946, in his concluding speech to the Peace Conference in Paris. Speaking of reparations, he said that from the outset the British view had been that it would be better in the general interest if reparations were restricted to deliveries which could not be said to interfere with the development of trade and reconstruction. "Indeed", he said, "I myself proposed at an early stage in our deliberations that the Great Powers at any rate should make a kind of self-denying ordinance and agree to demand no reparations for themselves." He was thus in effect saying to the U.S.S.R.: "You may have been bled white by the Germans, and may be in urgent need of the reparations on which, as we have agreed, you have a right to insist; but it would be a nice gesture on your part to forego them altogether, so as to help in the development of the trade and the reconstruction of those who have done you these terrible injuries, whilst you endure for a good deal longer the hardships which reparations would help to diminish." (He did not improve the position by going on, in the same speech, to demand the agreement of the other delegations to the British claim to take reparations from Italy!)

This resistance to the Soviet claim for reparations was due not only to a desire to weaken the U.S.S.R. by any and every means, but also to the wish to help in building up swiftly a powerful and reactionary monopolist state in West Germany, under American or Anglo-American control. In pursuance of that wish, the payment of reparations had already been gravely neglected in Germany; only £1,000,000 had so far been paid to the U.S.S.R., and only 24 out of 284 war factories had been dismantled in the British Zone. *The Times* of the 24th March, 1947, notes that, according to the Anglo-American plan, "in effect reparations from West Germany's current production could not be paid for nearly fifteen years". Bevin's argument was that the Soviet Union ought to "share all expenses, past, present, and future" in relation to Germany. This would involve her not only in foregoing her reparations from current production, but also in sharing in the burden of Britain's costly mismanagement of her Zone. Through her maintenance of reactionary Junker and ex-Nazi saboteurs in the controlling organs, Britain had incurred a net loss of £38 million in Germany in 1946; and Bevin's principle of "sharing" meant that the repayment of this £38 million was to take priority over the Soviet claim to receive something on account of the £2,500 million agreed at Yalta to be paid by way of reparation in respect of the £32,000 million damage done by the Nazis in the Soviet Union.

As Palme Dutt put it in the Notes of the Month in the *Labour Monthly* of May, 1947, the Soviet claim was opposed—

"in the interests of building up a rich and prosperous monopolist Germany, whilst the Russians in the devastated areas live in holes in the ground.... Once again, as after the first world war, the aim is to build up a powerful reactionary Germany under Anglo-American control as a bulwark against the Soviet Union; and for this aim the Western Powers are prepared to repudiate previous agreements, wreck the Moscow Conference and let it end in deadlock, and even if necessary partition Germany so as to retain the rich industrial areas of the West, the base and power-house of German monopoly and aggression and domination of Europe, as the decisive base of the Western European bloc advocated by official Anglo-American expression."

OPPOSITION TO BEVIN

Opposition to this policy, and to Bevin's policy generally, still persisted in the Labour Party, although it never met with great success, being defeated by a combination of the prestige which still hung round Bevin, of the skill with which Labour and trade union leaders and officials "managed" conferences, and of fears of "rocking the boat". But, on the 25th April, 1947, at the Scottish Trades Union Congress, a resolution demanding a radical change in the Government's foreign policy "in the interests of peace and progress" was lost by the very narrow margin of 166 to 158. It was probably only prevented from securing a majority by an appeal not to condemn "Mr. Bevin's and the Government's foreign policy". On the same day, a similar resolution was put forward at a delegate conference of women members of Bevin's union, the Transport and General Workers, and secured 25 votes against 64. Arthur Deakin, who had succeeded Bevin as General Secretary of the Union, appealed to the Conference to defeat the resolution because it would amount to a vote of "no confidence" in the Government. Opposition at the Labour Party Conference, held at Margate on the 26th-30th May was defeated on a show of hands; Bevin and the Government generally were still able to command a great deal of support, particularly at conferences where the effectiveness of the opposition in debate was reduced by the ban on members of the Communist Party.

At the Co-operative Party Conference held in April, 1947, 3,250,000 votes were cast for a resolution condemning Bevin's foreign policy; it was lost by the tiny majority of 150,000—roughly 5 per cent.; and the resolution mentioned above condemning the Truman Declaration (and implicitly our Government's support of it) was carried by an overwhelming majority.

MOSCOW CONFERENCE DISCUSSED

The Moscow Conference was discussed in the House of Commons on the 15th and 16th May, the debate being both opened and wound up by Bevin himself. On this occasion, whilst stoutly defending his attitude on reparations—he was not among those who sometimes suspect that they might have been wrong—he did not indulge in any anti-Soviet tirade. (Note that he expressed his adherence to the principle of public ownership of the basic industries in Germany!)

GOVERNMENT EXCUSES

It was often argued in defence of the Government's subservience to the U.S.A., and of its support of that country's anti-Soviet policy, that it had no choice but to line up with the U.S.A., since it could not otherwise obtain sufficient money to tide over the first heavy years of reconstruction, and that in any case it was necessary to arm Britain to the teeth lest the Soviet armies should overrun Europe. Neither of these defences was sound.

The first, if it were well-founded, would in any case amount to a confession that the Government had abandoned its claim to pursue a socialist policy, and all hopes of socialist development, and had allied itself with the leading capitalist country against the socialist world, because it felt it had no option save to betray in that fashion every principle it professed. But in truth there was always an alternative course, in harmony with socialist principles, namely to insist on a return to Three-Power co-operation, in which Britain, the U.S.A., and the U.S.S.R., collaborating sincerely in the United Nations and making a democratic peace with Germany, could solve all their economic problems, put an end to the Cold War, avoid all armament races, release colossal sums for social development, and begin to "co-exist" in real peace in a world in which the main contest between the Great Powers would be competition to show whether a socialist or a capitalist economy can best succeed.

Palme Dutt, in the Notes of the Month which I quoted above, wrote thus of the opportunity Britain had at the Moscow Conference of March-April:

"Britain had the opportunity to play an independent role, to end the ignominious position of eternal lieutenant and junior partner of

American imperialism, to exercise effective counter-pressure against the tightening economic and financial stranglehold of American monopoly on Britain's life, to speak for Europe and democracy, and to compel a return to the principles of the United Nations, the treaties agreed at the Crimea and Berlin, and co-operation of the three Great Powers. Such a stand would have transformed the world situation. It would have rallied the immense majority of the democratic nations of the world. It would have completely changed the proceedings . . . at Moscow, compelling agreement in place of deadlock. . . . It would have isolated and rendered impotent the aggressive expansionist designs of American imperialism. For it must never be forgotten that American imperialism is dependent for its aims of world expansion on Britain's support. . . . Were Britain's support withdrawn, American aggression would be faced with the opposition of the entire world and would have to draw in its horns. In that sense Britain holds the key."

THE FICTION OF SOVIET AGGRESSION

As for the argument that it was necessary to maintain immense forces to deal with an impending westward rush of Soviet forces through Europe, this story that the U.S.S.R. wanted to attack Western Europe—a story originally invented by Hitler and Goebbels—was one which no intelligent student of politics could accept; it has, indeed, at various times since 1945 been rejected by many well-known anti-Soviet figures, including John Foster Dulles, Bedell Smith, and George F. Kennan. It was moreover a story which the Labour Party, professing to be a friend of the Soviet Union, should have been eager to repudiate. All the facts of the situation combined to deny it; the obvious need of the U.S.S.R. for peace in order to cope with its vast problems of rehabilitiation, its lack of any need for territories into which to expand, the modest scale of its defence expenditure (inconsistent with any intention of aggression), its knowledge that it is impossible to export ideologies by force of arms, its socialist principles, and if the Labour Party were prepared to believe its own propaganda in *Cards on the Table* one might add, its military and economic weakness, all went to show that there was no need to fear invasion from that quarter.

The Labour Government might—and should—have been able to convince itself that there was no danger, by the simple reflection that even the most stupid propagandist would never have taken the risk of advancing the constant American argument—one which amounted to an invitation to the U.S.S.R. to attack at once—that the U.S.S.R. could at that time sweep through Europe almost unresisted, but that within two or three years the West would grow strong enough to resist it, if he had not been quite sure that the U.S.S.R. had no intention whatever of attacking. The Government might equally have reflected that, if anything could have created a danger of Soviet attack, it was the incessant hostile propaganda and threats of war coming from the U.S.A., with the approval of Ernest Bevin. The plain reason for all this American propaganda against the U.S.S.R. lay in a fear that, unless desperate measures were taken, most of the countries in Western Europe would go socialist; in that, it resembles closely the hysterical measures being taken in America, over many years, to persecute members of the U.S. Communist Party. (This matter is discussed further in Chapter 21.)

THE MARSHALL PLAN

The next event of importance was the "Marshall Plan" which was introduced to the public in a speech made by General Marshall, the American Secretary of State, at Harvard University on the 5th June, 1947. According to the parliamentary correspondent of the *Daily Express*, it had in fact been "discussed unofficially in London and Washington before Mr. Marshall's speech"; and *The Times* parliamentary correspondent reported at the same time (issue of the 7th June) that "before Mr. Marshall's speech, there had been unofficial and informal exchanges of view between members of the British Embassy and members of the State Department and other administrative departments on this matter, and from these talks an outline was emerging of the procedure which might be adopted to give effect to this offer of financial aid". "These talks", he added, "will now be continued at an official level."

On its face, the Plan was a proposal to introduce a greater degree of system and co-ordination into U.S. aid to Europe; but there was more to it than that. Its function and purpose as another move in the Cold War became gradually clearer; at the outset, the main point of interest lay in the question whether it was intended to include the U.S.S.R. and other socialist countries in the Plan. Its introduction came less than three months after the birth of the emphatically anti-Soviet Truman Doctrine, which Marshall was known to approve; there was no hint in the speech of any departure from that Doctrine; there were some of the stock phrases used for the exclusion of socialist countries; and there was certainly not a word that suggested including the U.S.S.R. Moreover, as a writer in the City column of *The Times* explained on the 9th June, what weighed most with the American Government about the Marshall scheme was "the greater need for, and greater difficulty of maintaining, governments of a more characteristically European pattern in Western and Southern Europe"—a polite way of saying that the U.S. government was concerned to get rid of communist influence, or communist participation in government, in France and Italy, and to do all it could to defeat and destroy the halfway-socialist governments of the People's Democracies.

There were other signs that the Truman hostility to the U.S.S.R. was not being changed in the least. As reported in a cable from Washington to the *New Statesman and Nation*, "at the very time when the Marshall scheme is being put forward, the State Department is pursuing from day to day a policy so clearly conditioned by distrust of Russia that it gives support to reactionaries without distinction, and now finds no trace of Fascism in the immaculate Perón"—the then current fascist dictator of the Argentine Republic. (The Marshall Plan also resembled the Truman Doctrine in by-passing the United Nations; indeed, it also by-passed the United Nations Economic Commission for Europe, a body on which the U.S.S.R. was represented.)

TO INCLUDE THE U.S.S.R.?

Thus there seemed at the start no doubt that the socialist countries were to be excluded; and it was plain too, that American public opinion, assisted by the Truman Doctrine, had been brought to such a state of anti-Soviet hysteria that Congress would probably not have voted funds for Marshall aid if those countries were not excluded.

But on the 12th June, Marshall explained in a Press conference that when he had spoken on the 5th about aiding Europe, he had included Britain and the U.S.S.R. in the term "Europe", by which, he said, he meant "everything west of Asia".

As Mr. and Mrs. Coates say, at p. 257 of their book, "there can be little doubt that the postscript was made in response to representations from London and Paris"; and there is a good deal of evidence that the proposal for this "postscript" came mainly from Bevin, who probably thought that it was better tactics to give the U.S.S.R. an apparent opportunity to join the Plan, which would never come to anything, either because the U.S.S.R. would not accept Marshall "strings", or because in the end Congress would not sanction aid to that country.

The initial French reaction to the Plan had not been wholly favourable; Attlee told Francis Williams, (see pp. 172, 173 of *A Prime Minister Remembers*) that he had known nothing of the plan before Marshall made his speech at Harvard.*

Attlee added:

"Ernie Bevin came round to see me as soon as we got the first reports, and we talked it over. We both saw what it could lead to. Ernie took it up very quickly. Without him, in fact, it mightn't have come to anything. It was in very general terms, and there were quite a lot of the Americans who didn't want to go anything like so far. They'd have been glad to see it die. But Ernie got on to the French and the others right away, and gave it life, and that encouraged America to go ahead."

(Bevin himself, in his speech in the House of Commons of the 19th June mentioned below, said: "When the Marshall proposals were announced, I grabbed them with both hands.")

HOW TO GET AN INVITATION REFUSED

At any rate, the U.S.S.R. was by the 12th June listed as a possible recipient, and had to be invited to the conference on the plan.† Bevin, faced with the odd task of pretending that the Americans wanted to help the socialist country they were hoping to impoverish and "contain", and that he himself liked this American idea, started with a speech, on the 13th June, in which he said that "We were glad last night to know that misunderstanding has been removed by including Russia in the proposals", and then went on throughout the rest of the negotiations as if he were trying to give the Americans a lesson as to how best to insult the U.S.S.R. Probably no international conference has even been summoned with such an accompaniment of provocations and insults to one of the leading participants as Bevin produced. In the very speech of the 13th June just mentioned, he announced that, in order to explore how best to respond to Marshall's lead, the British Government was going to consult France in the first instance, and what he vaguely called "other European nations" later. To emphasise the point, he declared: "France, Great Britain, and the United States—

* This ignorance is curious in the light of the reports given above from the *Daily Express* and *The Times* parliamentary correspondents.

† The practical impossibility of the U.S.S.R. accepting any of the conditions imposed on Britain and other countries under the Marshall Plan can be seen by examining how those conditions worked out in practice; see Chapter 15.

almost in a direct line geographically—have a great common interest",
as though Britain, under Article V of the Anglo-Soviet Treaty of 1942
which Mr. Bevin had so recently told Stalin he adhered to, had not as
great a "common interest" with the U.S.S.R. On the 17th June, he
flew to Paris, and for two days the British and French Governments
demonstratively held a consultation in which they worked out all the
essential elements of the plan which was later presented, first to
Molotov and then to the Paris conference of fifteen governments, on
the 12th July. After these talks had begun, the British Ambassador in
Moscow, on the 17th June, was still confining himself to asking
Molotov whether the Soviet Government had any "observations"
which it "may care to offer"; and only after the Paris talks were
completed on the 19th June was the Soviet Government invited
to a conference to be held during the week beginning the 23rd
June.

Then, while the Soviet Government was considering the invitation,
the British Government did its best to compel it to reject it. On the day
of Mr. Bevin's return from Paris (the 19th June) a foreign affairs debate
was held in the House of Commons which was marked by a series of
the most violent and hostile attacks on the U.S.S.R. and on the new
democracies ever heard in Parliament. Bevin himself joined in attacks
on Hungary, Poland, Rumania, Bulgaria, and on "dictators" with
whom there was "difficulty in negotiating when there was an under-
lying ideology being pursued". As though to make assurance—or
distrust—doubly sure, Mr. Attlee on the 21st June made a vituperative
attack on the governments of Eastern Europe in a speech at
Barnsley.

Simultaneously it was announced that the U.S. Under-Secretary of
State, Clayton, had arrived in London, and *The Times* published a
message from its Washington correspondent explaining that this
"obviously has been timed to make him available for direct consultation there when the Soviet reply to the Anglo-French communication
on the subject of the Marshall plan is received". And, in fact, when that
reply was received, suggesting the 27th June for the three-Power
meeting, Attlee, Bevin, Dalton and Cripps held a series of meetings
with Clayton on the Marshall Plan—meetings that occupied the
greater part of three days. When Bevin left for Paris again, on the 27th
June, a clear demonstration of the line-up of the United States, Britain
and France, before ever the Soviet Union was taken into consultation,
had been given to the world.

GOVERNMENT EXCUSES

In the speech in the House of Commons on the 19th June, mentioned above, Bevin had said in so many words that "the beginning of all that trouble was Russia", and had wound up with the remark: "If there is to be a conflict between ideologies, I shall regret it, but if it is forced upon us we must face it."

Four comments, I think must be made here. The first is that there was already conflict, without any "if" about it, a conflict between the ideologies of socialism and capitalism, in the sense that there were capitalist and socialist countries in the world, each seeking to live by their respective ideologies, and that what was required of governments, above all of our government, elected to lay the foundations of a Socialist Britain, was to make every possible effort to achieve peaceful co-existence of the countries of the two ideologies. The second comment is that, in the conflict, Bevin never remembered that he was supposed to be on the socialist side. The third is that he was plainly implying that the conflict was being "forced upon us" by the wicked socialists in Eastern Europe, a statement particularly grotesque in its inaccuracy at that moment, when the immediate tensions were plainly the result of the Truman Doctrine and the Marshall Plan, neither of which came from the U.S.S.R. (Nor had it made a speech at Fulton.) The fourth comment is that the theme at any rate latent in the phrases about ideological conflict, implying that "one doesn't want the world to be divided into two camps"—when it plainly was already so divided—was a favourite of both Bevin and Attlee; it was also a favourite of Chamberlain and other Munichites about a somewhat different alignment of camps.

THE ESSENCE OF THE PLAN

The concrete proposals presented to Molotov on the 27th June showed how carefully the cards had been stacked. Already on the 7th June, *The Times* parliamentary correspondent had stated that the outline "emerging" from Anglo-American talks was that of (i) a conference of European powers, (ii) an assessment of Europe's needs for heavy equipment and agricultural engineering, to be bought from the U.S.A. with dollar credit, (iii) the creation of "an organisation charged with the responsibility of allocation . . . to the various countries in accordance with their needs", for which the European Coal Organisation was a suitable model. On the 17th June, the *Times* Paris correspondent reported that under the French scheme—which, he revealed, the French Ambassador in Washington had already been discussing with Marshall —a series of "international expert committees" should draw up a balance sheet of resources and needs for each country in four fields, (i) iron and steel, (ii) coal, (iii) transport, (iv) agriculture, a scheme similar to that which had "emerged" from Anglo-American talks, as we have seen, by the 7th June. By the 23rd June, the Paris correspondent of the *Times* was able to add to the French scheme the missing link of a "steering committee" to "regulate and co-ordinate" the procedure of the expert committees—corresponding to the earlier Anglo-American scheme of "an organisation charged with the responsibility of allocation". Two days before Bevin, Bidault and Molotov met in Paris, the *News Chronicle* diplomatic correspondent wrote that the British scheme, too, was for a number of committees—"coal, food, transport, steel, and so on", and a steering committee to co-ordinate their findings.

The Paris discussions revealed that what was at stake was the economic independence of the Soviet Union and the countries which had broken the power of monopoly capital and begun to plan their own independent economies. The Anglo-French proposal was to treat Europe as an economic whole; to investigate what was needed to ensure the development of *Europe's* "key industries", and in particular, what equipment was needed to ensure the development of production and staple consumption products "requisite to assure" the economic life of Europe; and to have a steering committee to draw up a report on these lines by the 1st September. The reports of the various sub-committees were to be drawn up, not on the basis of the *national* requirements of each people for the development and, if it thought fit, the readjustment, of its economy, but to suit the needs of "Europe". "Europe" plainly meant the particular distribution of productive forces as they stood before the war, a distribution in which the western countries—Britain, France, Germany, Holland, Italy—were industrialised countries with colonial empires, and the countries of Eastern Europe were backward, impoverished agrarian countries, entirely dependent upon the stronger Powers, and a prey to political reaction in its worst form.

Further, the British and French Governments let it be understood that the restoration of German industrial resources was also part of the scheme. This was no surprise; as early as the 8th May, Acheson had declared that one of the main aims of American policy must be:

"To push ahead with the reconstruction of those two great work-shops of Europe and Asia—Germany and Japan—upon which the ultimate recovery of the two continents so largely depends. . . . European recovery cannot be complete until the various parts of Europe's economy" (presumably the socialist part as well as the capitalist part, under "Western guidance") "are working together in a harmonious whole. And the achievement of a co-ordinated European economy remains a fundamental objective of our foreign policy."

This was by no means the only indication that the aim of the new European planners was to have "a co-ordinated European economy" largely dependent on German industry. But an economy of that type had been experienced before the Second World War; it was an econ-omy in which the countries of Eastern Europe, having no industrial basis of their own, and relying for their existence entirely on agri-cultural exports, were falling more and more completely under the economic domination of Germany.

The whole basis and object of the Anglo-French-American plans put forward at Paris were to break down the socialist framework of planned industrial and agricultural development which the countries were developing—and to operate this break-down in the name of "Europe" as a whole, of a "co-ordinated European economy"; and to concentrate on coal-mining, iron and steel production, engineering and transport equipment, continuing the production of raw materials in the countries which produced them before the war, all in the name of solving Europe's urgent needs. That was the essence of the Marshall-Bevin scheme, and its acceptance would have meant a return to ruin and misery for the East European peoples, and an end to all their socialist hopes. American and British spokesmen made it clear that they would get no "aid if they did not abandon 'totalitarian' [i.e. socialist], methods of running their countries and accept a more characteristically European pattern". ("European" means "capitalist", of course.)

The Soviet Union accepted the invitation to attend, in spite of all the discouraging preparations, and Molotov arrived in Paris on the 26th July, with a large number of officials. What he found on arrival can best be described in the words of Professor Fleming, which I give from the same passage of his book that I quoted a little earlier. He wrote:

"On arrival Molotov encountered the same atmosphere of 'take it or leave it' on the part of Bevin. Molotov also resented the prior conferences between the British and French, and disapproved of the plan they had ready for him, which required an overall European balance sheet, showing resources and needs of the Continent as a whole. The British and French felt that such a plan was necessary to meet Marshall's requirements, but Molotov objected to it on three grounds: (1) that it was an interference in the internal affairs of the European nations; (2) that there should be a distinction between former allied, neutral, and enemy states; (3) and that the German problem was an entirely separate matter to be dealt with by the Council of Foreign Ministers alone."

Molotov himself put forward a positive plan, which was described in an article by Quaestor in the August issue of *Labour Monthly*, as follows:

"A plain, consistent and truly internationalist proposal—that the programmes of economic aid required from America should be estimated in the first instance by the European countries themselves; that a summary should be drawn up on the basis of these estimates, bearing in mind particularly the needs of the countries which suffered from German aggression; [and] that a committee of the three Powers, with some other European states, after doing this work, should ascertain from the U.S.A. what 'appropriate economic aid' it could grant."

THE TRAP FAILS

It is not surprising that the socialist countries did not walk into the Marshall trap. Professor Fleming writes:

"The meeting came to a negative end on the 2nd July. In his final statement, Molotov condemned 'the creation of a new organisation standing over and above the countries of Europe and interfering in their internal affairs down to determining the line of development to be followed by the main branches of industry in those countries', and said that 'the European countries would find themselves placed under control and would lose their former economic and national independence because it so pleases certain strong powers'."

And when the socialist states were no longer there, American statements of the Plan's real purposes became more frank. Quaestor tells us:

"On July 14, at Salt Lake City, Marshall gave a still more authoritative confirmation of the real purposes of his 'plan' . . . . He spoke of 'the incalculable stake which this country has in the preservation of European civilisation'—it being well understood, as we have seen already, that on the lips of an American politician 'European' means 'capitalist'. Marshall also [said] that either America must 'assist its traditional friends among the nations of the Old World . . . or it must reconcile itself to seeing them move in directions which are consistent neither with their own traditions nor with those of this country."

This was one of those occasions when the speech as actually delivered varied from the printed text distributed in advance to the Press, and Quaestor tells us:

"From this we learn that Marshall has incautiously blurted out that the alternative to American help might be 'to throw the war-torn nations into the arms of Communism'."

REBUILDING GERMAN HEAVY INDUSTRY

Quaestor went on a little later:

"Yet another aspect of the Marshall scheme for promoting an economic agreement of Western Europe began to emerge directly the U.S.S.R. was out of the way: the plan for reconstructing German heavy industry. On July 9th the United States Secretary of Commerce, Mr. Harriman, assured the chief Burgomaster of Essen that he was impressed by his plea for a revision of the order to dismantle the Krupp works, and that the British and Americans would leave 'sufficient industries' in Western Germany to pay for food imports. . . . And new levels were also agreed upon for other branches of industry, and the list of works to be destroyed or dismantled was 'shortened'. It must be remembered, of course, that not half a dozen of the big industrial works promised as reparations from the Western Zones to Yugoslavia, Poland or the U.S.S.R. have ever reached those States. . . .

"Equally significant, the United States Government sent a 'directive' to General Clay, its Military Governor, ordering him only to 'eliminate industry used *solely* for the manufacture of arms, ammunition, and the implements of war, and to reduce but not prohibit production which supported these industries'."

In the following September, the *New York Herald Tribune* revealed a secret report of the State Department, to the effect that Marshall economic aid must be given to at least fourteen European countries "*to counter Communism*" (my italics).*

Quaestor was surely correct in summing up the Marshall Plan as follows:

"A plan to stop the advance of Socialism in Europe, and if possible to throw back the advance towards it already made by a number of countries . . . a plan to isolate the Soviet Union and if possible retard it in its economic reconstruction and deny it just reparation; a plan to rebuild, as the spearhead of the Western bloc, a highly industrialised and anti-communist Western Germany. . . ."

Such was the plan which the Labour Government "grabbed with both hands". Hugh Dalton, too, wrote of it that "like Lease-Lend, it was an act of the most imaginative generosity, coming only just in time to save its beneficiaries".

"Just in time" must be read cautiously, for most of the beneficiaries still had many months to wait before anything tangible reached them. I deal with Marshall Aid more fully in Chapter 14; two of the odd features of it was that few countries, with the possible exception of West Germany, seemed to become any stronger or more stable as a result of it, and that we had to cut down our social services severely to "deserve aid".

* According to Gordon Schaffer (*Cahiers Internationaux*, No. 115, November, 1960), one of the conditions agreed by our Government on Marshall Aid was that we would release the U.S.A. from a promise made by Roosevelt that the atomic bomb would never be used without British consent.

CHAPTER 11

Colonial Policy, 1946-7

COLONIAL problems arose not only in Palestine and India, but also in Malaya, a little in Tanganyika, and above all in Egypt, a country which, although technically independent, fell at the time more aptly into the sphere of colonial rather than that of foreign policy.

Britain had substantially occupied Egypt for a century; still exercised a "condominium"—a joint British and Egyptian rule, with the British predominating even more than they did in Egypt itself—over the Sudan; and British troops had, of course, fought over and through Egypt in both the world wars. Steady Egyptian pressure for complete British evacuation had been growing since 1946, and the British were obviously bound to give way to this pressure in the near future.

They were reluctant to do so. Whilst the Government had announced some time before its intention to withdraw troops from Egypt and to negotiate a new Treaty on the basis of absolute equality, and many Labour enthusiasts genuinely believed that the oil and imperial interests of the Middle East were being abandoned, the negotiations were kept in a state of permanent breakdown owing to disputes over the time-table for withdrawal of troops and over the British demand for a military alliance which would make Egypt a pawn of Britain's foreign policy. At the same time, new barracks were being built at Suez, and Palestine was scheduled to become a permanent strategic base—thus discounting all previous pledges for that country's evolution towards independence.

The British still had a large number of troops in Egypt and enormous masses of military stores. When I happened to be there in August, 1946, the General Officer Commanding the British Forces told me that he still had 60,000 troops under his command in Egypt (none of them counting as combatants); and when I was there again in February, 1947, defending a number of men in R.E.M.E. and R.A.O.C., charged with mutiny at the big ordnance base at Tel-el-Kebir, that base was still operating on a grand scale, with something like 3,000 men—British,

German prisoners-of-war, and Egyptian civilians—at work every day.

In this period covered by this chapter, nothing decisive occurred in the Egyptian matter. In March, 1947, the negotiations for withdrawal, which had been going on for nearly a year, broke down. In May, Egypt appealed to the Security Council of U.N., demanding the immediate withdrawal of British troops from the Nile valley, including the Sudan. But the story was by no means over, and I shall return to it in later chapters.

PALESTINE

The position in Palestine, with which I dealt pretty fully in Chapter 7, had deteriorated in the year that had passed. There was by now virtually civil war in the country, fought by powerful Jewish terrorist organisations (equipped largely through a black market by British and Australian troops in Egypt, who were "flogging" war material on a large scale) fighting against both the British and the Arabs.

INDIA

The long story of British rule in India, already mentioned in Chapter 7, was nearing its end. It was growing clearer in the early part of 1947 both that the peoples of British India would not be content with anything less than independence, and that it would be impossible, in the face of popular resistance, for the British to continue to hold and administer the country for very long. In February, 1947, Attlee announced a time limit for independence, saying that power would be handed over to "responsible Indian hands" by June, 1948. The communal tension and riots noticed in Chapter 7 continued, and the establishment of an independent state or states at a far earlier date than June, 1948, was seen to be inevitable. Lord Mountbatten, who had been selected to succeed Lord Wavell as Viceroy, went to India, and by June, 1947, he had worked out a plan which all parties in India disliked but all were prepared to accept; and it was enshrined in the Indian Independence Act, 1947, passed in July, 1947.

This plan, briefly, involved the partition of British India into two independent states; an Indian state, overwhelmingly Hindu in religion, but with a Moslem population which turned out in the end, after the Princes' states had come in, to be about 40,000,000; and Pakistan, a state overwhelmingly Moslem, although, after the details of partition had been worked out, nearly half the population of East Pakistan (itself more than half of Pakistan) was Hindu. The Princes' States (sometimes called Native States), with a total population of some 90 million, were left to decide between continuing as separate states or linking up with India or Pakistan; in the end, they all linked up with one or other of the two.

PARTITION OF INDIA

Partition led to trouble. Not only were there riots, migrations, and massacres after independence, but the economic effects were grave; for example, the highly important and valuable jute industry in Bengal was crippled for a long time by the boundary between the two States—who at first had no commercial relations with one another—being drawn so as to put virtually all the raw jute on one side and the mills for processing it on the other; and the partition of the Punjab cut through large irrigation canals, the water of which came from India but was essential to the cultivation of much valuable land in Pakistan.

The two States both remained in the Commonwealth, both as Republics. Their future history is not really part of this story of the six years of Labour Government.

Of events in other colonial territories, I ought to write a little of Malaya and Tanganyika.

MALAYA

Malaya presented a sad illustration of the fundamentally imperialist attitude of the leadership—and, I fear, of a good deal of the rank and file—of the Labour Party. Malaya was, to their mind, a colony; and—even more important—a colony producing a very large dollar income by its tin and rubber. The strong and growing demand of its population for independence was "naturally" resisted, not only because it was an independence movement but also because it meant a loss of valuable dollar exchange,★ and it was easy to label it "communist" as a means of reconciling public opinion to a long and costly civil war, fought largely against those elements of the population who had been praised by the British for their courageous struggles against the Japanese occupation forces during the war.

The Malayan struggle was well described and criticised by Michael Carritt, in the March, 1947, issue of *Labour Monthly*:

★ I remember that in the General Election campaign of 1950 I personally had some opposition from "Labour" electors in my constituency, who were indignant at my support of the Malayan demand for independence, attacking me for thus "sacrificing dollar revenue".

"Here the popular democratic movement reached a high level of anti-imperialist militancy during its three and a half years of guerrilla warfare against the Japanese. From the very day of re-occupation by British troops the whole of armed force was used *against* the people who fought for us against the Japanese, in order to restore the old *status quo* of colonialism. Under cover of armed forces the old vested interests and the old compromised administrators were brought back. The popular movement was persecuted, and hundreds of the guerrilla fighters have been arrested on charges of 'murdering' Japanese agents and policemen (in two cases the charge was 'altered' to stealing the machinery of a river dredger!).* Civil liberty is non-existent. Demonstrations are fired upon. Editors are arrested and newspapers suppressed.

"However, since the situation cannot entirely be dealt with by repressive measures, new constitutional proposals have now been published which . . . leave all executive authority with the Governor and provide him with a puppet legislative council, in the formation of which democratic elections play no part. In spite of a promise to consult the Malayans before publishing these constitutional reforms, no such consultation took place with any of the popular democratic organisations, but only with the Sultans and their reactionary organi-sation, the U.M.N.O."

GROUND-NUTS IN TANGANYIKA

What I have to recount of Tanganyika has nothing to do with an independence movement; it was indeed to be nearly fifteen years before that then apparently backward and acquiescent territory triumphantly secured independence, getting ahead of Kenya and Uganda in doing so. The story there was of ground-nuts.

A grandiose scheme for the cultivation of ground-nuts on a vast scale, almost wholly in Tanganyika, but to a small extent in Northern Rhodesia and Kenya, had been suggested to the Government in March, 1946, by the United Africa Company, a subsidiary of the great Unilever Combine which carried on a great deal of ground-nut and

---

* This reminds me of an incident in Gibraltar in the early stages of the Spanish Civil War, when the Republican government was still recognised by the British as the govern-ment of Spain, and Franco was classed as a rebel. The Gibraltar government had allowed Franco to establish a representative there as "Agent of General Franco", and he had hung out a sign. A Republican sailor who had landed in Gibraltar was so angry at seeing this that he tore the sign down and threw it into the sea. He was prosecuted for "insulting the emblem of a friendly power", and the charge was amended to "drunk and disorderly" when it was pointed out to the prosecution that a rebel against a "friendly power" could hardly be a friendly power.

other cultivation in Africa, mostly in the West. The proposal was to develop an area of over three million acres, three-sevenths under ground-nuts, one-seventh under an alternative crop, and three-sevenths under a grass ley. An official mission of three men, one of whom was the head of the Plantation Department of the United Africa Company, was appointed to investigate and report. It reported favourably in September, 1946, and its recommendations were accepted by the Government with little modification, the United Africa Company being asked to act as managing director of the scheme until the necessary legislation could be passed.

The story of what proved to be a sad fiasco, and any comments on it, must be left to later chapters, as the scheme took some years to develop and fail. I may quote, as a comment on it as far as it had gone, the article of Michael Carritt already notified. At p. 89 of *Labour Monthly* (March, 1947), he wrote:

"In Tanganyika the Government has a much-advertised scheme for the opening-up of a ground-nuts industry which, it is claimed, will rectify the unbalanced agricultural economy of that territory. But the benefits which might accrue from such development are nullified by the decision to entrust the development of this new industry to the United Africa Company, the African's most powerful exploiter."

CHAPTER 12

Economic and Industrial Affairs, 1946-7

THE year of 1946-7 was a period of one economic crisis after another—
fuel crisis, balance of payments crisis, and convertibility of sterling
crisis. They were all made more acute by the cruel weather, already
mentioned, which began in January and did not ease up until March;
and they were all indirectly, and the last two directly, caused or
exacerbated by the foreign policy, which involved terrible expenses in
the "defence" field, and pretty heavy expenses in foreign commitments,
particularly in Germany, Greece, Palestine, and Malaya, whilst at the
same time contributing to a grave shortage of labour due to retaining—
at the beginning of the period—over one million *more* men in the
armed forces than the pre-war figure, and taking many civilians out of
directly productive activities into the work of equipping and supplying
such forces; this shortage of labour had grown so acute that as early as
November, 1946, an agreement was concluded between Britain and
Italy for the importation of Italian foundry workers, and many similar
arrangements were proposed.

BALANCE OF PAYMENTS CRISIS

The balance of payments crisis can be read from the figures; in 1946,
there was a deficit on the balance of payments—i.e. the difference
between the payments made to and those received from foreign
countries, mainly the U.S.A.—of £450 million, which was met by
drawing on dollar credits to the extent of £280 million, selling gold,
silver and capital resources for £100 million, and accumulating £70
million of new sterling debt. This last item meant simply that we
incurred debts for supplies from the sterling area and put off payment
of those debts. Under the innocent title of "sterling balances", we had
used this method, all through the war and subsequently, to the extent of
thousands of millions, especially with India, paying them off slowly
over long years at a rate of exchange fixed by ourselves and not by our
poor creditors. Hugh Dalton describes it, at p. 83 of his book, in an

imaginary statement (the use of which he did not recommend) by Britain to India:

"For years you have been in debt to us, and you have paid up; our political control of you ensured that. Now the wheel of fortune has turned full circle; we are indebted to you. It is true that you are poor and we are rich, and that you need our funds for your economic development. But I am afraid we are not going to pay up."

COAL SHORTAGE

The first crisis element of the year was the acute coal shortage, which became obvious in December, 1946.

The causes of the shortage went back to before the war. Colliery owners had closed down a good many pits; and then, when the war began, first the Chamberlain and then the Coalition Government had allowed 100,000 mineworkers to leave the pits between the outbreak of the war and the end of 1940. The war brought a heavy drain on coal supplies, and a coal rationing plan prepared by Lord Beveridge in 1942 was not operated. By April, 1945, when Labour was about to take office, coal stocks had dropped from a peak of 18,880,000 in 1941 to 10,000,000 tons.

In July, 1946, Shinwell, the Minister for Mines, warned the House of Commons of the great danger of the situation; he proposed to bridge the gap by increased open-cast mining, the use of more oil fuel, and improved distribution. In October, he appealed for an all-round voluntary saving in consumption of at least 10 per cent., but met with no response.

On the 1st February, 1947, when the freeze-up had begun but had not yet produced its grave effects, Shinwell told the House of Commons that "we decided to adopt other measures . . . a scheme which would mean a reduction not only in solid fuel but in electricity and gas. . . . The intention was to put it into force on December 1st, 1946, but the employers did not consider it went far enough. As a result the scheme had to be revised. . . . Then the intention was to introduce it on January 1st, but eventually, because of the difficulties which emerged— all kinds of industrial organisations querying the plan itself—it was decided that it should operate from January 20th."

MILLS CLOSING DOWN

Meanwhile, the effects of the shortage were developing. Cotton mills in Blackburn and the surrounding district closed on the 26th

December for want of fuel, and on the 30th December a general call was made for reduction in fuel consumption. Early in January, 1947, large quantities of coal were diverted from government coal dumps, many trains were cancelled, and extensive electricity cuts were made. On the 15th January, an emergency plan was announced, to come into force on the 20th, for a 50 per cent. cut in the allocations of coal to industry, with priority to electricity and gas undertakings, in the hope of bridging or at any rate reducing the weekly gap between production and consumption of 300,000 tons.

On the 20th January, allocations to steel works were cut by 25 per cent.; and by the end of January some 300 factories in the North-West of England were faced with complete stoppage for want of fuel.

The terribly cold weather then began to take hold; it increased the demand for coal, and also for gas and electricity, which were almost wholly produced by or from coal; and it gravely hampered distribution. On the 1st February, the great Austin Motor works announced that it was closing down for lack of fuel, and within a day or two other industrial firms closed or went on short time.

On the 7th February, electricity supplies were limited to essential services, and domestic supplies were cut off for five hours a day. By the 8th February, many factories were closed, and unemployment mounted. Just before the crisis, it had been 397,000, $2\frac{1}{2}$ per cent of insured workers; at its peak, on the 22nd February, it was 2,300,000, or $15\frac{1}{2}$ per cent.; by the 12th March, it had declined to 785,000, or 5 per cent.

On the 11th February many railway trains, both main-line and suburban, were suspended to give priority to coal transport.

The situation had eased a little by the end of February; in the Midlands, for example, industry was allowed to use electric power from the 24th February, and on the same day it was announced that as from the 3rd March power would be available for industrial purposes. There was, in effect, a general resumption of work in industry on that date, but the direct and indirect results of the long cold spell and of the floods that followed represented, both industrially and agriculturally, very heavy losses indeed. There were critics in the U.S.A. who saw the heavy blow to our economy as at once revealing our weaknesses resulting from the burden of the war and increasing those weaknesses to such an extent as to rank us permanently as a second-class Power. But there was one very happy feature of the crisis, in the great upsurge of loyal support which the industrial workers gave to the Government which they had put into power, and in which they had not yet lost faith. There were countless stories of workers, especially coal miners, making their way from bitterly cold cottages to bitterly cold work places over miles of snow-bound streets and roads, to work extremely hard to try to keep up production. Palme Dutt wrote of this in the Notes of the Month, (*Labour Monthly*, March, 1947, p. 66):

> "The immediate outcome of the emergency has been very different from the sanguine calculations in which Toryism and the big moneyed interests indulged. Toryism anticipated an immediate uprush of feeling against the Government for the political benefit of Toryism .. But the first outcome has dealt a check to these calculations. .... The powerful and impressive response of the working-class transformed the political atmosphere from attempted Tory exploitation of the Government's embarrassment to a strengthened revival of Labour solidarity and militancy."

ELECTRICAL SUPPLY INADEQUATE

The Government attributed the "shut-down" to the cold weather and the great increase of the demand for coal by the electrical industry. As immediate causes, these were obviously correct; but there was a longer-term cause in the general backwardness of the development of electrical power. Between 1938 and 1946, the consumption of electricity had increased by about 68 per cent. whilst capacity had gone up by no more than 37 per cent.; thus, without any pressure from exceptional weather, the demand for electricity was permanently in excess of capacity; in the last week of January, electricity undertakings had consumed 727,000 tons of coal, compared with 576,000 tons in the same week of 1946.

PLANLESSNESS

There had undoubtedly been insufficient Government realisation of the dangerous position, and insufficient organisation to deal with it. Richard Crossman, M.P., writing in the *News Chronicle* of the 20th February, 1947, criticised the lack of a general economic plan:

> "Today, we have no less than eight Ministers concerned with Supply, all working on their own and without any central system of allocation. ...
>
> "Mr. Barnes very properly wants to improve train services; Mr. Wilmot wants to get goods into the shop windows. ... Mr.

Shinwell wants generating plant, but Sir Stafford Cripps controls its allocation and, since he is responsible for the export drive, is inclined to send it abroad.

"Mr. Isaacs, in charge of Labour, can refer to no central authority which co-ordinates the supply of labour with that of materials. Dr. Dalton, since last June, has been Chairman of the Cabinet Coal Committee in his spare time. . . ."

And he enumerated as contributing to the crisis:

"The decision to increase the train services last September, the unrationed production and sale of electrical appliances, the under-estimation of fuel consumption in a period of full employment, the wastage of the American loan on cigarettes and films, the complacency about increased coal output per man when what was required was an increase far beyond the capacity of the existing labour force in the coal mines. . . ."

MINE EQUIPMENT NEEDED

On the 22nd February, 1947, in their discussions with the Cabinet Emergency Fuel Committee, the officials of the National Union of Mineworkers emphasised the shortage of mine equipment, and pressed both for priority for the production of mining machinery and for improvements in wages and conditions for miners, which had been very bad for many years. These improvements were in any case necessary to attract more manpower; the government estimated that 65,000 more men must be recruited in 1947.

Transportation of coal was another weak link. According to Ernest Watkins, in *The Cautious Revolution*, p. 20, Shinwell had demanded from the Cabinet in December, 1946, that coal transport should be given priority over passenger traffic, but the Cabinet had refused.

ECONOMIC WHITE PAPERS

Turning from coal to more general crisis considerations the next important matter was the issue by the Government of two "White Papers" (Cmds. 7,018 and 7,046) in February: the first on "Economic Considerations" and the second as an "Economic Survey". The general criticism that can be made of both of them is that they in effect accepted the capitalist framework of our economics and thus sought to solve on a capitalist basis many problems which capitalism could never solve. On the first of these White Papers, I adopt the comments of

Palme Dutt, in the Notes of the Month for March, 1947, (*Labour Monthly*, pp. 66-7). He wrote (before the second White Paper was available) that the first

"may have emanated from the Ministry of Labour, but it was the voice and demands of Big Business that sounded through it. It assumed without argument all the world-wide imperialist commitments as a natural god-given dispensation, and then complained of the shortage of manpower. It assumed the squandering of the bulk of Britain's foreign exchange on military adventures and the subsidising of reaction and the black market abroad, and then complained of the size of the consequent deficit, and demanded as the only solution the expansion of British exports to a degree beyond the immediate prospective capacity of the world market, crippling to home development, and without consideration of the intensified offensive of American competition. It ignored the soaring rise of profits and capital appreciation, far beyond the level of any rise of money wages, and concentrated the limelight entirely on the rise of money wages, without allowing for the rise in prices, and implied the conclusion that the only way to lower costs and prevent inflation was to hold up any further rise in wages or improvement of conditions until the general productive level has increased."

The second White Paper, the "Economic Survey", was rightly subjected to similar criticism. Mr. Nicholas Kaldor, the economist, writing in *The Times* of the 25th February, commented:

"The really disturbing feature of the Government's Economic Survey is not what it contains but what it lacks . . . [It is] more in the nature of what is likely to happen if things go reasonably well than of intermediary objectives in a clearly conceived long term plan. . . . How many more crises are needed before it is recognised that it is not possible to pen a 'planned economy' without a plan?"

FRIGHTENED OF PLANNING

Mr. Kaldor was pointing to an essential weakness in the Government's approach to any control which could fairly be described as planning. It had been elected to establish a planned economy, and had professed to intend to "plan from the ground up"; and it was not only impossible to build socialism on the vestiges of a planless capitalist economy but it was not even possible—at that period of transition—to carry a capitalist economy forward without sure disaster unless a high degree of planning were adopted. Planning had moreover been essential during the war, and had been operated in Britain at any rate more efficiently and honestly than in any other capitalist country, so that much of the necessary machinery was to hand. But the Government was from the start timid and lukewarm about planning, for a variety of reasons.* It was too ready to accept the Tory idea that a "free" economy was *prima facie* the best one, and that controls were a necessary evil, to be used only when absolutely unavoidable; coupled with that was the thoroughly middle-class idea that the public resented control and that a government which wanted to retain its popularity must have as little of it as possible. Another reason lay in the anti-communist obsessions of the leadership; planning was used extensively in the U.S.S.R., and therefore extensive planning must be condemned as "totalitarian" and "undemocratic"; Cripps, for example, when opening the debate in the House of Commons on the Economic Survey, (*Hansard*, Vol. 434, Cols. 946 *et seq.*) said that the method of planning had to be worked out in accordance with our *democratic* (my italics) institutions and ideas, and emphasised the differences between what he called democratic and what he called totalitarian planning. He was following a long line of Tory predecessors in this, and giving the impressions they so often gave; firstly that they regard what they call democracy as actually a hindrance to good government, and secondly that they know the U.S.S.R. does things better and feel that they must produce some excuse for not doing as well. In truth, very often, the real defect, and the real reason for inadequate measures, is timidity in the presence of entrenched financial and industrial interests.

Whatever the reasons or motives, the slow and inadequate steps taken by the Government in the direction of planning were certainly productive, both directly and indirectly, of endless economic weakness and crisis. I would turn again to Palme Dutt (pp. 105-6 of *Labour Monthly* for April, 1947):

"The weakness of the . . . 'Economic Survey for 1947' is that it completely fails to face the realities of the present situation. It rehearses at length some of the most familiar superficial facts of the situation (while hiding the most important) . . . It stresses the urgency; it speaks of desirable aims and requirements. But by treating the whole problem as primarily an outcome of two wars it completely fails to touch the heart of the disease. It does not dare to face the real factors which are crippling reconstruction. It slides over

* Compare the "Four-year-Plan" discussed in Chapter 24.

the Economic Consequences of Mr. Bevin. It makes no attempt to set out a plan of action. Its 'targets' are only desirable requirements with no relation to a positive policy or plan. . . . The plea that the principles of so-called 'democratic planning' make it in practice impossible to plan only covers the surrender to big business interests at home and to the squandering of resources in imperialist adventures abroad. Britain alone among the progressive nations of Europe remains without an overall economic plan. . . .

"It does not make sense for the House of Commons to debate for three days on the desperate urgency of the economic situation, and then next day to vote eighteen million pounds of precious foreign exchange to maintain the monarchist ex-fascist armed forces in Greece. It does not make sense to speak of the urgency of increasing home production, and then to export three times the agricultural machinery of pre-war. It does not make sense to speak of the urgent need of coal, and then to export coal to Franco, or desperately needed mining machinery. It does not make sense to speak of the urgent need of raising productivity and then to place capital re-equipment low down in the list, below the requirements of military expenditure placed at the top of the list. It does not make sense to warn against increases of wages, and to ignore the enormously greater increase of profits and capital appreciations."

Further comment which seems to me most pertinent is to be found in an article by J. R. Campbell in the May issue of the *Labour Monthly*, at pp. 145-6, as follows:

"The plain fact is that the Government either does not grasp the planning implications of its own programme, or is spinelessly shying away from them. On the one hand it talks about the great complexity of its tasks, and the next moment suggests that 'a small tripartite planning board'* will see us through. Maybe it thinks that the capitalists will be reconciled to some kind of central planning authority provided it is only a little one. . . .

"This type of organisation is no use for a Government which is seeking to direct the economy of the country in order to ensure priority for a great housing programme, a tremendous programme of capital re-equipment particularly in the nationalised industries, a

---

* On the 27th March, the Government had appointed Sir Edwin Plowden, a director of Tennant & Sons, as "Chief Planning Officer", with Sir Robert Sinclair, Chairman of the Imperial Tobacco Company, as "Industrial Consultant".

great build-up of the export trade, and a more equitable distribution of wealth. The Government cannot leave it to the capitalists to ensure that labour and materials are forthcoming for these great projects. It must take its own planned measures to ensure that the proper allocation of labour and materials takes place and that one phase of the reconstruction effort does not get in the way of the others."

HOUSING ESTIMATES

The Economic Survey estimated the number of houses to be built in 1947 as 300,000, three-quarters only of the previous year's estimate. Housing, one of the most important and urgent of all human requirements, was thus being cut down by 25 per cent. to meet a crisis caused by our foreign policy and its military consequences. It was of course difficult to overcome shortages of material and labour; but the foreign policy both contributed to the shortage of labour and prevented our still great resources being used to make up the shortage of material.

THE BUDGET

I must now turn to the Budget, which was introduced by the Chancellor, Dalton, on the 15th April, 1947 (see *Hansand*, Vol. 436, Cols. 35 *et seq.*). The Treasury estimates were that, if the existing rates of taxation were retained, there would be a revenue of £3,429,000,000 including £292,000,000 of miscellaneous receipts in the nature of windfalls, to cover an estimated expenditure of £3,181,000,000; this showed a prospective surplus of £248,000,000, which on the taxation rates actually proposed was estimated to be increased to £270,000,000.

The main changes in taxation were a measure of income-tax relief, achieved not by altering the standard rate of tax but by increasing the earned income allowance from one eighth to one-sixth (with a maximum of £250 instead of £150) and by increasing certain allowances. Profits tax remained at 5 per cent. on undistributed profits, but was raised to $12\frac{1}{2}$ per cent. on distributed profits. The main change in indirect taxation was an increase of 50 per cent. in the duty on tobacco, which mostly comes from the U.S.A. and has to be paid for in dollars.

That there was a prospective Budget surplus did not affect the fact that the balance of payments, the deficit on overseas exchange, was not merely as bad as ever but was actually getting worse. And the American loan was being used up much more rapidly than had been expected, with dollar prices in general having risen by 40 per cent. since the loan had been negotiated.

On the loan, and on the budget, Palme Dutt wrote in his Notes of the Month for May, 1947 (pp. 138-40 of *Labour Monthly*), as follows:

"Nor can we fail to note the tightening American strangle-hold on Britain. It is the peculiar character of Britain's situation that the crisis of foreign policy is intimately bound up with the deepening crisis of Britain's economic problem. The recent White Paper on National Income and Expenditure has revealed that out of the total deficit of £400 million on the balance of payments last year no less than three-quarters or £300 million was due to overseas Government expenditure, of which £225 million is recorded as direct military overseas expenditure (this is apart from the net loss in Germany of £38 million). Here is manifestly the main source of the trouble, not only in respect of manpower (withdrawal of two millions from production) but in respect of the external deficit and rapid exhaustion of the American loan. The withdrawals from the United States and Canadian loans in 1946, amounting to £279 million, have been entirely used up, and have even less than sufficed to cover the Government overseas expenditure; not a cent of them has served for reconstruction or the civilian population at home."

Dutt then went on to quote the remarks of G. D. H. Cole, who had written in the *New Statesman* of the 5th April:

" 'The very existence of the loan has enabled the Americans to impose on us obligations which we should otherwise have been forced to reject, because they would have been altogether beyond our immediate power. We should have been unable to go on garrisoning Greece against the Russians, or dallying disastrously in Palestine, or acting as capitalist policeman throughout the Near and Middle East. . . . Rejection of the loan, had it been possible, would have forced us at once to restrict our military and imperial commitments and to come to terms with the Soviet Union.' "

Dutt pointed out, in the same article, that nearly one-third of the expenditure contemplated in the Budget, or £900 million, was devoted to the armed forces, and that the reliefs in direct taxation were more than offset by heavier increases in indirect taxation, which shifted the burden on to the mass of the people.

LABOUR PARTY CONFERENCE

The Labour Party Conference was held at Margate in June. The mood both of the leaders and of the rank and file was not happy, in

striking but correct and inevitable contrast to the mood at Bournemouth a year before; but there is no need to write of it at any length,
since nothing was said or done to help the country or the Labour Party
out of the crises which were oppressing them, or to bring the leadership
to any change of policy. The quite natural reluctance of most critics to
rock the overloaded boat in a rough sea really prevented left-wing
delegates from making any headway, although the Executive was
defeated on important home issues, such as tied cottages in agriculture
and equal pay for women. (The motion for the latter was carried against
the executive by a four-fifths majority, but the Cabinet immediately
rejected it on the ground that it would cost £24 million and thus
carry with it a danger of inflation; £24 million is less than $\frac{1}{36}$ of the
amount then being expended on the armed forces, regardless of
inflation or other economic or financial damages.)

Palme Dutt, at p. 257 of the *Labour Monthly*, described the conference thus:

> "Margate revealed that the main body of Labour supporters still
> slumbered in a dreamland of confiding trust in right-wing leadership,
> cheering the empty theatricalities of Bevin even more thunderously
> than MacDonald used to be cheered, swallowing the suicidal dose of
> '*Cards on the Table*', Foreign Office poison, triumphantly routing the
> left and banning the Anglo-Soviet friendship movement—without
> the slightest realisation of the rocks in front."

CONVERTIBILITY CRISIS

The next crisis was that which arose out of "convertibility", i.e. the
undertaking—given as part of the agreement for the American loan of
1946—that on and after the 15th July, 1947, sterling should be made
freely convertible into foreign currency for all current, as opposed to
capital, transactions, so that debts, for example, to the U.S.A. would
have to be paid in dollars. This crisis, which as will be seen blew up
with great speed early in August, 1947, must be studied side by side
with the rapid exhaustion of the American loan itself and of the
Canadian loan that was made at the same time.

THE LOAN IS VANISHING

As recently as the 20th January, 1947, Dalton had warned his
colleagues that the loan—originally expected to last five years—might
be all used up by early in 1949. By the beginning of March, he was
telling them that it would be all gone by February, 1948, or June of

K

that year at the latest. And when the crisis blew up at the beginning of August, Attlee told the House of Commons that it would be gone by the end of 1947; but Dalton said in the same debate (on the 7th August) that it would be gone by October, leaving us with nothing to draw from abroad except £125 million still available in the Canadian loan, plus what rights we had to draw on the International Monetary Fund, £320 million over four years,* and our own gold and dollar reserves of £600 million,† whilst our liabilities for sterling balances amounted to £3,600 million. No money was to come by way of Marshall "aid" until well into the following year. (It can at any rate be understood, given the capitalist anti-Soviet framework within which the Government was working, how it "grabbed with both hands" the Marshall Plan, announced on the 5th June.)

In that perilous situation, the 15th July arrived, the Government allowed sterling to be freely converted, and oddly enough there was no *immediate* alarm; the Government went ahead with the plans for Parliament to go into recess for the summer, which it did on the 7th August, after a debate in which the Government proposed cuts in food imports amounting to £144 millions, cuts in other imports of about £50 millions, and an attempt to increase our exports in a world situation in which the post-war "seller's market" was beginning to disappear and every other country was also striving hard to increase its exports. The only proposals for reduction in "defence" expenditure were to reduce the 500,000 men stationed overseas to 300,000, and to cut the total under arms on the 31st March, 1948, by one-fourteenth, from 1,087,000 to 1,007,000.

CONVERTIBILITY SUSPENDED

But by the 15th August, 1947, the "run" on sterling had become so strong that Cabinet Ministers were recalled from their holidays, and met on the 17th August; and by the 20th August convertibility was suspended. Parliament was not recalled, and did not meet again until the 20th October, when it met simply to end the Session. The figures then given to Parliament were that our gold and dollar reserves had fallen from £552 millions on the 31st March, 1947, to £473 millions on the 30th June and to £437 million on the 30th September. In the

---

* The (American) controllers of the International Monetary Fund immediately repudiated the suggestion that it was available to meet expenditure of the sort Dalton had in mind.

† It is not clear why the figure of £600 million was given. As will appear in a moment, the true figure at that moment must have been little more than £400 millions.

second quarter of the year the drain had averaged about \$75 million a week, in July \$115 million, and in the last full week before suspension it was \$237 million.

The suspension of convertibility halted the specific drain on sterling, but solved no other problem; the cuts proposed in Parliament early in August did not go nearly far enough and the question was, what was the Government now to do.

It went about the problem, as it had done with previous problems and was destined to do again, by cutting imports, attempting to increase exports, and seeking to keep down wages, just as any Tory government would have done. On the 12th September, Cripps announced various proposals. One was for cuts in capital investment totalling £200 millions; and another was an attempt to increase exports, which then averaged £93 millions a month, by £31 millions, or one-third. He said:

"We must use every device of efficiency to reduce our costs. We do not want to reduce the workers' earnings, indeed we would gladly see them go up if production increased in line with them. But I am certain that we cannot look to higher standards through ever-rising spirals of prices and wages. . . . We should rather look to price decreases by means of more efficient methods."

WAGE CUTS? DIRECTION OF LABOUR?

He explained that wage cuts would only be introduced as a last resort, which is, alas! just what is said by every Government or employer who means to introduce them. Cripps estimated, too, that the cuts in capital expenditure—which included substantial cuts in house-building—would amount to £250 millions per annum. Truly, as Palme Dutt put it, "the price of Bevin abroad was Cripps at home"; and, one may add, the price of Bevin and Cripps was stalemate at the next General Election and defeat at the one after.

Another proposal was for the re-introduction of the war-time direction of labour, to prevent workers drifting from essential but poorly paid industries to less important but more attractive work; a better remedy would have been a wage policy which would attract them to the essential industries, but the Government was by this time thinking of a wage freeze, coupled with the familiar "appeal" to industrialists not to pay too large dividends. (An analysis prepared by the Labour Research Department shortly after this date showed that three textile concerns, five engineering and shipbuilding firms, and five iron and steel works had made profits, after taxation, of just over £18,000,000 as compared with £13,380,000 in the previous year.)

These "appeals" to powerful interests, well trained to prefer their own advantage to the public good, always accompany wage freezes or cuts that are applied in binding fashion to the workers. This is not really surprising but it is disconcerting, even to the most hardened politician, to find such a course actually defended by those who are supposed to lead us into battle against the capitalists. To illustrate this I will move a year ahead for a moment, to the Trades Union Congress of September, 1948. Emile Burns, in *Right Wing Labour*, at pp. 39-40, writes of a resolution which was moved at that Congress, calling on the Government to introduce the statutory control of profits and dividends.

T.U.C. SUPPORTS PROFITS

Opposing this resolution, Sir George Chester, of the Boot and Shoe Operatives, told the Congress:

"Do ask yourselves what profit is. . . . Few of us realise that marginal surplus or profit is essential to the conduct of British industry, whether it be nationalised or in private hands. . . . Examine this question of profit if you like in relation to the policy of full employment, and you will find it awfully difficult to restrain or limit profit."

Burns adds:

"In practice the Labour Government took the same view: wages were restrained with the help of the right-wing trade union leaders, but the Government found it 'awfully difficult' to do more than make appealing gestures to the capitalists as prices and profits rose.

"This is the fate of all promises of 'equal sacrifices'—the workers to freeze wages, the capitalists to freeze prices and profits. Repeatedly the right-wing Labour leaders have used this appeal—under Tory as well as Labour Governments—to damp down the pressure for increased wages. And when protests are made that the capitalists show no sign of keeping their side of the proposed bargain, these are met by saying that profits are essential, and the higher they are the more British industry will expand and the more employment there will be."

THE CRIPPS PLAN CRITICISED

The whole plan was justly criticised by Palme Dutt in the Notes of the Month for October, 1947 (*Labour Monthly*, pp. 289-90), as follows:

"The Government entered into close confabulation with the Federation of British Industries and the National Union of Manufacturers. On September 12 the outcome was announced in the Cripps Plan. The Cripps Plan seals the alliance of a Right Wing Labour Government and Big Business to seek to solve the crisis along orthodox capitalist lines at the expense of the workers. Slashing cuts in living standards, in social re-construction and in the re-equipment of industry; a feverish drive, with obsolescent industrial equipment, to force up exports in a shrinking world market; obstinate maintenance of excessive armed forces and overseas commitments; no change in the disastrous imperialist foreign policy mainly responsible for the crisis; no proposals for limiting profits, already soaring to fantastic heights. Big business reaction voiced by Tory M.P.s thinly disguised as industrialists, purrs approval. 'They were grateful to Sir Stafford Cripps; industry would welcome his sincere and courageous approach,' declared the President of the Federation of British Industries. 'They were at last facing realities', declared the President of the National Union of Manufacturers. Such is the outcome of two years of the rule of Social Democracy."

THE TWO VOICES OF BEVIN

Dutt went on to relate that on the 3rd September, Bevin, addressing the Trades Union Congress, had protested against the charge of tying Great Britain to America, saying: "My God, I am here this morning to appeal to you to fight for our independence in the workshops. Who can accuse me of wanting to be subservient to East or West?"

But on the 10th September, one week later, he addressed the American Legion at a dinner party at the Savoy Hotel, and declared:

"My dear Americans, we may be short of dollars, but we are not short of will. . . . We won't let you down.

"Britain is a great bastion of civilisation. Our Western civilisation cannot go, unless Britain falls, and Britain will not fall.

"Standards of life may go back. We may have to say to our miners and to our steel workers: 'We can't give you all we hoped for. We can't give you the houses we want you to live in. We can't give the amenities we desire to give you. But we won't fail'."

This servile assurance of devotion, that "Britain won't let the United States down" meant, as Dutt pointed out, that cuts and austerity without limit were to be imposed on the people in order that Britain might continue to serve as the "bastion" of "Western civilisation", i.e. of monopoly capitalism and imperialism under the American leadership.

WHERE THE BLAME LIES

There were no more crises before the parliamentary session ended on the 20th October. But the crises I have already described were more than enough! How much blame ought to be attached to the Labour Government for this appalling series of crises? Plainly, it could not be blamed for the terrible economic position in which the country stood when it came to power—the world shortage of food, the devastation and destruction of war, in Britain and elsewhere, the appalling difficulties of making the country's ends meet. Nor could it be blamed for the dreadful weather of January-March, 1947. It could, moreover, claim credit for efficiency in a good many departments—by no means all—in actually dealing with situations when they arose, even if it failed to foresee them.

But it is clearly to be blamed under three heads. The first was that it never did anything fundamentally socialist to give the economy a new orientation. The second—serious enough in its own field—was that it never showed any sign, any more than Tory governments have ever done, of seeing a crisis ahead. Just as some of the great financial and industrial magnates whom we are, or used to be, asked to admire failed to see the mighty slump of 1929 coming even a month ahead, so the Labour Government of 1945 onwards never saw any of the series of crises more than a few weeks ahead (or, if they did, they pretended not to do so).

Palme Dutt, in the Notes of the Month (pp. 133-4 of *Labour Monthly* for May, 1947), written just before the Labour Party Conference at Margate, pointed to the very different atmosphere from that of the Conference at Bournemouth a year previously. There was no longer room for the complacent illusions and self-satisfaction which had made easy the domination of the right wing, the rejection of Communist co-operation and working-class unity as superfluous, and the absence of any major challenge to official policy. The position was now very different, and—as Dutt wrote:—

"At Bournemouth Herbert Morrison could describe with lofty superiority the impotence and lack of foresight of the Labour Government of 1929 as a striking contrast to the situation of the present day:

" 'The Government is rapidly building up an overall planning organisation. I compare it with the complete lack of economic planning organisation in the past. . . .

" 'When we went into the economic and financial smash of 1931 we did not know we were going there. We ought to have known what was ahead, but we did not, because there was no proper machinery of State to tell us, and when we got there we did not fully know what to do about it.

" 'The real problem of statesmanship in the field of industry and economics is to see the trouble coming and to prevent ourselves getting into the smash.'

"Yet it is possible to read the ministerial pronouncements of the Bournemouth Conference in vain to find the slightest inkling of the real character of the critical economic situation which was to develop within a few months in the winter and to transform and dominate the whole perspective of 1947. Nine months after the pompous announcement of 'overall planning organisation' at Bournemouth, twenty months after the return of the Government supposedly on a programme of planning, only after the crisis had broken, in March, 1947, the Government suddenly announces the decision to call in a Big Business head as 'Chief Planner'. What, then, had been happening during twenty months?"

After quoting the comments of Harry Pollitt on the 1946 Conference, which are given above in Chapter 6, Dutt went on:

"It was the communist predictions of the deepening gravity of the economic situation ahead which were proved correct by the event, and not the rosewater pictures of complacency. And when the crisis came, it was to the communist Arthur Horner that Ministers turned for help and guidance; it was the communist miners who took the initiative in organising Sunday work for the emergency and speeding up effort and raising production figures; it was the communists at the key points of industry who stood in the forefront in the production drive, no less than in rallying working-class opinion to stand solidly behind the Government against the Tory attempts to exploit the crisis."

The third head of blame is, of course, the most serious; it lies in the foreign policy, which cost us incalculable millions in the economic field by tying us up to the U.S.A., cut us off from useful and profitable trade with the socialist world, forced us into ruinous military expenditures, produced crises both of labour and manpower by keeping up large armed forces, and led us into endless waste of money and resources in Germany, Greece, Palestine, Malaya, and many other areas.

DALTON'S WARNING

Even inside the Cabinet there was at any rate one warning voice against the military expenditure, and of the coming economic crisis. Dalton, at pp. 194-9 of *High Tide and After*, quotes a Note which he sent to the Prime Minister on the 20th January, 1947, just as the terrible freeze-up was beginning. This was three months before Palme Dutt wrote the passages I have just quoted, and six weeks after he had written (at p. 5 of the Notes of the Month for January, 1947):

"The fight that is now opening is a fight to save Britain; to end a course which leads to bankruptcy; to end the burdens of an imperialist policy which is strangling recovery; to carry through the home reconstruction which is imperative; it is a fight for the economic and political future of Britain, for the employment and standards of the people, for the lives of men and women and the young generation which is growing up."

Dalton's Note of the 20th January ran:

"I had already stated in a recent paper to my colleagues that this year 'we cannot afford either the money or the men for which the Minister of Defence asks. . . . We are vainly trying, in every sector of the national economy, to do more than we can. Unless we relax, the result will be rupture. We must think of our national defence, in these hard and heavy years of transition, not only against the more distant possibility of armed aggression, but also against the far more immediate risk of economic and financial overstrain and collapse.'

"I stand by that, and I regret that you and others of my colleagues seem so completely unmoved by these considerations.

"What shall it profit Britain to have even 1,500,000 men in the Forces and Supply, and to be spending nearly £1,000 millions a year on them, if we come to an economic and financial cropper two years hence? . . .

"And I am told in Cabinet that to have only 1,400,000 Service and Supply personnel and to spend only £750 millions on them is 'unilateral disarmament'.

"We are, I am afraid, drifting in a state of semi-animation towards the rapids. We had started our course, since the last election, wonderfully well. But we look like finishing wonderfully badly—worse perhaps than in 1931."

Dalton desrves praise for having seen the crisis coming; and the Government as a whole must bear even heavier blame for either not heeding his warning or concealing the facts from the public. But Dalton did not, alas! appear to move an inch towards realising that a change of attitude towards the socialist world would have transformed the situation. His justified warning could have been written by any Tory Chancellor.

TRADES UNION CONGRESS

The Trades Union Congress met at Southport in the first week in September. It was again dominated by Bevin, and there was little sign of revolt against Government policy, although plenty of opposition to our dependence on the U.S.A.

MARSHALL AID REQUIREMENTS

In this autumn of 1947, the sixteen "Marshall Plan" countries met in Paris to discuss the "shopping lists" which they had prepared as a statement of what they really needed to assist their economies under Marshall aid. They reported that Western European food production was less than two-thirds of the 1938 level; that 30 million tons of food would be needed annually from the U.S.A. until 1951; and that 40 million tons of American coal would be needed in 1948. When these countries put forward their "shopping lists" on that basis, they were told bluntly by the Americans that they must go back and "think again", and put forward more modest requests and that all requests for machinery and other capital goods were excluded! Some months were still to elapse before the hungry sixteen received anything at all.

"PALACE REVOLT" AGAINST ATTLEE

There was in this autumn a sort of "palace revolt"—a scheme put forward by Cripps, and discussed with him over some weeks with Dalton, Morrison, Bevin and Attlee himself—for the removal of Attlee from the office of Prime Minister, with Bevin as the probable replacement. As told by Dalton in Chapter 29 of *High Tide and After*, it makes a sorry story. Almost the only concrete result of the long manœuvres was that Cripps became Minister for Economic Affairs, with responsibility for such planning as was achieved. At about the same time, there were various other changes in the government, which were not of much importance.

TRADE WITH THE U.S.S.R.

Negotiations for a trade agreement with the U.S.S.R. started in the middle of April, 1947, in Moscow, and went on until the beginning of the second week in May; they were resumed on the 21st June and lasted until the 25th July when they broke down again. The U.S.S.R. could supply timber, which we urgently needed for our housing programme, and wheat and other grain which we would otherwise have to buy with dollars; and there was a good deal of machinery—including timber-cutting machinery—which we could supply and the Soviet Union greatly needed.

When the negotiations broke down, the British Press, on government inspiration, produced a series of excuses, which were mutually contradictory and in fact untrue; and it was obvious that the long-standing hostility to the U.S.S.R. was really at the root of our rejection of something which might have been of very great help to our economy. The actual point on which the negotiations broke down was British reluctance to reduce the rate of interest chargeable on a 1941 war credit. This reduction would have cost us £4 million, spread over a period of some years; £4 million at that time was less than the amount of the *daily* withdrawals on the American loan. (Compare what we were prepared to do for Tsarist Russia; for a long period of the First World War we gave her unsecured credits of £100 million every month, the rough equivalent of £100 million a week in 1947.)

However, later in the year, on the 27th December, 1947, after three weeks of negotiation in Moscow, a short-term agreement was signed, under which we obtained large quantities of barley, oats and maize, to be delivered before the autumn of 1948 and to be paid for by deliveries, spread over two or three years, of several varieties of machinery, besides a large quantity of steel rails.

As was pointed out by Harold Wilson in a debate in the House of Commons in March, 1948, there was not only no question of our giving credit to the U.S.S.R. under this agreement; in truth, the reverse was the case, for the Soviet deliveries of grain were being made some time before the goods which were to be delivered by us in payment.

The two sides, it was agreed, were to meet again not later than the 31st May, 1948, to negotiate a more comprehensive agreement. I will come back to this in Chapter 17.

HOUSING

As for housing, the great social importance of which needs no emphasis, the Government's housing programme for 1947 (Cmd. 7,021) aimed to complete not 400,000 the amount estimated in 1945 to be constructed every year—in itself inadequate in relation to the needs of the population—but 300,000 houses, of which 60,000 would be temporary; but even this programme fell away all through the year. There was an acute shortage of bricks, and a somewhat acute shortage of timber. The weather and the resulting fuel crisis of January-February, 1947, created additional arrears, and the August balance of payments crisis led to pressures to cut investment on all forms of building, including homes. In October, 1947, local authorities, except in mining and rural areas, were instructed not to enter into any contracts for new houses, and not to grant any licences for new houses to private builders; and the Ministry of Labour adult training scheme for building craftsmen was completely stopped.

CHAPTER 13

The Third Session, 1947-8

THE 1947-8 Session began on the 21st October, 1947, (the day after the end of the second session), and lasted until the 13th September, 1948.

The main burden of the King's Speech (see *Hansard*, Vol. 443, Cols. 4-7) was the country's economic difficulties, and the measures—not, alas! including either trade and friendship with the socialist world or a reduction of our colossal military expenditure—proposed for easing those difficulties. The primary aim expressed was "to reduce the adverse balance of payments", particularly by expanding exports—the difficulty of which, within the strait-jacket of the tie-up to the U.S.A., I have already described; this was correctly stated to involve increased production and the sale abroad of a larger share of what was produced.

Aid was promised to increase the home production of food.

REMEDIES FOR ECONOMIC ILLS

In order to increase exports and save imports, steps were to be taken to ensure the best use of our manpower, and in particular to increase the numbers working in coal-mining, agriculture, and the textile industry. The operation of labour controls—which are necessarily unpopular, but may be justified in emergency—was to be "closely watched", and measures would be taken to bring into essential work those making no contribution to national well-being—which would have been admirable if it had been carried into effect.

Close joint consultation in industry, which was necessary for maximum production, would be encouraged.

Attention would be given to securing essential foodstuffs and raw materials from overseas, everything possible being done to find new sources of supply; and further long-term agreements with overseas countries would be sought; at the same time there would be legislation to promote the expansion of production within the Empire.

On foreign policy, there was to be continued participation in the work of European reconstruction put in hand at the recent Paris Conference (i.e. the "Marshall Plan" meeting discussed in Chapter 10).

The Government would support the United Nations Organisation in the effort to promote mutual trust and tolerance. And the hope was expressed that the forthcoming Conference of Foreign Ministers, to be held in November, 1947, would result in an agreement leading towards a democratic and self-supporting Germany, which would not threaten world peace, and to a satisfactory settlement of the international status of Austria.

A treaty of peace with Japan was hoped for at an early date. There would be legislation to provide for the government of Burma in accordance with the free decision of the elected representatives of the Burmese people; and discussions were under way to enable Ceylon to have "fully responsible status within the British Commonwealth".

There was to be "accelerated release of men and women from the Armed Forces to the maximum extent consistent with the adequate fulfilment of the tasks falling to the Forces"—which reminds one of an habitual drunkard promising to maintain his family at the maximum level consistent with the continued satisfaction of his thirst. The Government was to press on with the re-organisation of the Forces on a peace-time basis, and would seek to obtain the necessary volunteers to build up our Regular and Auxiliary Forces.

LEGISLATION

There would be legislation to amend the Parliament Act, 1911; to abolish the Poor Law and provide a comprehensive system of public assistance; to nationalise the gas industry; to reform the franchise and electoral procedure; and to achieve a substantial number of other useful reforms of no particular political importance.

Gallacher spoke in the Debate on the Address (*Hansard*, Vol. 443, Cols. 179 *et seq.*). He criticised the failure to include the nationalisation of the steel industry in the programme outlined in the King's Speech, the policy of relying on the U.S.A. and of subordinating our policy to that country, and the attempts to solve our economic and financial crises by cutting back capital expenditure, thus reducing the supply of schools, hospitals, and homes.

Of the legislation actually carried through I should mention the Burma Independence Act, 1947, the Ceylon Independence Act, 1947; the Overseas Resources Development Act, 1948, which I will discuss in Chapter 16; the Palestine Act, 1948, which provided for our giving up the Palestine mandate—see Chapter 16; the Gas Act, which I will discuss at once; and the Parliament Bill, 1947, which I will also discuss in this chapter.

NATIONALISING GAS

The Gas Act, 1948, introduced on the 21st January and passed on the 30th July, 1948, was said by Gaitskell in the debate introducing it to rest on three propositions: "first, that the present structure of the industry is not conducive to maximum efficiency; second, that the present legislative framework is a major obstacle against achieving great efficiency; third, that from every angle the most suitable structure for an efficient gas industry can be achieved only by organisation under public ownership."

These arguments, which could equally well have been advanced by a Liberal government, were drawn from the Report of the Heywood Committee that had been set up in 1944.

There was some vigorous Tory opposition to the Bill, basically directed against the principle of extending nationalisation rather than against the particular arguments put forward in support of the Bill.

The provisions for compensation were the same as those for electricity under the Electricity Act, which I stated in Chapter 9.

But the administrative provisions were different; the industry was placed under the control of twelve area Boards, which were to be directly responsible for organising "an efficient co-ordinated and economical system" of gas supply in their areas and for developing "the efficient and economical" production of coke. And a National Gas Council was set up, mainly "advisory and federal" in character; this was in effect a co-ordinating committee, composed of the chairmen of the area Boards, with a full-time chairman and deputy chairman.

PERSONNEL OF BOARDS

As for personnel, the position in September, 1949, was that one of the twelve chairmen was a retired Indian Provincial Governor, one was a director of the Co-operative Wholesale Society, one was a Town Clerk, and the rest were executives from the gas industry, save one who was a managing director of Coal Wharf and other companies.

PARLIAMENT ACT

The Parliament Bill, 1947, was introduced on the 31st October, 1947, but did not become law owing to obstruction in the House of

Lords. Its object was to reduce the time during which the House of Lords could hold up legislation. The House of Lords was until 1911 constitutionally entitled to reject any Bill (except "money Bills"), and thus to veto progressive legislation, however important it might be and however great the popular demand for it; in practice, with an eye to preserving their own anachronistic existence, the Lords were generally a little hesitant about rejecting important legislation, so that their functions might be described as veto limited by fear. But in 1909 they had rejected important legislation introduced by the powerful Liberal Government of that time, and as a result Parliament had passed, the Parliament Act, 1911, providing that, if the Commons passed for a third time a Bill which had twice been rejected by the Lords, the Bill should become law, in spite of the Lords' rejection. The Lords could, constitutionally, have rejected that Parliament Bill, but had they done so it was pretty clear that the King would have created enough new Peers to provide the necessary majority to pass it; accordingly, the veto was cancelled by fear, and the Bill passed.

Now, in 1948, the Labour Government's Bill sought to make a modest enough provision, that such Bills need only be passed twice instead of three times; the Government was probably anxious to make sure that, when they would finally bring in the long-delayed measure for the nationalisation of Iron and Steel, there would still be time within the life of the Parliament to pass it over the Lords' veto. But, as I have said, obstruction prevented the Bill going through for the time being. It was passed for a second time in the short fourth Session of the Parliament, (September-October, 1948) and for a third time in the fifth Session; see Chapters 19 and 20.

CHAPTER 14

The Witch Hunt, 1947-8

A NATIONAL and international witch hunt against Communists and Communism, accompanied by general anti-Soviet hysteria, was such a pervading characteristic of the year under review that I must devote a chapter to the development of that disquieting medieval activity.

The first shot in the campaign was fired by Morgan Phillips, the Secretary of the Labour Party, in a circular issued on behalf of the National Executive Committee on the 21st December, 1947. Phillips in effect called upon trade unions to turn out all elected officials who were Communists. (It was a curious imitation on a small scale of the pressure that the U.S. government had been bringing for some time on France, and to some extent on Italy too, with the threat that unless all Communists were removed from their government American aid would be cut off.)

Phillips advanced no valid argument or evidence, but asserted that "we can expect a campaign of sabotage"—a somewhat serious allegation to make, even by the Labour Party leaders, who are habitually pretty reckless in attacking anyone to the left of their party—"by the Communists and their fellow-travellers. . . . We can expect Communist-inspired attempts to foment discontent in the factories. . . . We can expect intensified attempts to undermine and destroy the Labour movement from within."

COMMUNIST PARTY POLICY

The nearest approach to even a "peg" on which to hang an attack on the Communists was that Harry Pollitt, the general secretary of the Communist Party, in a then recent report, had enunciated a change in the Party's policy in relation to production. But it is important to know precisely what that change was; it is well explained by J. R. Campbell at p. 49 of the *Labour Monthly* for 1948:

"It does not consist of the Communists saying that increased production is no longer important to Britain. For the Communists cannot fight for Britain's independence without fighting for its economic recovery, and they cannot fight for its economic recovery without supporting under proper safeguards measures for increased production. . . .

"The essence of Harry Pollitt's thesis on production is that we cannot obtain sufficient production to guarantee national recovery and independence unless there is a complete change in the policy of the Government:

"'Without a decisive change in Government policy no solution to the crisis is possible, however hard the workers strive.

"'Any tendency to separate the issue of production from the main issue of the change of policy necessary can only result in trailing behind the Government's reactionary policy.

"'Now this question is being placed in still sharper terms because of the way Britain is being tied behind the Marshall plan; production increases will not be utilised for the benefit of Britain or the people, but will be subordinated to the general aims of American policy.'

"Throughout the whole post-war production drive", Campbell went on, "the Communist Party has always claimed that increased production was not a matter of fiercely speeding up the workers but on the contrary was primarily to be secured by the modernisation of industry with improved wages and conditions for the workers.

"The workers in all industries cannot, of course, be provided overnight with new machines, and so the Communists asked the workers to help production along until the new machines came along. They asked them to reduce absenteeism and co-operate with the employers in making, on the basis of existing equipment, such small changes as would lead to increased production, until the modernisation programmed could be put through."

ATTACK UNJUSTIFIED

Phillips' attack was in any case particularly unjustified, since it was well-known that for many years Communists in the trade unions and the factories had been of invaluable help in convincing their fellow-workers of the necessity of achieving maximum production in spite of difficulties, at first to win the war and later to give all possible help to the Government which the workers had elected to lay the foundations of socialism; but the attack was naturally hailed with joy by the Tory press, and supported by a Manifesto signed by Lady Violet Bonham-Carter, Mr. Clement Davies, and Lord Vansittart. Phillips

L

made himself a little ridiculous by asserting that Communist influence in certain trade unions was much greater than their real strength, because not enough trade unionists attended their branch meetings; "Communists thrive on apathy", he wrote, and the remedy was to be found in "Labour Party members playing an active part inside their respective trade unions". The answer to this was that, so far from "thriving on apathy" the Communists were busy, year in and year out, urging trade unionists, including Labour Party members, to play an active part in their unions! It was indeed by setting an example of playing an active part in union affairs that Communists won the respect of their fellow members and were often chosen to represent them.

Arthur Horner, writing in the *Labour Monthly*, criticised the tactics of such moves as this of Phillips as bound to have a grave effect in splitting the working-class movement. He wrote:

"It is not arguments, however, which matter in this document issued with the authority of the Labour Party Executive, but the intention behind the arguments. The intention to introduce splitting tactics is the sinister feature. Faced by the growing resentment of the trade union movement at the abandonment of the General Election programme and the ill-concealed endeavours to keep wages pegged while profits riot unchecked, Right-Wing Labour leaders, so far from paying heed to those who elected them, have set themselves to disorganise the movement.

"But there is a still more disquieting feature in this move, and more sinister forces lie behind it. Irving Brown and other emissaries of the American Federation of Labour, working hand-in-hand with the U.S.A. Department of State, have their fingers in this pie. It is they who have urged and stimulated this move in Britain following on the moves they had made in other countries of Europe." (This was presumably a reference to the American move against Communists participating in European governments, mentioned above.)

"Therefore, the challenge to the unity and strength of the British trade unions has to be taken up with a full understanding of the dark and vicious transatlantic forces that are the original inspiration of this move. That is to say; the workers in the trade unions of this country will not resist this splitting move with full success unless they tackle also the policies that have been thrust upon them, or upon so many of their leaders. Let no one imagine that this splitting move arises from the spleen of [Phillips]. The reasons lie deeper than that. The policy of Cripps has its own logic. Once the decision was taken to accept the proposals of the Federation of British Industries in regard to capital investment, etc., the rest of the outlook of the F.B.I., with its opposition to militant trade unionism, had sooner or later to follow as a matter of course. . . .

"Had the British Government and the British Labour Party joined with the progressive and democratic forces, both this country and all of Europe would be in a better position today; but by throwing this country into the arms of the American millionaires, the most profoundly anti-working class and anti-trade union forces in the world were given their chance."

ATTLEE ATTACKS AGAIN

Morgan Phillips' circular was the beginning; within a fortnight Attlee played the same tune in a New Year broadcast.

Attlee's broadcast was an indiscriminate attack on the U.S.S.R., and praise of the U.S.A. as a country "standing for individual liberty in the political sphere and for the maintenance of human rights"; he seemed to forget that it was a land of colour bars, of lynching, and of witch hunts against even the palest of "Pinks", and the main bastion of reaction against any advance towards the socialist system which he professed—and had been elected—to advance.

WHITE PAPER ON INCOMES

On the 10th February, 1948, the White Paper on Wages and Personal Incomes was published.* It was not of course specifically part of the Witch Hunt, but witch hunts against the political and trade union forces most likely to resist efforts to lay upon the working class the economic burdens resulting from bad foreign policy and capitalist crises, with a view to splitting opposition and putting over unpopular policies, are so common a feature of reaction that it will be useful to examine here to some extent what the White Paper provided.

SEEKING A WAGE FREEZE

It began with the proposition that "there should be no futher increase in the level of personal incomes without at least a corresponding increase in the volume of production". This is almost the classical formula for introducing a wage freeze (which can largely be made effective), coupled with an appeal for limitation of profits, interest and capital gains (which is not easily made a reality—as I noticed in Chapter 12).

* This White Paper is dealt with further in Chapter 17.

In the debate in the House of Commons on this White Paper on the 12th February, 1948, Cripps, by now Chancellor of the Exchequer, gave the Government's reasons for the policy outlined in the White Paper; (see *Hansard*, Vol. 447, Cols. 591 *et seq.*) Inflation, he said, would make it impossible to give fair shares to all, and any further increase in prices would lead to loss of export markets and thus to unemployment. And it was impossible to end the inflationary situation by putting more goods on the home market because "we have not finished our export task". The Government accordingly intended to bring about a standstill in wages and profits, so far as possible by consent. He had asked the Federation of British Industries(!) to produce a scheme for reducing prices and profits wherever possible. "If wages and salaries are not to be increased generally," he said, "there must be a halt in price increases."

Some cases of wage increases, according to the White Paper, could be justified, for example, to attract labour to an under-manned industry, or to meet a marked increase in the cost of living, or in cases where an increase in production had come about, or where wages were below subsistence level.

OPPOSITION TO WHITE PAPER

Eight Labour members tabled an amendment calling for the withdrawal of the White Paper, on the grounds that "it perpetuates the anomalies in payments, earnings, conditions and status of people, and contains fallacious economic ideas", and for the adoption in its place of a "constructive economic policy based upon the layout of a national industrial plan that will lead to increased output". But, under the parliamentary procedure which the Labour Government had inherited (and not altered) it lay in the Government's power to prevent any discussion that was unwelcome to it by simply not "giving time" for it; and this course was adopted on this occasion. Opposition to the policy was however fully expressed in the debate by Piratin (*Hansard*, Vol. 447, Cols. 647 *et seq.*)

A number of trade unions reacted unfavourably to the White Paper, insisting that all wage claims should go ahead; but the General Council of the T.U.C. accepted it.

CIVIL SERVICE PURGE

The next move in direct witch-hunting was the announcement on the 15th March, 1948, of a "purge" policy for the Civil Service. On that day, Attlee stated in Parliament (*Hansard*, Vol. 448, Cols. 1703 *et seq.*) that the Government had decided "to ensure that no one who is known to be a member of the Communist Party, or to be associated with it in such a way as to raise legitimate doubts about his or her reliability, is employed in connection with work the nature of which is vital to the security of the State. . . . The same rule will govern the employment of those known to be actively associated with Fascist organisations."

The immediate reaction in Parliament was that forty-three Labour members put down a resolution regretting the statement, on the ground that there were already in existence adequate safeguards; but another resolution signed by thirty-one Labour members congratulated the Prime Minister.

There was much indignation in Parliament over the decision, and great pressure from members of all parties for a debate. The Government refused to grant time for the discussion of the critical amendment, but advantage was taken of the Easter adjournment on the 25th March, 1948—one of the peculiarities of parliamentary procedure is that any topic can be discussed on the motion for adjournment—to have a short discussion of the matter (*Hansard*, Vol. 448, Cols. 3389-426) in the course of which Gallacher made a spirited attack on the whole "purge" policy, coupled with a defence of his party.

The opposition would, I think, have been much stronger if the Government had not succeeded in giving the impression that the civil servants affected would have all proper safeguards in the way of knowing the case against them, confronting the witnesses, and having the opportunity to make a defence with trade union or other assistance. It was only some time after the debate that it transpired bit by bit that those affected were not even to be allowed to see and hear and contradict the witnesses against them, nor to see in written form the whole of the evidence, nor to be represented by their trade unions or by anyone else.

In any view, the whole proposal was in the worst traditions of American witch-hunting, and was calculated to have very grave repercussions and extensions; and, as time went on, private employers working on government contracts were found in many cases to be using the policy as a pretext to get rid of excellent workers.

There was opposition outside Parliament, of course. The Co-operative Party Conference met within a fortnight of the 15th March, 1948, and on the 28th March a resolution was moved asserting that the purge was a "violation of the democratic traditions of the country"; it was unfortunately defeated by a large majority. On the same day, the Conference of the Clerical and Administrative Workers Union held a special session on the matter; it drew a distinction between civil servants who "accept the democratic premises"—a formula designed to group all capitalists and social-democrats in one anti-communist camp—and those "prepared to endanger the security of the State in the interests of any foreign power"—a formula expressing the most extreme and bigoted anti-communist attitude—and considered that the latter group should be withdrawn from positions affecting security. But the Conference did at least pledge its support to the Civil Service Clerical Association and other unions concerned in securing for those involved full protection and preservation of civil rights. And on the 31st May, 1948, the Institution of Professional Civil Servants went on record against the purge.

T.U.C. ON THE PURGE

At the Annual Conference of the T.U.C. in the following September, a resolution demanding that victims of the purge should have the right to be represented by officers of their union was moved by several unions; but the "platform" succeeded in getting it defeated by a narrow majority (3,841,000 to 3,467,000) on the ground that negotiations on the matter were proceeding. By then the poison of the Witch Hunt had gone so far that public reaction against this fundamentally unfair and illiberal procedure was lamentably weak. The only feature of the story that was even partly pleasant was that very few civil servants were in the end affected.

THE NENNI TELEGRAM

The next incident in the Witch Hunt was the expulsion of John Platts-Mills, M.P. for Finsbury, from the Labour Party, on the 28th April, 1948.

The Italian General Elections were being held at the time; and the Italian Socialist Party—a Social-Democratic Party—had some little time previously split into two sections; the main part, five or six times as large as the other, was presided over by Pietro Nenni, and was still in official relations with the British Labour Party, but was also on friendly terms with the Italian Communist Party. Platts-Mills and a number of other Labour M.P.s had sent a personal telegram of good wishes to the Nenni party for success in the elections; this excited the hostility of the leaders, who passed a resolution supporting the small "Saragat" social-democrats; and repudiated the action of those who had sent their good wishes to the main party. And on the 28th April, 1948, the National Executive Committee of the Labour Party expelled Platts-Mills and warned the other signatories that they too would be expelled unless they undertook to desist from "such conduct". Mr. S. O. Davies, M.P. for Merthyr Tydfil, as good a Labour democrat as one would wish to meet, bluntly asserted that Attlee had "responded to the panic and nightmarish conditions laid down by the American Embassy in London".

ATTLEE ATTACKS YET AGAIN

Within a day or two, Attlee took the occasion of a Labour Party May Day demonstration at Plymouth to make a savage and un-provoked attack on the U.S.S.R., saying, as reported in *The Times* for the 3rd May, 1948:

"Russia was always in my young days"—this would be, say, about 1905—"the supreme example of the police state; the land of fear and suppression; the land where free speech, free thought and free press were banned. *It is the same today as it was then, only with a different set of rulers. It has yet to overtake several centuries of progress which have left their mark on Western civilisation.*"

This "Western civilisation" theme was by now becoming common form among leaders of the Labour Party; it combines two defects, that of grouping fascist Germany, Italy, and Spain, and Greece and Turkey, on the side of the angels of democracy against the U.S.S.R., and that of grouping Britain and the U.S.A. against the socialist world. It was scarcely what the electorate had voted for in 1945.

That was the insult which the Prime Minister of the Labour Government chose to hurl at the Soviet Union on May Day, the great international workers' day. He had visited that country once only, in the 'thirties, when I happened to see quite a bit of him there, and he had then told me how favourably impressed he was by the country. All that had happened since then was, on the one hand, that the U.S.S.R. had given magnificent help in the Second World War to the side on which Attlee was working, had suffered greatly in doing so, had caught up a good many centuries of development, and had a civilisation which every socialist in the world thought superior to the Western civilisation of British dole queues, American negro-baiting, and German Belsens

and Buchenwalds, *and* further that Attlee had won a General Election
on the basis of claiming to be friendly to the U.S.S.R.

(At that same meeting, Attlee also discussed the left wingers in the
Parliamentary Labour Party, saying with apparent gusto: "We have
excluded Mr. Platts-Mills from the Party, and we have given a clear
warning to the rest of them". What a happy topic for a Socialist May
Day!)

U.S.S.R. "UN-EUROPEAN"

Nor was Attlee content with what he said at Plymouth; within a day
or two he carried his comparisons of civilisations to the House of
Commons, where he said:

"In the nineteenth century to a large extent we had in Western
Europe a broad general acceptance of moral values. The difficult
thing is that we have not got that common acceptance by the Soviet
Union, and therefore we have to deal with it on a different basis.
We want to have the most friendly relations with them, but we have
to recognise that their views are not our views, and that there is that
breach in the general sense of values of European civilisation."

This was almost saying everything that could be said to revile the
people of the U.S.S.R. Clearly implied was the old fascist sneer that
they were "not Europeans, only Asiatics", and had no moral values;
much more profound in its hostility and anti-socialism was the further
implication that the only "moral values" worth having were those
built up by the capitalist world of the nineteenth century. I would like
to adopt the criticism of this speech made by Mr. and Mrs. Coates in
their book, at p. 286:

"'Nineteenth-century Western European moral values'—had Attlee
ever read even elementary history?

"Did he know of the innumerable colonial wars waged in the
nineteenth century by the countries of Western Europe against
relatively unarmed peoples?

"Had he not heard of the artificially manufactured famine in
Ireland, which cost the lives of hundreds of thousands of Irish men,
women and children?

"Had he never heard of the battle of Omdurman, which was not
a battle, but a massacre?

"Did he not know that in all the colonial countries ruled by

Western Europe the natives were robbed of more than half their natural span of life by undernourishment?

"And what about Tsarist Russia with her repression of all freedom, her virtual serfdom, her Rasputins, her corruption in court and government circles? With her we nevertheless could have normal relations,* was she too a representative of nineteenth-century moral values?"

THE NATIONAL COUNCIL OF LABOUR JOINS IN

On the 28th July, 1948, the National Council of Labour contributed its ration of anti-Soviet poison, making the extraordinary declaration on the question of Berlin which I will quote and discuss in the next chapter.

It is hardly surprising that Winston Churchill should also lend his voice; he probably thought that he could do it better, and had had longer training for it, than "these Labour fellows". On the 9th October, 1948, he addressed the Conservative Party Conference at Llandudno as follows:

"We ought to bring matters to a head and *make a final settlement* (my italics). We ought not to go on jogging along, improvident, incompetent, waiting for something to turn up. . . . The Western nations will be far more likely to reach a lasting settlement without bloodshed if they formulate their just demands while they have the atomic power, and before the Russian Communists have got it too."

One could almost include an account of the Labour Party and T.U.C. Conferences in this "Witch-Hunt" chapter, so strongly did they tend in that direction; but it is better to deal with them in Chapter 18.

HOW SILLY CAN ONE GET?

I end this chapter with an account of a less serious but revealing incident in which I happened to take part about this time. A schoolmaster, a member of the Labour Party living near Newbury, in Berkshire, organised a "Mock Parliament" in that town one Saturday afternoon. He invited me, and a certain Labour M.P. of a fairly progressive outlook, to take part, and we did so. It was open to anyone who chose to attend, and Tories, Liberals, and Labourites did so, to the number of a hundred or more. The "Parliament", like all such mock

---

* And, remember, as already mentioned, could lend her £3,000,000 every twenty-four hours during the First World War, until 1917.

parliaments, was organised as a rough copy of Parliament itself; the three parties debated a Bill, and after a number of speeches, a division was held at the close. The only remarkable feature of it was that, when the division took place, it was found that—in a great Tory area—the Labour Party arguments put forward by the Labour M.P., supported by myself and others, had prevailed so well that the majority of those present voted Labour! This should have been a matter of some mild rejoicing for the Labour Party; it was as good as two or three well-attended Labour meetings, (and no Labour meeting there, between elections, would in fact get a good attendance); and it was fully reported in the local weekly Press. But how did the Labour Party *leaders* in fact receive it? Well, this gathering having taken place on a Saturday, and no Press report of it having, to the best of my belief, appeared by the following Monday, my friend the Labour M.P. was sought out in the House of Commons on that Monday by the Home Secretary, and rebuked for "attending a communist meeting". So far as I could see, there was no justification for describing the gathering as communist, (unless it be, as one was sometimes driven to suspect, that anyone who displayed any real zeal or activity in the Labour Party was at once suspected of communist infection); but the serious point is that, for all this to have happened so quickly, some kind of police snooper must have attended the gathering, concluded that it was "reportable communism", and sent up a report quickly to his superiors in London; that they in their turn must have thought it important enough to pass it at once to the Home Office; that the upper Home Office civil servants must have thought that it should be put before the Home Secretary at once, and, finally, that he must have thought it important enough to call for the immediate administration of a rebuke to the Labour M.P., and for heaven knows what other precautionary measures! Had the Labour Government, in that troubled year, really nothing better to do with its resources?

CHAPTER 15

Foreign Policy, 1947-8

THE long-awaited resumed meeting of the Council of Foreign Ministers opened in London on the 25th November, 1947, and ended in failure on the 15th December. Both the behaviour of the American and British representatives at the Conference and the statements of their governments before it had even begun compel the conclusion that they had no wish for it to succeed.

PEACE TREATY WITH GERMANY?

The most important topic on the agenda was that of a peace treaty with Germany; and the obstacle to any such treaty from the point of view of the U.S.A., Britain, and Germany was not just a question of terms; it lay in the fact that by this time they had decided to preserve at any rate the Western Zones of Germany as capitalist, anti-Soviet, and anti-communist. For this they needed separate zonal governments, and were unwilling to make a treaty with a single undivided Germany. This was made clear by a good many indications; for one, the Marshall Plan—to which I will return shortly—had already been drawn up on the tacit assumption that one of the beneficiaries would be a West German State. For another, as recently as the 18th November, Mr. Marshall had declared that "the revival of Germany was indispensable to the revival of Europe" (and no one imagined that he was including the revival of the Soviet Zone of Germany in that declaration).

NEW CURRENCY FOR NEW STATE

For an even more striking indication, one can turn to the question of currency; if—and only if—there was to be a West German State, it would need a currency, which would have to be prepared and printed in sufficient quantities. As is now well known, this had been secretly done in the U.S.A., some months before; the Associated Press disclosed the fact in the middle of the Foreign Ministers' Conference. Mr. Marshall, head of the U.S. delegation, immediately denied it, but the

Press at once emphatically re-asserted it, the *New York Times* on the
11th December, 1947, stating: "Responsible government officials
confirmed the action after keeping it a top secret for weeks because of
the Foreign Ministers' Conference in London."

It is hardly surprising that the Western delegations to the Conference
struggled to keep the question of a Peace Treaty with Germany at the
bottom of the Agenda; but Mr. Molotov succeeded in forcing it to the
top. Discussions went on for some days, with no great likelihood of
success; and spectators derived some wry amusement from watching
Mr. Bevin opposing one of his own proposals in order to keep in line
with the Americans when he found that they opposed it; he had put
forward a reasonable proposal for financial reform in Germany—one
which he had in fact already put forward at the Moscow meeting in
March-April 1947 (see Chapter 10)—and Molotov accepted and
supported it. Marshall, however, opposed it, moving an amendment
which would largely destroy it. Bevin accordingly shifted his ground,
and spoke in support of the opposition to his own proposal (leading
to a cynical question from Mr. Molotov, whether Mr. Bevin would
again oppose what he was now supporting if the U.S.S.R. were to
support it!)

REPARATIONS AS OBSTACLE AGAIN

Even at that stage there looked to be some prospect—or danger—
that agreement might be reached; but then the three Western delegations announced, on the 12th December, that they would never agree
to reparations being paid out of current production. As I explained in
Chapter 10, the Soviet Union's claim to such reparations was a just
one, from which it could not well recede, and this Western declaration was especially hypocritical and irritating in the light of the fact
that the French were all the time drawing reparations from current
production in their zone, as was no doubt intended. Thus all hope of
agreement was destroyed, and on the 15th December, after the weekend,
Marshall officially declared the Conference "indefinitely adjourned".
A day or two later, he gave as the "most fundamental reason for
the failure of the Conference" the existence of a political vacuum in
Western Europe, and asserted that no agreement would be possible
until the vacuum was "filled by the restoration of a healthy European
community". The "vacuum" was presumably the absence of a
capitalist government in Germany, and "healthy" in American jargon
means "having a policy agreeable to Washington and Wall Street".

MARSHALL PLAN DEVELOPMENTS

I pass to the developments of the Marshall Plan, with which I last dealt in Chapter 10. The story of how Great Britain tied herself more closely—and in ever-increasing servitude, political and economic—to the U.S.A., and laid the foundations of her close links to the new resurgent Germany, and how little she gained, even indirectly, by it, is a long one.

During the year in question, 1947-48, the first development in the Marshall Plan project, just before the meeting of the Council of Foreign Ministers, was the Report of the Harriman Committee on Marshall Aid, published on the 9th November, 1947. This Report made it clear that the amount of aid proposed to be granted in answer to the requests of the "sixteen participating nations" who—as we saw in Chapter 10—had been called together in Paris to consider and plan what they really needed, long before legislation was even introduced into Congress to start the plan, had already been scaled down to three-fifths of the amounts requested; and, further, that the American Government was contemplating altering the allotments of aid by giving some countries greater and others smaller proportions of what they had asked, or rather of the three-fifths thereof that was to be granted. Western Germany in particular—plainly to be split off very soon from Eastern Germany which was not to receive aid—was probably to get a good deal more than had been contemplated.

The Report further demonstrated the political motives of the Plan— proving step by step every criticism which socialist countries and left-wing elements in capitalist countries had made—by proclaiming that "continued adherence to basic democratic principles is an essential condition for aid", and that the aid should be given on a year to year basis. That of course meant that no country could receive aid unless it was clearly and consistently anti-Soviet and anti-communist, and that —in order to make certain that they should continue to display these characteristics—all the beneficiaries were to receive their aid on the basis of short periods, without any guarantee of continuance or possibility of planning steadily ahead, lest any of them should ever be incautious enough to lean towards the Left.

MARSHALL INFRINGES SOVEREIGNTY

Moreover, aided countries might be called upon to cut down their national programmes of housing or other capital development, but they were expressly informed that they were not to reduce the expenditure on their armed forces, for "to reduce the cost of European recovery in dollars by limiting the economic resources absorbed by military and political purposes would cost America" (note that, quite naturally, it is America that is considered) "many times what it saved not only in dollars but in security"—a singularly frank avowal of the true intentions of Marshall Aid, namely to build up a great military force against the U.S.S.R.

Among the expenditures to be discouraged on the part of the "aided poor" was the consumption of finished steel, particularly in shipbuilding. This was part of a plan to keep the aided countries from becoming formidable competitors of U.S. industries, and in particular to maintain the U.S. merchant fleet and find a market for U.S. surplus shipping (consisting almost wholly of war-time mass-produced vessels with a very short expectation of life). "The United States", the report ran "needs . . . an active merchant marine for national defence, and we must not create conditions in which that merchant marine cannot survive." It was proposed that the aided countries should buy or charter some of the surplus U.S. ships and should reduce correspondingly their own construction of modern vessels, at the price not only of weakening their transport position in the world market but also of creating unemployment in their shipbuilding industries. One result of this proposal—for it was at the moment no more than a proposal—was that the British Government at once reduced by 20 per cent. its allocations of its own steel to its own shipbuilding industry.

In general, the "slant" of the Report was in favour of increasing the proportions of food and other consumer goods asked for by the aided countries, and cutting down sharply their requests both for capital goods and for raw materials for industrial production.

LEGISLATING FOR MARSHALL AID

On the 19th December, 1947, the draft of an "Economic Co-operation Act", intended as the legislative foundation of Marshall Aid, was put before the U.S. Congress. It carried out in the main the various changes in the original plan which were contemplated in the Harriman Report.

It proposed the establishment in Washington of an "Economic Co-operation Administration". The aided countries were to submit periodical statements of their needs, which would be "screened", first by American "Economic Co-operation Officers" in the respective countries, and then by a U.S. "Ambassador at large". And it required every country receiving aid to sign a separate agreement with the United States, pledging itself:

(1) to take the necessary measures to increase production in industry and agriculture;

(2) to take proper measures to stabilise its currency and maintain proper exchange rates;

(3) to co-operate to reduce trade barriers;

(4) to agree to the full use of the resources of all participating countries and to make efficient use of all goods and services provided;

(5) to stimulate the production of specific raw materials and to facilitate the procurement of such materials by the U.S. for stock-piling;

(6) to deposit in a special account amounts of its own local currency equivalent to the amount of aid furnished in the form of grants, such amounts to be used only in a manner agreed on with the U.S. Government; and

(7) to publish at home, and to furnish to the U.S., details of the use made of all aid.

Marshall stated at the time, as reported in *The Times* of the 20th December, 1947, that the success of the programme "would necessarily mean the establishment of a balance in which sixteen Western nations . . . would be rehabilitated, strong in forms of government which guarantee true freedom, opportunity to the individual, and protection against the terror of governmental tyranny".

To those who have not learnt the shorthand of modern politics, and who might think that Marshall was preaching equality of opportunity for Negroes in the Southern States, political freedom for communists in the U.S.A. and Western Germany, and freedom for West Germans to take part, for example, in the peace movement, I should explain that in this formula "true freedom, etc." meant quite simply capitalism and anti-communism.

FOREIGN ASSISTANCE ACT

Marshall Aid took its final legislative form in the "Foreign Assistance Act of 1948", passed by the U.S. Congress and approved by President Truman on the 3rd April, 1948. It was followed on the 16th April by the signature in Paris of the "European Recovery Pact" by the original sixteen participants plus representatives of the Western Zones of

Germany. The Act comprised in itself four separate Acts, of which the first, the one covering the Marshall Plan, was the "Economic Co-operation Act of 1948".

TRUMAN DOCTRINE AND MARSHALL AID

Two of the other three Acts—the grouping gives some indication of the U.S. foreign-policy setting of the Marshall Plan—dealt with "Greek-Turkish Assistance", i.e. the Truman doctrine already mentioned in Chapter 10—and "China" (i.e. Chiang Kai-shek) aid. That this was a real linking of these apparently unconnected elements, and not just an oddity of legislation, can be seen from the comment of the New York *Nation* on the 10th April, 1948;

> "The degree to which politics and military plans today dominate economic aid is illustrated by the inclusion in the final E.R.P. Bill of the military appropriations for Greece and China. This chunk of $425 m. links Truman Doctrine to Marshall Plan in an indissoluble whole. Guns, goods, dollars—all are lumped together, along with the military-political purposes they represent."

With the passing of the Economic Co-operation Act, one gets the one authoritative declaration of the purposes and conditions of Marshall Aid. These were not well-known in Britain, and the Government—both in and out of Parliament—so systematically concealed them, in its efforts to persuade the public that Marshall Aid did not impose any restrictions on our freedom of action, that I must state the provisions of this Act at some length, to give the true picture of what was being inflicted on us all.

I can do this best by quoting much of what I wrote in the *Labour Monthly* (at pp. 170-6 of the 1948 volume).

DECLARED OBJECTS OF MARSHALL PLAN

"The politicians who described it as the greatest act of generosity in human history will feel that the draftsman of its title missed an opportunity to mention its altruism. It is in fact called:

> " 'An Act to promote world peace and the general welfare, national interest, and foreign policy of the United States through economic, financial, and other measures necessary to the maintenance of conditions abroad in which free institutions may survive, and consistent with the maintenance of the strength and stability of the United States.'

"So, what is its declared purpose? We may perhaps pass over 'the promotion of world peace', which is of course claimed as the primary object of everybody whose conduct brings about war; and what is left is this:

"The object of this Act is to promote the welfare, the interest, and the foreign policy of the United States (this last being to fight communism everywhere).

"This object is to be sought by using the economic, the financial, and the 'other'—i.e. military—power of the U.S.A. to maintain in other countries—perhaps even whether they want it or not— conditions in which 'free institutions' may survive—i.e. conditions of private enterprise, monopoly capital, free entry into all countries of American investment and American imports, and 'Western civilisation' generally.

"Further, the 'conditions' thus to be maintained abroad must be consistent with the maintenance of the strength of the United States —of which we are well aware—and of its stability—of which we at times have doubts.

"The undoubted generous instincts of great masses of the American people—which would be most useful if they had any power—have certainly had to give way in this title to the 'hard-headed realism' of the American ruling class.

"So much for the title. What of the body of the Act? It begins with a declaration of policy which uses the well-known catch words about individual liberty . . . free institutions and genuine independence. It goes on to a clear declaration of the need for 'equitable rates of exchanges' and the 'progressive elimination of trade barriers'; in other words, free trade, free entry into European markets for powerful United States exporters, and American control over currency.

"'Individual liberty, free institutions, and genuine independence in Europe' are to be sustained and strengthened by assisting European countries which participate in a joint recovery programme based upon self-help and mutual co-operation.

"That constitutes a definite policy of assisting certain countries, for certain motives; and at once, as if reactionaries had taken fright and called a halt, there is a proviso: the assistance must not seriously impair the economic stability of the United States, and 'continuity of assistance' is to be dependent upon continuity of co-operation among the participating countries.

M

"The countries eligible for aid are defined; they . . . expressly include 'any of the zones of occupation of Germany'. . . .

"Then the office of 'Administrator for Economic Co-operation' is created, and endowed with considerable powers. Among other things, he can 'review and appraise' the needs of the various countries for assistance, draw up programmes of assistance, and *put an end to assistance*. . . . The Administrator (Mr. Hoffman of Studebakers) and the Secretary of State (Mr. Marshall) are to keep each other fully informed in all matters, and whenever either of them thinks that any activity or inactivity of the other is 'inconsistent with the foreign policy of the United States'—i.e., that it might help any Communist State—he may object, and if necessary the President must decide. . . .

"The next provision worth notice is one designed to establish in each assisted country a special American mission for economic co-operation, to assure 'the performance within such country of operations under the Plan.' . . .

WHAT AID YOU GET

"Then, at rather long last, we reach something concrete as to how assistance may actually be given. Mr. Hoffman may give assistance, when he thinks fit, on various conditions, in various ways, the principal ones being as follows:

"1. The supply of goods;

"2. Processing, storing, transporting, or repairing goods, or rendering any other services. But 'as far as practicable' he must ensure that at least half the tonnage of goods carried abroad from the U.S.A. under the plan must be carried in U.S. ships at market rates— a great help to the American merchant fleet, a possible blow to other merchant fleets, and a considerable drain on dollar resources, for American freight rates are hard and high;

"3. Technical information and assistance.

"In this work, Mr. Hoffman is to 'facilitate and maximise' the use of private channels of trade.

"The assistance is to be financed either by establishing accounts which may be drawn on, by utilising the services or facilities of any U.S. Government agency, or by guaranteeing investments in connection with projects approved by Mr. Hoffman and by the assisted country.

BEGGARS NOT CHOOSERS

"It will be seen at once that there is nothing definite to be found here—and there is in fact little anywhere in the Act—to indicate how much any particular country is to get, nor what quantities of what kinds of goods are to be supplied either to all countries or to any particular country. That is a matter to be negotiated between Mr. Hoffman and the various countries. Beggars can't do much choosing, but the most unfortunate form of negotiation to which a beggar can be committed is to start with a general scheme which leaves all the details to be filled in by free and equal negotiations between the begger and the rich man; and that is the sort of blank chequelessness to which we have been so committed in advance by entering the Marshall Plan. If we want to know how much mining machinery we shall get; whether we shall have to take more Virginia tobacco than we want and not nearly enough machinery; whether we shall get ingot steel or merely steel products such as motor vehicles; whether Western Germany—Mr. Dean Acheson's famous 'workshop of Western democracy'—will get more iron ore and steel scrap than we do; whether we will really have the opportunity to rebuild our industrial plants so as to make them fairly equal competitiors of the U.S.A., or will on the contrary be treated more on a relief basis and kept as a somewhat colonial country that will continue to need large quantities of U.S. manufactured goods—what is called 'exporting American unemployment'—to all these and similar questions, we can find answers indicated in the recommendations of Congress Committees or the statements of American ministers, and plenty of those pronouncements give us good ground for anxiety; but we cannot be sure of anything until we come to make a free and equal agreement on the topic with Mr. Hoffman.

HOW YOU REPAY

"The next question on which the Act throws a certain amount of light is the much-discussed one as to whether and to what extent 'Marshall Aid' has to be paid for or not. It provides that Mr. Hoffman, when giving assistance in the forms already mentioned, may do so by way of grant, or for cash payment, or on credit terms, or on any other terms of payment he likes. This expressly includes the transfer to the United States—terms and amounts to be agreed between Mr. Hoffman and the country concerned—of materials 'required by the United

States as a result of deficiencies in its own resources'. This is the famous 'stock-piling' provision which may be used to strengthen enormously the war-making power of America and to keep other countries short of essential raw materials.

"Then there comes at any rate a little light as to the sort of goods the assisted countries may get. Under the head of 'Protection of Domestic Economy', Mr. Hoffman is directed that his procurement of goods in the U.S.A. for Marshall Aid is to be so managed as to minimise the drain on U.S. resources and the impact on U.S. economy and to avoid impairing the fulfilment of vital needs of the United States—and who can be surprised an industrial ruling class should do this? In this connection, petroleum and petroleum products are to be got 'to the maximum extent possible' from outside the U.S.; and even then Mr. Hoffman has to consider the present and anticipated shortage in this field, and the consequent undesirability of expansion in petroleum-consuming equipment where alternatives are available. . . .

GETTING RID OF SURPLUSES

"There are next provisions designed to get rid of any agricultural products which are available in excess of American domestic requirements. Such products are to be shipped (i.e. 'supplied') in general from the U.S. only; the assisted countries will not be allowed to have them supplied from other countries, however great the saving might be for them if they could. . . .

"Then, some way through the Act, we find the outline of what the assisted countries have to do to receive their aid. Agreements may be made by Mr. Marshall, after consultation with Mr. Hoffman, with any of the countries 'or with an organisation representing any such countries'. These agreements are to cover a variety of points, some of which call for notice.

"The first point covers the promotion of industrial and agricultural production in the assisted country in order to enable it to become independent of extraordinary outside economic assistance. Those who have heard rumours of proposals for keeping these countries under control, and preventing them from becoming so highly productive of finished goods as not to remain good markets for American products, will want to know how far the agreements are to go on such matters. The answer is that, under the agreements envisaged, the countries are to propose specific projects, to be submitted for Mr. Hoffman's approval, and that these projects, whenever practicable, are to include increased production by the assisted country of the basic raw materials, coal, steel, transportation facilities, and food; in other words, they are to be encouraged to become good semi-colonial countries.

FINANCIAL CONTROL

"The next point to be covered by the agreements is the stabilisation of currencies, the establishment of 'valid' rates of exchange, the balancing of budgets, and the restoration or maintenance of confidence in their monetary systems. This goes far beyond mere efficiency and being a 'good debtor'; it can easily involve complete financial control, and the permanent opening of markets to full U.S. invasion. This is another point at which many questions arise, and many suggestions have been made, as to what degree of control or interference in either British finance, colonial finance, or the much wider sterling area is contemplated. Once again, the answer is: wait and see, it is all to be agreed. And once again the reports from America are ominous; taking only the more solid and serious suggestions, we find that we may be called upon to transfer to Mr. Hoffman the control over all dollar expenditure by Great Britain in the sterling area, and perhaps also to submit to a veto on all British capital investments—even in sterling— in the sterling area; there is even talk of an intention to break up the sterling area entirely. . . .

"Another point covers the tracking down and utilisation for the Marshall Plan of all assets of citizens of the assisted countries that are in the U.S.A. or in its possessions. . . .

"The next point provides for the deposit in a special account in the assisted country, in its own currency, of funds to match, on an 'agreed' basis, the goods or services furnished under the plan. These deposits are to be held or used for 'agreed' purposes of various kinds, 'including local currency administrative expenditures of the United States' incident to operations under the plan; and the ultimate balances are to be disposed of, subject to the approval of Congress, on an 'agreed' basis. It is easy to see that the power over local currencies which will be secured in this way by the U.S. Government must constitute a strangle-hold on any country's finance. . . .

INDUSTRIAL CONTROL

"The last of the points to be covered by the agreements is a little more complicated; but it is important. The assisted countries are to agree to negotiate 'a future schedule of minimum availabilities to the

United States for future purchase and delivery of a fair share of materials required by the U.S. to meet potential deficiences in its own resources, 'so as to protect the access of United States industry to an equitable share of such materials'; and they are equally to agree to negotiate a 'schedule of increased production of such materials' in their own countries and the delivery of an agreed percentage of such production to the U.S.A.

"It is clear that provisions of this kind make it possible for the United States Government in large measure to determine what we are to produce and to whom we are to deliver the bulk of what we do produce. This amounts not merely to an interference with sovereign independence, but substantially to a shaping of our industrial future by our most powerful competitor.

"A provision for substantial control of the running of our industries comes next, in the shape of a direction to Mr. Hoffman to give his encouragement to a joint organisation of all the assisted countries, which it is proposed to set up, to see that each country uses its resources efficiently 'by observing and reviewing such use through an effective follow-up system approved by the joint organisation'.

STOPPING REPARATIONS

"Then, without any mention of the Potsdam agreement, Mr. Hoffman is to ask Mr. Marshall to get all the countries to weaken themselves and strengthen the new Washington-controlled Germany by agreeing:

" 'that such capital equipment as is scheduled for removal as reparations from the three Western Zones of Germany be retained in Germany if such retention will most effectively serve the purposes of the European recovery programme.'

MAY WE TRADE WITH EASTERN EUROPE?

"There are still most important provisions to consider. One relates to the much discussed question whether assisted countries are to be allowed to trade with Eastern Europe. The provision on this point is obscurely worded; but its effect is pretty clear. If an assisted country— say Great Britain—wants to supply to any 'non-participating European country'—say, the U.S.S.R.—any commodity—say electrical plant—is it forbidden to do so? No, not in so many words. But this is the problem it will have to face: if the commodity is one which the U.S. 'in the interest of national security' would not license for export from the U.S. to the country in question, then the penalty to be laid upon us for supplying it ourselves will be that Mr. Hoffman must 'as far as practicable' refuse to deliver to us any goods which go into the production of the commodity. So, if any manufacturer here wants to bid for the supply of electrical plant to the U.S.S.R., he will have to face the risk that if, by the time he comes to deliver the plant, the U.S.A. has concluded that *it* won't license electrical plant for export from U.S.A. to the U.S.S.R., he and everyone else here will be cut off from supplies under the Plan of American copper and any other material that goes into such a plant. It will in effect be impracticable to contract, or even to allow any of our producers to try to contract, for a wide range of supplies to the East, except in so far as Mr. Hoffman chooses to tell us that it will be permitted.

"Then there is the question of time. To give Britain and other war-battered countries a real chance to plan their reconstruction, there ought to be some definite period during which a continuation of aid may be relied on. But in fact we are treated like a small shopkeeper trying to build up a business in premises on a quarterly tenancy. Mr. Hoffman is not merely to take into account the extent to which assisted countries are complying with their undertakings when he is deciding on the form and measure of assistance they are to have. He has a much bigger task. He is definitely ordered to 'terminate the provision of assistance' to any country not merely when he thinks it is not keeping its bargain or is making any wrong use of any assistance it has received, but also whenever 'because of changed conditions, assistance is no longer consistent with the national interest of the United States'. Such termination includes stopping the delivery of all supplies not already delivered before the termination. This of course amounts to the imposition of a complete veto—by crushing economic sanctions—on any political development in any assisted country that may not suit the changing hysteria of American foreign policy. M. Molotov was indeed prophetic—or just plain intelligent—when he announced in the summer of 1947 that the Marshall Plan involved an inadmissable infringement of sovereignty."

I quote from a further article which I wrote in *Labour Monthly* in May of the following year, 1949. For a full understanding of the evils of Marshall Aid—evils which emerged slowly, whilst the Government did its best to conceal them—is necessary to the history of the Labour Government, and the article in question put the position as I would put it today if I came to write a fresh criticism. I wrote:

STRINGS TO MARSHALL AID

"The Government continues blandly to deny that there are any strings to Marshall Aid. It tells us that we are benefiting by a great act of free generosity from 'the Americans', that is, from the eight mighty interlocking groups that run the United States—the same people who cut off lease-lend, fixed up the Loan and then took off price controls, and produced the Truman doctrine to finance the Greek and Turkish fascists. And it asserts too that we are able to carry our the investment policy of our long-term programme without American approval or control. . . .

"It is thus useful to make a practical test, and an interesting field for this was provided by Mr. Thomas K. Finletter, Chief of the Special Mission of the European Co-operation Administration to the United Kingdom, when he testified before the Foreign Relations Committee of the U.S. Senate some weeks ago—well before the opening of the Cripps misery budget.* I take the account of this from the official report of the United States Information Service.

"Mr. Finletter attended before the Committee to tell it how 'the large amount of money which was being made available to the United Kingdom for its first E.C.A. year' . . . . had been dealt with and controlled, a matter of importance to the members of a legislature which would soon be considering what it would vote for its second year. He began with a short analysis of Britain's financial difficulties, which he ascribed to the loss of invisible earnings and to the consequent large deficit, which was made more serious by being allowed to the Western Hemisphere. (He did not mention armament expenditure, or colonial wars, or the Berlin air-lift.) This deficit, he explained, the British Government was setting out to cover by high taxes and sharp restriction of expenditure, involving 'the holding down of increases in wages and salaries and in dividend distribution'(!) He said, however, that it would be difficult to resist all wage increases, and thought that 'only a most vigorously pressed policy . . . will be able to maintain . . . the excellent record'. Excellent for whom?

CUTTING BACK SOCIAL PROGRAMMES

"He went on to explain how this policy was designed to step up exports to meet the deficit:

" 'The austerity programme is part of the broad policy which Britain has adopted to funnel as much of her total annual resources as

* I.e. the Budget of April, 1948; see Chapter 17.

possible into exports, especially to the dollar area, and into capital. She is trying to hold down her consumption, that is to say, her personal . . . and her governmental consumption, to the minimum possible so that as much as possible of what is left over will be available for capital formation and exports. . . .

" 'In other words . . . her policy is to step up her gross national product by increasing her production to the maximum, to hold down governmental consumption *by cutting back social programmes instituted when the Labour Government came into power*, [my italics] and then to divide up what is left between exports and capital formation.'

"He did not of course add that to restrict working-class consumption in order to provide the maximum amount of goods for export was traditional *capitalist* policy in Britain, nor did he explain that the percentage of our total national production to be invested in capital expenditure —viz. 20 per cent.—was inadequate for any serious capital rehabilitation. He just left the facts of reduced consumption and cutting-back of the social programmes to commend our country to the representatives of American generosity as worthy of further 'aid'—aid which should have as its by-product postponement of the American slump and the implication of Britain's economy in expensive and suicidal preparation for service as an advance base for bombing (two-way bombing, of course) in the war that Washington and Wall Street are preparing against the U.S.S.R.

"But one or two Senators seemed unwilling to believe that our social programme was being properly cut back, and asked Mr. Finletter to be more specific. He was quite willing. He pointed out that 'governmental consumption'—which, to him, varies mainly with the expansion of social programmes—had been only 14.7 per cent. of our total annual resources in 1938, but by 1946 had 'worsened'* to 26.2 per cent, due in part to 'carry-overs from the war',† but also in part 'to the British social programme of that year'.

" 'I ask you', he goes on, 'to look at the year 1947; already that percentage has been cut to 20.7; and in the year 1948, it has been cut to

---

* An illuminating word. To an American class-warrior, expenditure on housing, medical treatment and health generally, education and insurance against the worst evils of accident, illness, and unemployment, benefiting the working majority of the people, is a "worsening".

† Another illuminating class-war contribution; workers are more urgently needed in war, and so more social expenditure on them is necessary, and must be put "right" after the war.

18.2. It is going steadily down. As programmed for 1952, it comes to 16.8. That is giving effect to the policies announced in the long-term programme, of giving priority to all users of resources within the United Kingdom which will tend to create exports and go into capital formation *at the cost of social service programmes.*' [My italics.]

" 'That . . . is quite clearly indicated in the long-term programme of the British Government, and is official British Government policy and practice.'

"Even this was not sufficient to satisfy some Senators; a cut of nearly 36 per cent. on social services in six years left them only partly convinced that the British Government had really and sincerely betrayed the social service programme which it had been elected to carry out. So they asked for more; *what* programmes, they asked, were being cut? Mr. Finletter was quite ready with the information:

CUTTING HOUSING, HEALTH, AND EDUCATION

" 'The housing programme has been quite seiously cut back. So has the health programme, and so has the programme for education.'

"Mr. Finletter made it clear that even our 'quite seriously cut back' housing programme had given our American paymasters ground for anxious thought. He put it thus:

" 'We were somewhat troubled about the percentages devoted to housing in the capital formation part of the British investment programme. Twenty-one per cent of that total investment' (i.e. 21 per cent. of the 20 per cent. of national production mentioned above) . . . 'goes into new housing. We examined that proportion with some care. We came to the conclusion that . . . that was a justifiable figure, for this reason. Four hundred and seventy thousand houses were destroyed in the United Kingdom by enemy action. There are at the present time half a million houses which have been classified as unfit for habitation. Despite that fact, and in the carrying out of this cut-back programme on housing, there are fewer houses being built in Britain today than there were in 1938; and, more than that, a smaller proportion of the national product is being devoted to housing in the year 1949 than in the year 1938.'

"So, Mr. Finletter approves, and asks the Senate to approve, the conduct of our Government in cutting expenditure on health—reducing the number of the much-needed health centres, for example, to a handful for the whole country; and on education:—'fewer new schools and fewer goods and services going into schools', as he puts it; and on housing—the cuts he describes, which the queues waiting for houses know so well. And can there be any doubt what would have happened if he had not brought himself to approve our cuts on the ground that we were really doing—our war losses considered—so little that the Senate need not be alarmed? If he had, instead, concluded that we did not deserve further 'aid' unless we cut still more, it is obvious that, in spite of the advantages to the U.S.A., direct and indirect, of continuing Marshall Aid, we should have been compelled to cut our programme still further, on the threat of a reduction or stoppage of 'aid'. That this is the reality is in a sense established by the Government's denials. A question was put last month to the Chancellor of the Exchequer asking when this policy of cutting back the housing, health and education programmes was approved by the E.C.A. What purported to be an answer was given with such insolent disregard of what was actually asked that the question was put down again; and as it is generally not possible to avoid answering a question twice running something had to be said the second time. Cripps on this occasion blandly said that there was no question of approval, that what Mr. Finletter had said was not approval, and that 'nothing would have happened' if he had disapproved. (As the French cynic said, nothing is true until it has been officially denied.) . . .

AVOIDING COMMUNISM

"Finally, Mr. Finletter speculated on the effects of the Marshall Plan in helping Europe to avoid communism and the United States to maintain its exports! But all that is of less interest than the demonstration, which grows clearer and clearer as one reads the report, that in reality all the main lines of our economic policies and programmes are now subject to veto—in the true sense of that abused word—in Washington or Wall Street. We know now that, when the Labour Government and the Chancellor of the Exchequer appear to be cutting the throat of the working class and betraying all the principles they ever professed, they are acting under the orders of the ruling class of a capitalist country which dominates Britain just like Britain used to dominate smaller countries.

"This sacrifice of our independence, this dependence on the most ruthless capitalist ruling class still remaining in power anywhere in the world, the price of whose aid is not only the loss of our independence but our active participation in the crime against humanity and social-ism involved in lending our territory for use as a United States military base against the great socialist country, is in truth wholly vain. For we do not only contribute our ground, our honour, and our pride; we have also to shoulder—as part of Marhsall Aid and the Atlantic pact—a rearmament programme vast enough to render us economically poorer than if we had no Marshall Aid at all and retained merely our independence and our socialist initiative. Let us hope that the clever but difficult propaganda work of concealing this humiliating sacrifice of the honour and independence of the great British people breaks down before it is too late for the people to reverse the engine and rid us of our chains."

From all this, one gets a true and very disquieting picture of the handcuffs, to enlarge a metaphor, which Bevin "grabbed with both hands" when it was first offered, (see Chapter 10) and which both he and Cripps and the Government generally presented to the public as a happy escape from an economic ruin, kindly provided by "the Ameri-cans". To mix the metaphor a little, one may ask what sort of a "pig in a poke" did Bevin, with his hands in these handcuffs, expect to get for us, in return for pawning much of our economy, our trade, and our industry, including the immense possibilities of trade with Eastern Europe, with the hysterical controllers of American foreign policy? This can well be seen from the speech of Cripps in the previous January, in which he confessed that, even if we were to succeed in our ambitious projects to increase both our exports generally and our exports to the dollar area by large percentages, we had still to expect a deficit in 1948 on our dollar trading of £300 millions. And all that it seemed possible to hope for from Marshall, if we remained obedient anti-socialists, not attempting to reduce our arms expenditure or to increase our trade with Eastern Europe, was £625 million spread over four and a quarter years (if not "vetoed" by Mr. Hoffman at any stage), or about one-third of the visible deficit; and of that £625 millions nearly one-third had to be taken in American tobacco.

When the allocations finally became known, it turned out that West Germany was receiving well over 50 per cent. more Marshall Aid than Britain, and France 10 per cent. more. The net result was sufficiently discouraging to lead *The Times* to publish a leading article on the 30th June, 1948, explaining that our existing dollar deficit was running at an annual rate more than double the aid we were to receive in the first year, and that in reality Britain might be as well off, economically, without the Aid as with it. (But it let a cat out of the bag with the remark that such a weighing of economic advantage "is not the final consideration. The Marshall Plan is designed to be a great unifying force in Europe, binding the Western countries together.")

GERMANY

Developments in and in connection with Germany in 1948 were to be decisive in many respects. The rulers of the U.S.A., as leaders of the capitalist, anti-socialist, anti-Soviet world, had already gone a fairly long way—as we have seen—in the direction of so dividing Germany as to ensure that at least the three Western Zones should be neither socialist nor neutral, but should become a strong—and strongly armed —element in a Western capitalist bloc aimed against the U.S.S.R. This involved the complete defiance and betrayal of the letter and the spirit of the Yalta and Potsdam agreements, especially in the rearmament of Western Germany and the restoration of its industries to the old capitalist rulers of Germany who had worked under Hitler, and in the indefinite abandonment of any idea of retaining (or re-creating) a single Germany with which a peace treaty could be made (and that, too, at a time when German public opinion was so strongly in favour of the reunification of the country that 15,000,000 signatures were given to the petition of the German People's Congress for referendum on unity).

The Labour Government of Great Britain supported this American policy; there can be no doubt that, if they had opposed it, it could never have been carried through; but their history as we have been able to follow it since 1945 had by 1948 made it clear that they were too closely bound to the U.S.A. by such ties as Marshall Aid, and that they were too hostile to the Soviet Union, to conduct themselves as if they were on the side of socialism and not on that of capitalism. The story of their behaviour in specific relation to German affairs, as we shall see, was of the same pattern as that of their behaviour over the Witch Hunt and the Marshall Plan.

The German story moves forward with the air of inevitable doom associated with Greek classical tragedy. On the 22nd January, 1948, Bevin opened a two-day debate in the House of Commons (*Hansard*, Vol. 446, Cols. 383 *et seq.*). After such remarks as "the Communist process goes on ruthlessly in each country", he announced that as the U.S.S.R. had refused to accept the terms presented by the three Western Powers, steps were being taken by Britain and France to make

new treaties with the "Benelux" countries for a "consolidation of
Western Europe". The treaties were to aim at a "brotherhood rather
than a rigid system", and were to include Italy later. He added that this
Western Organisation of Europe must be supported by the closest
possible collaboration with the Commonwealth and overseas territories—not only British, but also the French, Dutch, Belgian and Portuguese overseas territories, for these areas were primary producers
capable of vast development. (I shall return to this scheme for saving
Europe on the backs of the colonial peoples in the next chapter.)

Bevin also announced that the British, French and American governments were to have a conference in a few weeks' time on the three
zones of Germany with the aim of making them work economically
and of introducing a currency. Bevin made one bitter attack after
another in this speech on the Government of the U.S.S.R. and of her
allies; he was loudly cheered by the Tories.

Gallacher also spoke in this debate, saying (at Col. 482):

"What a shame it is that the Socialists should be looking to Mr.
Marshall and the monopoly capitalists of America, instead of to the
mass movement of the working class in this and other countries to
bring freedom to us and to Europe."

And adding, in answer to the often repeated and ignorant sneer that
communism was some kind of a foreign doctrine:

"It is a foolish lie that communist ideology came from Russia to this
country. It is the other way round. . . . There is not a revolutionary
idea in existence which has not had its birth in this country."

And a back-bench Labour member, not of the left wing, Mr. C.
Shawcross, was moved to say (at Col. 489):

"We must all confess that during the election campaign we assured
the electorate . . . that only a Socialist government could maintain
friendship with Soviet Russia, . . [and] that only a Socialist foreign
policy could restore Europe and bring permanent peace. . . . That
is about the only thing which has been contradicted by events, but
does anything else matter? Nationalisation, housing, full employment, social welfare, all these are nothing if we are steadily and
maybe rapidly drifting into an economic disaster of the first magni-
tude, or if we are heading, it may be tomorrow or in five, ten or
twenty years for a third world war. If these are the prospects as I
see them, what is the cause? I believe the cause is mainly . . . that this

Socialist government has never yet had a real Socialist foreign policy."

Attlee replied to the debate, playing on the old theme of "Western civilisation", (i.e. capitalist U.S.A. and Western Europe, treating the socialist world as either non-European and therefore second-class, or uncivilised, or both). He was as abusive as ever.

BIZONIA

Within a few weeks "Bizonia"—the fusion of the American and British Zones, whose administration was to be largely financed, and therefore controlled, by the Americans—and the establishment of a Central Bank for Bizonia with powers of note issue, were successively announced.

In March, a Western Military Pact was signed in Brussels by the five Western Powers, pledging mutual assistance against an unnamed aggressor.

WEST GERMAN REPUBLIC TO BE SET UP

By the 2nd June, 1948, the London Conference of Six Powers— U.S.A., Britain, France, Holland, Belgium and Luxemburg—really determined *inter alia* on the creation of the West German Republic, the formal establishment of which comes in Chapter 21. Among the recommendations of the Conference were that the proposed transference of the Ruhr industries to public ownership—earlier strongly supported by Bevin, and now opposed by the U.S.A.—should be dropped, and that there should be no withdrawal from Germany "until the peace of Europe was secured". The British Government, the U.S.A., and the Benelux countries accepted the recommendations. In France, the General Assembly accepted them—with some reservations—by the narrow margin of 300 votes to 286.

NEW CURRENCY

On the 18th June, 1948, the new currency was actually introduced in West Germany (having, as already mentioned, been printed in the U.S.A. months before), with an announcement by the Military Governors of the three Western Zones; it was to come into effect on the 20th June, and was not for the time being to apply to Berlin. There had up to that time been one currency for all Germany—the four zones and the City of Berlin; the new currency was of course just one more symptom and element of the determination to create two Germanys.

A NEW CURRENCY FOR BERLIN

It must have seemed quite impossible at that moment to think of attempting to apply this new currency in Berlin, which was no part of any of the three Western Zones but lay deep within the Soviet Zone and was economically part of it; it was under joint administration by all four Powers. But, however impossible it was, the Western Powers in fact announced within a few days the introduction of a separate currency for their sectors of Berlin. Economically and financially, it was like the introduction of a separate currency for two-thirds of the metropolitan boroughs of London by authorities who were governing, say, Wales and the North of England and had no power in the Midlands or the Home Counties. What those on the spot in Berlin thought of it may be judged from the fact that, after the "Air-lift" (to which I will come in a moment) had begun, the Municipal Council of the city decided to recognise only the Eastern currency in the city.

The insistence on establishing a separate currency in the Western sectors may have seemed to border on insanity; but it was worse than mere insanity, for it involved inevitably that huge sums of the old common currency, freely available throughout Berlin and the Eastern Zone and able freely to come into Berlin by the various lines of communication between that city and the Western zones, would have flooded from the West into East Germany. This would have created economic chaos and disaster there, for currency is curious stuff, and if one suddenly enormously increases the amount of it available it has the same effect as increasing the amount of, say, potatoes available. The value of currency, like that of potatoes, drops when there is too much of it about; and a drop in the value of currency really means a sky-rocketing of the price of everything people want to use money to buy. The Soviet government in the Eastern Zone, confronted with this emergency, was compelled to cut off communications with West Germany for the time being, and also to introduce a new currency in the East, which it did at first by stamping a certain amount of the old currency to validate it, and shortly afterwards (on the 7th July) by issuing new currency.

SOVIET PROTEST

The Soviet Government put the matter very clearly in a note which it sent to the British Government on the 14th July:

"The Government of Great Britain declares that the temporary measures introduced by the Soviet command for restricting transport communications between Berlin and the Western Zones have created difficulties in the supply of the Berlin population of the western sectors. . . . These difficulties were caused by the actions of the United States, British and French Governments, and above all by their separate actions in introducing a new currency in the Western Zones of Germany and a special currency in the Western sectors of Berlin.

"Berlin is in the centre of the Soviet Zone and is part of that Zone. The interests of the Berlin population do not admit of a situation where there has been introduced into Berlin, or even only into the Western sectors of Berlin, a special currency which is not in circulation in the Soviet Zone. Moreover, the introduction of a separate currency reform in the Western Zones of Germany placed Berlin, and with it the entire Soviet Zone of occupation, in a position where the entire mass of currency notes invalidated in the Western Zones threatened to pour into Berlin and into the Soviet occupation Zone of Germany.

"The Soviet command was compelled therefore to adopt urgent measures to safeguard the interests of the German population as well as the economy of the Soviet Zone of occupation and the area of 'Greater Berlin'. The danger of disruption of the normal economic activity of the Soviet Zone of occupation and Berlin has not been averted even yet, since Great Britain, the United States and France continue to maintain their own special currency in Berlin.

"At the same time, the Soviet Command has constantly manifested, and continues to manifest, concern for the well-being of the Berlin population and for ensuring it normal supplies of everything necessary, and is striving for the speediest elimination of the difficulties which have recently arisen in this matter. Moreover, if necessary, the Soviet Government will not object to ensuring sufficient supplies for the whole of 'Greater Berlin' by its own means."

THE WEST HAD NO RIGHTS IN BERLIN

It only adds to the horror of the use by the West of the Berlin problem to bring the world to the brink of war and keep it there for years on end, to realise that there is not even a sound foundation for the claim of the Western Powers to retain either officials or troops in Berlin, or indeed to have any status or function there. They were there, originally, by virtue of the Potsdam Agreement; and there was then something for them to do—for Berlin, as the capital of Germany, was made the seat of the Four-Power Government which was to administer the country until, as was hoped and intended, a democratic government of Germany could be established and a peace treaty made with it. In those conditions the Four Powers could together both administer the City and take part in making decisions relating to the military government of Germany as a whole. But by 1948 there were two clearly fatal objections to the continued presence or operation of the three Western Powers in Berlin. The first was that all pretence of seeking to establish one German government, or even one state of all Germany, had been abandoned, or rather destroyed; there was thus no possibility of Berlin or any other city becoming in the foreseeable future the capital of a whole Germany, and there was no purpose or function for the Western Powers to fulfil in Berlin (unless one counts the preservation of "face" and the work of espionage). The second objection lay in the principle, sound in law and in common sense, that no one can simultaneously tear up an agreement by breaking all his duties under it, and also claim to have the benefit of those parts of the agreement that give him something. As it was put in the Notes of the Month in the *Labour Monthly*, at p. 226:

"In vain the Western conspirators seek to invoke . . . their 'legal' right to participate in Four-Power control of Berlin. They have driven a coach and four through every agreement for Four-Power control of Germany by their unilateral decisions in the Western Zones, their repudiation of Potsdam decisions, their establishment of a West German currency. . . and their establishment of a West German State. They have met with derisory scorn every Soviet protest and demand to return to the basis of Four-Power agreement. When now they suddenly invoke the sanctity of Four-Power agreement for their 'legal right' to be in Berlin, they are in the position of burglars invoking the sanctity of the rights of private property."

JOHN FOSTER DULLES IS FRANK

The horror is increased a little more when one reads how the motives of the U.S.A. in the whole Berlin operation were admitted by John Foster Dulles, in a talk with the Overseas Writers' Association on the 10th January, 1949. He said that it would be easy to solve the Berlin

question at any moment by agreeing on the currency question. "But",
he added with sudden frankness,

"the deadlock is of great advantage to the U.S. for propaganda
purposes; and secondly the danger in settling the Berlin dispute
resides in the fact that it would then be impossible to avoid facing
the problem of a German peace treaty. The U.S.A. would then be
faced with a Soviet proposal for the withdrawal of all occupation
troops and the establishment of a central German government.
Frankly, I do not know what we could say to that."

THE WARSAW PACT

The "Warsaw Pact", a direct response of the Socialist States to the
Western policy of a split Germany and a militarised Western Bloc
(soon to be called NATO) was signed on the 23rd June, 1948. I
quote part of its programme from the Official Declaration:

"In accordance with the Yalta and Potsdam Agreements on
Germany . . . the following problems should be settled in the first
place, without any delay:

"1. Implementation of the measures ensuring the final demilitarisation of Germany, by agreement among Great Britain, the U.S.S.R.,
France and the United States;

"2. Institution for a definite time of control by the four Powers . . .
over Ruhr industry and preventing the re-establishment of
Germany's war potential;

"3. Establishment, by agreement among the (four) Governments
of a provisional democratic, peace-loving Government for the
whole of Germany, composed of representatives of the democratic
parties and organisations of Germany, for the purpose of creating
a guarantee against a repetition of German aggression;

"4. Conclusion of a peace treaty with Germany in accordance
with the Potsdam decisions, so that the occupation troops of all
Powers should be withdrawn from Germany within one year
after the conclusion of the peace treaty;

"5. Elaboration of measures for the fulfilment by Germany of her
reparations obligations towards States which suffered from German
aggression."

WHAT SHOULD THE GOVERNMENT DO?

Which policy ought a British Labour Government to have
supported? This one, or the policy of re-arming Western Germany

that has led us to the position as it stands today? And how much happier would the world have been by now if the British Government had followed the Yalta, the Potsdam, and her socialist obligations?

THE "AIRLIFT"

But by this time the American rulers had taken the bit between their teeth. General Clay was only prevented by British and French reluctance from attempting to take a military convoy through to Berlin by force of arms, at the risk of starting a third world war; and on the 28th June, 1948, the well-known "Airlift", destined to last for ten and a half months, was started.

This was an operation whereby, at fabulous expense (the cost of carrying coal by this means, for example, was £24 per ton), a continuous stream of freight aeroplanes was flown from the Western Zones to West Berlin, in order to keep the population supplied, after a fashion, with the necessities of life—not including light, power, or the provision of employment—although the government of the Eastern Zone was and remained at all times both able and willing to supply what was needed—it did in fact, for months on end, make good the deficiences of the airlift by supplying 900 tons of necessities a day! This the British Government had the insolence to describe as "blockade", and when in the House of Commons I asked one of the Ministers why he called such a state of affairs a blockade, he was taken aback at being asked to justify the jargon of his trade, and finally said: "I call it 'blockade' because they do not supply as much as we want of all the things we want."

U.S. BOMBERS COME TO BRITAIN

It is part of the same pattern that, on the 16th July, 1948, the first contingent of U.S. Air Force bombers arrived to take up stations—which they still hold—in Britain. More followed on the 8th August.

Attlee, in *A Prime Minister Remembers*, at p. 171, gives Francis Williams his reason for consenting to this occupation:

"We had to face this possible danger of the Russians sweeping right across Europe, and we had to have something to hold them. One way was air power, where the West was superior to the Russians because of the atom bomb. But the American planes had to be based somewhere—they couldn't fly from across the Atlantic. So we based them here. Obviously it added a certain amount of danger to our own position, but we couldn't have asked other countries, continental countries, to put themselves in a dangerous position while keeping ourselves out. It was a case where one had to take unpleasant decisions—realistic decisions."

If one once concedes the baseless idea that the Soviet Union was contemplating an invasion of Western Europe—with which I dealt in Chapter 10—it is relatively easy not only to talk revealing nonsense like this of Attlee's but also to put one's own fellow countrymen into appalling danger by making them a front-line target in the event of war. But it is interesting, if tragic, to see what these fellow-countrymen were told by their government when this "realistic decision" was taken to endanger their lives in order to assist the great capitalist state of the U.S.A., governed by a hysterically anti-socialist ruling class, in planning to destroy the leading socialist state.

WHAT THEY TOLD THE PUBLIC

According to the official announcement, these U.S. bombers were coming to Britain "for a short period of temporary duty, as part of the normal long-range flight training programme instituted over a year ago". But the account given by Forrestal in his diaries was that the U.S. request for atom-bomb bases was made in the latter part of June, 1948, and was instantly accepted by Bevin; that the Americans had considerable doubts as to what the reaction of British public opinion would be, but that Bevin had none; that the American decision was taken on the 15th July, and the bombers arrived on the 16th. Forrestal also related that in the following October, Cripps told him that "Britain must be regarded as the main base for the development of American power, and the chief offensive against Russia must be by air".

Forrestal could easily be repudiated as unreliable; but neither in his two autobiographies nor in any other writings has Attlee suggested that there was any inaccuracy in Forrestal's account of the matter.

On the 24th July, the *Economist* wrote of the airlift a strong article under the title of "A Bitter Choice":

"Events in the last week have only served to underline the strength of the Russian position in Berlin. The Soviet rejection of the Allied Notes leaves the Western Powers, not the Russians, in a quandary over what to do next. The Russian offer to feed the Western sectors of Berlin in exchange for Eastern currency weakens the Allied accusation that it is Russia's aim to starve out $2\frac{1}{2}$ million Germans. . . . It is no use minimising the Russian advantage. . . . The airlift cannot be maintained indefinitely on the present scale. . . . At some point the airlift will cease to be enough to hold the position."

The only practical alternatives seen by this editorial writer, as stated in the Notes of the Month (*Labour Monthly*, 1948, p. 259), were war or withdrawal (since the only real alternative of a return to a Four Power co-operation and wartime agreements could not of course be envisaged by these disciples of the Western Block and the Marshall Plan); and both looked equally unpromising. The unfavourable conditions for war at this point over this issue were recognised:

"Such a war might not be either quickly or easily won. Too much reliance can easily be put in the atom bomb . . . If the quarrel over Berlin is to be resolved by force, the responsibility for firing the first shot may lie with the West. This is one more illustration of the tactical strength of the Russian position."

And the conclusion of this sapient commentator?

"It is, then, a very bitter choice that the Western peoples may have to make. It is not the purpose of this article to say what the choice should be. *Frankly, we do not know*. The Western countries have blundered into this crisis and are only just beginning to realise the intensity of the dilemma with which they are faced. They have every right to be furiously angry with the so-called leaders who put them there."

The *Economist* writer was not absolutely correct when he wrote that the airlift could not "be maintained indefinitely" and that at some point it would "cease to be enough to hold the position"; for, although it might have failed utterly if the U.S.S.R. had refused to continue supplies, it did in fact run for many months, including right through the following winter. Modern technical achievement, if you don't mind how much you spend and what risks you run, can do a great deal in its own fields. It cannot make peace; it cannot make sense if its managers have no sense; but it can make a large number of planes fly. (It gives a modern version of the remark of Bismarck—who would have made a very good Nazi or a very good General Clay—that "You can do everything with bayonets—except sit on them!")

NATIONAL COUNCIL OF LABOUR IN HYSTERICS

There followed a period of many months in which the less foolish or embittered of the Western leaders tried to get out of the impasse by negotiation with the Soviet Union, whilst the rest tried to sabotage those negotiations. I will come to these in a moment, but I must first record a fantastic outburst of anti-Soviet hysteria from the National Council of Labour (the supreme representative, in theory, of the Labour Party, the Co-operative Party and the Labour Parliamentary Party). On the 28th July, it proclaimed:

"Once again a totalitarian flood threatens to engulf the last island of liberty in Eastern Europe.
"The obligations resting on the West today are as compelling as they were in 1938. . .
"Berlin is a symbol of the conflict between two systems of belief and action. Any show of weakness would be a fatal shock to world confidence.
"Further discussion cannot begin until the Russian blockade is lifted. The Council expresses its appreciation of the courage shown by the people of Berlin."

This outburst would presumably not have been made if it had been thought that the Government would disagree with it; and the Government certainly never expressed any dissent from it. It deserves a little analysis; to what does "once again" refer? Probably, to those who know the mentality of its authors, the previous "threats of engulfment by totalitarian floods" they had in mind were Nazi threats, for many of them by now had grown accustomed to attributing to the Soviet Union (with whom we had a Treaty of Alliance, and with whom the Labour Party had proclaimed friendship at the General Election) all the wickedness of the Nazis (and the reference to 1938, the period when most of the Labour leaders were at any rate sometimes opposing Chamberlain's Munich policy, confirms that view). But to think of Berlin, to which "the West"—i.e. capitalist U.S.A. and Labour Britain—had forfeited all right in the manner I have just discussed, as the last island of liberty in Eastern Europe, as if everything capitalist was "free" and everything socialist was slavery, is something that might at least have been left to the Tories. The contrast between "two systems of belief and action" is, again, a comparison between capitalist America and Labour Britain on the one side and socialist states on the other; and to demand that there be "no show of weakness" goes if anything further than the editorial written in the *Economist*, quoted above; for he at least admitted that he did not know what could be done, whereas the National Council seemed to have a firm policy that carried with it a grave danger of war.

NEGOTIATIONS IN MOSCOW

The demand, too, that the West should not even hold discussions with the U.S.S.R. until it conceded the whole of the Western case by calling off the non-existent blockade, was in line with the intransigent attitude taken up by the West shortly before the outburst; but unfortunately for the National Council of Labour this proved to be out of date, for on the very day of their outburst, the 28th July, 1948, the less foolish elements in the Western leadership prevailed sufficiently to secure a decision that negotiators should be at once sent to Moscow to discuss the position. And relatively quickly, namely on the 30th August, 1948, to the horror of those who did not want the Berlin crisis settled, an agreement was reached, or apparently reached, for the simultaneous ending of the transport restrictions around Berlin, and the acceptance of the new East German currency as the sole currency of the whole of Berlin, to be circulated under Four Power auspices—a fairly simple and certainly a reasonable settlement. On the following day, the 31st August, the four military governors met to prepare an agreed directive carrying out the Moscow terms and, to the delight of the more extreme Western elements, disputes arose as to the interpretation of the agreement, and the settlement broke down; talks were then resumed in Moscow, and finally failed on the 22nd September, 1948.

U.N. GENERAL ASSEMBLY MEETS

The day before, on the 21st, the General Assembly of the United Nations met in Paris. On the 4th October, although U.N.O. by the terms of its Charter was not entitled to deal with the German problem, the Security Council insisted on discussing the Berlin situation; it was perhaps well that they did so, for the unreasonable attitude of the Western Powers was thereby exposed once more. The smaller States called for some compromise, and the Soviet representative said that they were ready to negotiate on the basis of the terms that had already been agreed in August. Dr. Bramuglia, the President of the Security Council, took up the negotiations, and by the 24th October agreement was reached between Vyshinsky on behalf of the U.S.S.R. and Dr. Bramuglia on behalf of the three Western Powers, for the simultaneous removal of the transport restrictions and negotiations for the introduction of the Eastern Mark as the sole currency in Berlin; both these operations were to start at once, and were to be completed by the 20th November; neither was to be valid without the other; and negotiations on all other questions outstanding in relation to Germany were to begin between the four Powers by the 30th November.

Here, once again, was a reasonable settlement of this most dangerous problem; and, once again, within twenty-four hours, the enemies of peace in the Western delegations repudiated the settlement. They put forward a proposal of their own which followed very closely the terms agreed by Vyshinsky and Dr. Bramuglia, with one vital and insolent variation, namely that whilst the Eastern Mark was still to be introduced by the 20th November the transport restrictions were to be removed at once. That meant that the Western Powers were insisting on a month's opportunity to flood the Soviet Zone with their old currency, after which they would agree—or might agree, if they found no new excuse for not doing so—to the introduction of the Eastern Mark into the economic chaos which they would by then have created.

The General Assembly gave at least one more clear proof of its understanding of the grave danger of the Berlin position. On the 3rd November, it passed a resolution appealing to the four Great Powers to renew their efforts to compose their differences, and thus hasten the final settlement of the (Second World) War. This resolution was passed unanimously, the British, American and French delegations voting in its favour. Ten days later, on the 10th November, the President of the Assembly, the Australian leader Dr. Evatt, and the Secretary-General, Trygve Lie, wrote a letter to the four Great Powers, urging upon them "the desirability of immediate conversations and of taking all other necessary steps towards the solution of the Berlin question, thus opening the way to a prompt resumption of negotiations for the conclusion of the remaining peace settlements for Germany, Austria, and Japan".

This reasonable appeal for some reason angered the Western Governments, particularly that of Great Britain. The *News Chronicle* of the 15th November reported that it had "caused great embarrassment and some indignation", since "it will certainly be interpreted as a criticism of the determination of the Western Allies not to negotiate under duress" (i.e. their determination to disorganise the economy of the Soviet Zone, and to keep the running sore of Berlin open indefinitely rather than accept a perfectly reasonable settlement which had apparently been accepted twice already). But it is difficult to see why they should have felt so embarrassed at being asked to do little more than live up to the spirit of the resolution for which they themselves had voted on the 3rd November.

NATO

The next stage of this story belongs to the following year, 1948-9, and I will return briefly to it in Chapter 21. But it is noteworthy that the Brussels Pact signatories announced on the 26th October that they had reached agreement on a "North Atlantic Defensive Pact", i.e. on a military alliance with the U.S.A., which was behaving towards the U.S.S.R. in a manner that could scarcely be called defensive.

INCREASING OUR ARMED FORCES

And on the 14th September, 1948, the day after the Parliamentary session of 1947-8 came to an end, the Government announced a general delay of three months in the release from the armed forces; this was followed on the 23rd September by the announcement of arrangements for the registration of ex-service men and women willing to rejoin "in an emergency". Even before the session ended, Shinwell as Secretary of State for War had made an appeal for 100,000 recruits to the territorial army. (Earlier, the "Defence White Paper" of the 19th February, 1948, had planned to reduce the total strength of the armed forces, by further stages of demobilisation, by 224,000 to 716,000 by the 31st March, 1949, and to reduce the total expenditure for 1948 by about £200 million to £692 million.)

CZECHOSLOVAKIA

Apart from the endless troubles in Greece, the only other important matter in the field of foreign affairs in 1947-8—there were already too many—took place in Czechoslavakia. This advanced industrial country in the socialist camp was one which the Americans and British had never given up hope of seducing. It had a somewhat complicated system of government under which four parties (or six, including some slightly different groupings in Slovakia), representing agrarian, middle-class, Social-Democrat and Communist outlooks, shared the government between them, and all questions of policy had to be determined by agreement of all of them. Such a system seemed to outsiders to be almost unworkable, but it had in fact worked pretty well from 1945 until the beginning of 1948, when—in February—a group of some twelve right-wing ministers, believing that they could thereby force a crisis and secure a reconstruction of the government and the system which would reduce very greatly the strength of the left, resigned in a block. They had, however, miscalculated, forgetting—like many other such people—the working-class forces of their country. The correct response to such resignations was that the Prime Minister, a Communist, supported by a majority in the Parliament, should reconstruct the government without the twelve right-wing Ministers, aligning it further to the left. This he was both able and willing to do; and when the old Liberal President Beneš hesitated, the working class displayed its power, and proved unmistakably to the world that the Prime Minister and his party had the support not only of the majority in the popularly elected Parliament but also of the workers. On an appeal by the Communist Party, the organised workers, in tens of thousands, poured into Prague in an orderly, non-violent and overwhelmingly impressive demonstration of their will. Within a week, without a shot being fired, the twelve resigning Ministers passed into history's waste-paper basket, and the government was reconstructed with a great increase of the power of the Communist Party, half the Ministers in the new government being Communist.

The British Government and the British Press proceeded to give the most fantastic misdescription of these "February days", alleging that Soviet armed forces had marched into the country and the capital and carried out the changes by armed force; it was not even possible to discover, in the legends they invented, the fact that the twelve right-wing Ministers had started the story by resigning. On the 26th February a joint statement of the three Western Powers, and on the 2nd March the National Executive Committee of the Labour Party, condemned the "seizure of power by the Communist faction in Czechoslovakia" as a crime.

The comment of Palme Dutt in the Notes of the Month (*Labour Monthly*, pp. 100–1) is illuminating. He referred to:

"The extraordinary maniac outburst of rage which has greeted the victory of the working class and popular forces in Czechoslovakia. It might have been thought that the establishment of a united Socialist-Communist Government on the basis of an indisputedly freely elected parliamentary majority, with the backing of a united trade union movement and the factory councils throughout the country, engaged in nationalising the whole field of industry, would have been regarded by every man and woman of the labour movement as a marvellous triumph of democracy, socialism, and the peaceful transition to the new socialist order. On the contrary, it has been met with a universal howl of despair and lamentation, not merely from the *Daily Mail* and the Kemsley Press and Mr. Churchill and the Economic League, but equally and in identical terms from the *Daily Herald* and the 'socialist' *Tribune* and Mr. Attlee and Mr. Morrison and the entire leadership of the Labour Party, as if the end of the world had come. Indeed, Mr. Morrison has gone so far as to call for a 'resistance movement' against the new government in Czechoslovakia, 'with the same resources and initiative and sacrifice as in the war against Hitler'—in other words, for an illegal fascist movement to revolt against a government based on an elected parliamentary majority."

I had at this time a personal experience of no great importance, but illuminating as an indication of the general political attitude created by these stories in Britain. I was invited by the British Broadcasting Corporation to debate the Czechoslovakian situation with a Tory M.P., who had a freer and less hide-bound mind than many Tories, and was likely to give a vigorous and not just a stereotyped or conventional presentation of the matter.

In those days, the B.B.C. practice was that the speakers in such discussion should rehearse their arguments in considerable detail, and in the first presentation of his argument at the rehearsal the Tory M.P. referred to "the presence in Prague of large contingents of the Red Army, overawing the government of the people and imposing a Communist government on them by armed force".

When we had finished this first "draft presentation", I spoke to him in a friendly fashion, explaining that this statement was totally untrue, that there had been no Soviet troops anywhere, that the facts were well-known, and had been verified to me by Englishmen who had been in Prague at the time; and that he would only make a fool of himself, at any rate in Europe, if he repeated such a statement. He looked a little mulish and unconvinced, and we went through two more draft presentations, in which he repeated his statement, and I repeated my friendly protest, with the same negative result. As we finished the rehearsal, I told him that I had, of course, no power to stop him making a fool of himself if he insisted on doing so, but that it would be a pity in the actual broadcast, when time was precious, to take up even a little of our time in him making this baseless statement and my explaining its baselessness. He said nothing as to what he would do, and I waited with interest to see what he would do "on the air". He had obviously given thought to the matter, and tried to reach a happy medium between what he wanted to believe and what I had pretty well convinced him was the truth; for all that he said was that "over all, in the background, there loomed the mighty force of the Red Army"!

In the course of our conversations, this M.P. perhaps gave me the true reason why the whole British "establishment" was so angry over the "February days", when he said: "One thing is certain, Pritt. We weren't sure whether the 'Iron Curtain' ran on the east or the west of Czechoslovakia. Now we know quite definitely that it runs on the west."

CHAPTER 16
Colonial Policy, 1947-8

THE conduct of colonial policy in this period was inevitably "all of a piece" with the Witch Hunt, the reception of Marshall Aid, and the rest of our foreign policy; policy is never really partly good and partly bad.

Although two countries, Burma and Ceylon, found their way to their inevitable independence in the year, the essentially imperialist attitude of the Government became ever clearer. It was now more than two years since the Second World War, with its great weakening of capitalist strength, had ended, and further substantial areas had moved into the socialist camp. The national independence movement among colonial peoples was developing strongly and rapidly in all parts of the colonial world, and the old rulers were by now plotting to save something of their power—military and economic—by planning great developments in Africa, which many of them thought of as more backward than Asia, and by no means irrevocably lost to them. They sought not only to preserve indirect economic control in Africa, but also to found great industrial enterprises and great military bases, in order both to replace some of their lost wealth and to equip themselves to fight the U.S.S.R. (However much the story of these ambitions may sound illusory today, they had a slight air of reality then.) Bevin, always able to express Tory views and ambitions better than most Tories, put the plan very neatly to the House of Commons in the Foreign Affairs debate on the 22nd January, 1948 (*Hansard*, Vol. 446, Cols. 398-9), quoted in the previous chapter. It came into the sphere of foreign affairs for him, because he worked it out as part of a plan for "Western Union", a union, in substance, of the Marshall Plan countries. He said:

"DEVELOPING" AFRICA

"Western Union . . . is its right description. I would emphasise that I am not concerned only with Europe as a geographical conception.

Europe* has extended its influence throughout the world, and we have to look further afield. In the first place, we turn our eyes to Africa, where great responsibilities are shared by us with South Africa, Belgium and Portugal, and equally to all overseas territories, especially of South-East Asia, with which the Dutch† are closely concerned. The organisation of Western Europe must be economically supported. That involves the closest possible collaboration with the Commonwealth and with overseas territories, not only British, but French, Dutch, Belgian and Portuguese. . . . If Western Europe is to achieve its balance of payments and to get a world equilibrium, it is essential that these resources should be developed and made available, and the exchange between them carried out in a correct and proper manner."

(It was interesting to notice that at this time Bevin had not only the Tories to support him, but also the Fascists; for Sir Oswald Mosley had said a month or two before: "Our first aim is to bring about a union of the European peoples, all those in the West willing to join—Europe and the British Dominions will be asked to join in developing Africa.")

Mr. Brady, in his *Crisis in Britain* (pp. 594 *et seq.*), commented:

"The phraseology with which Labour spokesmen advocated colonial development in Africa and elsewhere is almost indistinguishable from that of the Liberal and Conservative Opposition. The same seems to be true of Labour's actual plans. . . . The Labour-sponsored Acts . . . are devoted almost exclusively to economic development, and where attention is paid to social welfare at all it has been virtually without exception justified on the grounds that it is absolutely essential as a condition to getting more efficient work out of the African natives whom development projects must employ in large numbers. Throughout all the debates . . . there was but little difference of opinion between Labour and the Opposition, and that little was devoted almost exclusively to administrative and financial questions. Discussion was centered primarily on the prospective gain to Britain from these developments, and was conducted almost exclusively in terms of empire, in the ordinary and conventional sense of the word."

* Europe, here, was plainly a political conception, and meant capitalist Europe, but Bevin saw nothing odd in a socialist government embracing it.

† The Dutch were at this time busy, with active support from Britain, in military operations in what is now Indonesia, unsuccessfully opposing the national independence movement.

Mr. John Strachey had put one aspect of the matter even more crudely the day before in the House of Commons, in the debate on the third reading of the Overseas Resources Development Bill, which Bill I will discuss below. He then said that "to obtain by one means or another, by hook or by crook, the development of primary production of all sorts . . . is a life and death matter for the economy of this country". This harmonised with a Colonial Office Memorandum of October, 1947, which stated that

> "The United Kingdom has every interest in forwarding the production drive in the Colonial territories, for the double purpose of enabling it to procure from them the commodities which it has now got to buy in dollars, and of enabling these territories to earn more dollars."

PALESTINE

I return to Palestine, with which I have already dealt in Chapters 7 and 11. In this year, 1947-8, the decision to give up the mandate and withdraw from Palestine was formally announced to the United Nations on the 13th November, 1947, by Sir Alexander Cadogan on behalf of the British Government; he gave the date of the proposed withdrawal as the 1st August, 1948, but in the end it took place on the 14th May, 1948.

The problem of the future administration and status of the country still had to be settled. Probably the best solution in the long run would have been that supported by the U.S.S.R., of setting up a bi-national State; but the only solution—if it can be called a solution—for which a U.N. majority could be found was that of "partition", i.e. of the establishment of a Jewish State and of an Arab State. This was adopted by the U.N. on the 30th November, 1947.

The country was still in turmoil. Throughout December and January, and indeed later, there was confused but serious fighting between Jews, Arabs, and British troops. In March, 1948, the Palestine Bill for the termination of the Mandate was debated in Parliament; it provided for the termination of the mandate, but was silent on the question to whom authority was to be handed over.

On the 19th March, 1948, at the Security Council, the U.S.A. proposed that partition should be dropped, and a temporary trusteeship set up; according to the *Economist*, the change was made because the Americans feared that partition would involve increasing Soviet influence in the Middle East.

STATE OF ISRAEL SET UP

The Jews were, however, determined to establish a Jewish State, and on the day the British gave up the mandate they proclaimed the new State of Israel, comprising territories going beyond the boundaries allocated by the U.N. for partition. Partition, in the sense of establishing two States, was not carried out, for the Arab State was not set up. The U.S.A. recognised the new State *de facto* immediately, and the Soviet Union did the same within a few days.

The Arabs at once declared war on Israel, and the British Government, in effect seeking to use Arab puppet troops armed and officered by the British to reconquer the territories which Israel had encroached, transferred to the Arab Legion forty-eight heavy guns with their ammunition, and 225 tons of war material. As Mr. Lyall Wilkes, M.P., pointed out in a letter to *The Times* of the 22nd May: "Every tank and aeroplane now being used by the Arabs has been supplied by the United Kingdom; the British Air Mission is still functioning in Iraq; British missions are now working, training and re-equipping Arab armies in Saudi-Arabia and Iraq; the Arab Legion now waging war is wholly subsidised by us with £2,000,000 a year and is commanded by thirty-eight British officers; and Transjordan, under the March, 1948, Treaty, is bound to 'undertake not to adopt in regard to foreign countries an attitude which is inconsistent with the alliance'."

Hostilities were interrupted by a truce at the end of May and the last British troops left Palestine on the 30th June; but in July the truce broke down and more fighting followed. In May, at the Labour Party Conference at Scarborough, with which I will deal in Chapter 18, Palestine had been kept off the Agenda!

PALESTINIAN ARAB REFUGEES

The British Government had thus rid itself of direct responsibility for the administration of the territory, but not of any other problem. It went on to serve its imperialist interests by putting the rest of Palestine into the puppet State of Jordan, thus in effect completing the operation of partition. A huge band of Palestinian Arab refugees, expelled from their lands in the areas taken by Israel, found themselves in a miserable and virtually hopeless position, which is much the same to-day, as I write in 1962, as it was in 1948. But Bevin declared in the House of Commons that his conscience was clear.

o

GROUND–NUTS

I pass to another large-scale activity, not so tragic in loss of life or the creation or maintenance of insoluble problems, but nevertheless thoroughly colonialist, and disastrous and humiliating in its outcome— the Ground-nuts Scheme, with its legislative parent, or uncle, the Overseas Resources Development Act, 1948 (introduced on the 23rd October, 1947, and passed on the 11th February, 1948).

This Act was put forward as designed to accelerate economic development of various kinds, under the sponsorship of either British or colonial authorities; it established for the purpose two government corporations, the Colonial Development Corporation and the Overseas Food Corporation. The former had "the duty of securing the investigation, formulation and carrying out of projects for developing resources of colonial territories with a view to the expansion of production therein of foodstuffs and raw materials, or for other agricultural, industrial or trade development therein". And the latter, whose officers were to be appointed by and be responsible to the Minister of Food, was to devote itself to "projects for the production or processing in places outside the United Kingdom of foodstuffs or agricultural products other than foodstuffs and the marketing thereof".

The purpose of both Corporations was stated to be a "three-way" partnership between the British Government, colonial governments and private enterprise.

The Colonial Development Corporation had as its Chairman a Peer who had been both a Liberal and a Labour M.P., as its Deputy Chairman a colonial civil servant, and as its directors two big figures from colonial private enterprise, two bankers, an investment trust manager, a director of the Co-operative Wholesale Society, and a director of the National Physical Laboratory.

The Overseas Food Corporation had as its Chairman a former director of Express Newspapers, as its Vice-Chairman a director of the Co-operative Wholesale Society, and as whole-time members the Economic Adviser to the East African Governors' Conference, a banker who was a member of the original Ground-nuts Committee (mentioned in Chapter 11), and a former director of agriculture in Tanganyika. There were two part-time members, one the managing director of the United Africa Company—a vast private-enterprise organisation virtually ruling some West African colonies—and Lord Rothschild. The Ground-nuts Scheme was its first project.

This grandiose scheme, destined—as will be seen later, in Chapters 22, 32 and 40—to become a total and very costly failure, was a terrible example of how things should not be done. From all points of view, that of a Labour Government professing to speed the advance of the colonial peoples, that of private enterprise seeking to use public funds and resources to aid the winning of profit from colonial peoples and raw materials, that of feeding the population of Britain, and that of mere efficient administration, it is not easy to imagine anything that could have been done worse.

A great point was made from the start that the scheme would bring substantial social and economic benefits to the peoples of territories involved (mostly Tanganyikan but in part Kenyan); "the health, nutrition, housing, welfare and labour policies of the scheme will", it was said, "raise the standard of life of the undertaking's employees and their families"; and the increased national income, and revenue from taxation, would, it was claimed, make possible higher standards of living and better social services, eradication of the tsetse fly and a revolution in agricultural technique. Such claims have always been made, by private enterprise and by governments alike; and it is often true that, when colonial development schemes succeed, there are crumbs from the exploiter's table for the innumerable servants who create his wealth. But that has long been seen to be not enough in the middle of the twentieth century. To form a judgment on the scheme from the point of view of the colonial peoples, who were looking to an independent future of their own and expecting that a Labour Government would help them towards that future, much more than crumbs had to be considered. They would want to know who was to be in charge, what part in the adoption of the scheme, its planning, development, and administration, was to be played by Africans; and how Africans would benefit by the establishment of processing or other subsidiary or satellite industries. These were the questions that have to be asked, and satisfactorily answered; but the answers were uniformly unsatisfactory.

THE GROUND–NUTS SET–UP

As to who was to be in charge, I have already given the personnel, which included no Africans and scarcely a single European with a progressive background. Moreover, Unilever, in which the United Africa Company, the authors of the original scheme, was merged were "suspect by virtually all natives . . . with having a primary, if not sole, interest in exploiting native natural and human resources at the expense of the resident population" (Brady, op. cit.). There was little in all this to convince any African that there was anything new or different in the scheme from the development schemes of half a century earlier.

As for the part to be played by Africans, immediately or even later, the picture was no better. There was of course not even a dream—or would it have been a nightmare?—of consulting the Africans as to whether they wanted such a development at all, and if so where, on what scale, in what hands, or for what crop. As for employment, some Africans were to be trained as tractor-drivers, mechanics, clerks, etc., but all higher posts were to remain in European hands. On the U.N. Trusteeship Council, to which the British Government was responsible so far as it concerned Tanganyika Territory (the former German East Africa, administered under Mandate), the British delegate reported that native opinion had not been consulted in the preparation of plans for the scheme, and that he could not say at the moment how the project was to be handed over to the native population. (It had been stated by the Government that the long-term aim was the taking over of the scheme by the Africans themselves, but "no date for the transfer could be suggested or even ventured, since it would depend entirely on the economic condition of the peoples concerned. In other words the African communities must prove their ability to conduct such ventures for themselves." It is just as well that, thirteen years later, in December 1961, the African people of Tanganyika, having taken note of the utter inability of the Europeans "to conduct such ventures" for themselves, or anyone else, secured their independence!

With regard to the establishment of processing or other industries, it is scarcely surprising to learn that the proposal was for the ground-nuts to be exported whole; there was to be no local processing industry, and thus—*inter alia*—no cattle-food for African cattle as a by-product.

AN IMPERIALIST SET-UP

In truth, the whole character of the scheme was the traditional imperialist one—the production of a primary product for export, with no change in the existing one-sided economic development, and the continuance of government by the Europeans of the Africans for the Europeans. It is all of the same pattern to realise that at that time the Oils and Fats Division of the Ministry of Food was still almost wholly staffed by Unilever employees, paid by Unilever; and that nearly

95 per cent. of the imported edible oils and fats consumed in Britain were processed and distributed by Unilever subsidiaries. As Mr. Brady put it: "Through these employees, lent so to speak to the Government to run the division whose policies affect it most directly, Unilever gets almost exactly what it wishes in terms of controls."

As Mr. Brady points out, it must have suited Unilever very well that the Ground-nuts Scheme as a whole should be run by the Government, and not as a purely private enterprise. The scale of investment involved was gigantic, especially in such concealed costs as the destruction of the tsetse fly over vast areas, and in supplementary expenses like railway construction, roads, docks and watershed control. And United Africa was primarily a *trading* corporation.

"Thus," wrote Brady, "the government, in taking over the Ground-nuts Scheme, is not only saving Unilever vast conditional and primary development expenses on which no direct return may be expected, but it is shouldering a supply problem which Unilever simply could not handle on its own—yet one which it has a very great interest in seeing solved adequately on a large scale."

For the further, and economically disastrous history of the Ground-nuts Scheme, we must wait for later chapters.

THE GOLD COAST (GHANA)

Another unhappy activity of the Government was to be seen in the Gold Coast, which is now independent Ghana. The developments there give a picture in miniature of many of the features of colonial interest and development.

During the year under consideration—1947-8—there was a good deal of unemployment, wages were low, and prices were high; and producers, largely of cocoa, were dissatisfied with the prices they received for their products. This soon linked itself with the demand for national independence; and in August, 1947, the "Gold Coast Convention" was formed, and soon won mass support for its independence campaign.

In the early part of 1948, a country-wide boycott was organised against imported goods, as a protest against high prices; the boycott started on the 26th January and achieved substantial success by the 28th February, when the Government reduced prices by one-third. On that date, the African Ex-Servicemen's Union, *with permission from the Governor*, held a demonstration and march, with a petition. The police stopped this, firing both bullets and tear-gas—two traditional methods of meeting economic and political hardships; rioting followed, 22 Africans being killed and 228 Africans and 13 Europeans injured. The Government turned to another traditional remedy; it suspended the sittings of the Legislative Council, arrested the Secretary of the Ex-Servicemen's Union, and detained six leading members of the political party, the United Gold Coast Convention. A Committee of Enquiry was set up, and reported in the same year with an analysis of the basic causes of the trouble which, as Mr. Brady put it, included an "amazing cross-section of the maladies of Empire". These embraced the following features:

ENQUIRY COMMITTEE'S REPORT

1. A large number of Gold Coast Africans, who had served in the Armed Forces during the war, and had lived under better conditions than at home, had developed a political and national consciousness as a result of their contacts with other peoples. They were disappointed with the conditions they found at home on their return, and thus constituted a focal point of unrest and of a general movement against the existing authority.

2. Educated Africans had a feeling of political frustration because they saw no prospect of ever winning political power under the existing conditions, and regarded the constitution given in 1946 as mere window-dressing designed to cover, but not to advance, their political aspirations.

3. The failure of the government to realise that, with the spread of liberal ideas, increasing literacy, and closer contact with political developments in other parts of the world, the idea of rule by Chiefs was fading out. The winning of self-government in India, Burma, and Ceylon, had not passed unnoticed.

4. The feeling was universal that "Africanisation" was merely a promise, and not a driving force in Government policy.

5. There was a general suspicion of Government measures and intentions.

6. There was increasing resentment at the growing concentration of certain trades in the hands of foreigners, and particularly at the increase in the number of Syrian traders.

7. There was indignation at the announcement by the Government that it would remain neutral in the dispute between traders and the people over the high prices of imported goods, which had led to the boycott of January-February, 1948, at the continuance of war-time

control of imports and the high price of consumer goods, and at the alleged unfair allocation and distribution of goods in short supply.

8. The policy of the Government in cutting out trees affected by "swollen shoot" disease was exciting resentment.

9. The degree of control exercised by the Cocoa Marketing Board, limiting the power of cocoa farmers' representatives to control the vast reserves of cocoa accumulating under the Board's policy, was also causing resentment.

10. There was a feeling that the Government had not formulated plans for the future of industry and agriculture, and was in fact luke-warm about any development except production for export.

11. There was alleged to be too slow development of educational facilities, and an almost complete failure to provide any technical or vocational training.

12. There was a shortage of housing, and a very low standard of housing for Africans compared to that for Europeans.

13. There was a fear of wholesale alienation of tribal laws; and, one has to add:

14. The legal powers of Government to deal with speeches designed to arouse disorder and violence were inadequate.

The Committee recommended various changes in the Constitution; but it is typical that the Government, instead of accepting its recom-mendations, set up another committee—this time with 39 African members and an African chairman—which did not report until the following year, in September, 1949.

It is not surprising that Ghana became independent a few years later.

MALAYA

The problem of Malaya came to a head in this year, with the start of a civil war which lasted for some years. The Malay Peninsula has wealth in rubber and tin, which had made many British investors between the two world wars fantastically rich—and at other times only moderately rich, as world slumps reduced the demand for these commodities. During the war, the European inhabitants made a very poor showing against the Japanese invasion and conquest, the only resistance—a glorious one—being shown by the native "Malayan People's Anti-Japanese army", the leaders of which were decorated after the war and took part in the Victory March in London.

After the war, the position was as follows:

Malaya, including Singapore, had been freed from the Japanese. The British attached great importance to its rubber and tin, the value of which was now enhanced by the fact that the greatest demand for them came from the dollar area; they attached equal importance to Singapore as a naval base, particularly as any bases in India, Ceylon, and perhaps even Hong Kong, might well cease to be under their control. On the other hand, the native population (Malay, Tamil and Chinese) not only felt the general post-war desire for independence, but had also an additional cause for pride and insistence having regard to their own war record (and that of the Europeans). Economically, there had been a steep rise in prices and very little even nominal rise in wages, leading to many strikes even as early as 1946.

The British, in the effort to keep Singapore as a naval base, whilst also holding on to the Malay Peninsula as long as possible, "rearranged" this part of their colonial empire by separating Singapore from the other "Straits Settlements" and keeping it separate from the rest of Malaya, as a Crown Colony, and by making the whole peninsula into a "Federation of Malaya", which was to become gradually "independent", with as much "dependence" as could be managed.

The native population soon secured representation, in the Advisory Councils which were set up, for their Communist Party, trade unions, Youth League and Women's Federation; and when the new Constitution of the Federation of Malaya that had to be drafted was seen to be thoroughly undemocratic they staged a twenty-four hour strike against it. This Constitution, which came into force on the 1st February, 1948, contained no provision for elections to the Central Legislative Assembly. Of the 75 members, 14 were to be officials and the rest were to be appointed by the High Commissioners. Singapore did *a little* better with its Constitution; six out of the 22 members of the Legislative Council were to be elected; but only British citizens, just over one in five of the electorate, were entitled to vote. Singapore, too, had a twenty-four hour protest strike.

SUPPRESSION AND CIVIL WAR

It was not long before matters came to a head in the Federation of Malaya; the heroes of the war were now—it is a familiar pattern—"bandits", "gangsters", "terrorists", and "communists" to the Labour Government, just as they would have been to a Tory Government; in June the Pan-Malayan Federation of Trade Unions with its 300,000 members was banned, and within a few days the same fate struck the

Ex-Servicemen's Association of the Malayan People's Anti-Japanese army, the Communist Party and the New Democratic Youth League. In July, 1948, a State of Emergency was declared, with sweeping powers of arrest, detention, banishment, and execution.

There was a division of troops in Malaya, 12,000 armed police, rocket-firing Spitfire aeroplanes, and units of the Navy; and the public at home was fed with stories of "Communist plots to seize Malaya". After a time, the troops were reinforced with a Brigade of Guards, with Gurkhas, with Dyak head-hunters, with members of the disbanded Palestine Police, and with Alsatian dogs.

THE COMMUNIST BOGY

What the Labour Government attributed to "communism", less bigoted critics thought to be due to the high price of rice and the low wages; but the peninsula was by now fully launched in a civil war that was to last for several years, carried on by the Army, the Air Force and the Navy, with their miscellaneous auxiliaries just mentioned, against the Malayan people.

IRAQ

The only other colonial area of trouble in the year in question was Iraq. It had been a British colony for some time after it had been taken from Turkey at the end of the First World War, but had a little later been erected as a puppet kingdom, complete with British troops, Royal Air Force stations and other insignia of puppet independence; this was a convenient and a much cheaper method of keeping a grip on the country's petroleum supplies.

With Iraq the British Government negotiated a new Treaty, signed on the 15th January, 1948, and called the Treaty of Portsmouth. It was a pseudo-progressive treaty; Britain surrendered the right to maintain troops in Iraq which she held under the Anglo-Iraq Treaty of 1930, "but only when the Allied Forces are withdrawn from ex-enemy countries"; she was to surrender also the right to maintain two air bases, but she was to continue to provide technical staff, installations and equipment, and to use the bases. She was to have the right also, in the event of war, to send in troops of all arms, and to have all facilities for the use of ports, railways, airfields etc.; and Iraq was to have British military instructors and to send military personnel to Britain for training.

When the terms of this Treaty were disclosed in Baghdad, hundreds of thousands of people demonstrated against them, strikes were called, and it looked as if there might be a revolution.

Bevin told the House of Commons on the 22nd January, in the speech from which I quoted above, that when the Iraqi Premier, who had come to England to sign the Treaty, returned to Baghdad, he would be able to explain its terms and thus put an end to the demonstrations, which were caused by a few "innocent students instigated by" —can you guess it?—"disruptive elements". But when the Premier did get home, he found a vast national demonstration of over 300,000 people. He hurriedly left the country again by plane, the government resigned, and ratification of the Treaty was refused on the ground that it "does not assure the rights of the country and its national aspirations". The people were not prepared to accept the unctuous assurance of Bevin (*Hansard*, Vol. 446, Col. 400) that "neither I nor the Iraqi Prime Minister would have set our signatures to any document which ignored the aspirations of the people of Iraq".

The Iraqi people had scored a victory; but they achieved for the time nothing more. The new government was no better than the old, and ten years were to pass before a popular uprising got rid of the Kingdom and of its puppet status to Britain.

The wholly gloomy imperialist picture of Britain's relations with the colonial world in this year was of course lightened by the concession of political independence to Burma and Ceylon. This was important, even if inevitable; a Tory Government would have had to do the same, but at least it was done.

CHAPTER 17

Economic and Industrial Affairs, 1947-8

THE story of affairs at home is once again dominated by the twin problems of the balance of payments and the dollar shortage which had come to a head in the previous August (see Chapter 12) and by the high level of overseas expenditure coupled with the retention of large numbers of men in the armed forces.

WAGE FREEZE

One of the Government's attempted remedies for these problems was the typically Tory one of a wage freeze. On the 1st October, 1947, the Prime Minister met the General Council of the T.U.C. to discuss a letter which had been sent by the Minister of Labour (George Isaacs) to all joint wage-negotiation bodies, asking them to keep in mind the Prime Minister's appeal, made on the 6th of the previous August, that workers should refrain from pressing for wage increases. At this meeting, Attlee agreed that this letter should be withdrawn, but asked the General Council to have a further discussion on wages, which took place on the 14th October, 1947. Cripps and Isaacs then asked the Council to consider the possibility of securing "greater stability" of wages, and it agreed to do so.

A few days later, on the 23rd October, 1947, in the House of Commons, Cripps reviewed the whole economic position. He painted, correctly enough, a gloomy picture of our economic position, stating once again that the root of all our troubles lay in the overseas balance of payments, and in particular in the dollar balance. He made no mention of the true cause of the lack of balance, nor any suggestion for easing it by reducing our military expenditure, either at home or abroad; and he preached the orthodox Tory remedy of curing the problem by importing less, consuming less, and exporting more (*if* export markets could be found; as he put it at Cols. 269 and 288 of Vol. 443 of *Hansard*: "[I am] assuming for the moment that the export programme will be achieved. It is not possible, of course, to make any very accurate forecast as to how much of those exports will in fact find their way into markets which would enable us to earn dollars, or how far we shall be able to supply the actual goods. . . . We are proceeding frankly on an optimistic basis so far as the saleability of our exports is concerned—optimistic because . . . there may well be a growing tendency for all nations to restrict imports and to attempt to force their exports.").

Cripps added oblique hints that, if we did not solve our economic problems, the whole of Europe would become communist, and concluded what was in truth one long betrayal of socialist principles with an appeal to the country for a "deep draught of Christian faith". (*Hansard*, Vol. 443, Col. 294.)

The details of the policy he put forward were:

1. Further cuts in imports, over and above those, amounting to £228 million yearly, that had been already decided on up to the previous August (see Chapter 12). The new additional cuts were to be £100 million a year for non-food goods, including timber, steel, tobacco and machinery, and £66 million for food, involving reduced consumption of sugar, dried eggs, meat and bacon.

2. Exports were to be increased—if, as I have mentioned, buyers could be found—by the end of 1948 by £31 million a month (a one-third increase over the figure at the end of 1946, and 60 per cent. over that of 1938); both materials and finished goods were to be diverted from the home market for the purpose.

3. Capital construction and equipment were to be cut by £200 million a year—nearly one-fifth of the rate of capital expenditure then running.

4. The purchasing power of the mass of the people was to be reduced by wage freezing, removal of some subsidies, and further indirect taxes.

Part of the loss to home consumers may be measured by the facts that the then average consumption of food, 2,870 calories, was to be reduced to 2,700 (pre-war, in spite of massive unemployment, this figure had been 3,000), and that new house construction was to be reduced to 140,000 a year, about half the rate then prevailing.

STILL DEPENDENT ON U.S.A.

Even with all that austerity, Cripps said that we would still be heavily dependent on American aid; by the end of 1948, he said, our gold and dollar reserves would have fallen from £580 million to £270 million, and the dollar deficit would still be running at £250 million a year.

The cause of the trouble was as plain as ever; in the then current financial year government overseas expenditure was £175 million, compared with £16 million in 1938; we were exporting not only to pay for food and raw materials but also to maintain large overseas armed forces; and we still had over 1,000,000 men in the forces. But the Government was still refusing to break away from the American stranglehold, to look for economic and political co-operation with the socialist world, to control profits, to tax the rich more severely, to speed up nationalisation, or to plan industry.

On the 29th October, 1947, the Trades Union Congress General Council's Special Committee on the Economic Situation, which was dealing with the Government demand for a wage freeze, was instructed to prepare a report on cost-of-living subsidies, profits, price control, and wages, for submission to a Conference of Executives of Trade Unions.

SUPPLEMENTARY BUDGET

On the 12th November, 1947, Dalton introduced a Supplementary Autumn Budget, for the second time in three years, as he pointed out (*Hansard*, Vol. 444, Col. 39) to "strengthen budgetary defences against inflation", since, if goods were diverted to the export market as proposed, the amount of goods available for sale in the home market would be reduced without any corresponding reduction in purchasing power.

The more important measures he proposed were the doubling of profits tax, which was to be 10 per cent. on undistributed and 25 per cent. on distributed profits, with only half (instead of all) of advertising expenditure to rank as expenditure deducted from profits before tax. Interest at 3 per cent. per annum was to be charged on outstanding arrears of income tax.

Purchase tax was to be increased, and so were the duties on beer and spirits, and a 10 per cent. tax was introduced on bets on football pools and dog race totalisators. The subsidies on leather, cotton and wool were abolished; the large and very important subsidies on food were left untouched at their then current rate of £392 million a year, but they were not to be increased if prices rose.

REGRESSIVE TAXATION

The general trend of the taxation was regressive, for it involved an addition to indirect taxes—of which the highest proportion always falls on wage and salary earners—three times as great as the addition to direct taxes. Dalton pointed out that there had been a continued tendency to declare increased dividends, and that profits were still running at a very high level; but he did nothing—beyond the increased profits tax —to check them, and as the *Financial Times* put it, "the Budget contains no shock for the market".

Piratin spoke in the debate (at Cols. 615-16 of Vol. 444 of *Hansard*), claiming that the crisis could have been averted "by a vigorous implementation at home and abroad of Labour's 1945 programme. Even now it is not too late to revise the policy from that of the F.B.I. to that of Labour." He added that half of the military expenditure of £900 million a year could be cut "possibly not immediately, but very quickly", and that the Chancellor had "no right to call upon the people to make sacrifices, as he is calling now and as he will be calling further, on the ground that we are facing what has been called 'economic strangulation', when in fact we are lavishing £900 million on military expenditure which is not in the interests of this country".

Palme Dutt, in his Notes of the Month (*Labour Monthly*, for December, 1947), written on the 17th November, summed up the Budget as placing "three-quarters of its additional burdens on the shoulders of the workers and lower incomes in order to pay for a reckless and extravagant foreign and arms policy absorbing one-third of the State's expenditure".

It was in connection with this Budget that Dalton incautiously disclosed some details of his proposals to a journalist a very short time before he began his speech "opening" his budget—but just in time for the Press to report them before he actually announced them in his speech; as a consequence, he resigned and was succeeded by Cripps.

T.U.C. GENERAL COUNCIL REPORTS

In December, 1947, an Interim Report of the T.U.C. General Council was circulated to the unions, demanding (1) the maintenance of the existing subsidies, (2) the exercise by union executives of "even more restraint" in wage claims, (3) no interference by the Government in wage negotiations, and (4) stricter control of prices and a reduction of profits.

WHITE PAPER ON CAPITAL INVESTMENT

In the same month, December, 1947, the Government published its White Paper (Cmd. 7,268) on Capital Investment, giving proposals for investment cuts. Its plans for reducing investment in nationalised industries were quite definite, whilst all that it did with private industrialists was to appeal to them not to endanger the plan by indiscriminate spending on capital equipment. Housing was to be slowed down, and all building of community centres, youth clubs, and adult education centres was to be postponed, as were major schemes for nursery schools and school meals.

The best comment that can be made on this, and indeed on the whole of the end-of-1947 plan for cutting down, is to be found in an article by Maurice Dobb in the *Labour Monthly* of January, 1948, at pp. 12, 13. He wrote:

"To give precedence to an over-all scaling-down of an already limited programme of equipment and maintenance, while leaving the inflated unproductive expenditure on the armed forces, and in particular overseas expenditure, almost untouched, would look to any sober observer like the economics of Bedlam. It is noteworthy that those who have clamoured most loudly in recent months for cutting investment have been silent about expenditure on the armed forces; and some of them . . . have shown signs that they would strenuously resist any curtailment of our foreign commitments. In this connection it is significant that the recent Labour Party pamphlet, *A.B.C. of the Crisis*, all but completely ignores this aspect of the question (hastily referring in one half-sentence to additional cuts being made in the Armed Forces, without stating that the additional cuts so far announced are quite negligible in amount).

"In other words, it is abundantly clear that at the heart of all discussion of economic policy today lies a political question; and that we are being asked to accept investment-cuts and housing-cuts and deflation of working-class spending power in order to support a particular foreign policy and to fall in with American standards of what is extravagant expenditure when indulged in by European countries and what is not. Moreover, as a means of relieving inflationary pressure, reduction of the armed forces is particularly suitable on purely economic grounds."

STEEL ALLOCATIONS CUT

On the 12th January, 1948, allocations of steel for building, ship-building, and the gas industry were reduced, whilst those for engineering, transport and agriculture were increased. The steel industry was still in private hands, waiting for what proved to be a very half-hearted measure of nationalisation. The shortage of steel was by now probably the country's most serious single industrial handicap; and the steel industry was still following its traditional policy—natural enough, from its point of view, but very injurious to the national economy—of keeping its capacity relatively low so that there should be less plant standing idle during slumps.

WHITE PAPER ON INCOMES, COSTS, AND PRICES

The next step was that, on the 4th February, 1948, the White Paper (Cmd. 7,321) on "Personal Incomes Costs and Prices", was published, which I have already discussed in Chapter 14; this came without any detailed discussion with the T.U.C. General Council, notwithstanding that the Council and the Government were in the middle of negotiations about the Wage Freeze policy. The General Council announced that it had "great difficulty" in accepting this White Paper because of the "limited and weak character" of its reference to profits.

CRIPPS TALKS TO T.U.C.

The Special Committee of the T.U.C. General Council, mentioned above, met Ministers on the 11th February, 1948, and received what they held to be "greater assurances" on prices and profits. Cripps described to the Committee the Government's interim plan to freeze the prices of controlled goods, and *to ask* (!) the Federation of British Industries and employers' organisations to make "specific and practical proposals for limitation of profits and reductions in prices". These proposals, said Cripps, would come before him in time to decide, if he did not consider them satisfactory, to take action to deal with the matter in the Budget which he would be introducing in April. The Special Committee stated that it would have preferred to have the F.B.I. proposals before deciding its policy on wages, but it felt that the Government's proposals had been put in a more favourable light—an unconscious tribute to Cripps' skill as an advocate—and it emphasised that no authority could enforce restraint on wage demands unless profits and price increases were limited.

WHITE PAPER: ECONOMIC SURVEY

The next step came in March, 1948, with the White Paper "Economic Survey for 1948". This showed that the results of the year 1947 had been worse than forecast. The survey for 1947 had foreseen a deficit of about £350 million on the balance of payments, but the actual figure—notwithstanding the drastic cuts made in the course of the year in the imports of food and raw materials—proved to be £675 million. The reason for this was partly that exports had been less than planned—only 20 per cent. above pre-war volume instead of 40 per cent., and partly the increase of world prices, especially in the U.S.A.

Government overseas expenditure for military purposes totalled £211 million, nearly one-third of the deficit of £675 million, apart from the loss of production due to the retention of manpower in the forces.

The White Paper stated the plan to keep total imports for the first half of 1948 at about the 1947 volume, with less from the dollar area, more from the sterling area, and a little more from the rest of the world, than before.

It was no longer expected that a balance of overseas payments would be reached in 1948, as Cripps had forecast in October, 1947; the overall deficit for the first half of 1948 was estimated at £136 million, and that for the whole year at £250 million. The dollar deficit in the first half was estimated at £183 million; this was to be met by drawing on the remaining U.S. and Canadian credits, by a gold loan of £80 million from South Africa, by further sales of overseas investments, and by running down gold and dollar reserves from £680 million to £450 million by mid-1948. After that, reliance was to be placed on Marshall Aid; if that were not forthcoming, the remaining reserves would be gone by the end of 1948.

Trade strategy was to increase exports, cut down imports, concentrate on selling to dollar markets, create new non-dollar sources of supply, ask other sterling countries to adopt similar methods of saving dollars, and help to restore multilateral trade.

The main problem of home production lay in the shortage of raw materials, especially steel, but no drastic proposals were made for overcoming this.

REDUCING LIVING STANDARDS

Living standards were expected to be further reduced. Supplies for home consumption would be 3 to 5 per cent. less than in 1947; food

P

supplies per head would go down; there would be less meat, fat, fruit, vegetables, and potatoes, with increases in cereals and (slightly) in eggs.

T.U. EXECUTIVES CONFERENCE

Hard on this publication there came, on the 24th March, 1948, the Special Conference of Executives of Trade Unions, called by the T.U.C. General Council to discuss its attitude to the policy of Wage Freeze.

There was a good deal of controversy at this Conference, but in the end the Report submitted to it was adopted by a card vote of 5,421,000 to 2,032,000; the minority including—as reported in the Press—the Amalgamated Engineering Union and the Electrical Trades Union.

The Report stated that the principles of the White Paper on wages were acceptable to the trade union movement to the extent that they—

(*a*) recognised the necessity of retaining unimpaired the system of collective bargaining and free negotiation;

(*b*) admitted the justification for claims for increased wages where they were based on the fact of increased output;

(*c*) admitted the necessity of adjusting the wage of workers whose incomes were below a reasonable standard of subsistence;

(*d*) affirmed that it is in the national interest to establish standards of wages and conditions in under-manned essential industries in order to attract sufficient manpower; and

(*e*) recognised the need to safeguard those wage differentials which are an essential element in the wage structure of many important industries.

The Report stated:

"It is clearly the view of the Government that the principles of the White Paper must be applied in the light of the overriding necessity to restrain as far as possible any further rise in the level of all incomes. But, as it applies to wage movements, the White Paper is not a law imposing rigid and specific restrictions upon wage claims and negotiations; it is a request to unions to restrain wage claims within the principles laid down by the White Paper."

The policy proposed in the Report was to endorse the policy of general stabilisation as set forth in the White Paper "on condition that the Government pursues, vigorously and firmly, a policy designed not only to stabilise but to reduce profits and prices". This policy was to be reviewed after the Budget and thereafter at intervals of not less than three months.

On the 9th April, 1948, the Minister of Labour, perhaps half-encouraged by this half-support from the General Council, issued a further letter to wages councils and wages boards saying that, while the White Paper had no statutory force, he asked them to accompany all awards in the future by a memorandum to him showing that the points set out in the White Paper had been taken into consideration by them in making their awards.

BUDGET OF 1948

Just before this, on the 6th April, Cripps introduced his Budget. He said that the Budget had two main objectives, firstly to obtain, with equitable distribution of taxation, a real and substantial surplus to counter inflationary pressure, and secondly to adjust taxation so as to encourage production—the typical Tory argument by which industrialists always call for the reduction of taxation falling on themselves. He budgeted for a surplus, after meeting all current expenditure and all government capital expenditure, of £338 millions.

He proposed reductions in income tax, increases in indirect taxes, and a special "once-for-all" levy, largely payable out of capital, based on the investment income of individuals in 1947-8, in cases where the total income exceeded £2,000 and the investment income exceeded £250; the actual bearing of this tax—a sort of token capital levy—was not heavy; the rate of contribution ranged from 2s. in the £ on investment income between £250 and £500 to 10s. in the £ on investment income over £5,000.

The proportion of indirect taxation to direct was increased—just as had been done by Dalton in the previous Autumn—and in the debate on the Budget, several speakers pointed out that the majority of workers with children—the group most hardly pressed by rising prices—would not benefit by the reduction in income tax but would have to pay more in indirect taxation. (I myself had been earning throughout the period of the Labour Government a relatively large income, eminently suitable for tax, and I noticed that each successive Budget *reduced* by more than a negligible amount the taxation I had to pay.)

Piratin spoke in the debate (*Hansard*, Vol. 449, Cols. 230 *et seq.*). He criticised the lack of effective planning proposed, and the excuse advanced by Cripps—as by Ministers generally, whenever challenged for their failure to introduce the "planned economy" promised in 1945—that "because we are a democracy" we cannot effectively plan. He also attacked the weakness of the Government in doing no more to control profits than "appealing to the directors of companies not to increase the distribution of profits", and the failure to develop exports to the socialist countries.

Profits were in fact still growing remarkably. In the first quarter of 1948, the profits of the companies appearing in the *Economist* records rose sharply; with 1945 as 100, and 1947 as 125, the gross profits in that quarter were 150·7; and the companies in question raised their dividends from £59 millions in 1947 to £61 millions in 1948. It is not surprising that by May, 1948, a number of unions were proceeding with wage claims, including the Confederation of Engineering and Shipbuilding Unions, covering some 3 million workers. (One sees at once the sad parallel between the Labour Government in 1948 and the Tory Government in 1962. In each case they were confronted with an economic crisis; in each case they sought to "cure" it by a wage freeze, coupled with no more effort to control the vast profits of industrialists than appeals for voluntary limitation of the profits, or rather of the distribution of profits. And in each case the working class reacted with strikes or threats of strikes—to which I will now come.)

STRIKES

Naturally, in the face of the economic stringency, and of the Government policy of rejecting the remedies of cutting down military expenditure and of developing trade with the socialist world, following instead the policy I have just described, there were a good many strikes at this period, mostly unofficial. One of them, the London dock strike of June, 1948, had as its immediate cause dissatisfaction over some disciplinary measures; it started on the 14th June, spread to the Mersey on the 28th June, and in the end involved some 30,000 men. On the 22nd June, the union (Transport and General) called a meeting at the Albert Hall, attended by 3,000 men, who agreed to return to work; but at the same time a meeting over twice as large, called by the strike committee, decided to continue the strike. On the 23rd June, the Government brought in troops to unload perishable foodstuffs. On the 25th, Arthur Deakin, General Secretary of the union, was shouted down at a strike meeting; and three members of the strike committee resigned on the old cry of "communist influence". So baseless was this allegation that, even after these three anti-communists had gone, the

Committee consisted of 27 non-political, five Communist and ten Labour Party members).

On the 28th June, the Government proclaimed a state of emergency under the Act of 1920 (already mentioned in Chapter 8), and the Prime Minister broadcast an appeal to return to work; and on the following day the strike was called off.

TRADE WITH U.S.S.R.

The position of such trade as there was between Britain and the U.S.S.R. is described at pp. 314-17 of Mr. and Mrs. Coates' book. As I mentioned in Chapter 12, an agreement had been signed in Moscow on the 29th December, 1947, under which, so far from Britain giving credit, it was given credit in the sense that the U.S.S.R. undertook to ship grain in advance of receiving the goods which it was to have in return. It was provided in the agreement that the parties were to meet again not later than the 31st May, 1948, to review the payments position and to negotiate a more comprehensive agreement; but by mid-June they had got no further with that than an announcement by Mr. Harold Wilson that trade talks were to be resumed "very soon". But the position as to our deliveries to the Soviet Union was by no means satisfactory. The U.S.S.R. had agreed to ship 750,000 tons of grain by instalments, with a right to withhold 200,000 tons if it proved impossible to place half their contracts for British goods (which had of course mostly to be placed with private suppliers) by the 1st May. The position as it stood in June was set out in an article in the issue of *Soviet News* dated 23rd June, 1948:

"By June 12, 1948, the U.S.S.R. had sent to Great Britain about 400,000 tons of grain, or 53·5 per cent. of the total provided for by the Agreement.

"Thus the U.S.S.R. in four and a half months had delivered more than half the grain provided for in the Agreement, and consequently had accurately fulfilled its obligation.

"Great Britain's obligation under the Agreement was, first of all, to supply to the Soviet Union 35,000 tons of light rails with fish-plates, bolts and nuts for narrow-gauge railways, including 25,000 tons from Government military surpluses and 10,000 tons from current production.

"Up to the present time Great Britain has delivered to the U.S.S.R. 12,200 tons from surpluses, and contracts have been concluded for the supply of 13,000 tons out of current production by the end of 1948.

"According to approximate figures, by June 1, 1948, the Soviet side has been able to place orders for only 10·5 per cent of the total value of the equipment. This unsatisfactory situation is explained by the one-sided nature of the tenders submitted by British firms, which seek to retain rights for the supplier while placing all the obligations on the purchaser.

"As a rule the proposed prices are unjustifiably high, considerably exceeding world price levels. Sometimes this excess amounts to 40 or 50 per cent. However, in the Agreement it is clearly stated that 'prices to be charged by the seller to the purchaser for the goods to be delivered in accordance with Article I of this Agreement shall be based on world prices'.

"It can be stated without exaggeration that the terms offered to the Trade Delegation of the U.S.S.R. by British firms are worse not only than the terms of its trade in Great Britain in pre-war years, but also in the post-war period, and that they are considerably worse than the terms of its trade with a number of other countries at the present time.

"Many British firms explain their unaccommodating attitude in regard to Soviet orders by references to materials in short supply, above all steel, and the vagueness of the British Government's guarantees regarding such supplies."

Talks were actually resumed in June, but little progress was made by the end of the year. The U.S.S.R. in fact delivered all the grain it had undertaken to deliver by the end of the year, without exercising its right to withhold 200,000 tons, but the contracts which it was able to place by the end of December, 1948, amounted to only a little over 15 per cent of the total contemplated in the agreement.

ECONOMIC POSITION WORSENING

Coming back to the economic position, it was unhappily clear by July, 1948, that the economic situation was developing worse than had been forecast. Cripps had given figures in June showed a deficiency in our "visible" trade not only with the dollar area but with the whole world. *Labour Research* for July gave figures for the first four months of 1948, showing that "the map laid down in the Economic Survey and Capital Investment White Paper no longer charts the course". And on the 5th July Cripps admitted in the House of Commons that our gold and dollar reserves were already down to £473 million. The first six months of the year were dealt with by J. R. Campbell in an article in the *Labour Monthly* for September, showing that exports in that six months were 30 per cent. above 1938 and 1946, and in July were 45 per cent. above, so that the target of 50 per cent. increase by the end of 1948 might be reached; but the "terms of trade" had turned unfavourably, import prices rising more than export, so that the balance of payments deficit was running at the rate of £300 million instead of £250 million. Prices and profits had both been rising faster than wages. In the Notes of the Month, in the same issue of *Labour Monthly*, the position was described thus:

> "Real wages have fallen; even according to the official figures, the past twelve months show a rise in retail prices by ten per cent as against a rise of wage rates by six per cent. Profits have continued to soar; in his mid-July report on the economic situation Cripps declared that 'profits declared this year have been considerably higher than in the past twelve months', and that, despite the appeal for voluntary limitation of dividends, one-quarter of the companies declaring results in the previous three months had increased their dividends'."

NATIONALISED INDUSTRIES

On transport, I need only mention that the 1st January, 1948, was the "vesting date" for railways, canals and the London Passenger Transport Board.

COAL

Coal had of course been nationalised earlier, and it was possible for the Coal Board to make a report on its first year's working—that for 1947—as early as July, 1948. It showed an improved output, and more men joining the industry than for many years past; but it was not surprising that there was a deficit of £23 million, made up mainly by heavy payments of "interim income" and compensation to ex-owners; £1,600,000 had been lost on importing coal from America and Poland at prices much above our home prices, and then disposing of it at low prices. (The loss on U.S. coal was £2 5s. 10d. per ton.) The net operating loss was £6,200,000.

The report made the point that "a joint stock company could have covered part of the deficit" (on colliery working) "by not distributing any dividend. This expedient was not open to the Board. They must make repayments of capital and interest each year, whether good or bad".

HOUSING

As I have mentioned above, the White Paper on Capital Investment of December, 1947, envisaged cuts in building, with a net reduction of building workers by 31,532 by June, 1948, and of further reductions thereafter; and the numbers of approvals for new housing, then standing at 261,826, were to be scaled down to 210,000 by June, 1948, and 140,000 by June, 1949. Preliminary work on New Towns was cut, except for those needed for immediate industrial needs or for mining.

In June, 1948, by which time the number of new permanent houses under construction had fallen to 218,044, Aneurin Bevan, the Minister in charge of housing, revised the programme upwards; local authorities were told to work on the basis that the figure of 180,000 under construction at any one time would be maintained, and the figure for all house construction was to be about 200,000; this compared favourably with the figure of 140,000 estimated six months before, but it was considerably less than the current labour force was capable of building.

There were, however, great increases in building costs; building materials were costing double the pre-war prices, and both manufacturers and merchants were making large profits. Interest rates on housing loans were also starting on what proved to be a long upward journey.

SOCIAL SERVICES

In the field of social services, it was a great step forward that on the 5th July, 1948, four Acts, National Insurance, National Health Service, Industrial Injuries, and National Assistance, came into force. But much of their operation was badly affected by the cuts. In January, 1948, the construction of Health Centres, publicised as an essential measure of the Health Service and twice previously postponed, was now treated as "not desired"; and in fact practically none has ever been built.

Nevertheless, it was by this time clear that, with all its deficits, and the inroads made upon it by crisis measures, the National Health Service was a great advance, for which the Labour Government is entitled to credit. I will write more of this in Chapter 26.

EDUCATION

Education also suffered, although it had some positive achievements; the Annual Report of the Ministry of Education, published in August, 1948, showed advances in some raising of the school-leaving age to 15, an increase in the supply of teachers and of State scholarships, more financial assistance to those winning scholarships to universities, better salaries for teachers, and marked improvements in school health services, including an increase in the numbers getting school meals and milk (the latter free).

But there were still many shortcomings. The capital expenditure cuts of December, 1947, brought the expansion of nursery schools to a standstill; the provision of such schools was about 1 per cent of what was required to implement fully the Education Act. (In January, 1947, the number in nursery schools had been only 19,000.) Over one million children were still in "all-age" schools; 650 black-listed schools were still in use; 30,000 primary school classes had over 40 children; and school meals were provided for only 52 per cent. of all children, whilst the effective demand was officially estimated at 75 per cent.

Since August 1945, only sixteen new schools (catering for 4,000 children) had been completed, although many others were under construction. There were long delays in the construction of those for which plans had been approved; on the 31st March, 1948, for example, plans had been approved for schools costing £28 million, but those under construction or completed accounted for only £13 million.

In some primary schools, children were actually being refused admission when they reached the entry age of five, for lack of accommodation and of teachers; in January, 1947, there were 2,036 primary school classes of over 50, and 31,949 of over 40.

There was still no indication as to when the school-leaving age was to be raised to 16 as provided by the Education Act.

CHAPTER 18

Labour Party Policy, 1947-8

In the sphere of Labour Party policy in this period, there come the Labour Party Conference, held at Scarborough at Whitsuntide, and the Trades Union Conference, held at Margate in September, 1948.

At the first of these Conferences, a resolution was passed welcoming "the initiative of the Government in attempting to establish a policy for wages, profits and other incomes, designed to prevent inflation", but insisting that "the basis of such a policy must be the stabilisation of the cost of living". In the same resolution, "the increase in commodity prices, with the consequent effect on the standards of living" was "viewed with grave concern", and the Government was called on to take action to "curb exhorbitant profit distribution". A resolution which "viewed with grave concern the publication of the Government White Paper on Wage Stabilisation unaccompanied by specific proposals for the limitation of prices and profits", was lost.

CONSOLIDATING "GAINS"

The Government line of covering the virtual abandonment of attempts to fulfil the policies for which the Party had been returned to power three years earlier, with talk of "consolidating our socialist gains", was put forward, particularly in a speech by Morrison; this was linked with appeals not to "rock the boat" however badly it was navigated, since there was bound to be a General Election, at the very latest, early in 1950.

It was on the whole a "flat" Conference, but the Left opposition, not too well co-ordinated and vulnerable to manœuvres by the government machine, was nevertheless strong—if not nearly strong enough.

TRADES UNION CONGRESS

The Trades Union Congress was much more alive and intense than the Labour Party Conference had been. No doubt the exclusion of communists from the Labour Party Conference, which cannot be

carried through to the Trades Union Congress, is one of the reasons
why the latter is often more significant and revealing.

Margate showed the same picture as Scarborough of conflict
between Left and Right, but showed it more starkly and vividly;
the Left was stronger although never strong enough, and the Right
was more extremely right. The Conference was to a large extent shaped
as an anti-communist demonstration, indeed as an attempt to blame
communism and communists for the economic and other troubles of
the Government. It showed also the beginnings of the manœuvre to
break up the world trade union unity achieved by the World Federation
of Trade Unions and to found as a rival body the "International
Confederation of free Trade Unions".

Cripps was a prominent figure at the Conference, using his great
ability as an advocate to forward the ever more right-wing—and
essentially Tory—policy which had to be "put over" to win support for
the Government's plans to freeze wages, obey America, and conciliate capitalists. He appealed—as any Tory minister might have done—
for more production, the removal of restrictive practices, and restraint
on wage demands. He said:

> "If . . . we were to regard the increased difficulties of paying our way,
> as individuals or nationally, as a reason for making the cost of produc-
> tion go up, we should simply be making a certainty that the real value
> of wages went down."

Cripps sought to deflect indignation at mounting profits by compar-
ing the £320 million distributed in dividends by certain companies
with a wage total of £3,260 million in the whole field of employment.
Even £320 million would represent £6 a head for every man, woman
and child in the country; but the comparison would have been more real
if he had substituted for £320 million the figure of £2,588 million,
the total *after taxation* of rent, interest and profit received in 1947.

Wages and prices were dealt with in a Supplementary Report on the
economic situation by the General Council, whose main conclusions
were:

> 1. The increase of two points in prices since the White Paper on the
> stabilisation of wages was recognised; this was largely due to extra
> taxes and withdrawal of subsidies and "it is extremely doubtful if
> the Government were wise to provoke increases in those items". . . .
> On the other hand the rate of subsidies had been increased in recent
> months, and the Government could take credit for some voluntary

price reductions; but even more vigorous steps should be taken to secure lower prices.

2. Reduction of profits by direct legal limitation would be difficult and would "create inequalities and bitterness of a kind similar to the inequalities and bitterness which would be created by direct legal limitation on wage increases".

3. Voluntary dividend limitation was proving increasingly successful.

4. Wage rates for men had risen by only 1 per cent. and for women by 2 per cent. since the White Paper. "It is clear that there is no wage freeze, and equally clear that unions are acting with the restraint and high sense of responsibility which was the essence of the policy adopted by the Special Conference in March."

The General Council recommended that the wage stabilisation policy be continued, but reiterated that no authority could restrain demands for increases unless a limit were imposed upon profits and prices.

A resolution urging the Government to take more effective action to control price movements and to impose stricter limitations on profits was carried by an overwhelming majority.

But a resolution stating that, so far, the Government had not prevented a decline of wages in relation to profits and prices, which were still rising, calling on the Government to introduce statutory control of profits and dividends, and declaring that Congress could not support a policy designed to stabilise wages at their present levels, was lost on a card vote by 5,207,000 to 2,184,000. (This latter figure represented the voting strength of the Left in the Conference, which fluctuated between two and three millions.)

Palme Dutt wrote in his Notes of the Month in *Labour Monthly* for October, 1948:

"The Right stood for the sanctity of profits, the foregoing of wage demands, co-operation with the master class, war on militant trade unionism, disruption of international unity, and dependence on the American colossus of Big Business. The Left stood for trade union unity at home and abroad, resistance to the employers' offensive, the fight to win improved wages and living standards at the expense of profits, and the strengthening of trade unionism through the methods of class struggle for which the unions were founded."

It was at this Conference that Sir George Chester explained the importance of allowing profits to be made, as mentioned in Chapter 12.

CHAPTER 19

The Fourth Session, 1948

THE fourth Session of Parliament lasted only six weeks, from the 14th September, 1948, to the 25th October.

It was held, as the King's Speech explained, for the sole purpose of giving "further consideration to the Bill to amend the Parliament Act, 1911, on which there was disagreement between the two Houses in the third Session".

This quite legitimate procedure was required, as explained in Chapter 13, if the Parliament Act was to be amended against the resistance of the House of Lords, for the Amending Bill had to be passed in three consecutive sessions; this session was held in order to constitute the second of the three.

The Bill was presented on the 16th September, given a second reading on the 20th, passed, and sent up to the House of Lords, which again disagreed. And the session then ended. (The Bill was passed for the third time on the 10th December, 1949. See the next chapter.)

Had the Government taken stronger steps against the House of Lords in the first or second sessions, they would probably not have ventured to resist. But by now they had the measure of the Government's timidity and "respectability".

During the brief Session, some other matters were discussed. On "Defence", Parliament was told that all men in the Armed Forces due for release in the next following three months, were to have their terms of service extended by three months, so that there would be 80,000 more men under arms at the end of 1948 than had been planned.

CHAPTER 20

The Fifth Session, 1948-9

THE fifth session—effectively the fourth year of the Government—began on the 26th October, 1948, and ended on the 16th December, 1949. It was destined to be the last session before the General Election of February, 1950.

By this time, the Government was tired, and not inclined to any great activity. It had carried out most of the specific promises of its 1945 Election programme (without of course doing anything appreciable to advance towards socialism). As I noticed in earlier chapters, it had started in mid-1948 talking of a phase of "consolidation", partly as a cover for its own internal doubts and disputes over the desirability of further measures of nationalisation (including desirability from the point of view of winning the "middle-of-the-road" voter to vote for it in the next General Election), and partly probably from fatigue and inertia. And it had become, beyond any hope of early reform, "set in its ways" of anti-Soviet, pro-American policies, and thus condemned to the series of financial and economic crises that those policies brought with them.

The King's Speech (*Hansard*, Vol. 457, Cols. 5-8) had little in it, apart from promises of the Bills to amend the Parliament Act and to nationalise the iron and steel industry, and a number of useful minor reforms. It read like a right-wing political manifesto, at least as acceptable to Tories as to socialists. The Brussels Treaty, Germany, Berlin, the airlift, the balance of payments—"will continue to tackle the problem, fortified by generous U.S. aid"—the maintenance of the Armed Forces with a lengthened period of conscription and the organisation of Civil Defence, held the field.

I need not write at great length in this chapter about the legislation passed in the session, as the more important Acts will be dealt with in their place in later chapters. The Parliament Act, 1949, introduced on the 28th July, 1949, for its third presentation, received the Royal assent on the 10th December, 1949.

Of the other legislation, I should mention the Legal Aid and Advice Act, 1949, a useful measure—even if the actual bringing into force of an important part of it was postponed to meet one of the "crises"—and the Juries Act, 1949, designed to do something, but not nearly enough, to amend the qualifications of jurymen which had hitherto practically ensured that juries should never have more than one or two working-class people sitting on them.

CHAPTER 21

Foreign Policy, 1948-9

FOREIGN affairs, including developments in the economic field at home which were directly linked to our subservience to the U.S.A., occupied as usual a large field in the politics and the problems of the year.

NATO

I will deal first with the development of NATO (The North Atlantic Treaty Organisation) and then with Marshall Aid. In both of these, one saw not only a closer subordination of British policy to U.S. ambitions for capitalist domination of the world, but also a growing bipartisanship of the Labour Government and the Tory opposition. Mr. Milliband wrote, at p. 303 of his *Parliamentary Socialism*, of "an even more substantial measure of agreement between the Labour leadership and its Conservative counterpart, most of all in regard to foreign policy. This was not due to any Conservative shift to a distinctive Labour foreign policy. There was no such policy. Winston Churchill was not vainly boasting when he said, as he often did, that the Government had consistently followed his own recommendations and proposals."

Milliband quoted Churchill as saying in the House of Commons in 1952 that the policy he had outlined at Fulton (on which see Chapter 6, above) had been effectively adopted by the Labour Party, and that that Party had in particular followed his policy in the Brussels Pact and in NATO. "With NATO," adds Milliband, "for the first time in twentieth-century British politics save in time of war, the most important factor in foreign policy was now agreed to be above and beyond 'partisan' debate." He should have added the qualification: "except from the two Communists, and a few left-wing members".

And what, in reality, was the essence of NATO? Here we have one more example of the dishonesty which is displayed by too many governments, for NATO was "put over" to the British public as something fundamentally different from the reality. It is particularly easy now, fourteen or fifteen years later, to see the reality and the swindle, but at the time it was perhaps easier for most people to suspect than to be sure.

It would be hard to deny that it was fundamentally a breach of the United Nations Charter, as well as—so far as Britain was concerned— of the 1942 Anglo-Soviet Treaty of Alliance. Nor can it be denied that the rulers of the U.S.A. intended from the start to build up under NATO a vast military force of all Western powers who could be trusted to serve American anti-Soviet policy, and to include in that force a powerful new West German army—although it is clear that in the early stages of the story neither the British nor the Germans themselves wanted that particular development.

And only those who were in a high degree gullible, or anti-Soviet, or pro-American, or all three, would think of NATO as even mainly defensive—for the evidence that the U.S.S.R. had no aggressive intentions was overwhelming. In truth, NATO was part of the wide general policy of the rulers of the U.S.A., intoxicated by economic power and by fear of socialism, to dominate the world and to defeat or destroy the U.S.S.R. by a mighty political, economic and military combination or conspiracy. The European satellites of the U.S.A. were to be kept from becoming socialist by economic aid through the Marshall Plan, carefully made conditional on their keeping their skirts "clean"; they were to be built up by military development and co-ordination through NATO; and they were to provide bomber bases from which the supposed monopoly of the supposedly invincible atom bomb could be conveniently applied against the encircled U.S.S.R., by threat or by action, at any time. This reactionary, costly, dangerous, illusory, anti-socialist scheme was enthusiastically adopted by the Labour Government of Great Britain.

But it had to be "put over" to the British public. How exactly was this done?

"PUTTING NATO OVER"

The picture of NATO presented to British public opinion in 1948 and 1949 is quite unrecognisable by anyone who has the knowledge available fourteen or fifteen years later. The story of its conception, leaving out of account the many private talks of ruling politicians which must have led up to it, began, in a sense, with a resolution of the U.S. Senate in June, 1948, proposed by Senator Vandenberg, welcoming the (possible) association of the U.S.A. with regional agreements. Then,

Q

on the 20th October, 1948, the Foreign Ministers of Britain, France, Belgium, Holland and Luxemburg, the five Powers associated in the Brussels Pact, itself part of the U.S. conspiracy for the development of the great anti-socialist policy, agreed at a meeting in Paris to the formation of a North Atlantic Treaty. The official communiqué announced "complete agreement on the principle of a defensive pact for the North Atlantic, and on the next steps to be taken in this direction".

Discussions then went on in private, as is usual in such conspiracies, and on the 18th March, 1949, the terms of the Treaty which had been negotiated were made public.

By Article 5, an armed attack against any one or more of the Parties to the Treaty in Europe or North America was to be considered as an attack against them all; and such an armed attack was to justify—if not actually to compel—the others to "take such actions as (they) deem necessary, including the use of armed force, to restore and maintain the security of the 'North Atlantic Area'", the action being merely reported *ex post facto* to the Security Council of the U.N.

("The North Atlantic Area" had as its southern geographical limit the Tropic of Cancer, which runs through North Africa. No boundaries were set to the North, West, or East; after February, 1952, it presumably included Turkey, which then became a NATO power, thus bringing the frontiers of Armenia, Iraq and Iran into the area—and the perils—of the North Atlantic!)

The interpretation put upon these terms in his public statements by the American Secretary of State, Dean Rusk—with a good deal of justification from the words of the Treaty—made it clear that not merely aggression from outside but any internal revolt could be treated as armed attack and made the excuse for starting what would soon develop into a third world war. This was particularly serious when one remembers that the government of Greece, which came into the Pact in February 1952, could not last a week in the face of popular discontent without military support from Britain or America, and that already in 1948 the positions of the American-supported governments of France and Italy were by no means secure against left-wing popular pressure in those countries.

As these Treaty terms were made public, arrangements were being made to fly (destined to be the first of many) an American atom-bomb long-range bomber contingent, with thirty planes complete with atom-bomb equipment and a personnel of nine hundred, into Britain. Its departure was announced in a press statement of the U.S. Air Chief with the phrase ("purely defensive", no doubt) that: "The shadow of United States air power can be cast over any part of the world." (He might almost have been copying Mussolini: "The shadow of our planes will darken the sky." But the British Government would have been wise to recall a statement by the Chinese Ambassador to Britain at the time of Munich: "The sky is black with chickens coming home to roost.")

Just as in the case of Marshall Aid—and indeed of every other manifestation of anti-Soviet policy—Bevin was not merely acquiescent but enthusiastic. He described the Treaty to the House of Commons as "a powerful defensive arrangement", "not directed against anyone", not "ganging up against any country or group of countries". But when he had been asked a Parliamentary question on the 9th February "whether he would give an assurance that no obligations would be entered into under the terms of the proposed Atlantic Pact whereby this country would *automatically* become a belligerent in the event of hostilities between the U.S.A. and the U.S.S.R.", he had answered quite simply "No, sir", and said nothing to suggest that he had any reluctance to sacrifice an essential part of our sovereignty, and risk the deaths of millions of his fellow-citizens, by committing the country in advance to war in the service of the capitalist U.S.A. against the socialist world.

U.S.S.R. REACTS

The Soviet Union reacted quickly enough. On the 1st April, 1949, it delivered Notes to the Governments of Britain, the U.S.A., France, Canada, and the three "Benelux" countries, asserting that the Treaty contradicted both the principles and aims of the United Nations Organisation and the commitments of the U.S.A., Britain and France, under other treaties, including the Anglo-Soviet Treaty and the Yalta and Potsdam Agreements, and that the Treaty was plainly directed against the U.S.S.R.

NATO TREATY SIGNED

The Treaty was signed in Washington on the 4th April, 1949, by the U.S.A., Canada, Belgium, Denmark, France, Iceland, Italy, Luxemburg, the Netherlands, Norway, Portugal, and the United Kingdom. All of these countries ratified it at the latest by the 24th August, 1949; Greece and Turkey acceded to the Treaty in February, 1952. Bevin's biographer, Francis Williams, wrote of the ceremony at

Washington, which was given a great radio and television ballyhoo: "As I watched (Bevin) put his signature to the Treaty, I could not help but know that this was, as he had said to me, 'one of the great moments of all my life'."

On the day of the signature, in the House of Commons, Mr. Mayhew, Under-Secretary of State for Foreign Affairs, asserted that the Treaty was compatible with the Anglo-Soviet Treaty of Alliance, and on the 11th April he said that there was no intention of inviting the U.S.S.R. to join the Treaty. The British Government, in a Note to the Soviet Government, asserted that it was not contrary to the Anglo-Soviet Treaty and was in conformity with the spirit and letter of the U.N. Charter.

NATO AT THE U.N.

On the 13th April, 1949, speaking at the U.N. General Assembly, Mr. Gromyko said:

"The circumstances which accompanied the preparations for the North Atlantic Treaty, as well as the composition of the parties to this treaty, show that this new military bloc of States situated on both shores of the Atlantic Ocean is aimed against the U.S.S.R. This is borne out by the fact that the North Atlantic Treaty, similar to Western Union, denotes the creation of a limited grouping of States and excludes the participation of only one great Power— The Soviet Union. . . .

"It cannot be regarded as fortuitous that the initiators of the North Atlantic Alliance take such interest in the inclusion in it of States bordering on the Soviet Union. . . . This pursues the aim of securing the possibility for creating on the territory of these States military bases including air bases for attacking the Soviet Union. . . .

"Inasmuch as the North Atlantic Treaty is aimed against the U.S.S.R., it contradicts the aims and purposes of the Anglo-Soviet Treaty of 1942."

The U.S. Senate having ratified the Treaty on the 21st July, President Truman four days later asked Congress, as a first instalment of the arms programme under the Treaty, for $1,450 million for the current fiscal year; (the allotment, so far as concerned the North Atlantic countries, was cut to $1,000 million by the time the Bill passed the Senate on the 22nd September, 1949).

On the 29th July, General Bradley, the U.S. Chief of Staff, said that the U.S. share of the joint strategy of NATO was to deliver the atom bomb; the American and Western Union Powers were to keep the sea lanes clear; and the bulk of the responsibility for short-range *attack*, bombardment, and air-defence was to fall on Britain and France. And a day or two after this statement, the American joint Chiefs of Staff arrived in London to discuss the organisation of "defence" under NATO.

I turn now to consider the falsity of the claims and assertions made by the British Government in relation to the North Atlantic Treaty.

GOVERNMENT MISREPRESENTATIONS

The thesis that it was in accordance with the Charter of the U.N. was almost ridiculous. It was said to be a regional pact; but from Seattle— or indeed Alaska—to the borders of Iran is a funny sort of region; and this defence was seen to be so weak that it was very soon dropped. In any case, under Article 52 of the Charter, the function of regional "agencies" was laid down to be the pacific settlement of *local* disputes. Even more destructive of any plausible argument for the "U.N. legitimacy" of NATO, however, are the provisions of Article 53 of the Charter, which says in terms that "no enforcement action shall be taken under regional arrangements or by regional agencies without the authorisation of the Security Council, with the exception of measures against any enemy State as defined in the Article". (And "enemy State", however much the rulers of the U.S.A. may have felt that the words should *exclude* Germany and *include* the U.S.S.R., did in fact mean, under the Charter "any State which during the Second World War has been an enemy of any signatories of the present Charter".)

Then, as to the suggestion that the Treaty was not a violation of the Anglo-Soviet Treaty of Alliance, Article VII of that Treaty contains an undertaking by each of the parties "not to conclude any alliance, and not to take part in any coalition, directed against the other". The argument advanced by the British government was that NATO was purely a defensive alliance and could not therefore offend against the Treaty. I shall come to the argument about NATO being "purely defensive" in a moment; but it is surely indisputable that an alliance or a coalition, although defensive, may still be "directed against" the one State which is alleged to be "offensive" enough for a defensive alliance or coalition to be prepared against it.

NATO "DEFENSIVE"

Coming to the question whether NATO could be described as defensive, the first point to consider is that the claim that one's actions or intentions are defensive is at the best rather weak, for there has never been any offensive force in the world that has not been called "defensive" by its authors; even Hitler's army was *die Wehrmacht*, which means "the defence power". The question whether the true purpose of NATO was defensive or potentially aggressive depends not on the declarations of the British Government but on the attitude, actions and policies of the American Government; and that these were extremely aggressive can be seen from what I have written on many pages of this book, and indeed, from post-Second World War history generally. A good deal depends, too, when one is considering the alleged defensive character of an alliance obviously directed against one Power, on whether that Power has shown any sign of aggressiveness; for it is improbable that any sensible persons, acting in good faith, would spend thousands of millions on elaborate preparations for defence specifically directed against someone who has no intention of attacking them.

As I mentioned above, in Chapter 10, most of the most hostile critics of the U.S.S.R. throughout the period covered by this book have frankly admitted that it had no intention of starting a war. Beyond that general statement, I would refer to some observations to be found at p. 518 of Professor Fleming's *The Cold War*. It had been plain for some years after 1945 that Soviet military power exceeded anything that could be mustered against it in Western Europe, so that, if the rulers of the U.S.S.R. had been lunatic enough, and false enough to their principles, to want to make the whole of the masses of Europe—including the masses of their own people—hostile to them, and to socialism, by "marching to Calais", it was militarily possible for them to do so; and one of the arguments often advanced to show that they had no intention of doing so was the fact that America and Britain kept asserting that this invasion was not only possible but easy, but that with the passage of time—if the "aggressive" Soviet Union would kindly wait—it would become less easy and finally impossible. (As I pointed out in Chapter 10, it may be doubted whether even the hysterical and largely second-rate brains that controlled so much of Western policy would have gone on issuing what practically amounted to invitations to "attack us now, before it is too late", if they had not been sure that the U.S.S.R. would never do anything of the sort.)

Professor Fleming—in a passage in which he demonstrated the non-sense, from a military point of view, of the whole NATO strategy—wrote that the really intelligent American military critic Max Werner "noted that Western diplomats are tortured by the question: 'Why don't the Russians attack now?'" Soviet military power . . . was "immeasurably superior to that of Hitler in 1939", but the absolute military weakness of Western Europe had not provoked Soviet aggression. Instead of launching her armies, Russia was making tremendous investments in long-range projects, huge factories, big dams, irrigation, reafforestation, and the rebuilding of cities—all of it pure waste if the Soviet believed war inevitable in the near future. This decade was "decisive for Soviet industrialisation". It was highly unlikely that Soviet leaders would willingly imperil it by invoking the devastations of war, of which they had recent first-hand knowledge. Moreover, Soviet military doctrine rejected the blitz idea; it was based on protracted effort in a long war, the kind which defeated Napoleon and Hitler. Yet aggression could not "start without belief in a blitz, since it makes no sense to attack in order to wage a long, expensive, and dangerous war".

"ALL OF A PIECE"

The whole NATO policy of building up huge armies in Western Europe, to carry the main burden of the war against the U.S.S.R., and against socialism generally, which too many strategists and politicians in America foresaw and foretold as part of their future, was in truth part of the whole pattern of rejecting disarmament proposals, rebuilding Germany, keeping the Berlin dispute alive, carrying on the Marshall Plan—all at the price of infinite danger of war, and certainty of infinite and crippling expense; but it is interesting to notice that even as late as the end of 1949 the proposal to rearm Western Germany—which really meant recreating Hitler's armies—did not appeal either to the German or to the British Governments.

STILL NO REARMAMENT OF GERMANY

On the 22nd November, 1949, the three High Commissioners of the Western Powers in Germany and the Chancellor of the West German Republic signed an agreement in which the Federal Government declared its earnest determination to maintain the demilitarisation of the federal territory and to endeavour by all means in its power to prevent the recreation of armed forces of any kind. Then, on the 16th

December, 1949, as *The Times* reported on the following day, "all parties in the Bundestag joined . . . in repudiating the idea of rearmament. Whatever their motives, the result was to put on record the West German Parliament's opposition to, and even detestation of, a revival of the Wehrmacht". And on the 18th December, the Government coalition parties of West Germany published a statement to the same effect. On the following day, a *Times* editorial stated that "the leading statesmen of the Western Powers have denied that there is now or ever has been any intention of re-arming Germany", (but added some cryptic words hinting that this attitude might well change).

THE ATOM BOMB IN U.S.S.R.

There were both in U.S.A. and Britain a good many people, anti-Soviet enough, who nevertheless thought that the whole conception of building up NATO was strategically wrong and useless; but their views did not prevail. All the U.S. strategy of the period was still based on two fundamental conceptions or misconceptions, the first that atomic power could win a war by itself, and win it quickly, and the second that the U.S.A. would preserve the monopoly of the atom bomb for some years to come; and many Americans thought that the U.S.S.R. could be intimidated by this great U.S. advantage into making concessions of all kinds. Whether or not there was any foundation for the first conception, the second—as to which it must be said that a good many people believed that the U.S.S.R. had already, at least a year or two earlier, learnt the whole know-how of making atom bombs—was definitely destroyed on the 23rd September, 1949, when the American and British Governments announced that "within recent weeks an atomic explosion occurred in the U.S.S.R.". This statement was confirmed by a TASS news agency announcement in Moscow on the 25th September.

U.S. REACTIONS

The reaction in the U.S.A. was one of astonishment and dismay; but although the whole basis of their policy had in effect been destroyed, the rulers of the U.S. made no move to change it; this was partly due— it may be suspected—to the fact that in truth they were both determined to continue the armament race against the U.S.S.R., in the forlorn hope of destroying it, and dismayed at the prospect of upsetting their economy and losing their profits if armament expenditure had to be reduced. But it was also partly, even largely, due to a sort of mental paralysis, an inability to pull themselves together, make an intelligent assessment of the wholly new military situation, and adjust their military policy accordingly. This last was the view taken by Mr. Walter Lippman, the most intelligent of the American commentators. In the *New York Herald Tribune* of the 30th September, 1949, he wrote:

"In the event, the phantom policy, under which the Soviet régime was supposed to break down by containment all around the periphery, is now blown away—first by its total collapse in the Far East*, and then by the Soviet achievement of the bomb. There is no alternative to the negotiation of a *modus vivendi* based on the balance of power and reciprocal advantages.

"The American plan . . . had as [its] major premise an American monopoly of the bomb and of the technological knowledge and measures to make the bomb. It was a plan for the regulated sharing of the monopoly. All the conditions we asked for assumed that the Russians must pay a price—in the form of inspection and control—to get their share of our monopoly. . . .

"Now that the Russians have broken the monopoly, the basic premise of the American policy has disappeared. A totally different policy, based on the radically new condition, will have to be formulated."

An estimate of the impact which this news must have been made on the rulers of the U.S.A.—and equally a picture of the sort of military position they were seeking to create in Europe under their Marshall-NATO-bomber-base complex of "defensive" preparation—may be gathered from a disclosure made by Joseph and Stewart Alsop in the *New York Herald Tribune* of the 21st September, 1949, two days before the announcement of the first Soviet atom bomb explosion. These well-informed commentators reported that the plan of the joint chiefs of staff for "the defence" of Western Europe was based—by a majority of the planning experts—on the view that the expenditure of $8,000 to $10,000 million, coupled with a major effort by the West European countries, could create an army of 45 to 50 divisions in West Europe, even without German rearmament, by 1954—that year being selected on the footing that the American monopoly of the atom bomb

---

* He was referring to the Chinese People's Republic, which formally proclaimed its foundation on the following day, the 1st October. It had been clear for many months before this proclamation that Chiang Kai-shek, in spite of mammoth American support, was losing the whole mainland of China, and that the Chinese People's Republic had "come to stay".

(which in fact was already at an end) would last until then. (A minority of the experts held that the "defence" of Western Europe was wholly impossible unless Germany was rearmed.)

It must be rare, even in military matters, for a plan worked out for five years to become obsolete in two days, and equally rare for the controllers involved to be apparently too paralysed to start again and work out something new and pertinent.

The same two Alsop brothers wrote in the same paper on the 3rd October:

> "The trance-like reception of the news that the Soviets had exploded an atomic bomb is a bitter commentary on the quality of American leadership. . . . The plain truth is that the United States and the Western world are totally unprepared for the new situation that has now arisen."

U.N. NOT AWAKE

The reaction of the General Assembly of the U.N., which was in session at the time, was equally modest. A few hours after the American and British announcements, and two days before an official announcement was made in Moscow on the subject, Mr. Vyshinsky on behalf of the Soviet Union (without mentioning the explosion in his country) tabled a proposal calling on the assembly to:

(1) Condemn the preparations for a new war which were being conducted in the United States, Britain and other countries.

(2) protest against further delay in completing treaties banning atomic weapons and establishing international atomic controls; and

(3) call for all nations to settle their disputes peacefully, and for the five Great Powers to conclude among themselves a pact for the strengthening of peace.

On the 26th September, after the Moscow statement had been printed in full in the morning newspapers of Europe and the U.S.A., Bevin spoke in the General Assembly in answer to Vyshinksy. He made exactly the same speech as he would have made if no announcement of a Soviet explosion had ever been given, rejected Vyshinsky's proposals, denounced the U.S.S.R. for not having accepted the Baruch Plan—the utter inacceptability of which, even before the U.S.S.R. had the atom bomb, is explained in Chapter 6—and by implication appealed to the country now to accept the Baruch Plan, which he described as "the only workable effective system yet devised".

The *News Chronicle* of the 29th September wrote of this and other exhibitions of mental paralysis on the part of the delegates to the Assembly:

"The news of Russia's possession of the atom bomb has set everybody asking: 'Where do we go from here?' But the world statesmen at Lake Success [the then meeting place of the United Nations] have so far shown a pathetic inability to come to grips morally and intellectually with the master problem.

"[Bevin's speech] was little more than a repetition of what he has been saying for the last two years.

"If we believe (as we must surely do) that control of the atom is the most pressing business facing us all, then the debate at Lake Success has been so far a confession of the bankruptcy of statesmanship. Has nobody any new ideas to contribute?

"There is a mocking unreality in the sight of the United Nations passing on to discuss other subjects . . . leaving the tremendous life-and-death issue of atomic control hanging (like the smoke over Hiroshima) in the air."

On the 28th September, 1949, forty Labour Members of Parliament signed a motion—couched in terms conciliatory to the Government—to the effect that the House

"affirms its belief that the Prime Minister should take the initiative in proposing a Conference between the heads of the States concerned, particularly the U.S.A. and the U.S.S.R., for resolving the existing deadlock and ending the race for the production of atomic and other weapons of mass destruction."

Such motions cannot be debated unless the Government chooses to give time for debate; and the Government gave no time for this.

It would have been pleasant to be able to say in extenuation on behalf of the British Government that most of the stupid, incompetent, and war-dangerous things that were done in connection with NATO and the new position relating to the atom bomb were American crimes rather than British; but our Government was an accomplice in everything the Americans did, and it was British people and British soil, not American, that were being turned into primary targets.

It is as well to note what an intelligent socialist commentator was able to see, and to write, in relation to the NATO project, as early as the 16th February, 1949. On that day, Palme Dutt wrote in his Notes of the Month for the March issue of *Labour Monthly*, as follows:

"The Atlantic Pact, if it is signed (and neither parliament nor people will have any say in the matter till the deed is done) will bind this country to an automatic commitment for war, not under the control and decision of its own government and parliament, nor by the authority of an international organ for collective security, but under the effective control and decision of a foreign Power which is openly pursuing the most ambitious operations for world expansion and eventual war. . . .

"The purpose of the . . . Pact is inescapable. It is to undermine the United Nations and to replace it by a sectional war bloc. Every attempt to utilise the United Nations as an instrument for war, as an instrument for imposing the domination of the Western Powers on the basis of an artificial majority of puppet states, and for aligning an anti-Soviet coalition, has foundered against the immovable rock of the principle of unanimity of the great Powers. The drafters of the Charter built well. The so-called 'veto' stands as the bulwark of peace. So long as the 'veto' stands—and no provision of the Charter permits its removal or revision—the United Nations can never be used as an instrument for a third world war.* No wonder the advocates of war rage against the 'veto' as the obstacle in their path. Having failed in all their attempts to circumvent it within the United Nations . . . they now openly turn to build their war coalition outside the United Nations and in defiance of the United Nations. That is the Atlantic Pact."

Dutt went on to quote a statement by Hector McNeil in the House of Commons (*Hansard*, Vol. 461, Col. 15) on the 7th February, answering a question put to Bevin, to the effect that it would never have been necessary to negotiate a North Atlantic Pact if the Soviet Union had not made "all attempts to organise collective security directly under the United Nations" impossible. The Government did not realise, apparently, what Dutt saw clearly enough, that by this (false) accusation they were betraying the real plan to substitute NATO for the U.N., and incidentally making further nonsense of their plea that NATO was not an infringement of the U.N. Charter, but a regional defence pact under and consistent with the Charter.

* This was written before the U.N. came very near to being so used in the Korean War. See Chapter 30.

THE MARSHALL PLAN

On the Marshall Plan, there is less to report in 1949 than in the previous year—see Chapter 15—for one has to observe no more than its development, not its establishment. The Plan in this year had no effect whatever in preventing crises; indeed the only countries in Europe that were prospering were those that stayed out of the Plan.

In matters on a smaller scale—but not unimportant—some of the story of the year can be told chronologically. As early as the 25th February, 1949, after Mr. Mayhew, the Under-Secretary for Foreign Affairs, had asserted at the United Nations that Britain had now achieved a balance in its foreign trade, the Foreign Relations Committee of the U.S. Senate—illustrating the jealousy with which it always watched any expenditure of U.S. money not directly and solely applied for internal purposes—decided to reopen public hearings on the question of Marshall Aid for Britain. Within twenty-four hours, Cripps as Chancellor of the Exchequer attempted to counter this by announcing that our recovery was not complete—this at any rate was tragically correct —and depended on the continuation of American aid.

In May, 1949, the Report of the U.S. Council of the International Chamber of Commerce, under the heading "The Spectre of 1953", stated that the Marshall-aided countries of Europe must expect a lower standard of living by 1953.

FINLETTER'S FETTERS

On the 16th June, 1949, Cripps spoke of Mr. Finletter, the Marshall watchdog over our economy, who held the strings I discussed in Chapter 15, in the following unctuous terms:

"Tom—he's the sort of man you just have to call by his Christian name the second time you see him—Tom has won his way deep into the hearts of everyone who has come into contact with him.

"He could have done anything with any of us, but I realised that he was not that sort of person—the more you live with him the less he asks of you. That is the perfect type of man with whom to co-operate, because it makes you want to offer him more."

The thought that Cripps wanted to offer the Americans even more by way of sacrifices of our housing and other social services must have seemed a little unattractive to the toad beneath the harrow; but Mr. Finletter did not seize the opportunity to call Cripps "Stafford", or to insist on taking less from us. On the contrary, he gave a jerk to the harrow by pointing out that "never before in history have the representatives of one Government [the U.S.A.] been given the duty of reviewing in detail and in public the acts of another country [Britain] in dealing with its own affairs"; and he went on to advise us, firstly, that the West must no longer be divided into two currency areas—in other words, the sterling area, our main financial safeguard, must go, leaving us still more defenceless against the dollar; secondly, that dollar investment in European countries and in the sterling area must increase, and governments must facilitate it—in other words, American finance must have an ever-increasing control over what we produce in competition with American industry, already alarmed by its own developing slump, over what steps we take to limit or abandon production, and over our conditions of work; thirdly, that "impediments to trade" must go—in other words, we were not to protect our industries or markets by protective tariffs or quotas against American dumping; and finally that all the forces of the West must be combined, in the political military and economic fields, for we could no longer afford the luxury of going our own industrial way—in other words, our politics and policies, our military expenditure, development, strategy, and even equipment, in effect our whole economy, were to be directed by a sort of partnership in which capitalist Washington and Wall Street had more than 50 per cent. of the votes.

Developing these ideas, Finletter spoke of a "solid Atlantic community", created by the Marshall Plan, working in concert with the Atlantic Pact and the military programme; note the use of the singular number; the programme was conceived as *one* programme for all the Marshall countries; and note, too, how he confirms what I have written above as to the positions and functions of NATO and the Marshall Plan.

It is difficult to know what "more" Cripps would then want to offer him.

AMERICAN SLUMP

By August, Britain and other European countries were beginning to suffer from the American slump. In the U.S., the official unemployment figures—always for various technical reasons substantially below the truth—had passed the 4,000,000 mark; surplus goods were piling up; the steel industry was working at only 85 per cent. of capacity and expecting to drop to 65 per cent. And in Britain there was some "redundancy", short-time working, and the closing of some factories for lack of orders; our dollar deficit for the second quarter of 1949 was at the rate of over £600 million per annum, and our gold and dollar reserve at the end of June was down to £406 million, £950 million below the minimum level set by the Government's Economic Survey for 1949. But on the 19th August the British delegate to the Council of the Organisation for European Economic Co-operation was resisting an American proposal to cut our Marshall Aid dollars for 1949-50, and Mr. Hoffman, the Marshall Administrator for Europe (mentioned in Chapter 15) was saying that British industry should treble its dollar exports—finding somehow three times as much buying capacity in an American market unable to sell its own goods in a slump. At the time, American imports were in fact decreasing rapidly, as were British exports; but American exports were scarcely decreasing. Thus, we were not capturing the American market, but on the contrary America was capturing something of ours. (Those who call this sort of performance the economics of Bedlam should consider whether they are not insulting the certified mentally ill.)

In September, the pound sterling was devalued; I will deal with that in Chapter 24.

EAST–WEST TRADE OPPOSED

By this time, there was—not unnaturally—a wider and more active demand in Britain for an increase in East-West trade in Europe. It was met, if you please, by an indignant campaign in the *Observer* and other circles, in which it was asserted that, whilst it was easy by such trade to reduce the dependence of Western Europe on American foodstuffs and thereby the dollar deficit, "the political results would be disastrous" and that we should not aim at "European independence by 1952", but at reliance for an indefinite time on the economic strength of the U.S.A. Thus was the British public, which had voted for socialism four years before, expected to play the roles of satellites and beggars in a capitalist soup-kitchen, rather than win independence by trading on equal terms with their socialist neighbours. And the Government obeyed.

GERMANY

The story of Germany—including Berlin—in 1949 is a long one. It included a settlement of the Berlin "blockade", the establishment of both the Federal Republic of Germany (the West) and the German Democratic Republic (the East), and some agreement relating to the Ruhr.

THE RUHR

Already in June, 1948, the Western Powers had reached in principle an international agreement for the Ruhr. This heavy industrial area, the core of Hitler's armament production, lay in the British Zone; but it was of exceptional importance for all the four Powers, who had agreed at Potsdam on the destruction of German armament production, the "de-cartelisation" of German industry (which had been very heavily centralised and "combined" under Hitler), and the limitation of the total volume of German industrial production. The British were moreover interested in staving off the menace of German export competition, based on ample steel supplies, low wages, and efficiency; but the Americans were interested in developing German industry with their own finance for their own profit, and as a longer-term objective in rebuilding the military power of Germany. The Soviet Union was interested in preventing such re-militarisation, and generally in the fulfilment of the Potsdam Agreement. And, finally, the three Western Powers were all hopeful of keeping the U.S.S.R. out of all say in the future of the Ruhr.

The agreement of June, 1948, accepted the principle of an international régime for the Ruhr, but on the vital question of the ownership and management of the Ruhr industries the negotiators could not reach agreement, and left the matter to be discussed at a new conference to be held in London on the 11th November, 1948. On the day before this conference, General Clay announced the passing of a new Law, vesting the ownership of the industries in German trustees until their final disposition was decided (decided that is, by the Government of the West German State which was to be, and was, established in 1949). This torpedoed the conference, put an end to hopes of the nationalisation of the Ruhr, and roused great indignation, particularly in France. It led, inevitably, to the Ruhr industries remaining in the hands of Krupp and others who had owned them—to their own great power and profit—under Hitler. The nominees for the board of trustees had all been Nazis, and were all steel "bosses" or financiers.

The London Conference went on, nevertheless and agreed on a Statute for the Ruhr.

On the 28th December, the Brussels Powers: Britain, U.S.A., France and the Benelux countries, agreed on an international authority for the Ruhr.

A NEW WEST GERMAN STATE

Meanwhile, the operation of setting up a strongly capitalist pro-American State and Government in West Germany, involving the temporary or indefinite splitting of Germany (without the agreement of the Soviet ally, and without any peace treaty with Germany), pursued its course. As early as September, 1948, a West German "Parliamentary Council" had been at work preparing a draft Constitution for a West German State; the draft was completed in March, 1949, amended to some extent at the request of the Western Powers, and approved by them. In May, a federal Statute for Western Germany was proclaimed by the military governors of the Western occupying powers, who described it as a combination of "German democratic tradition, representative government, and the 'rule of law'". Anyone reading the Constitution would think that all parties concerned were primarily interested in peace; it is outside the scope of this book to examine the militarist and neo-Nazi oligarchical finance dictatorship, called the "German Federal Republic", which has grown out of it, and claims to be the sole government of all Germany.

The actual date of the establishment of this Republic was the 20th September, 1949; this was followed, on the 2nd October, by a Note of the Soviet Government, protesting against the formation as:

"the culmination of the policy of splitting Germany which has been pursued by the Governments of the United States, Great Britain, and France during the past few years in violation of the Potsdam Agreement, under which these States, jointly with the Soviet Union, undertook to regard Germany as one single whole and assist its transformation into a democratic peace-loving state."

One month later, on the 7th October, the German Democratic Republic was established, covering what had until then been the Soviet Zone.

"BLOCKADE" OF BERLIN ENDED

The Berlin "blockade" and airlift, described in Chapter 15, went on all through the winter, for as already explained the Western Powers thought there were considerable advantages to be gained by prolonging it. It was, however, settled in the end. Negotiations to that end began (or rather, began again) on the 15th February, 1949, between Mr. Malik, Soviet delegate to the U.N. Security Council and Dr.

R

Jessup, "roving Ambassador" of the U.S.A., acting for the three Western Powers; and an agreement was reached on the 4th May, for—

(1) the removal on the 12th May of all restrictions imposed by the U.S.S.R. since the 1st March, 1948, on communications, transport and trade between Berlin and West Germany and between East and West Germany;

(2) the removal on the same 12th May of all restrictions imposed by the Western Powers since the same 1st March, 1948, on communications, transport and trade between Berlin and East Germany and between West and East Germany;

(3) a meeting on the 23rd May of the Council of Foreign Ministers in Paris, to consider questions relating to Germany and Berlin, including the question of currency in Berlin on which the Western Powers had established or purported to establish West German currency as the only legal tender in West Berlin.*

In the short interval between this agreement and the date—23rd May—fixed for the meeting of the Council of Foreign Ministers, the Western Powers hurried through various measures. On the 5th May, the Statute of the "Council of Europe" was signed in London, the proclamation of the Federal Republic (already mentioned) came on the 12th May; and on the 14th a statute for West Berlin was proclaimed.

COUNCIL OF FOREIGN MINISTERS

The Council of Foreign Ministers duly met on the appointed 23rd May, and sat until the 20th June. After a good deal of difficulty it arrived at an agreement (in addition to a limited arrangement about Austria) that:

(a) every effort should be made to establish trade and generally normal relations between East and West Berlin and East and West Germany;

(b) in the forthcoming fourth session of the General Assembly of U.N., the four Powers would exchange views regarding the date and other arrangements for the next session of the Council of Foreign Ministers on the German question.

REPARATIONS CLOSED

The last incident that needs to be reported in connection with Germany in 1949 is that, on the 6th December, it was announced in

* But the operation of the air-lift did not actually end until the 1st October, 1949.

Frankfurt that the Inter-Allied Reparations Agency had decided to make a final allocation among themselves of the equipment in Western Germany earmarked for reparations. In breach once again of the Potsdam Agreement, the U.S.S.R. was not consulted, and no allocation was reserved for that country.

It was about this time, too, that suggestions were being made that the Western Allies would re-arm Western Germany without previous consultation with the U.S.S.R. But, as I noted earlier in this chapter, both Germany and Britain were opposed to this move.

DEFENCE POLICY

I come now to the developments in "Defence" in the year under consideration.

As early as September 1948, some measures of further armament were announced, including another slow-down in demobilisation, a doubling of jet-fighter production, an increased quantity of fighting vehicles and munitions, and the acceleration of the naval programme. In line with that, but more sensational, was the announcement in November, 1948, of a 50 per cent. increase—from twelve months to eighteen—in the length of conscription service. This was duly passed into law, after a stronger challenge from Labour M.P.s than any other measure since 1945; forty Labour M.P.s voted against the Bill, thirty abstained "positively" by not going into the division lobbies, and seventy more managed to be absent.

As for defence costs, the Chancellor in his 1949 Budget estimated expenditure at £760 million, saying:

> "We obviously cannot look for any marked reduction for some years, unless there is a complete change in the international situation. Indeed, we may have to face some increase as a result of our co-operation in making the defences of Western Europe more effective and efficient."

It was later announced that expenditure would have to increase; but in the economic difficulties—more acute even than usual—that had to be dealt with in the following October (1949) (on which I will write in greater detail in Chapter 24) cuts in "defence" expenditure of £30 million (nearly 4 per cent.) were sought to be achieved by a substantial reduction in Headquarters Staff, a reduction in the training, maintenance and administrative establishments, and a slower intake of recruits;

the total strength, as a result, was expected to be less than 730,000 by April, 1950, instead of 750,000.

WORLD PEACE MOVEMENT

As part of what one might call the military history of the year, one has to reckon not only the direct "Defence" matters just recounted, and the developments in Germany, but also the "emergency" of the Soviet atom bomb, already discussed, and the birth of the new World Peace movement. After a "Conference of Intellectuals for Peace" had been held in Wroclaw in the summer of 1948, a large general Congress was held in Paris in April, 1949, with a "parallel" Congress in Prague of the many people from socialist countries who had been prevented from attending in Paris by the refusal of the French Government to grant them visas. These two Congresses made a great impression on world opinion, and led to the formation of the World Peace Council, now an important factor in world politics. The reaction of the Labour Party was to "ban" all its members from associating themselves with the movement.

CHINA: THE AMETHYST

Developments in China were also important in 1949. I have already mentioned the establishment of the Chinese People's Republic, and the sweeping victories over the Kuomintang forces under Chiang Kai-shek that led up to them, and to the final elimination of any trace of foreign rule, influence, or investment in China, and I must deal with the curious part played by Britain in the later stages of the civil war.

In April, 1949, the victorious advance of the Communist armies had reached the mighty Yangtse River, pursuing the forces of the Kuomintang (or "Nationalists"—it is curious how often the word Nationalist is used to describe those who sacrifice their own nation to its oppressors). Suddenly, on the 20th April, the British sloop *Amethyst* sailed up the river between the two armies, thus "intervening" in the most literal sense of the word in a civil war which was surely no affair of Britain, even if the U.S.A. was supporting, supplying and financing —with thousands of millions of dollars—the side that was going down to defeat. The intervention could only help, and could only be designed to help, the Kuomintang, whom the communists were attacking.

Such an intervention in a Chinese war could have been well understood a century, perhaps even fifty years, earlier; and there may well have been people in the Foreign Office and the Admiralty who had not observed the passage of time. But the operation was stupid and insolent beyond belief. The inevitable result—since the time had gone by when "foreigners" engaged in warfare could be expected to stop their advance for the benefit of an English warship navigating in the heart of their own country—was that the unfortunate crew of the *Amethyst* suffered losses of 17 killed and 20 wounded, and the ship was put out of action. On the following day, the communist crossing of the river was carried out, and another British ship, H.M.S. *Consort*, which also put itself in the line of fire, was holed by gunfire, with 15 killed and 17 wounded.

There arose in Britain a tremendous outburst of public indignation, fomented by the Government and the Press; this was perhaps easy to understand if the story was presented—as it was—without any true explanation of the background. And it was not until the 30th July that the *Amethyst* succeeded in sailing down the Yangtse. According to communist government reports, she sank a Chinese merchant ship, causing heavy loss of life, on her way down the river.

But two months later, in June, when a British ship near Shanghai was bombed by the Kuomintang forces, who warned British ships to leave communist ports, the mild reaction of the British Government reminded one of the days of the Spanish Civil War, when Franco's forces—"nationalist", of course—bombarded British ships with impunity.

The British Government behaved better than the Americans, and incurred their displeasure, by recognising the Chinese People's Republic *de jure* on the 6th January, 1950; but to this day it has not followed this up either by exchanging Ambassadors or by opposing the U.S. policy of excluding the Republic from its place in the U.N., on the childishly ridiculous theory that the Kuomintang is the real government of China.

GREECE

The problems of Greece continued to give trouble in 1949. The Greek Government went on with its practice of trying its citizens for alleged political offences, sentencing them to death, and—not always but far too often—waiting until just after the U.N. General Assembly had finished its sittings to execute them. In the first seven months of the year, 700 prisoners taken in the civil war that was still raging were executed; and it was not until the 31st October, 1949, that British troops were finally withdrawn.

PALESTINE

Palestine (which by 1949 should logically be dealt with as a matter of foreign affairs and not of colonial) also continued to cause trouble. In January, 1949, Britain was protesting that the Israeli forces had shot down five R.A.F. planes near the Egyptian border, and the Israeli Government complained to the Security Council of U.N. about alleged British "intervention". At the end of the month, Israel was recognised *de facto* by Britain; and both Israel and Transjordan (now the Kingdom of Jordan) were recognised *de jure* by the U.S.A. On the 11th March, 1949, there was a cease-fire agreement between Israel and Transjordan, followed on the 2nd April by an armistice agreement; and on the 23rd March an armistice agreement was signed between Israel and Lebanon.

TRADE WITH THE SOVIET UNION

I conclude this chapter with a short account of trade between Britain and the U.S.S.R., to which I last referred in Chapter 17. In the early summer of 1949, there was a good deal of pressure, in the light particularly of the slump in the U.S.A. and of our own growing economic and export difficulties, for increased trade with the East, and for the removal of restrictions on the export of various types of machinery which our government had imposed at the request—or instruction—of the U.S.A. This pressure came in particular from several of the larger trade unions, and as a result Bevin, on the 18th July, 1949 denounced the idea of *not* trading with the U.S.S.R. Negotiations began, and met with some success. In particular a contract was signed in August for the supply of 100,000 standards of hardwood (enough for the building of nearly 70,000 houses) by the U.S.S.R., and another in September for a million tons of grain. (This latter was signed shortly before the announcement of devaluation, which I have already mentioned.)

CHAPTER 22

Colonial Policy, 1948-9

THE Government's colonial policy in this year ran on the same lines as before, aiming in particular to increase the production of raw materials in the colonies to ease our economic problems—calling in the black world to redress the imbalance of the white. U.S. participation in colonial investment was expected, and indeed welcomed. The importance attached to this form of exploitation of colonial resources and labour to the profit of the British economy is illustrated by a leading article in *The Times* of the 1st March, 1949:

> "For this country the disturbances in the Asian area spell insecurity along the Commonwealth life-line. . . . They have put in peril the rich supplies of raw material which this country, France and the Netherlands desperately need. From the half million tons of rubber which Malaya produced yearly before the war and the 60,000 tons of tin, and from the Burmese rice, minerals and timber, this country gathered a large part of the sterling area's dollar surplus. . . .
>
> "Eastern Asia is a main base of Western Europe; and . . . further reverses in South-East could undermine the West European prosperity which is America's first defence."

In the Four-year Plan produced by the Government in the Spring of 1949, it was stated that "the plans described contemplate a large increase in the contribution of the colonies to European recovery". In this Plan, the requirements of the U.S. Government were given a special place; the Plan stated in paragraph 191:

> "Under Article V of the Economic Co-operation Agreement" (see Chapter 15) "the United Kingdom Government for their part intend in collaboration with the colonial governments to take all possible steps to increase the production of materials which the United States Government may require, and are already considering the measures to be taken for this purpose. They recognise the

importance which the United States Government attach to chrome and manganese."

The plan envisaged the following increases in output:

Ground-nuts: (East and West Africa), production in 1946, 385,000 tons; target for 1952-3, 880,000 tons;

Sugar: (West Indies) production in 1947, 740,000 tons; target for 1952-3, 1,400,000 tons;

Rubber: (Malaya) production in 1936, 400,000 tons, target for 1952-3, 830,000 tons;

Tin: (Malaya, and a little in Nigeria) production in 1947, 27,500 tons, target for 1952-3, 94,500;

Copper: (N. Rhodesia and a little in Cyprus) 1943 production 195,000 tons, target for 1952-3, 340,000 tons;

Cobalt: (British Guiana, Gold Coast and Malaya) target for 1952-3, 2 million tons (previous production not stated);

Lead: (Nigeria) production in 1947, 16,000 tons, target for 1952-3, 35,000 tons.

I must quote once again the comments of Mr. Milliband. At p. 304 of his *Parliamentary Socialism* he wrote:

"Nor, from the time Labour had taken office in 1945, had there been any serious disagreement over the management of the Colonial Empire. All that *Let us Face the Future* had said on the subject was that the Labour Party would seek to promote 'the planned progress of our Colonial Dependencies'. Both parties were agreed on the need for 'Colonial Development', and Labour Ministers made no bones about the fact that the purpose of such development was to help alleviate Britain's economic and financial difficulties. As John Strachey, then Minister of Food, put it in 1948 [20th January, 1948; *Hansard*, Vol. 446. Cols. 140-1], to obtain, 'by one means or another, by hook or by crook', the development of primary production of all sorts everywhere in and outside the Empire, was 'a life and death matter for the economy of this country'. . . . As Conservatives were delighted to point out, the Government's plans were quite in tune with traditional Conservative colonial policy, however different the colonial rhetoric of each party might be. . . .

"The Government's response to the anti-colonial challenge it faced was a mixture of minimal constitutional reforms on the one hand, and of repression on the other, including, as part of the defence of the 'free world' against Communism, the waging of a fierce colonial war in Malaya."

One of the fields in which colonial policy remained particularly unchanged was that of trade unionism. In virtually all colonies—under Tory and Labour governments alike—a show was made of encouraging trade unions, safeguarded by provisions as to registration which ensured that only docile organisations, preferably split up into many small bodies without any central organisation to which they could affiliate, should be allowed to operate; and "trade union advisers" were appointed from among right-wing trade unionists in Britain.

In Malaya, the Pan-Malayan Federation of Trade Unions, representing 91 per cent. of organised workers, was banned, and its former President sentenced to death for possessing a revolver; and in 1949 one hundred and eighty-six trade union officials were arrested. The practical effect of such handling of the unions is well illustrated by the statement of the Chairman of a Malayan Tin-mining Company at the Annual General Meeting of the Company on the 9th December, 1948:

"Trouble was experienced due to interference by the local branch of the Miners' Union, which dominated and intimidated our workers. Immediately the Union ceased to function, the labour force returned to work and operations have since been carried on without interruption. . . . It was only after the Emergency Orders came into operation and the majority of trade unions as such as a result ceased to function that the workers were allowed to settle down free from intimidation."

For a sample of the trade union advisers, I refer to the adviser appointed in Kenya—who once expressed great pleasure at meeting me there, and sought to enlist my help in persuading such clients of mine as Tom Mboya to be "more moderate". This gentleman said to a meeting of settlers:

"I cannot imagine anything more disastrous to the progress of a Colony than the development of trade unionism by uneducated people, and it will be my constant endeavour to prevent such a possibility."

His biggest task, he said, was trying to restrain a variety of people—quarry workers, painters and so forth—who wanted to be recognised as trade unions and given that status without the necessary qualities of leadership and organisation.

Asked if he had met one African capable of being a real trade union official in Kenya, he said: "Honestly, no!"

GROUND-NUTS

The outstanding features of the year were the developing fiasco in ground-nuts, the long-continuing war in Malaya, and disturbances in Nigeria. I will deal at once with ground-nuts (last mentioned in Chapter 16). The Plan had contemplated the clearance and planting of over 3,000,000 acres by 1952, harvests of 56,920 tons in 1948 and 227,676 tons in 1949, at a total cost of £24,000,000. By the end of March, 1949, it was known that the 1948 planted acreage was 7,500 and in 1949 was expected to be 49,620, about 1·6 per cent. of the total; the 1948 harvest was 1,566 tons of ground-nuts, somewhat over 3 per cent. of the estimate; and the 1948 harvest was expected to be 2,150 tons of nuts and 800 tons of sunflower seed (ton for ton, somewhat over 1 per cent.). But the amount already expended by March, 1949, was £23,000,000, about 95 per cent. of the total.

By October, 1949, it was decided to replace ground-nuts by sunflower seed over a large area; and in November, 1949, the first Annual Report was published. In this report, the setbacks were attributed to a drought in the 1948-9 season, and to the fact that when the scheme began there were no heavy tractor units of the right type available in Britain and only a few new machines could be acquired in the U.S.A. A search had been made for used vehicles and a number gathered from U.S. Army surplus stores in the Philippines and the Middle East, and the Valentine tank was adapted as a tractor.

A new railway line built in 1947, 16 miles long, from Mtwara to Kanga, had been partly washed away in the annual floods. Part of the crop was attacked by rosette disease. Facilities for repair and maintenance were inadequate.

It was pretty obvious by now that the scheme had been launched on too large a scale, with inadequate study; it was typical of the sort of enterprise of which a large private concern would be delighted to allow a government to carry the initial burdens.

The Government rejected all demands for an Enquiry into the scheme. Two members of the Board of the Overseas Food Corporation were dismissed; Strachey expressed his complete confidence in the reconstituted Board, and undertook to spend another £25,000,000, and to have 600,000 acres to show for it (one-fifth of the contemplated acreage for twice the contemplated cost). But, as we shall see in Chapter 32, Strachey's successor as Minister of Food, Maurice Webb, had to write the scheme off wholly.

MALAYA

In Malaya, where living standards had fallen far below 1939, and the Report of a Joint Wages Commission in July, 1947,—accepted as correct by a Government Report of November, 1948—had attributed the unrest to "disappointment and disillusion, shortages of supplies, lack of houses and amenities, high prices and low wages, and the ferment of new political ideas", the British Government continued to carry on a civil war, blaming "Communism" for all the unrest.

A review of the war was published in *World News* in July, 1949. At the start, 50,000 men, consisting of British troops, Gurkhas, special police, and armed civilian units were engaged; these were later reinforced by Guards sent out from Britain, troops from Hong Kong, and Gurkhas, the total engaged rising to 70,000. Attacks were made by land, sea and air, and whole villages were destroyed.

In the autumn of 1948, the British Commander-in-Chief estimated that the war might last another fifteen months; bombing raids on villages were intensified, "head-hunters" were brought in from Borneo, and a large offensive was launched. From June, 1948, to May, 1949, the British combined forces' casualties were said to be 614 killed, but 9,265 civilians had been imprisoned or deported. In August, 1949, the monthly remittances from our hard-pressed financial resources were £4,000,000 as payment for the forces and £5,000,000 to the Malayan Government for "police operations", the total cost of the war thus being not less than £100,000,000 a year. And at the end of 1949 it was announced that civilian volunteer forces were to be mobilised for "intensified operations" against the "rebels".

So the war went on and on, for the Government was planning to help British economy, and in particular our dollar position, by raising rubber output from 435,000 tons in 1946 to 830,000 tons in 1952, and tin from 27,500 tons in 1946 to 94,500 in 1950.

NIGERIA POLICE SHOOTINGS

Nigeria, which had not for some time been prominent in the news, achieved unhappy distinction in 1949, with the shooting dead by the police on the 18th November, during a strike at the government-owned colliery at Enugu, of 21 miners and the wounding of 51 others, (those were the official figures; the workers asserted that there were sixty dead, and eighty taken to hospital with injuries). No policeman was killed or injured.

The incident aroused great indignation among Africans, and widespread disturbances followed at various other places, with large demonstrations, stoning of the police, police baton-charges, tear-gas, and shootings. Government property was attacked, and European shops were looted. A state of emergency was declared on the 27th November, and a Commission of Enquiry appointed, which reported in June, 1950. According to this Report, the trouble had developed as follows:

Throughout 1948-9 the average daily wage of hewers was 6s. or above, going up as far as 6s. 2d. or 6s. 6d. in most months; tubmen averaged 4s. 1d. per day. The "figures . . . of incapacity arising from accidents and diseases . . . appeared to be extremely high".

In July 1949 the Secretary of the Colliery Workers' Union put forward claims at a meeting of the Colliery Whitley Council. On most of the demands the two sides failed to reach agreement, but some concessions were granted to certain grades other than hewers. When it became known that only a few workers would actually benefit there was considerable disappointment. The Commission blamed the Secretary of the Colliery Workers' Union, described by them as a dishonest and worthless person, for not making the position clear to the hewers.

On the 8th November, the hewers started a "go-slow". On the 10th November, notice of summary dismissal of 50 hewers was posted up and this was followed by similar notices on the following days; "this action can only be described as a major blunder", said the Report.

On the 13th November, the Chief Commissioner called a meeting to discuss the possibility that the go-slow strike might develop into a stay-in strike. On the 17th, he decided to remove explosives from the mines on the grounds that these might fall into the hands of agitators. The Commission stated: "We consider that the Chief Commissioner . . . erred in diagnosing and treating the miners' dispute as a political agitation rather than—what in our opinion it was—an industrial dispute. If he had treated this as an industrial dispute . . . he would have been aware . . . that the reason why the miners objected to the removal of the explosives was because they feared that if once the explosives were removed nothing stood in the way of the management closing the mine and thus effecting a 'lock-out'."

On the 18th November, two parties of armed police went to remove the explosives. About 1,500 miners were standing about and Superintendent Philip ordered the police to cross a footbridge and line up on a hill; he stated that the attitude of the miners was becoming more and more menacing, and while the police were moving across the bridge he gave the order to open fire.

The Report went on: "Some evidence was given that the mob was armed . . . we are forced to the conclusion that the only weapons possessed by the miners were sticks, which they always carry for walking on that sloping ground, and the implements of mining, such as pick handles and picks. . . . What is significant is . . . that the crowd was assembled there for some hours and yet there appears to have been no attempt whatever to use any force against the police. . . . If the crowd were bent on using force against the police nothing could have saved these policemen from grave injury, whereas in fact they were not injured at all. . . . Mr. Philip has failed to satisfy us that he could not have removed those 35 or so men to the other side of the bridge, without resorting to the extreme measures which he took. . . ."

Following on all this the Commission made the mild stricture that Mr. Philip "made an error of judgment".

The Commission condemned the demonstrations which followed the Enugu shooting, as being ones to further "purely political ends", and considered that the people were inflamed by "mischievous speeches"; but it also considered that the police action was entirely unjustified.

Following the findings of the Commission the Governor of Nigeria supported the Chief Commissioner, saying that: "My own view is that the Chief Commissioner regarded and treated the dispute as an industrial dispute until disorder occurred and a threat to public security developed." However, Mr. Philip, the Chief Superintendent of Police responsible for the shooting, went on leave and did not return.

The facts as presented in the Report of Enquiry were bad enough; but they were put in a worse light by the fact that before the Report was published, M.P.s had had difficulty in getting the Government to make any admissions; e.g. Mr. Creech Jones, the Colonial Secretary, replying to Questions in the House of Commons on the 28th November, 1949, said (*Hansard*, Vol. 470, Col. 787) that to the best of his knowledge there had been no negotiations with regard to wages, no trade dispute had been declared, and this was not a normal breakdown in labour relations as understood in this country.

Conditions in general in Nigeria were disclosed to some extent in the Fifth Report of the Select Committee on Estimates 1947-8 on Colonial Development, which ran:

"In Nigeria as a whole there is one doctor for every 133,000 people, and one hospital bed for every 3,700 compared with one doctor for every 1,200 people and one hospital bed for every 250 people in the U.K. There are 10 dentists. Over 20 million people are living on an agricultural subsistence of a very low order, and malnutrition and disease are widespread. Health statistics for the country are not available. The infant mortality rate in Lagos is stated to be 110 as compared with 40 to 50 in European countries, and from post mortem examinations together with notifications from private practice it has been estimated that tuberculosis accounts for 9 to 10 per cent. of all deaths. There are no sanatoria in the country; tuberculosis is treated in ordinary hospitals. There are only three asylums; in every prison a ward is set aside for those suffering from mental disorders. Long waiting lists exist at all the hospitals, and in some it is necessary to put patients on the floor. Out of about 8 million children under the age of sixteen, 660,000 are receiving primary education in various forms. There are about 10,000 children in secondary schools; technical education is totally inadequate."

One can get a clear idea of the conditions under which the Enugu coal miners existed—living mostly in abominable shacks at a rent of 25s. to 30s. per month—from the report on *Labour Conditions in West Africa* written in 1940 by an eminent government servant, Major Orde Browne. He stated that the diet of the average worker was such that "he shows clear signs of deficiency as soon as he accepts employment involving strenuous exertion. Consequently, there is a marked degree of inefficiency obviously due to lack of stamina; in the case of exacting tasks, such as coal hewing, men will profess themselves unable to work every day, so that employment may only amount to 15 or 16 days a month."

That was nine years before; but by 1949 it was estimated that to secure even that diet, pay rent, and buy the scantiest clothing, a man would need to earn £7 a month. The average earnings of underground workers were given by the Nigerian Department of Labour in 1948 at 3s. 4d. per day. The arithmetic is simple enough. On the basis of 26 working days a month, at 3s. 4d. a day the average worker would get £4 6s. 8d. towards the £7 needed (and the less than average worker would get less); if he were only able to work for 16 days he would get £2 12s. 8d. If the full demand for 5s. 10d. a day had been met in cash instead of by bullets, the figure would have been £7 7s. for 26 days and £4 8s. for 16 days.

Other colonies were presenting difficulties at this period, which were being countered by the British Government on orthodox conservative lines.

CHAPTER 23

Nationalisation and Nationalised Industries, 1949

As I have mentioned, the only measure of further nationalisation undertaken in 1949—and the only specific measure outstanding from the 1945 election programme—was that of iron and steel.

DIFFICULTIES WITH IRON AND STEEL

There were a good many differences between this nationalisation and those carried through earlier. To begin with, there was very real and determined opposition from the owners, reflected in the readiness of the House of Lords at the least to oppose many of the provisions of any Bill that might be brought forward, if not to reject it outright. Further, there was at all stages some opposition to it in the Cabinet; according to Dalton's *High Tide and After*, p. 136, Morrison had even sought to have it excluded from the election programme in 1945. In addition, there was some fear that the Americans might threaten to refuse Marshall Aid if the Government proceeded with so "socialistic" a measure. All these considerations were among the reasons why the Bill was not brought forward until 1948-9.

The opposition of the owners, and of the Tory party, was natural enough. Iron and steel was not as "sick" an industry as, say, coal; nor did it have the characteristic, to be found both in coal and transport, of being an essential service to other industries, not easily capable of itself producing rich returns, and imperatively needing heavy further investment. It was on the contrary a highly profitable stronghold of monopoly, with many ramifications. There was also the feature, as Anthony Eden described it in the Commons debates, that "there is no point after this at which the advance towards the extinction of private capital in British industry could be halted".

The reality of the House of Lords opposition is well explained by Brady, in *Crisis in Britain*, p. 188:

"The debates in the House of Lords over the Gas Bill showed a determination to put a stop to any further nationalisation at all costs, and so the Labour Government was forewarned that its plans to nationalise steel, against which even more determined opposition was certain, were impossible of fulfilment unless the power of the House of Lords to delay legislation was curbed. Hence it came about that the question of what to do about the House of Lords began by the middle of 1948 to take precedence over all other issues."

It was mainly as a result of these difficulties that the Parliament Bill was introduced in 1947 and finally passed in November, 1949, as I have already related. (In the end, as we shall see, the Iron and Steel Bill was passed before the Parliament Act Amendment Bill.)

The problem of possible American interference was well described by Brady, at p. 189 of his book just mentioned:

"Sir Stafford Cripps has knowingly made himself responsible for the fixed belief that without Marshall Plan aid Britain could not solve the problem of the import-export gap, and that this solution holds the key to Britain's post-war revival—not to mention the success or failure of the Labour Government's whole economic and social programme. If, then, American aid is indispensable, and if this aid—proffered by an American Congress dominated by American business interests, and to be administered along business lines by an American business man, Paul G. Hoffman—can be received only on American conditions, what is to be said about American disapproval of the nationalisation of steel, advertised as it was as a major step on the road to the socialist society which American business abhors?

"At a critical point in the steel discussions in Britain the news came that, when questioned about 'his attitude towards British national-isation policies', Hoffman had said 'that if the British Government asked for E.C.A. shipments to modernise the steel industry and then announced that the industry would be nationalised, the shipments would probably be denied' (Daily Telegraph, 14th May, 1948).

"Though this opinion was delivered, as it was later explained, quite obviously to quieten a Congress which was out of sympathy with the socialist programme of the British Labour Government, and though it did not specifically say that aid to Britain would not be given because of its nationalisation measures, nevertheless the damage had been done. The statement was received in London by government spokesmen with stunned silence.

"While, as subsequent events established, it was the official

s

position of both British and American governments that the Marshall Plan was to involve no interference in the internal affairs of recipient countries, yet the Italian elections showed clearly the American intention not to give aid where it suspected the political intentions of the dominant party. The Opposition was gleeful. . . .

"It is in the face of facts and events such as these . . . that the Labour Government toyed for three years with its programme for national-isation of the iron and steel industry, and finally brought in a measure which represents a compromise that it evidently thought would extricate it from the most trying of its numerous postwar dilemmas."

I need only note on these passages, firstly, that I have explained the reality of the story about "no Marshall interference in internal affairs" in Chapter 15, and secondly that in the Italian elections the American interference to avoid any Communist success had been open, shameless, and on a very large scale.

The case in favour of nationalising iron and steel, apart from any argument based on socialist principles, was a strong one. Steel was basic to our economy; almost every industry depended on an adequate supply of good quality steel at a reasonable price. It was moreover a restrictive private monopoly; half the productive capacity was in the hands of six concerns, who were linked to one another by interlocking directorships; and the same directors controlled most of the smaller concerns. All the concerns were further associated in monopolistic trade associations catering for different sections of the industry.

On the top of the whole structure was the British Iron and Steel Federation, which Brady described as "a supercartel of the type which not even the Germans succeeded in effecting for any major industry until the rise of the Nazis". The Federation maintained high prices through the exercise of cartel controls; its general principle was to fix prices enabling the least efficient of its members to make a profit, leaving all the more efficient to make vast profits. Competition was eliminated, so far as foreign producers were concerned, by an agree-ment with the International Steel Cartel, and at home by preventing new concerns from entering the industry. Such a "set up" provided little incentive to eliminate obsolete plant or methods, and the industry was in truth very backward.

IRON AND STEEL NATIONALISATION PROPOSALS

The Bill to nationalise the industry, brought in in October, 1948, proposed to take over the industry from the stage of iron ore production to that of semi-finished products. All companies with an annual production of over 50,000 tons of ore, or 20,000 tons of pig iron, ingot steel, or hot-rolled products, were to be taken; those with less production but not less than 5,000 tons would remain un-nationalised but would work under licence from the Ministry of Supply, controlling their output and maximum price. Producers below 5,000 tons were left wholly free.

The effect was to "catch" 107 concerns with a total capital of £195 millions, producing 97·5 per cent. of iron-ore production, 97·6 per cent. of pig iron, 99·6 per cent. of carbon steel ingots, 93·7 per cent. of alloy steel ingots, 93·1 per cent. of re-rolling, 94·1 per cent. of sheet steel, 97·3 per cent. of steel plate, and 88 per cent. of tinplate. As the industry was highly integrated "vertically", large sections of finished steel and heavy engineering were also brought in.

But a good deal was still left free; where the steel-producing portions of a concern were financially and technically divisible from the other portions, the latter were severed and remained free; for example, the English Steel Corportion was taken, but its "parents" Vickers Ltd. and Cammell Laird & Company Ltd., remained out; and Thomas Firth and John Brown Ltd., were taken, but not their owners, John Brown Ltd.

In the matter of ownership and control, the Government seemed anxious to make its omelet in such a way that the eggs *could* be put back in the shells—which the Tories later did!—for the method adopted was to transfer the entire stock ownership of the concerns taken to a new government corporation called the Iron and Steel Corporation of Great Britain, with a board of a Chairman and not less than four nor more than ten other members, who were to "have had wide experience of, and shown capacity in, the production of iron and steel; industrial, commercial or financial matters; administration; or the organisation of workers". The concerns taken were to retain their identities and names. George Strauss, the Minister of Supply, said in the debates that it was proposed "to keep intact the identity of the individual concerns. Their personnel and internal organisations, and such *esprit de corps* as they had achieved, will be unaffected. Indeed, on the morning after vesting day, the only difference for them will be that the ownership of the securities has changed hands. The companies will continue to win ore, produce iron and steel and sell their products as before." They were to carry on under the existing directors and managements. The Corporation had power to make changes in the

Boards of Directors, but no wholesale changes appeared to be contemplated. The Government submitted no plan for the re-organisation of the industry at all.

The Corporation was to pay the shareholders the market prices of their shares as they stood in the period the 1st–25th October, 1948, or on certain dates in the first half of 1945, whichever was the higher.

Dividends from the date of the introduction of the Act to the take-over date were to be limited to the 1947–8 level or to 4 per cent. whichever was higher. The interest to be paid on Corporation stock was to be determined by the general level of government securities at the time of acquisition.

The shares in iron and steel companies had risen sharply as soon as the Bill had been presented.

One result of the Bill having been brought in as late as the end of 1948 was that "timing" became difficult. It was necessary not only to pass the Bill before the General Election, of the outcome of which no one felt any certainty, but also if possible to fix the "vesting date"— i.e. the date at which the Act and the nationalisation would actually become effective—so as not to give the Tories too much of a chance of repealing the Act before it ever operated. And, if it proved necessary to use the amended Parliament Act to get the Bill through, that Act itself would have to be passed.

This timing worked out as follows. In October, 1949, the Commons were faced with some sixty amendments made by the Lords, the most important of which was one to postpone the vesting date from the Government's proposal of May, 1950, (i.e. within the five years of the possible life of the Parliament), to a date after those five years. If they did not accept the amendments, the Bill would lapse at the end of the 1948–9 session. If they sought to avoid this by applying the amended Parliament Act which in fact became law on the 16th December, 1949, they would have to hold a further session of Parliament in 1950, making it impossible to hold the General Election before April, and impracticable to hold it before May or June because of the need to pass the Budget.

The final result was that the Government amended the Bill to provide that the Corporation should not come into existence until October, 1950, and that the vesting date should not be earlier than January, 1951; in the end it was the 15th February, 1951. The Bill received the Royal Assent on the 24th November, 1949.

I must now turn to the Reports of the two major nationalised industries, Coal and Transport.

COAL

The Coal Board Report for 1948 was published in June 1949. It showed a *surplus* for 1948 of £1·7 million compared with the deficit of £23¼ million the previous year. The deficit carried forward, therefore, was £21·8 million.

There was a large profit on the operation of the collieries and ancillary businesses (17½ million as against a loss of over £6 million in 1947) but £15·6 million of this went in compensation charges of various kinds, ("interim income" to former mine-owners; interest to royalty owners, compensation for loss of office to former directors, etc.). Profitable collieries had made a profit of £41·9 millions, whilst others made losses amounting to £25·7 millions. Thirty-seven unprofitable collieries had been closed during the year. Production was 5½ per cent. above 1947. As the report said: "There has not often been a greater increase from one year to another." Part of the increase was due to increased manpower, but the main cause was the greater output per man.

Manpower increased only by 7,763, less than one-third of the increase in 1947, and at the end of the year was 24,000 behind the Government target. But for 8,700 foreign recruits, the industry would not even have replaced the men who left.

Output per manshift at the end of 1948 was about 4 per cent. higher than a year before, but wages did not increase during the year. Since the last wage increase in November 1947 the official cost of living index had risen by 8 per cent.

Mechanisation and modernisation had not advanced greatly during the year: £5·2 million had been spent on major reconstruction schemes but these had been centred on the highly productive regions rather than on the more backward coalfields.

The Report pointed out the extreme difficulty of formulating any plan under the existing economic system. The plan had to depend on "the general state of trade", and forecasts of demand were "fraught with difficulty and uncertainty, overseas demand particularly so".

TRANSPORT

The British Transport Commission report for 1948 was published in September, 1949. It showed a deficit for the year—its first year of work —of £4·7 million.

The British Transport Commission Report for the first year's working showed a deficit of £4·7 million.

The total net traffic receipts after paying running expenses were £36,360,000, to which was added income from rents and other sources, making a total of £45·2 million.

Against this had to be set interest on transport stock and other interest of £42·3 million, administrative expenses of £705,812 and almost £4 million to the Freight Rebates Fund. (In 1929, when the railways were relieved of part of their rates, they had been instructed to use the saving to give rebates on certain freight charges, e.g. coal, coke, milk and livestock.)

This left a net loss of £1·7 million, raised to £4·7 million by a number of miscellaneous payments, of which the most important was nearly £2½ million for redemption of British Transport stock. Of the £42·3 total interest payments, £33·1 was interest on Transport Stock.

The major reorganisation work had taken place on the railways. A good deal of over-age stock was broken up during the year, including 769 locomotives, and the Railway Executive planned to break up in the following three years 85,000 mineral wagons, "practically all former privately owned vehicles, advanced in age and expensive to maintain and difficult to traffic".

CHAPTER 24

Economic Policy, 1948-9

THE year's economy followed the pattern of misfortune and crisis set in the previous year or two, sharpened by an American slump which led to the devaluation of the pound in September, 1949.

The first important event of the period was the publication in October, 1948, of the White Paper on European Co-operation and the share of Britain in the European Recovery Plan (Cmd. 7,545). "Recovery for the U.K.", it announced, "means the recovery of the balance of payments at a reasonable level and the restoration of external financial strength. This is the central objective of all the United Kingdom's economic policies"; and it enunciated the principle that through "Mutual Aid" and "Self-help" the countries in the European Recovery Programme should do everything possible to satisfy one another's needs before making claims on Marshall Aid for their net deficiencies. (The total of Marshall Aid authorised by Congress was $4,875 million, of which Britain expected to get $1,263 millions under the European Recovery Programme.) Under the Intra-European Payments Scheme certain countries were given the right to draw on Britain in sterling, while Britain was given the right to draw on Belgian francs; this amounted to an agreement to net drawings on the U.K. of the sterling equivalent of $282 millions. The Organisation for European Co-operation estimated the net deficit with the sterling area of all other European Recovery Programme countries at $491 millions. The difference between this and the net drawing rights of $282 millions was to be financed by drawings against the sterling balance of "E.R.P." countries which hitherto had not been available for purchases of sterling area goods. The sterling area was therefore to export goods to E.R.P. countries other than Britain, which would be paid for by writing off $282 million from Britain's E.R.P. dollar receipts and by writing down sterling balances to the equivalent of $209 millions. Thus there would be $491 millions (£122¾ millions) worth of "unrequited exports", i.e. exports of goods for which no goods would be received in return by Britain.

ANGLO–AMERICAN PRODUCTIVITY COUNCIL

The Anglo-American Productivity Council, "an autonomous body," as Cripps explained, "set up by employers and trade unionists in British and American industry (it was not a government committee and the Government had no responsibility for its composition or terms of reference)", held its first meeting on the 25th October, 1948. In its first report, in which it emphasised that the outstanding cause of the difference in productivity between the U.S.A. and Britain was the higher degree of mechanisation which the former had been able to achieve, it wrote:

> "Every possible measure should be taken both by industrial management and by the Government not merely to maintain the present level of mechanisation but also to increase the power and modern tools available to British workers. Much can be done without waiting for complete re-equipment."

The report, however, contained no specific suggestions beyond "clear thinking, continued hard work and competent leadership of management and labour".

BRIEF OPTIMISM

In the early part of a year which was destined to end in economic near-disaster, some optimism was displayed for a time. In November, 1948, it was announced that the trade returns for October showed rising exports and a decrease in the adverse balance of trade; that steel output in October had run at a record rate;* that more newsprint would be available for newspapers in 1949; and that various controls were to be relaxed.

A FOUR–YEAR PLAN

Then, still optimistically, on the 30th December, 1948, the "Four-year Plan", i.e. a provisional economic programme for the ensuing four years, submitted to the Organisation for European Economic Co-operation, was published as a White Paper.

Let us first see what was actually being "planned", or rather hopefully foreseen.

Agricultural production was to be increased so as to give a 30 per cent. rise in home consumption and to save 4 million tons of imports.

* The steel industry, it was suspected, was driving its machinery as hard as it could in order to "window-dress" itself with good returns for the coming battle for compensation.

Coal exports were to rise to 40 million (metric) tons in four years, involving a 5 per cent. increase in productivity, a substantial rise in production, and an investment of £600 million. Oil production was to be doubled by creating a large refining industry (under the control of the private oil giants) in the United Kingdom, capable of treating 20 million tons of crude oil per annum (as compared with 2½ million in 1947). Steel production was to rise to 17 million tons by 1953. In engineering, production was to be 70 per cent. above 1938, and to provide 40 per cent. of our total exports. Textile exports were to earn more than three times as much as in 1938. And shipping was to earn $360 million in 1952-3.

Industrial production as a whole was to be increased to 40 per cent. above pre-war, 25 per cent. above 1947; and exports were to be 50 per cent. above pre-war, 30 per cent. above 1947.

"Invisible income"—interest and profits on overseas capital investments, and returns from shipping and other services rendered to overseas countries—was to rise to £250 million.

Great increases were equally foreseen in colonial production, as I have already set out in Chapter 22.

Investment was to be maintained at the rate of 20 per cent.(!) of the national income—£2,000 million in 1948; the national income was to rise by 12 per cent. with a corresponding increase in investment.

In spite of all the need for increases in production, needed and contemplated—dependent of course on markets—no development of East-West trade was foreseen; "the general scale of trade with Eastern Europe envisaged in these estimates is appreciably less than that ruling before the war". This stubborn attitude, due partly to anti-Soviet obsessions and partly to fear of incurring American displeasure, has to be seen in the light of the statement of the United Nations Commission for Europe that that continent *could not recover* unless there was a development of East-West trade very much greater than before the war.

On the other hand, what was to be done for the people at home in Britain was much more meagre. Housebuilding, still desperately short, was to be fixed at about 200,000 houses a year, compared with the average of 358,611 a year in 1935-9. There was to be little or no increase in the very low rate of construction of schools, hospitals, and other social buildings, "new general hospitals, urgently required in a number of districts, must . . . wait until towards the end of the period".

Home consumption per head was promised to increase by 1953, not only beyond the somewhat meagre standards of 1947, but in many respects beyond pre-war levels. Clothing and household goods were to be available somewhat above the pre-war level; and consumption of food as a whole was to approach that level. Wage increases were to depend on increased production.

There was no attempt in the Plan to estimate the increase in the overall standard of living; the highest unofficial estimate gave an overall increase of 5 per cent. on the basis of an increase of 15 per cent. in the output per head.

Perhaps the most extraordinary feature of the Plan was that no allowance was made for government overseas expenditure, particularly military expenditure, in the figures relating to the balance of payment. This military expenditure had amounted in the three years 1946-8 to £745 millions, 57 per cent. of the balance of payments deficit of those years. The Plan, it seemed, failed to count the cost of the Cold War whilst plainly contemplating its continuance.

INCREASED PRODUCTION: BUT HOW?

How was all this increase in production and export to be achieved? Mainly, it seemed, by hard work—increased production per head—and by finding, of course, buyers for our products. In this, there was apparently infinite faith in the ability of the U.S. and Canada to sustain a high capacity to purchase goods, coupled with a readiness to admit imports. The Plan assumed, for example, that our total exports to North America would rise to £167 million in 1952, as compared with £92·8 million in 1947, (and £44 million in 1938). As J. R. Campbell wrote in *Labour Monthly* for January, 1949, p. 44:

"This . . . remarkable increase . . . is based on three improbabilities: (1) . . . No U.S. crisis on the scale of 1929; (2) . . . not even a substantial recession of business activity; . . . (3) U.S. industry will not be able to saturate the domestic market with U.S. goods. Whatever their views of the first probability, no U.S. business man would bet even a counterfeit dime on the last two. Note that the U.S. is not only expected to open its markets to an even greater quantity of British goods, but it is also expected to absorb an even greater quantity of colonial goods and also spend a lot more on holidays in Britain."

As we shall see, probability No. 2, an American recession, was to be a reality by the middle of 1949.

PLANNING FOR A CAPITALIST FUTURE

The Plan is extremely interesting from several points of view; not the least is that of the assumptions on which it is plainly based. These include the continuance of the Cold War and of the colonial system, and the absence of any further nationalisation of major industries for at least the period of the Plan.

All these assumptions constitute basic defects of the Plan, from the socialist point of view, but there was another defect which really deprives the Plan of any right to be called a Plan at all. This rests on that curious belittling of democracy common to both Toryism and to right-wing Labour,* under which every bold measure to relieve or improve any difficult situation is described as "undemocratic" because it interferes unduly with "the freedom of the individual". For the Tories this is natural enough, for to them the freedom of the individual connotes the sacred right of capitalists to run the capitalist system for their own profit at the cost of the real freedom of the masses of individuals whom they exploit. For right-wing Labour, the matter is not quite so simple; but the result is the same, since so long as they are attempting to run a mixed economy on the basis of co-operation with powerful capitalist concerns their power to interfere by real planning is limited by their need to secure this co-operation and their reluctance to face a show-down by seeking to eliminate or coerce capitalist concerns. Accordingly, one should not be surprised to find that the Plan is really not a plan. It is stated in the Foreword not merely that:

"Any programme of economic planning must be . . . sufficiently flexible to meet unpredictable and rapidly changing events. It is not possible to establish firm and definite plans which would bind the United Kingdom economy to a pre-determined course of action so far ahead as 1952-3 or even eighteen months hence.

"Neither programme" (i.e. short 1949-50 or long 1949-53) "is intended as a detailed forecast of what will actually happen."

but also:

"No other method of programming is possible in a democratic community. For, quite apart from the unpredictable impact of external events, policies can be fulfilled only if they gain the voluntary co-operation of people as groups and individuals. The means of control which can effectively be used within a democracy are limited."

* Already discussed in Chapter 12.

The authors of the Plan sought to explain—or to cover up—their subjection to capitalism and their inability to make a genuine fight for socialism by such phrases as:

"It must never be overlooked that for a democracy economic planning is a means to an end and not an end in itself."

"Even in purely domestic matters the means of control that can be used within a democracy are limited."

"Powers of prohibition and compulsion, though they must be used to set limits to economic freedom, must not be allowed, except in very special circumstances, to infringe the freedom of the individual."

J. R. Campbell, at pp. 45-6 of the article from which I quoted above, was right to observe that "the late Ramsay MacDonald in his most verbose mood never produced anything so platitudinous"; and that "such statements as they stand are almost meaningless; but substitute 'capitalism' for 'democracy' and 'capitalist' for 'individual' and the whole thing becomes clear."

As we shall see, the developments of the year made nonsense of this plan; but optimism continued, at any rate on the surface. In January, 1949, it was announced that industrial production in October, 1948, had been higher than in any previous month, and that iron and steel production for 1948 showed a record of 14,877,000 tons, 2,000,000 more than in 1947, although coal production was more than 2,500,000 tons below its target. And a good many rationing controls were removed on the 31st January. On the 20th January it was announced in the House of Commons that the trade deficit for 1948 had been £432 million (a decrease of £165 million) and was reduced by "invisibles" to perhaps less than £225 million. The serious and obstinate dollar deficit, however, although better than 1947, was still over £400 million.

In March, 1949, it was announced that the steel output for February was again a record; on the 14th March the rationing of clothes and textiles was completely abolished. Many trade controls, too, were dropped, but on the 17th March the meat ration was reduced to 10d. per head per week.

ECONOMIC SURVEY FOR 1949

In the same month of March, the Economic Survey for 1949 was published. It showed that the national income, in terms of money, had risen by 11 per cent. in 1947-8; 7 per cent. of the rise was accounted for by increased prices, so that the "real" rise was 4 per cent. The wages bill had risen by 12½ per cent., salaries by 6 per cent, company profits by 17 per cent., farmers' incomes by 22 per cent., and the profits of individuals and partnerships by 10 per cent. compared with 1938, wages were up by 129 per cent., salaries 67 per cent., company profits 202 per cent and rents only 9 per cent. Capital investment had risen from £2,040 million in 1947 to £2,353 million in 1948; the total government expenditure "plus surplus" was £3,689 million; defence in 1948-9 was costing about £752 million; and taxation was £39 per head in direct and £30 in indirect.

1949 BUDGET

The Budget came, as usual, in April It was preceded by a clamour from bankers and economists for reductions in expenditure, particularly on education, health services, national assistance, and food subsidies, which mean less to bankers and economists than to most of us.

It ran true to right-wing Labour policy. Defence was estimated to cost £753 million; Cripps said:

"We obviously cannot look for any marked reduction for some years, unless there is a complete change in the international situation. Indeed we may have to face some increase as a result of our co-operation in making the defences of Western Europe more effective and efficient."

Foreseeing an "inevitable increase" over the next five to ten years in the cost of education, health, insurance and national assistance, costing in 1949-50 £763 million, he said that there was "a very good argument for imposing some special charge or tax in connection with the Health Services, both to help finance them and to bring home to people generally the simple fact that they have got to be paid for out of taxation". No Tory Chancellor could have put it better.

Cripps then dealt with food subsidies, something of infinite public value, the loss of which would inevitably involve great wage claims to make up to household budgets the resulting difference in the prices of basic foodstuffs. He said that the cost of the subsidies had risen from £63 million in 1940-1 to £265 million in 1945-6. A year before, the attempt to peg them at £400 million a year had been abandoned because a campaign had just been launched to stabilise wages, costs and prices. As a result the subsidies had risen to about £485 million, and the prospective total for 1949-50 was about £568 million. He said "We must call a halt"; hence it had been decided to "peg" the subsidies at £465 million and to increase the price of cheese and meat by 4d. a lb., butter by 2d. a lb and margarine by 1d. This would mean an immediate rise in the cost of living index of almost two points, with a further increase if prices continued to rise. He justified this rise, and the lack of concessions on purchase tax, income tax and other taxes by the somewhat astonishing assertion that "a very great and highly desirable redistribution of wealth . . . has already taken place over the last few years", and he said, too, that "there is not much further immediate possibility of the redistribution of the national income by way of taxation in this country".

But he had to admit that, with the total of local and national taxation running at over 40 per cent. of the national income, the redistribution of income entailed in the payment for the social services was already falling to a considerable extent on the recipients of those services.

REGRESSIVE BUDGET

In truth, the Budget tended to swing the redistribution to some extent against the poorer sections in favour of the richer. It gave relief to the latter in increased depreciation allowances, amounting to £75 million in a full year, offset by an increase in death duties of £20 million; and as a result of the "pegged" food subsidies and the taxes on insurance contributions, matches and football pools—offset by a reduction in beer duty—it added over £60 million to what the people had to pay. It is not surprising that the *Observer* remarked: "some people might even say that he had taken over Conservative policy"; and the City in particular was delighted with the repeal of the duty on issues of bonus shares.

The results of the changes in taxation were tabulated as follows by *World News* of the 16th April:

What the People Would Pay:
Increased food prices, as a result of reduced subsidies: £67 million;
Income tax increase on one-seventh of contribution (allowing for tax exemption on benefits): £10 million;
Increased tax on matches: £5 million;
Increased tax on football pools: £6 million;
Total 88 million Less reduction in beer tax: £20 million.
Net loss for the people: £68 million.

What the Rich Would Get:

Increase in tax-free wear and tear allowance for plant and machinery: £75 million.

Removal of tax on bonus issues: £1 million.

Repeal of other stamp duties: £1 million.

Special depreciation allowance for overseas mining companies: £1 million.

Less increase in estate duties: £1 million.

Net gain for the rich: £58 million.

U.S. RECESSION KILLS OPTIMISM

It was not long before the mood of optimism had to give way before various harsh realities. Already in April there were signs of a recession in the U.S.A., which—or even the threat of which—was bound to have a terrible effect on Britain, owing to the policy of pinning virtually all its hopes on the U.S.A., not just as a kind uncle but much more as a purchaser with a long purse. These signs grew and grew in the weeks and months that followed. In May, the motor, cotton, wool textiles, engineering and whisky industries all suffered big drops in their exports to U.S.A. And in his "State of the Union" message to Congress, as at the 30th June, President Truman wrote:

"We are now in a transition period. . . . . Employment is still high, but it is lower than it was last year. Business investment is at a high rate, but plans for new investments are being made with caution."

SHADOW OF DEVALUATION

Talk soon grew about a probable need to devalue the pound sterling; it was becoming increasingly difficult to find markets for our exports, particularly in the U.S.A., and Japanese competition was developing. The trade returns for June, announced on the 20th July, showed the largest adverse balance for 21 months.

By the beginning of July our dollar reserves were diminishing so rapidly that Cripps announced in the House of Commons on the 6th July that all new dollar purchases must be postponed for at least three months, and on the 14th July the House debated "medium-term" measures to stop the drain on dollars. Four days later, at the conclusion of a meeting of Commonwealth Finance Ministers in London, a statement was issued recommending all the Commonwealth governments to take immediate steps to check the drain on the sterling area reserves.

Our main sources of dollars, the export of food and raw materials from the Empire, rubber and tin from Malaya, jute from Pakistan or India, wool and hides from South Africa and Australia, and cocoa and tea from West Africa and Ceylon, were all suffering through most of 1949, in terms both of quantity and of price. In the second quarter of the year, dollar exports of rubber, tin, cocoa, diamonds and wool from the sterling area fell from $120 million per quarter (in the year ending March 1949) to $60 million. As the *Manchester Guardian* reported on the 6th July:

> "Something like two-thirds of the American imports from the sterling area are primary products—notably rubber, jute, wool, cocoa, tea, precious stones and tin. The sharpest part of the business recession in the U.S. has been the fall in commodity prices, and this has hit our exports without saving much of the cost of imports. Cocoa has slumped to half its price last autumn. Raw rubber, the greatest of all the sterling area's dollar earnings, is now 25 per cent. below its average price last year. Jute and wool fetched about 20 per cent. less in the U.S. than they did during 1948. Tea and tin have not yet become cheaper, but price reductions are expected soon. The American demand for rough diamonds has shrunk by more than one-half since the beginning of the year."

All this gives one main cause of the fall in the gold reserves of the sterling area to little over £400 million; but there was also present an element of attempts by enemies of the Labour Government to "get out of sterling".

The immediate reaction of Tories, and particularly of employers, was to call for lower wages, in order to reduce costs; but the official index showed that wage rates were lagging behind prices. In June, 1949, in terms of June, 1947, as 100, prices stood at 111, and wages at 108, and in the Notes of the Month in the September *Labour Monthly* Palme Dutt pointed out at p. 267 that, whilst real wages had been cut by 3 per cent. since the wage freeze, production had risen by 17 per cent. and profits and interest by 24 per cent.

DEVALUATION

The urgency of devaluation grew swiftly in the end; by September, 1949, the gold and dollar reserves of the sterling area had fallen below £400 million (by the 30th September they were £351 million, just over half the level of the end of 1946) and the drain on them was running at the rate of £600 million a year. Whether the decision to devalue was taken on American orders or not was subsequently a matter of considerable controversy, but is relatively unimportant since it was plainly inevitable. There had undoubtedly been pressure in the U.S.A. for devaluation of the pound, and the Secretary of the U.S. Treasury had visited Britain and discussed the matter with the Government as early as July. But the Government asserted that it took the decision independently, before Bevin and Cripps went to Washington in the first week of September for the Conference attended by representatives of U.S.A., Canada, and Britain to consider what was to be done to meet the situation. Devaluation was actually announced on the 18th September, after the Conference, the dollar parity of the pound sterling being reduced from $4·03 to $2·80. (The dates should be noticed; the decision was taken in the first week of September, before the Trades Union Congress met at Bridlington, and it was announced after that Conference was over. Thus everything that took place at Bridlington was based on false assumptions. I shall deal with that Conference in the next chapter.)

The true direct cause of the devaluation—the "last straw" cause, coming on top of a highly vulnerable position brought about by the crushing expense of our overseas expenditures on military and colonial adventures, our huge defence costs, and our insistence on trying to trade with the difficult dollar markets to the virtual exclusion of trade with the socialist world—was the American slump, which led to the Americans buying much less from the sterling area, and paying lower prices for it. (It was not the case that we had had adverse trading balances with most overseas countries; we had credit balances with the sterling area and with some European countries, but our debits in dollars—the currency to which our government's policy directed almost all our energies—was overwhelming.)

WASHINGTON CONFERENCE

The Washington Conference, described by advocate Cripps as "the most successful we have ever had", and as producing "unprecedented agreement", resulted in what was called a "ten-point programme"; indeed, he said that it had "brought our reserves position into a manageable condition". When examined, six of the points were no more than declarations of intentions to "study" or "explore" questions —a common means of concealing the absence of agreement; they

T

included American tariffs, American world investment, sterling balances, petroleum, shipping, and European trade and payments. The remaining points included permission to the British to use Marshall dollars in part payment of Canadian wheat, and promises by the U.S.A. to purchase more rubber and tin and to review American customs procedure. The wheat concession was of some value; in a sense it was worth £44 million; but it was offset by an undertaking by the British government to buy £10 million additional imports of U.S. wheat and fruit. The most optimistic calculation suggested that we had gained concessions worth £84 millions to cope with the gold and dollar deficit, already mentioned, running at the rate of £600 million a year, or—after allowing for Marshall subsidies—£360 million; this was scarcely a "manageable position".

Both the devaluation itself, and the remedies necessary to meet the grave crisis which had brought it about, were debated in the House of Commons on the three days beginning on the 27th September, 1949 (*Hansard*, Vol. 468, Cols. 7-154, 157-290, 310-439). The debate was opened by Cripps, who insisted on dollars, dollars, and more dollars. We must expand our dollar earnings, he said, by increasing exports to the dollar countries from Britain and the sterling area; we must not confine ourselves to the commodities we were already exporting, but must find new fields that might be opened up for us by the new exchange rate; for example, the birth-rate had risen in the U.S.A., and we might be able to sell things for children. (He dealt with the obvious disadvantage that every pound's worth of goods we might succeed in exporting would bring in far fewer dollars than before by saying that the "increased volume of goods we should have to sell in the dollar market to offset the fall in receipts due to the lower rate of exchange . . . should be less than the calculated maximum figure of 44 per cent.")

The workers, who had already raised productivity by 4 per cent. in a year (over an already good figure), were to raise it still further. The cost of living would inevitably rise,* but "nothing, literally nothing" must be done to increase personal incomes arising out of profits, wages or salaries. As for wages, this meant that there must be a wage freeze, absolute save for very narrowly limited special cases, and workers were not to attempt to get rises to recoup themselves for increases in the cost of living; i.e. wages, already lagging, as I shall show in a moment,

---

* The price of bread rose at once by 33⅓ per cent. This was later reduced to "only" 25 per cent.

behind the increased cost of living, were to diminish further in real terms.

Those who lived by profit were dealt with differently. As Cripps pointed out, their profits for various reasons would often be increasing, but he *earnestly begged them* not to pay out increased dividends. He said that many of them had been ignoring similar requests in the past; and he warned that, if they went on doing so, he—terrible threat—would "*consider himself at liberty* to introduce legislation to restrict dividends in the next Finance Bill" (in six or seven months' time!). Meanwhile, he increased the profits tax from 25 per cent. to 30 per cent.

His other proposals were to cut down capital investment and to reduce government expenditure, *not* including defence expenditure.

Both I myself and Gallacher were able to speak in this debate. I pointed out (*Hansard*, Vol. 468, Cols. 60-70) that there was no element in the Government's proposal of any socialist attempt to find remedies for the situation; that efforts to export to the U.S.A. during a slump in that country were unlikely to succeed to any extent; and that to seek to avoid unemployment by keeping wages down and thus diminishing the purchasing power of the bulk of the population was a classical contradiction and futility of capitalism. I added that Marshall Aid, which was supposedly designed to help the countries of Western Europe, including Britain, seemed to have had little success; the countries of all Europe could by now be divided into two groups, those who had no Marshall Aid and were improving their positions, and those who had Marshall Aid and were in trouble.

Gallacher (Cols. 225-33) spoke on somewhat similar lines. (Indeed, by that time, debates on foreign affairs, financial crises, and economics generally, had fallen into a set pattern. Bevin would make a very long speech blaming the U.S.S.R. for everything that was going wrong, or, in economic matters, Cripps would speak at less length and with greater plausibility to the same effect; the Tories would then praise them; and one or two speakers would present the point of view of the Communist Party or of left-wing Labour, which in its turn did not vary greatly from debate to debate, since it was after all both simple and correct. It was thus difficult not to repeat oneself.) Gallacher emphasised that the policy of the Government amounted to a demand that the workers should produce more and consume less in order to make profits for both British and American capitalists.

NEW CRISIS

Devaluation, however inevitable, was at best no more than a partial remedy, and it was not long before a new crisis loomed up, calling for further expedients. Within five weeks of devaluation there came one more in the series of emergencies, inevitable and yet not apparently anticipated by the Government, which Cripps had so aptly described in a Press Conference just after devaluation, in the phrase:

"We have been trying to deal with things by a series of temporary expedients which have led to a series of crises."

Attlee and Cripps announced a number of further economy cuts, designed to save £250 million a year. The measures proposed included economies in current government expenditure, which together with the increase in taxes mentioned below were expected to save over £100 million a year, and cuts in capital outlay amounting to £140 million in a year. In addition, the savings in defence expenditure which I described in Chapter 21 were estimated at another £30 million a year.

CUTS

The capital cuts proposed included £25 millions on fuel and power; £10 millions on transport and communications; £35 millions on housing; £7,500,000 on school building; £1,000,000 on universities; and £35 millions on miscellaneous building work and plant. (How far away it all sounds from the "Four-year Plan" of less than a year before!)

The cuts in fuel and power expenditure were to fall mainly on electrical distribution development, which meant in particular the postponement of schemes of rural electrification. In transport and communications, the principal items were a reduction in the standard of maintenance on the railways, and the restriction of much-needed development work. The housing cuts involved a reduction of the already severely diminished programme of 200,000 houses a year to 175,000; it was stated that the reduction was to fall solely on private enterprise house-building. The education cuts fell both on capital outlay and current expenditure; the aim was not to build fewer schools, but to reduce the cost per place, from about £200 to about £170 for primary schools, with a rather smaller reduction for secondary schools. All new building for the school meals service was postponed indefinitely.

Local authorities were to cut their administrative, inspectorial and clerical staffs. There was to be a uniform charge of 6d. per meal for school meals, to replace the then current charges, which averaged 5d. Expenditure on recreation and physical training was to be reduced. Distinctive school clothing was to be stopped. Economies were to be made in the transport of children to and from school. Fees for evening classes were to be raised, on an average, by 10s.

Other economies in administration were estimated to save £40 to £45 million; and £6 million was to be saved on agriculture, £10 million on the National Health Service, £7 million on food subsidies, and £36 million on animal feeding-stuff subsidies. A charge of not more than 1s. was to be made on every National Health prescription (except for Old Age Pensioners). Price controls on fish were to be removed, together with the subsidy on fish.

Everything cut was socially useful, and nearly everything socially useful was cut.

The tax on distributed profits was raised, as I have already mentioned, from 25 per cent. to 30 per cent. with an estimated yield of £24 million gross and £13 million net after loss on income tax. The Capital Issues Committee was asked to hold up all future applications for the issue of bonus shares.

Imports from the dollar area to the sterling area were to be cut by 25 per cent., beginning in 1950; the chief cuts were to be in food (other than wheat and sugar), tobacco and raw materials. Sterling balance repayments, which had amounted so far in 1949 to £206 million and were said by the United Nations Economic Commission to have contributed largely to the crisis, were to stop.

For once the capitalist Press did not approve; its criticism was that the economies did not go far enough!

ATTACK ON WAGES

There was at the same time a further attack on wages. Devaluation, by bringing about price increases, had produced an automatic reduction of real wages, standards, and social benefits; and the government policy of "no increase in wages unless there is more production", prevailing before devaluation, was replaced by "no increase in wages even if there is an increase in prices".

In truth, even before devaluation, wage rates were lagging behind price increases. At June, 1949, the official price index showed an 11 per cent. rise over June, 1947, whilst the official wage index showed only

8 per cent. rise. At September, 1949, before devaluation had had time to show its effects, the price index was 112 and the wage index 109— June, 1947, being 100. But rent, interest, and profit had risen by 57 per cent. in 1948 compared with 1947, after payment of direct taxes. And the *Economist* index for 2,291 companies reporting in the year to September, 1949, showed an increase in profits of 14 per cent. after tax.

T.U.C. HELPS TO HOLD DOWN WAGES

As always, when a policy of "wage-freezing", with profits left free, has to be put over on the mass of the people, no government can get very far unless it can conciliate or bamboozle the official leadership of the organised industrial workers, the General Council of the Trades Union Congress. This is not easy, even for a Labour Government; but it is sometimes possible, given the relatively large representation of reactionary views among the members of the General Council. And at this period the operation succeeded; on the 23rd November, the General Council endorsed a statement to the following effect:

1. Devaluation has been adopted as an alternative to deflation. The dangerous inflationary tendencies which it inevitably intensifies must be countered by vigorous restraints upon all increases of wages, salaries and dividends.

2. The existing machinery of negotiation must be preserved.

3. The operation of wages policy is the responsibility of the unions themselves, but the unions must pay regard to the realities of the economic situation.

4. The General Council recognises that the problem of lower-paid workers may call for consideration in certain cases, but urges that in consideration even of such cases regard be had to the need for restraint and that attention be paid to helping lower-paid workers by incentive schemes.

5. The General Council recommends unions to reconsider existing wage claims and sliding scale agreements, with a view to holding agreed wage rates stable while the Retail Price Index remains between 118 and 106; when the index reaches the upper or the lower limits, both sides of industry to be free to open negotiations again, and sliding scales to operate. Reconsideration of these arrangements in any case by January 1, 1951.

6. More publicity for constructive suggestions on productivity, not excluding overtime working.

7. Each industry to try to extend payment by results over the widest possible range.

This represented in substance a complete acceptance of the stock Tory attitude to wage claims in time of rising prices due to crisis. It did not even contain a demand for an attack on high profits or for the stabilisation of prices. This policy would bear very hardly on many sections of the working population. Miners, for example, had had no increase in wage rates since October, 1947; the cost of living index had meanwhile risen by 11 per cent., but they were expected to accept what was in effect a cut of 17 per cent. in wage rates before they could claim an increase. It was, however, decided that this statement should be brought before a Special Conference of Trade Union Executives on the 12th January, 1950.

SPECIAL CONFERENCE OF UNION EXECUTIVES

At this Conference, whilst the government policy was endorsed by a small majority, the opposition was formidable. The miners, the engineers, the railwaymen, the electricians, the foundry workers, and the boiler-makers, the most decisive key sections of the industrial workers, cast their votes against the General Council, the Labour Government and the Labour Party; only two-thirds of a million remained as a majority. Moreover, the votes in favour of the government policy were cast by leaders who had not consulted their members. (The miners had consulted their members, with an interesting result. The Executive of the Union had endorsed the policy in November; even a delegate Conference had endorsed it by 406,000 to 273,000; but the workers rejected it by 518,000 to 147,000.)

The engineers and the railwaymen continued to press claims for increases. As always, when efforts are made to lay the burden of crises mainly on the working class, the mass of organised workers stand militantly against the manœuvre, even if trade union leaders go with the government, and even although their political representatives support the Labour Party for fear of "rocking the boat". We shall see signs of this militancy in the next chapter.

CHAPTER 25

Industrial Affairs, 1948-9

THE main events of the year in the industrial field were the Trades Union Congress which, as mentioned above, met in Bridlington in September, 1949, the disruption of world trade union unity by withdrawals from the World Federation of Trade Unions, and a number of strikes.

STRIKES

Taking strikes first, there came in May, 1949, months before the October crises, three industrial battles, after fifteen months of official "wage freeze" expounded and enforced by Cabinet Ministers, trade union leaders, and arbitration tribunals. These battles were fought by the dockers, the miners, and the railwaymen.

The dockers' strike, the second strike of dockers in twelve months and the second resort by the Government in the same period to a declaration of emergency and the use of troops as "blacklegs", deserves a full account, for it gives a sad display of the readiness of a Labour Government to betray elementary trade union principles if the anti-communist bogey is trotted out.

CANADIAN STRIKE

The strike developed out of a Canadian strike of merchant seamen, led by the militant "Canadian Seamen's Union". This, the then recognised union of seamen in Eastern Canada, was accused, like so many strong unions, of being under "communist influence". When the Canadian seamen, led by this union, struck against a demand for large wage reductions, their employers reacted in three ways. Firstly, they "recognised" a rival union, the "International Seafarers' Union", an American organisation affiliated to the American Federation of Labour, having very few members on Canada's Eastern seaboard, and being in conflict with the Canadian Trades and Labour Council (the Canadian equivalent of the T.U.C.); this union was much less militant than the

Canadian Seamen's Union, and had accepted conditions rejected by the latter. Secondly, they persuaded the Canadian Trades and Labour Council to suspend the Canadian Seamen's Union; this was agreed by the Trades and Labour Council on strong pressure from the American unions. And, thirdly, they hired strike-breaking crews, who, as is not uncommon in North America, were recruited not from the industry but from professional gangsters, who made their way on to the ships by violence, and beat up the members of the Canadian Seamen's Union who were on board. (I happened to be in Canada at the time, helping in the defence of a political case, and thus saw the Canadian side of the picture before I saw the British.)

CANADIAN STRIKE COMES TO BRITAIN

A dispute of merchant seamen is bound to impinge on foreign ports and by the 14th May, 1949, a Canadian ship arrived in Avonmouth, worked across the Atlantic by a strike-breaking International Seafarers' Union crew. Every instinct and tradition of organised industrial workers called aloud for this ship to be treated as "black", and the Avonmouth dockers refused to handle her. On the 16th May, the employers threatened to penalise the dockers for this refusal, whereupon the whole dock labour force struck; but on the following day work was resumed except on the ship involved. Next day the employers said that they would take on no labour for other ships until the dockers handled the "black" ship, which of course they did not do; and on the 22nd May, 600 men at neighbouring Bristol struck in sympathy with the Avonmouth men thus locked out. On the 25th May some lock-gate and tug-boat men in Avonmouth were suspended for refusing to handle any ships until the Avonmouth dockers were allowed to work again.

On the 27th May, troops were employed to unload a banana ship in Avonmouth; and the strike spread to Liverpool, where 1,000 men struck because 45 men were suspended for refusing to handle a "black" Canadian ship which had been sent on from Avonmouth.

On the same date, Canadian and American leaders of the International Seafarers' Union showed their true colours by cabling to Attlee that they would ask the International Longshoremen's Union (also affiliated to the American Federation of Labour) to boycott British ships in Canadian and U.S. ports unless the Canadian ships were handled in British ports. (A pretty blackmail: "If you don't force your dockers to handle 'black' ships, you will get your 'white' ships boycotted!")

THE STRIKE EXTENDS

Under such circumstances the strike could hardly fail to extend; that "black" ships should not be handled is one of the most sacred and important—and unselfish—rules of workers' solidarity. On the 30th May, 1,400 more dockers in Liverpool came out, and the Avonmouth men instructed their Lock-out Committee to seek support from other ports. On the 31st May the crane drivers at Avonmouth refused to work with troops, and the number on strike at Liverpool rose to 6,000. On the 2nd June troops began to unload all the ships lying at Avonmouth, and the total "out" at Liverpool rose to 9,500: on the following day the total was 11,000. On the 6th June, the crew of the British ship *Trojan Star* refused to sail her out of Avonmouth because the lock-gates were manned by troops; and on the 8th June the crew of another British ship struck when troops came to unload it.

On the 13th June, dockers on strike in Liverpool returned to work, and agreed to unload a British ship that had been transferred from Avonmouth; they still refused, however, to unload a Canadian ship that had come from Avonmouth.

On the 14th June, the Avonmouth dockers, after being out since the 18th May, returned to work on a guarantee of no victimisation (which the employers later asserted to apply only to permanent men), but said that they would not handle "black" Canadian ships diverted from other ports.

By now, London became involved. A Canadian ship had been lying isolated there since the 1st April, and on the 20th June dockers were asked to handle her. They refused; and three days later the employers said that they would not hire labour for newly-arrived ships until this Canadian ship and another one waiting to be handled were unloaded.

On the 24th June, an announcement was made that the Canadian strike had been settled, and the London dockers immediately proceeded to unload the two ships; but on the following day the Canadian owners announced that the settlement only covered the return voyages of the ships. Accordingly, on the 27th June, when a call was made for men to work the Canadian ships in London, 4,000 men stopped work; and within two days 5,500 London dockers were out and 44 ships were idle. The figure rose to 8,484 men by the 5th July.

TROOPS AS STRIKE–BREAKERS

On the 7th July, troops were brought in and started to unload ships; 250 more men came out, and drivers of meat haulage firms and fruit and vegetable firms said that they would not carry goods unloaded by troops.

"STATE OF EMERGENCY"

On the 8th July, the Government announced that it would proclaim a state of emergency on the 11th; 400 stewards of the Watermen, Lightermen and Tugmen and Bargemen's Union thereupon struck, and the total of dockers on strike rose to 10,213. By the 12th July (the first day of the Emergency), whilst the Government was pouring troops into the docks, there were 13,296 men out; the executive of the Lightermen's Union told their members not to work with troops; and French dockers said that they would not work ships coming from London. By the 14th July, the 13,296 figure had risen to 14,289.

Throughout the whole period—so strongly was the anti-communist bogey being used—the trade union leadership in general, including in particular Sir Arthur Deakin, was doing all it could to discourage strike action; and the tragic spectacle continued of a Labour Government using troops to help British employers to defeat by a lock-out workers who were observing the simplest and most fundamental loyalty and solidarity; and all this to help Canadian employers who were using strike-breakers to defeat their own workers.

The Government made things no better by staffing the Emergency Board appointed to take charge of the docks during the strike with, as chairman, a civil servant who had spent years in that stronghold of reaction, the Home Office, and as members one who in his capacity as British Government representative at International Labour Office meetings had always taken the side of the employers against the workers, one executive of a great petroleum company, one more (pensioned) high civil servant, and one trade union official.

The strike went on; and on the 19th July the National Dock Labour Board issued a statement saying that it appreciated the dockers' sense of loyalty, and that it was because many dockers feared that "this loyalty might be challenged by the operation of the dock labour scheme, now or in the future, that they were withholding their labour"; that the Board would not allocate men to jobs except in accordance with agreements and would not allocate men to a job in dispute if the proper machinery of negotiation was being followed. They then ordered the dockers to return to work by 7.45 a.m. on the 21st July, and said that "failure to return to work will jeopardise the very existence of the scheme".

This was suspected of being a threat to deprive the dockers of the security provided by the dock-labour scheme, which might well have led to the extension of the strike to every port in England; it may have been for this reason that the Government announced on the evening of that day that the Dock Labour Board's statement had been issued without consultation with the Emergency Board, and that there was no intention of ending the dock-labour scheme.

On the 20th July, the total of men out was 15,505. Two days later, on the 22nd, the Canadian Seamen's Union made a generous intervention, withdrawing their pickets from the ships and announcing that they were terminating their dispute so far as Britain was concerned, whilst maintaining it in the rest of the world. This enabled the dockers to return to work, which they did on the 25th July.

MINERS AND RAILWAYMEN

The strikes of the miners and railwaymen were neither so long or so sensational; it was sad that they both arose in nationalised industries, but it must be said that in most of the nationalised industries the new employers had proved to be little different from the old private ones.

The miners' strike, which came in May, concerned concessionary coal (coal supplied to miners at reduced rates) in some few districts in Lancashire where no such coal had yet been "conceded". The miners made their claim for it, which was rejected; and they thereupon put a ban on overtime. On that quiet beginning, trouble began when the employers attempted to put members of another union to do work normally done by members of the National Union of Mineworkers. A number of men came out at once, and by the 10th May every pit in the county but one was stopped. Faced with this, the employers "found a basis for negotiations"; the men went back, and secured substantial grants of concessionary coal.

The railway strike arose over the old complaint, fruitful of many stoppages, that inconvenient "lodging turns" had been fixed without proper consultation with the men. It took the form of Sunday strikes over a period of weeks in the summer.

SPLITTING THE W.F.T.U.

It was inevitable, in the anti-communist atmosphere of the time, that the World Federation of Trade Unions should become the object of attack by the leaders of the trade union movement and their friends in the American Federation of Labour and Congress of Industrial

Organisations. The W.F.T.U. had been founded in 1945, and embraced every trade unionist in the world, to the number of about 71,000,000, and was a force of infinite value for the advance of working-class strength in the world. To the British leaders, and still more to the Americans, it was anathema, for they were in a minority and the socialist countries were in a majority; but the latter had never attempted to get any decision by majority vote, and the non-socialists—as one is compelled to label them—had some difficulty in finding a pretext to walk out. They even complained that the Federation had refused to approve the Marshall Plan, notwithstanding that experience had shown both the "strings" in which that Plan entangled the economies of its European members, and its failure to bring them out of slump and crisis. But in the end, in July, 1949, the General Council of the T.U.C., without consulting its members, walked out on the simple if fundamentally anti-socialist ground that the majority of trade unions composing it had Communist leaders; in September, as we shall see, they got approval of their conduct from the T.U.C. at Bridlington. In October, 1949, the T.U.C. published a draft constitution for what can fairly be called a "breakaway" international, to be called the "International Confederation of Free Trade Unions", and in December, 1949, at a Conference in London, this organisation was definitely established, to the delight of the opponents of the working classes in all countries.

T.U.C. CONFERENCE

As for the Bridlington meeting of the T.U.C., it took place—as already mentioned—after the Government had decided to devalue the pound but before the decision had been announced. It had no knowledge that any such development, with its inevitable effect in raising the cost of living and thereby rendering general wage increases a measure of the barest necessity and justice, was on the point of arrival.

The general course of the Conference represented a victory for the Government. One of its more important resolutions pledged "continued support of the policy aimed at securing the greatest possible measure of restraint in seeking to increase personal incomes and expenditure unrelated to increased productivity". The "hedging" phraseology of this resolution shows that there had been a good deal of opposition, as did the rejection of proposals for lowering wages, lengthening hours of labour, or contracting the social services.

An opposition resolution, calling on the Government to introduce statutory control of profits and further control of bonus shares, and condemning the stabilisation of wages at their then levels, insufficient to maintain a reasonable or adequate standard of living, attracted a million votes. One can guess that a month later it would have been carried.

The action of the General Council in withdrawing from the World Federation of Trade Unions was, as already mentioned, approved; the Federation was alleged in the resolution to have become "the instrument of political aims to the detriment of countries striving unitedly to promote their economic recovery". The resolution was carried by over 6,000,000 votes to over 1,000,000.

"Countries striving unitedly to promote their economic recovery" was a typical right-wing description of the capitalist U.S.A. and its capitalist and Labour dependants in Europe with the Marshall Plan, NATO, and the Cold War round their necks, trying in vain to make capitalism work by, to quote Cripps again, "a series of temporary expedients which have led to a series of crises".

When this approval of the withdrawal was "safely" through, the Congress went on to pass an anti-communist resolution, against a minority vote of 760,000; it referred to "the malignant nature of Communist agitation and organisation", and said that "energetic steps must be taken to stop these evil machinations which threaten the economic recovery of the country". The Government was thus encouraged to pursue its Cold War policy of indefinitely postponing the economic recovery of the country.

It is odd, and something of a relief, to see that in that atmosphere the Congress also unanimously passed a resolution in favour of developing trade on a larger scale with the U.S.S.R.

CHAPTER 26

Social Services and Other Matters, 1948-9

I WILL begin with housing, the field of social activity where neglect is most easily productive of endless human misery, as anyone who has ever represented an urban constituency in Parliament knows almost as well as anyone who has ever waited years for a house.

At the start of the year 1948-9, the position was that by the end of October, 1948, 821,434 families had been rehoused since the end of the war. This included 387,502 in new permanent dwellings, 156,616 in temporary houses, and the remaining 277,316 in requisitioned dwellings or in uninhabitable dwellings which had been repaired.

The total number of dwellings built under the Tories in three and a half years after the First World War was 171,000. In a similar period therefore, Labour had built twice as many permanent dwellings, apart from temporary ones and other housing measures.

Moreover, nearly three permanent dwellings had been built by local authorities for every one built by private enterprise, whereas during the inter-war years only two local authority dwellings had been built for every five built by private enterprise (the latter were mostly for sale). In fact in 1948 local authorities completed far more new houses than in any previous year.

All this, therefore, was much better than the Tory record. Nevertheless, the total rate of new building in 1948 was considerably less than the building industry was capable of. In the four pre-war years, over 350,000 dwellings were being completed annually but in 1948 just under 230,000 dwellings were completed. This was also much less than the original target, which was set at four million dwellings in the first ten years after the war, i.e., an average of 400,000 dwellings a year. Had this been fulfilled, there would have been 1,200,000 new dwellings instead of 387,502. It will be remembered that the number of dwellings under construction had been reduced from 261,826 at October 1947 to 197,931 by September 1948. This was done by limiting severely the number of new dwellings the local authorities were permitted to start, so that each month the number begun was less than the number completed.

There had, of course, been many difficulties, in shortage of materials and the diversion of labour to export industries, but the most important cause of trouble was the excessive defence expenditure and the maintenance of the armed forces at a high level. The principal material shortage was of timber, which could easily have been drawn from the U.S.S.R., if we had supplied the timber-cutting machinery and light rails that were necessary for large-scale cutting.

The Government had, moreover, throughout its life failed in many measures that would have greatly helped housing. In *Let Us Face the Future*, it had promised to take drastic action to ensure an efficient building industry; to prevent restrictive price rings; to introduce modern building methods and materials; to maintain a due balance between housing, schools and factories (commercial work and private work not even being mentioned); to institute centralised purchasing and price control; and to create a Ministry of Housing and Planning. It had not fulfilled even one of these promises, and the building and building-material industries had been left pretty free to make their profits as they wished. Both men and materials had been diverted, by a tolerated black market and by generous licensing, to non-priority work in private houses, shops, showrooms, offices, and hotels; this had gone on to such an extent that not more than one-quarter of the building trade operatives had ever been working on new houses at any one time.

This complete failure to tackle price ramps was carried so far that in *Labour Believes in Britain* (see the following chapter) practically nothing was said about the building and building materials industry, apart from a promise to nationalise cement. The most that the Government did on this point in 1949 was to refer the activities of certain building-materials concerns to the necessarily slow machinery of the Monopolies Commission. And the subsidies, fixed in 1946 on the basis that the rent of a typical house would be about 10s. a week, remained unaltered while actual costs rose to such an extent that a house which would have a rent of 10s. a week would by 1949 require 14s. 4d. The cost of land, too, was allowed to rise unchecked.

The Tories, of course, sought to lay the blame for the rises in the cost of building on the building workers, accusing them of low output; in truth, in July, 1949, it was shown in the House of Commons that their output had risen by 40 per cent.

Through 1949, too, the number of buildings under construction was falling; at the 31st March the figure was 187,256, compared to 197,931 at September 30th, 1948, and 261,826 at the 31st October, 1947.

As already explained, further severe cuts came in October, 1949.

HOUSING ACT, 1949

Some help was forthcoming in the Housing Act, 1949, introduced on the 28th February, 1949, and passed on the 30th July, 1949. Its principal purpose was to provide for conversion of and improvements to existing houses. Two methods of achieving this were provided. Under the first, local authorities could acquire houses and carry out the work, receiving three-quarters of the cost from the Exchequer and providing the rest themselves. Under the second, private owners could apply to the local authority for a grant of half the cost of the work, the local authority getting from the Exchequer three-quarters of what it provided.

The Act also gave a number of useful powers to local authorities, e.g. to provide canteens or restaurants and laundry facilities for tenants of municipal flats and housing estates, and to sell them furniture.

The Act also removed the restriction placed by all earlier housing legislation on local authorities, which limited them to providing dwellings for the working class; the object of this was to enable them to develop mixed estates of houses of more varied sizes and types, attracting all income groups.

I had a half-amusing and half-infuriating experience in connection with this provision. To carry out its purpose, the Act removed provisions relating to the "working class" from the housing legislation, and thereby deprived working-class tenants of a very useful provision in an oldish "Housing of the Working-Classes Act", which had enabled tenants of any working-class house to recover damages from their landlords for personal injuries caused by defects in the premises (which could not be recovered under the ordinary law). Believing in my innocence that this was an oversight, and that the Minister—Aneurin Bevan, an intelligent man of working-class origin—would be glad to put it right, I drew his attention to the position, and found stout opposition. So far as the legal side of the matter went, he passed on to me a series of arguments from his department's lawyers, which he did not pretend to understand very well, and which I thought to be wholly wrong. On the broader point that anyway the provision should be kept alive because it would in any case benefit a good many tenants, he

U

astonished me a little by refusing to do anything of the sort, explaining to me that I was trying to apply "obsolete class distinctions".

NATIONAL HEALTH SERVICE

The National Health Service was by now in full running, and in February, 1949, a review of it showed that 40 million people (95 per cent. to 98 per cent. of the total) had put their names on doctors' lists, and that 18,000 out of 21,000 general practitioners had joined the scheme; of 10,000 dentists, 9,000 had joined.

There had been from the start a rush for dental and optical treatment; by the end of January, 1949, 2,500,000 people had had their sight tested, and 3,000,000 pairs of spectacles had been supplied or ordered. In one northern city of 100,000 people, over half the population had gone to oculists in the first four months, and the rush was scarcely beginning to fall off, and much more than half of that half was found to be in serious need of attention. Dental treatment had been given to 2,200,000 people, and 1,200,000 more were still under treatment. There were carpers ready to accuse people of "cashing in" on the free service, as if it were a pleasure to have oneself treated when there was no need of it; but the truth was that lack of money had previously prevented large sections of the population from receiving treatment they really needed. This was at once a reflection on past indifference and a measure of the value of the service. It may not have been socialism, but it was a very great achievement.

On the other hand, our economic insanities had produced defects. Health centres, at first publicised as not only a great forward step but essential to the proper working of the service, were almost not to be found, and there was no likelihood of their ever being built; and there were long waiting lists for hospital treatment whilst 57,000 hospital beds were empty through shortage of nurses, due mainly to their very low pay, which government wage policy made it impossible to raise. And, even if all the beds had been in use, the total number was grossly inadequate to the true needs now discovered, because government policy prevented new hospitals from being built, or old ones being improved.

As already mentioned, the crisis measures of October, 1949, included a charge on prescriptions of 1s., which was more of a hardship to the poorest people, who have a higher rate of sickness, than to the general mass of us, and was in any case an inroad on the principle that treatment should be free.

EDUCATION

Education, too, suffered from the cold war policy and crises. The 1948 programme had provided for an expenditure of £52 million on school building; and in December, 1948, the 1949 programme was stated as £55 million; but this was not as good as it looked, since the actual 1948 expenditure was only £26,000,000, and half the £55 million for 1949 included the missing £26,000,000 of 1948.

In July, 1949, the Annual Report of the Ministry of Education for 1948 gave a pretty distressing picture. There were still 32,925 primary school classes of over 40, and 27,647 secondary school classes of over 30; and 20 per cent. of all children were still being educated in "all-age" schools. There was no prospect for the time being of any further application of the Education Act, e.g. raising the school-leaving age to sixteen, or providing County Colleges. Nursery schools numbered only 398, with an approximate total expenditure of £20,343; and there were no projects for the extension of this service.

The number of male teachers had increased in the three years from October, 1945, to October 1948, by 33,000—not nearly enough—but the number of women had dropped by over 2,000.

Whilst 644 black-listed schools were still in use, there was very little new building; in the whole of 1948, only ten new secondary schools and fifteen new primary schools were completed and brought into use.

A fifteen-year plan for school building, to carry out the Education Act, was shown by the Committee on School Sites and Building Procedure to require the expenditure of at least £1,000 million over fifteen years, or £66,700,000 a year. The actual expenditure on such building in 1948 was much less than half that sum, whilst the Government was spending far more than ten times that amount on "defence".

That sad picture existed, of course, long before the crisis cuts of October, 1949, which aimed—as I have already mentioned—at lopping off a further 10 per cent. from the already miserably inadequate programme—from the results of which inadequacy we are now suffering.

NATIONAL ASSISTANCE

The Report of the first six months of the National Assistance Board—the 5th July to the 1st December, 1948, was mainly of importance as showing the inadequacy of the social service benefits, which I discussed in Chapter 5. By November, 1948, the number of continuing weekly allowances had risen to just under 1,000,000; with the dependants of the actual recipients, the Board was thus making provision continuously for nearly 1,500,000 people, say 3 per cent. of the population. By August, 1949, the number of actual recipients was stated in the House of Commons to have risen to 1,107,199; the number of dependants was not stated, but the proportion would presumably be much the same.

Something like 60 per cent. of those on National Assistance were insured persons who would not have needed Assistance if their benefits had been adequate. In May, 1949, of the total of 4,160,000 drawing retirement pensions, 630,000 were receiving supplementary allowances from the National Assistance Board. Others in receipt of such allowances included people receiving widow's allowances and pensions, sickness benefit, or unemployment benefit.

The Board operated scale rates which, however meagre, were much higher than in the past; for example, the rate for a married couple was 31s. a week before the new service started, and 40s. a week when it did start, plus an allowance for rent. In most cases where the applicant was a householder, the rent allowance was the actual rent paid.

FASCISM

There are one or two miscellaneous incidents in 1949 which I may report here.

On the 20th March, 1949, a provocative fascist march was held in North-East London. The Home Office, a stronghold of reaction, used large forces of police to protect the march, and as a result there were clashes between the indignant crowds and the police. The immediate reaction of the Home Office was to ban "all public processions of a political character in London" for three months, under powers given in the Public Order Act. As a result, all May Day marches—on what was to be the sixtieth world anniversary of May Day—were made illegal throughout London, a pretty step for a Labour Government! Some people were cynical enough to wonder whether the whole thing had been arranged between the fascists and their sympathisers in the Home Office, a suspicion which was increased in the following year, when a mere announcement by the fascists that they proposed to hold a march on May Day proved enough to lead the Home Office not to restrain or control the fascists but to ban all processions.* (It was on one

---

* In form, the ban is imposed by the Chief Commissioner of Police, with the consent of the Home Secretary.

of these occasions that I began a May Day speech in Trafalgar Square—for the Home Office could not ban *meetings*—with the observation that there were only two capital cities in Europe where the workers could not hold their traditional marches, namely Madrid and London.)

In this year, 1949, the London Trades Council decided to hold May Day meetings at each of the assembly points originally fixed for the march, in addition to a central meeting in Trafalgar Square. When some of those attending the meetings attempted to march, large forces of police broke them up and arrested numbers of them.

A Tory government could not have done more; it might even have found it difficult to do as much.

LYNSKEY INQUIRY

In November, 1948, there was an unpleasant judicial enquiry—called the Lynskey enquiry, after the judge who presided—into allegations of irregularities affecting public servants, including one Minister. It went on for some time, gave a very unpleasant picture of a lushly corrupt world of introductions, commissions, and wangles, which did the Government much less harm than might have been feared. And the Minister who was involved resigned. (It led to a riddle: "What is the difference between Old King Cole and Mr. Attlee?" Answer: "Old King Cole knew how many fiddlers he had!")

CHAPTER 27
Labour Party Policy, 1948-9

As a General Election was bound to come at the latest in the middle of 1950, the Labour Party and government had to devote a good deal of thought, in this terrible year of crises, NATO, and devaluation, to preparing a policy for the Election; in this Chapter I will deal with that preparation, taking in the Labour Party Conference at Blackpool at Whitsuntide as part of the story.

The work began with a conference held in February, 1949, at Shanklin, attended by members of the National Executive and a number of Ministers, for the purpose of drafting a policy statement. To tie this in somewhat with the general development of the Government's policy, I mention that it was just before the Shanklin meeting that Cripps delivered a speech in Washington in which he said that, if we "indulged" further social demands, "it would wreck all our hopes of recovery", confirmed that the needs, comforts, and amenities of the family "were a last priority coming after exports and capital investment in industry", and added that there must be no "unnecessary interference" with the (capitalist) ways of production of the export trades, and that non-nationalised industry must be given "all the stimulation and help that we could reasonably give it".

"LABOUR BELIEVES IN BRITAIN"

The results of the work of this Conference, in the form of a thirty-page pamphlet called *Labour Believes in Britain*, was distributed to constituency parties for their consideration in March, and on the 11th April was issued to the Press.

The pamphlet contained proposals for the nationalisation of industrial insurance, the cement industry, sugar refining and manufacture, the machinery of meat distribution, and water supplies; there was talk, in much vaguer terms, of "examining the chemical industry" and of setting up a development council for shipping. And it enunciated four basic principles on which "the socialist society should be based", containing little that any socialist would recognise. One of them did contain a condemnation of capitalism as inefficient and wasteful, adding that "we have set out, therefore to . . ."—and one might surely have expected at any rate lip-service to the idea of getting rid of it and putting socialism in its place; but all we get is: "to enlarge the productive power of the nation, to banish mass unemployment, and so to raise the standard of life of the people".

In a section dealing with the task of increasing production, the old dilemma of "planning without (capitalist) tears", discussed in Chapters 12 and 24, it is stated that:

> "Economic planning is essential to secure that the public interest always comes first. . . . but we will have no truck with totalitarian or strait-waistcoat planning. Our aim is to lead the world in evolving democratic planning. By that we mean the continuing consent and co-operation of the people in the objectives and methods of the plan."

Alas! One has to realise that the "people" whose consent and co-operation were most important were the capitalist producers who were not ready to consent to anything that interfered with their sacred "rights". And anyone who sought, either with hope or fear, to see what the Party had to say about the project of building a socialist Britain, would find in the very next sentence that:

> "We mean that both public and private enterprise shall serve the public interest";

And, a few lines further:

> "There can be no advance without an effective partnership between government and industry."

Later the same tune is played in another key:

> "The managers and owners of private industry are trustees responsible to the nation. . . . We cannot allow anyone to pursue his own selfish interest, guided *solely*" (my italics) "by the profit motive. There can be no sheltering behind price rings and rigged markets. . . .
>
>   "On these conditions Labour wants to continue and extend the fruitful partnership* between private and public interest and the State, begun during the last few years."

* A "partnership" that had been little of a partnership but extremely fruitful for takers of interest and profit, as can be seen from what I have written above.

The social services were—with good justification—praised, but the claim that "the people of Britain have taken a long stride towards social equality. Extreme poverty has been banished" was by no means just. And the warning was given:

> "frankly, that new commitments for further expansion of our social services can only be accepted as production goes up; indeed, more production will be necessary to underpin the immense changes on which we have already embarked".

On education and house-building, the pamphlet gave many promises of further development, without any apology for past failures or cuts, or any statement as to where the money was to come from.

On foreign policy, the opportunity was not neglected to make a savage and inaccurate onslaught on the Soviet Union, under the heading of "Russia Blocks the Road". Marshall Aid and the U.S.A. were praised, with no hint that Britain had had to pay any price by way of subordination to the U.S.A. There is much talk about the colonies, and we learn that "Labour always denounced the old Imperialism". We learn, too, that "Great Britain and the Colonies have gone into partnership to liquidate ignorance, poverty and disease". (I sometimes wish, as a lawyer, that people should be stopped calling themselves "partners" or "trustees" without first studying the law to see the high obligations partners and trustees undertake. If they did that, they would never again describe the big industrial and financial leaders as partners or trustees of the masses, or the people who shot the coal miners at Enugu as partners or trustees of the Africans.)

Mr. Miliband writes at p. 300 of *Parliamentary Socialism*:

> "The programme, whatever its merits, quite failed to conceal the fact . . . that Labour's leadership, should it be returned to power at the next election, was entirely prepared to postpone indefinitely any further attempt at the structural transformation of a predominantly capitalist economy, now increasingly and euphemistically labelled 'the mixed economy'. . . . Proposals for nationalisation were not entirely eliminated; but neither were the proposals . . . intended to make more than marginal inroads into the 'private sector'. They neither satisfied the activists nor made any marked impression on the electorate. But they also failed to pacify Labour's enemies or to attract that middle-class vote whose seduction had become a major obsession with Labour's electoral strategists."

LOCAL ELECTIONS

In April and May, 1949, in the Local Elections, the Labour Party—which had not lost a parliamentary by-election since it came into power in 1945—had net losses of 255 seats in County Councils and of 711 seats in Borough Councils. (In the Metropolitan Boroughs, which only vote once in three years, the control of six of the seven Councils won by Labour in November, 1945, was lost in 1949.)

LABOUR PARTY CONFERENCE

Then came the Labour Party Conference at Blackpool. I can describe it very largely in the words I used at the time in the *Labour Monthly* at pp. 203-6:

"The Conference . . . delegates . . . lent themselves to such actions as the approval of the wage freeze against which their brothers in the trade unions are threatening to strike, and the acceptance of the fundamentally unsocialist policies stated in *Labour Believes in Britain*. . . . Long speeches by men of experience and prestige from the platform, with no right of reply from the floor; short speeches from the floor by those—experienced or inexperienced—who catch the chairman's eye; some large blocks of votes negotiated in advance; the usual appeals 'not to rock the boat' or cause confusion in the face of the enemy—with never a thought to the point that draftsmen of programmes who ask the movement to be loyal to the programmes should see that the programmes are loyal to the movement . . . these and other old weapons of what is now called democratic socialism served to get rid of practically every resolution, to pass over with little trouble every awkward point, and to secure approval of the policy document by a voteless 'show of views', in the democratic formation of which 5 per cent. of the delegates managed to speak, and the platform took one third of the-time allotted.

"One wonders, in this 'planned economy' of expression, how many of the mostly militant socialist delegates realised, until it was too late, what they had done! On the face of things, four years after the great victory for a forward socialist policy achieved in 1945, they accepted a mixed economy, 80 per cent. capitalist, designed to remain virtually stationary for five years in a world which is turning over to successful socialist economy at such a speed that over half the world may be socialist before the five years are over. They endorsed the wage freeze, congratulated the trade unions on keeping wages down, and resolved to produce more for the same wages in the service of their capitalist bosses, with no guarantee of full employment or stabilised prices and no more provision for limitation of profits than is given by well-phrased exhortations to the wolf to consider carefully the true interests of the lamb. They accepted all the rubbish talked in the Tory Press and elsewhere against the U.S.S.R. without even realising—so far as one can tell—that that rubbish is at once the weapon of the monopoly capitalist war-mongers who dominate our country from Wall Street, and the forcing-ground of war preparations and the third world war. And they accepted uncritically Ernest Bevin's well-known speech, and with it a foreign policy that costs us £2,000,000 a day in preparation for a battle against the Socialist sector of the world in which we should be politically on the wrong side and strategically at the wrong end of the bomb track. . . .

"But far more remarkable and tragic is the fashion in which the Conference succeeded in ignoring almost all the realities—realities in part ominous and in part full of hope—of the political and economic situation.

"Perhaps the most striking omission was the effect of the tie-up with the 100 per cent. monopoly ruling-class of the United States. These ruthless gentlemen make it impossible for us to pursue any aggressive socialist policy; they condemn us in advance to joining their coming slump; it is their policy to ruin in the near future the very export drive in whose service the Conference pledged itself to keep down wages and produce more for the same pay. . . .

"There was not of course anywhere even a hint of any intention to transfer power to the working class; the brave souls who talked, for example, of taking the land were just brushed aside. . . .

"The greatest of all the omissions was probably the failure to realise that the whole mood of the country is changing, and that the political situation is becoming so lively and fluid that almost anything may happen except the relative stagnation and immobility which every platform speaker accepted as the basic assumption of his arguments. They all, apparently, took it for granted that they could continue the wage freeze, could somehow settle, crush, or otherwise dispose of the inevitably resultant strikes, could keep up the dollar export drive in face of the American slump by prayers and hard work—their prayers and your work—and could thus go into a General Election in 1950 in much the atmosphere of June, 1945, with their problems unsolved and their policies unaltered, relying for victory on the certainly remarkable confusion and policy-bankruptcy of the Tories."

(And, of course, few of them could foresee the devaluation of the pound or the crisis which followed in October.)

It may be worth noticing, in point of time, that this Conference took place about the time of a case in the Courts which marked another low point in the subjection of our government to the U.S.A. A militant German Communist, Gerhardt Eisler, had "jumped his bail" and slipped out of the United States on the Polish ship *Batory*, which was to call at Southampton on her way from New York. The Americans were very angry at his escape—although they did not want him, and had indeed made an expulsion order against him which he was willing to obey; and they accordingly requested—or ordered, whichever word one likes to use—the British Government to take him off the *Batory* when it called at Southampton and send him back to the U.S.A. The only method by which this could conceivably be done lawfully was by the process of "extradition", which provides by treaty for the return from one country to another of any person (not a citizen of the country returning him) to the demanding country *if and only if* there is evidence against the person to be extradited showing *prima facie* that he may be guilty of some offence *listed in the schedule to the Treaty* in question. In Eisler's case there never was a shadow of evidence that he had been guilty of any offence listed in the Treaty between Britain and the U.S.A.; the nearest the Americans could get—a fatally long distance away— was to suggest that he had committed perjury, an offence mentioned in the treaty. Perjury consists of giving false evidence on oath in legal proceedings; and all that could be plausibly alleged was that they held him to be guilty of having made a false statement in an answer to a questionnaire, *not on oath and not in legal proceedings.* The British Government should have refused absolutely to take him off the ship; instead they boarded the *Batory*, hunted him out, frog-marched him off (without even having the intelligence to make sure that the journalists were not photographing this gratuitous piece of brutality), and held him in custody. In due course he was brought before the Magistrate at Bow Street, where the U.S.A. sought an order for his extradition. It did not take long for the magistrate to see that it was impossible to make any such order, and he was released. The U.S. Press then started a campaign against the British Government, accusing it of "ingratitude" for obeying its own laws! (A story went round Parliament at the time that the decision to take Eisler off the *Batory* was taken by Ernest Bevin, who described the position as "one of the times when I 'ad to be Britain". Perhaps he was right, if by "Britain" he meant the Government.)

TORY PAMPHLET

In July, the Tory Party produced a counterblast to *Labour Believes in Britain*, called *The Right Road for Britain*. Critics noticed that there was a large "overlap" of common ground between the two documents. Such an overlap was bound to be present when the hard facts were that the party which in 1945 had flown the socialist banner and the party of capitalist reaction were now in agreement on a dozen major points of policy: the Atlantic Pact; the Marshall Plan; the wage freeze; the payment of colossal prices to landowners; the Cold War; American troops and bases on our soil; sanctity of the National Debt, of rent, interest, and profit; anti-communist witch-hunts and purges; police protection for fascists; war in Malaya; and rearmament.

After the devaluation of the pound there came demands from both Tories and some Labour circles for an early election; but the Cabinet decided on the 13th October that there should be no dissolution in 1949. (The announcement of a dissolution and election came—as already mentioned—on the 10th January, and polling day was the 23rd February 1950.)

Thus ended in tameness and uncertainty, with the Labour, Conservative and Liberal parties preoccupied with a coming General Election, a year of tremendous happenings. In that twelve months, socialists could count among their blessings the establishment of the Chinese People's Republic—surely the second greatest event of modern history—the foundation of the German Democratic Republic, the Paris-Prague Peace Conference, and twelve months of tremendous contrast between the development of the socialist countries and the growing crises of the capitalist world, including the ever more manifest fiasco of the Marshall Plan of salvation for capitalism.

Against those glories, they had to reckon with the establishment of NATO, the disruption of world trade union unity involved in the breakaway from the World Federation of Trade Unions, and all the miseries of devaluation, economic crises, wage-freezes, rising prices, and an arms race.

And, as we shall see, this great year was to be followed by what

Winston Churchill called a "demure" General Election, in which the two main parties, in sublime indifference to the great issues of the day, fought one another on such differences as they could find between themselves. They reminded one of the moment in Goethe's *Sorrows of Werther*, as "boiled down" by Thackeray:

> "Charlotte, having seen his body,
>   Borne before her on a shutter,
> Like a well-conducted person,
>   Went on cutting bread and butter."

CHAPTER 28

The General Election, 1950

THE announcement of the Dissolution and Election came on the 10th January, 1950; the polling-date was the 23rd February. The Election Manifesto of the Labour Party, called *Let Us Win Through Together* was published on the 18th January. It was a reduced version of *Labour Believes in Britain*, with one or two significant differences. It was silent, for example, on wages policy. It gave pride of place to the maintenance of full employment, as to which fears were entertained lest the developing slump in the U.S.A. would soon cause unemployment in Britain. (The Government claimed it as a very great achievement on its part that full employment had been maintained ever since it came to power; this was only partly justified, for even the capitalist system can give full employment during the years of reconstruction after a great war; and, indeed, Aneurin Bevan had rather spoilt the claim, in a speech defending our dependence on the U.S.A., by asserting that without American aid we would have a million or more unemployed!)

The Manifesto made one change in the nationalisation proposals, changing the "nationalisation" of industrial insurance to "mutualisation"; the effect was to substitute ownership by the policy holders for that of the existing proprietary companies, leaving unaffected concerns already mutually owned, such as the Co-operative Insurance Company and the Liverpool Victoria. There was no direct reference to the defence services or their cost, or to American aid; and no mention of foreign affairs beyond a condemnation of Munich and a promise to work "realistically" for peace. Still less was anything to be seen of the old stirring demands of the socialist past, in truth more important than ever in the present: no capital levy, no pledge of friendship with the socialist countries; no sweeping promises of large-scale housebuilding; no talk of health centres or new hospitals; no promise to cut military expenditure; no declaration of belief in land nationalisation; no repetition of the great declaration of 1945 that "Labour will not tolerate freedom to exploit other people"; not even an unqualified promise of equal pay to women for equal work; no further assertion of the 1945 "common bond with the working people of all countries who have achieved a new dignity and influence through their long struggles against Nazi tyranny".

The impression given was of a desire to confine the election fight mainly to domestic issues.

The Tory Manifesto—*This is the Road*—had an even greater area of common ground with the Labour one than had been the case with the longer pamphlets issued earlier.

A MILD CAMPAIGN

The campaign had, on the surface, at any rate, a certain mildness; it had great unreality, too, since both parties seemed anxious to avoid discussion of the vital issues of foreign policy, and the distortions of domestic policies which they caused, and to be more concerned with attacking one another on past records than on making serious provision for the great but precarious future. But party machines, even if they act in concert, cannot always—in spite of the immensely powerful propaganda apparatus at their disposal—compel the electorate to keep its mind off issues that it regards as vital. And, as this campaign developed, the electorate, greatly helped in this by the campaign of the Communist Party, which put up a hundred candidates, insisted on bringing up its anxieties about peace. Constituents began to worry candidates on this point, and on the effect of their leaders' policies on the preservation of peace. This led the adroit Winston Churchill, on the 14th February, to suggest at a meeting in Edinburgh "another talk with Soviet Russia upon the highest level . . . a supreme effort to bridge the gulf between the two worlds, so that each can live their life, if not in friendship, at least without the hatreds and manœuvres of the cold war".

Churchill was loudly applauded by his audience. His move was immediately denounced by Labour leaders as an "election stunt"; no doubt it was, but it would plainly never have been tried if Churchill had not seen that the electorate was much pre-occupied with the question of peace; and, as Mr. Milliband points out at p. 308 of his book, if it was a stunt, it is a pity the Labour leaders didn't think of it first! Their answer to it was merely a few anti-Soviet comments on the difficulty of "dealing with the Russians". But Churchill, realising how popular his suggestion was, took the matter up again in an election broadcast to the nation on the 17th February. On the next day, Mr.

Attlee, in his election broadcast, gave the lukewarm and little positive reply that "we are ready at all times to co-operate with Russia on equal terms in the comity of nations. But it must be on equal terms."

EXPECTING A CLOSE RESULT

The other interesting feature of the election was that towards the end most electors were feeling—and they proved to be right—that the result was going to be very close; this had two effects, firstly, that there was a large poll (84 per cent.), and, secondly, that most electors voted for the one or the other of the two main parties; as one of my own electors put it to me: "I want to vote for a man who I know for certain will always support the government, whether he thinks it is right or wrong." Most Labour electors, however disappointed they might be, were still latently conscious that there was a class struggle, and that their side of it was represented—however badly—in politics by the Labour Party; and they wanted to make sure of putting in to Parliament M.P.s who would always vote their way. One result was, naturally, to eliminate every independent candidate, as well as the two Communist M.P.s.*

RESULT

In the end the Labour Party had a small and unworkable "absolute" majority of six. The 624 seats (623 if one excludes the Speaker), and the votes were distributed thus:

	Seats	Votes
Labour	315	13,348,451
Conservatives, etc. . . .	297	12,441,153
Liberals	10	2,782,319
Irish Nationalists	2	65,211
Communists	0	91,815
Irish, Scottish & Welsh Nationalists .	0	93,421
Independents, etc. . . .	0	112,318

* I was one of the independents thus eliminated. I remember a conversation I had with an ordinary worker whom I met in the course of the campaign, running thus:

ELECTOR: "You're a good man, and I voted for you in 1945. But I'm voting official Labour this time."

PRITT: "You know, that means that you are in favour of the wage-freeze, the cold-war, anti-Soviet policy, inadequate housing, being tied to the U.S.A. instead of advancing to socialism, and all the rest of the bad policy I am fighting. Are you in favour of any of these things?"

ELECTOR: "Don't be daft. Of course I'm not. I agree with all you say, but I'm still voting official Labour."

The total poll was 84 per cent. as compared with 74·5 per cent. in 1945. The Labour vote had risen by 1⅓ millions; the Tory vote had risen by 2½ million. The percentage of the total votes cast which went to Labour had dropped from 48·5 per cent to 46·1 per cent.; the Tory percentage had risen from 39·9 per cent. to 43·4 per cent.; the Liberal percentage had risen one-tenth of 1 per cent. from 9·0 to 9·1. The "swing" in the vote was 3·3 per cent. The redistribution of seats had greatly favoured the Tories.

In truth, on ordinary professional electioneering calculations, the Labour Party had fared well to lose no more votes or seats than they did, after nearly five years of government at a period of great difficulty. But both the election and its result had taken place in a sort of vacuum remote from all the real political and economic facts and dangers of life. The Election solved no problem; it merely transferred the existing problems from a government which had a working majority to one which had not.

I wrote a comment at the time in *Labour Monthly*, some of which I will quote here (from pp. 174 *et seq.*):

"In 1945 the electorate had voted for socialism; it wanted the responsibilities, the anxieties, the glories of the fight for socialism, and sent the Labour leaders and M.P.s to Parliament to fight for them. The leaders promised to lead; they promised a policy of peace, of friendship with our ally the Soviet Union, of consciously created bonds of comradeship with workers everywhere, of rising standards of living, of ample housing.

"But the leaders broke their promises and deserted. They had excuses, explanations, alibis, denials, all plausible enough, but they deserted—in some fields, such as foreign relations, at the very start, in others more slowly. By the end of 1949, it was clear that their 'march to Socialism' had changed to a close economic tie-up with the convulsive capitalism of the United States, rendering any advance on the Socialist road both economically and politically impossible; their 'peace policy' consisted in being a junior partner—providing bombing bases and cannon-fodder—in the mightiest conspiracy for war that the world has ever seen, run by the terrified financiers and militarists of the Pentagon plus the State Department plus Wall Street; their 'friendship with the Soviet Union' took the form of propagating lies and abuse of the U.S.S.R. and of every socialist country in the world; their 'comradeship with the workers of the

W

world' embraced everyone except the two-fifths of the world which saw nothing wrong in Communism; and they sacrificed our hopes of rising standards of living and of housing to a colossal scheme of armament expenditure dictated by the U.S.A., with its logical consequence of the wage-freeze, the cuts in housing, a rising cost of living, and acquiescence in ever-increasing profit making. . . .

"In those circumstances, what sort of a General Election did we get? The two main parties were agreed on the whole foreign policy, the Marshall Plan, the Atlantic Pact, the readiness for an anti-Soviet, anti-communist armaments race—atom and hydrogen bombs and all—in short, a pure war policy. They were agreed, too, on the wage-freeze, on the imperialist grip on the colonies, on the policy of trade boycotts of the socialist world—in short, on every vital issue. They thus went to the electorate with all these vital issues masked by their agreement, and with the support of a high measure of success in the press and radio propaganda which had worked steadily for years to present their war-policy as one of defence of peace; and the stern reality of crisis, slump, and unemployment which must soon horrify and disillusion the younger generation of workers, to whom mass unemployment is as yet unknown, was kept off-stage, muttering in the wings, by the adroit manœuvre of holding the General Election before the slump developed.

"The Communists, the Labour Independents, and a few of the official Labour candidates (if they dared to speak up) had the right policy, and the great mass of the workers would have agreed with that policy if it had been presented to them on the scale on which the Labour and Tory policies were presented. They wanted peace; they knew a war policy when they saw it; they wanted increased real wages, a better standard of living, more and cheaper houses, limitation of profits, and a resumption of the march to socialism.

"What did the electorate do? The non-working-class electorate, completely bamboozled, was mildly interested in the contest between Tweedledum, who would hold them in the American war camp and the American economic whirlpool, and Tweedledee, who would hold them in the same place. The majority of the working class did better than that, and of course better than its Tweedleaders. It didn't want the Tories; it opposed in the main the Tory policy as put forward by the Labour leaders; and it was thus confronted by a choice of evils. The two (or three) party system was felt to bar the way to voting for the policy which represented true working-class interests; indeed, in most constituencies, it had only the choice of Tory, Liberal, or Labour, the last-named either right wing by conviction or compelled to support the right-wing policy of the leaders.

"What could the workers do? What did they do? They were of course better than their leaders . . .; both the consciously political and the more or less unconscious saw the class struggle which their leaders blandly deny, thought to use their vote against the Tory class enemy, and so polarised themselves on the one mass party whose true job it is to fight the Tories, the party which would at least keep the Tories out of office if it won enough seats."

CHAPTER 29

The 1950 Session

As is usual after a General Election, there was some reconstruction of the Government, but it was not on any great scale. Seven Ministers had failed to get re-elected; one of them, Creech Jones, was a Cabinet Minister, and one, Soskice, was Solicitor-General. No effort was made to find new seats for any of these except Soskice. The case of Silkin, who had been Minister of Town and Country Planning, was interesting. In the extensive redistribution of seats, his constituency had disappeared, and he had set about finding another one. It should not have been difficult, for he was a Minister and an able parliamentarian, and there were plenty of good constituencies looking for candidates; but wherever he went he found the central party machine working steadily to try to prevent him being adopted. Thus, he did not find a seat at all, was not given office in the reconstituted government, and soon afterwards went to the House of Lords. The reason for this virtual boycott of a good Minister was significant; he was friendly with the new government of Poland, and he had never been heard to say a word against the U.S.S.R.

None of the ministerial changes was important. Bevin and Cripps remained in their important offices, although both of them were by now in pretty bad health.

The new Parliament assembled on the 6th March, and the King's Speech was read on the 10th; the session ended on the 4th October, 1950. A majority so small as to be unworkable confronts a government with the not very pleasant choice of either "marking time" with unimportant and more or less uncontroversial measures and policies, or of going ahead with a strong programme, intending—if there should be a defeat on an important vote—to appeal to the country in a new Election in the hope of getting a larger and workable majority. The Government chose the former course, dropping all the proposed nationalisation or mutualisation measures, (but not abandoning the actual introduction of the Iron and Steel Nationalisation which had been provided for in the legislation of 1949).

THE KING'S SPEECH

The King's Speech began by noting that both industrial and agricultural production had increased, with the assistance of the Governments and peoples of the rest of the Commonwealth; and that the world dollar shortage had been eased by help from the U.S.A. and Canada. To this it added that renewed efforts were needed to balance our overseas trade and in particular to increase our earnings in North America.

Support was to be maintained for the Organisation for European Economic Co-operation, through which it was hoped to work out a new European Payments Scheme.

The opportunity for an exchange of views on foreign affairs provided by the recent meeting of Commonwealth Ministers in Colombo was welcomed, and the Government looked forward to co-operation with other Commonwealth governments in South and South-East Asia.

The inauguration of the Republic of the United States of Indonesia on the 27th December, 1949, was welcomed; diplomatic relations had been established with it. On the 6th January, the Government had recognised the Chinese People's Republic and on the 7th February the States of Vietnam, Laos and Cambodia as associate States within the French Union.

Full support was promised for U.N., and the hope was expressed of finding through that organisation a durable solution to the problem of atomic energy, so that international agreement for adequate control and supervision of the production of atomic energy might be secured; and the Government promised to do its utmost for the success of the Council of Europe.

The establishment of the Federal German Government was said to have made possible the progressive transfer of responsibilities from the Western Allies to the Germans, thus substantially reducing the cost of administration falling on the allies in Germany.

The Government promised to maintain the closest relations with the other signatory powers of the North Atlantic and Brussels Treaties; to play its due part in strengthening the common means of defence; and to take all necessary steps to ensure that the armed forces should be ready to meet their responsibilities in all parts of the world.

The new Civil Defence organisation was to be developed.

The Government was, it said, actively promoting the economic and social development of the colonial territories, and the Colonial

Development Corporation was proving a useful instrument. All practical steps were to be taken to increase agricultural output and to make better use of marginal land.

I wrote shortly after this speech, that:

"From the first moment of this Parliament, with its colourless King's Speech, it became clear that there is to be a move towards a Coalition-behind-the-scenes, a Coalition of policies."

The legislation proposed was, inevitably, of minor importance; it dealt with water supplies, medical education, midwives, the breaking up of streets, and the placing of cattle grids in highways.

CHAPTER 30

Foreign Policy, 1950

THE recognition of the Chinese People's Republic was an admirable step with which to begin the year which was to be darkened by the outbreak of the Korean war, the subject of the next chapter. It is tragic that this recognition was not followed—even up to 1962, as I am writing—either by the exchange of Ambassadors or support for the admission of the new government to its rightful position in the United Nations. As just mentioned, the recognition came on the 6th January, before the General Election.

The bad reasons which had led the Government to take this good step were given by Bevin in the House of Commons in the course of a foreign affairs debate on the 24th May, 1950. He spoke as nearly apologetically as one of his temperament could, and did not rely on any of the grounds traditionally recognised as just and adequate for the recognition of new régimes, such as the firm establishment of the government in effective and secure control of the country. Instead, he emphasised that Britain had many interests in China, and many of our citizens were there—it was interesting that he mentioned the "interests" before the citizens, like the group of Tory M.P.s during the war who put down a motion deploring some incident "which had led to the destruction of valuable property and to loss of life"—and that pressure for recognition had been brought upon the Government by "all our China interests and our experts". India, Bevin said, had recognised the new government earlier, and he had talked over the problem first with Nehru and later with the American Secretary of State, Dean Acheson; there had been some divergence of view between himself and Acheson, and of course a desire "to keep in step with the U.S.A.". But in the end the Government had decided on recognition without American concurrence, so as "not to let the Russians"—as he always called the U.S.S.R.—"assume that they were the only country who would do anything at all for China". He did say, earlier in his speech, that it was not for us to consider the political colour of the new government, thus correctly stating a sound principle of international law, if perhaps straining the credulity of the public.

CHINESE EXCLUDED FROM U.N.

Bevin also explained why the Government had, in spite of the recognition, voted against the admission of the Chinese People's Republic to its seat in the U.N. It will be remembered that the U.S.A. had executed a pretty outrageous manœuvre, which is still in effect as I write twelve years later, to keep the new régime in China out of its proper place in U.N. Under the U.N. Charter, China is one of the five permanent members of the Security Council; and until the establishment of the Chinese People's Republic in October, 1949, she was represented by the delegates of the Kuomintang, the then recognised government of China. From that date, it became ever more obvious that the rout of this gang was final; that it had lost its last foothold on the Chinese mainland; that it was confined to Taiwan (Formosa); and that even there, as it was soon clear, it only continued to exist by force of American arms. Every consideration of international law, reality, and commonsense required that "China" should be represented at the U.N. by the one indisputable Government of the country, recognised as such by Britain and most other countries, although not by the U.S.A. But the U.S.A. has succeeded ever since in compelling or cajoling the U.N. to keep this government out, and to admit the Kuomintang puppet delegates in its place.

Bevin asserted in his speech, by the way of giving a reason for our concurrence in this manœuvre, that the Government had been quite ready to vote for the admission of China, but that it had been prevented by the "Russian" boycott of the U.N. (The U.S.S.R. had refused to attend the meetings of the Security Council so long as China was represented there by the Kuomintang delegates; and this, in some way which Bevin did not succeed in making clear, rendered it impossible for us to vote for admission. The suspicion arises, naturally, that the Government had been bluntly ordered by the Americans to vote against the admission, and Bevin, having to find the best excuse he could, was delighted to blame "the Russians".

STILL AGAINST GERMAN REARMAMENT

When the new Session began, the first business that in reality concerned foreign affairs came in March, with the "defence" estimates of £899 million, destined as so often before to be greatly increased before the year was out. In the debate on foreign affairs at the end of the month, Churchill advocated the creation of a West German army, on the ground that Europe could not be unified or restored without Germany. In reply, Bevin declared emphatically against any German rearmament, as the French Government had already done. He was not to change his mind—or to have it changed for him—until September.

THE STOCKHOLM APPEAL

Another remarkable event of March, 1950, was the inauguration of the "Stockholm Appeal". The Permanent Committee of the World Peace Council, meeting in Stockholm, adopted two appeals. The first and most famous of them inaugurated a signature campaign for an appeal worded:

> "We demand unconditional prohibition of the atomic weapon as a weapon of aggression and mass annihilation of people, and that strict international control for the implementation of this decision be established. We shall consider as a war criminal that government which first employs the atomic weapon against any country. We call upon all people of good will throughout the world to sign the appeal."

The second appeal called for the holding of a second World Peace Congress.

The first appeal led to the collection of many millions of signatures in all socialist and "neutral" countries, and of great numbers in capitalist countries too. The British Peace Committee, a relatively young body, with no large organisation and deprived of the help of almost all Labour Party members owing to its being proscribed by the Labour Party—"peace is a dirty word"—collected 823,000 signatures by the middle of July; it found that practically everyone who was approached was ready to sign, but it was hampered by the limited number of people who could find time for the work of collection and who—if they were Labour Party members—were prepared to face expulsion from the party for taking part in it.

At the beginning of April, 1950, the Defence Ministers of the NATO countries met at the Hague and approved plans for "collective self-defence". (At about the same moment, it was announced that a new "atomic energy" establishment was to be built at a Berkshire village called Aldermaston. This is now known as the "Atomic Weapons Research Establishment", and its name has been made world famous by the work of the Campaign for Nuclear Disarmament.)

NATO COUNCIL MEETS

On the 15th May, the Council of NATO held a meeting in London, preceded by an important meeting of the Foreign Ministers of the U.S.A., Britain and France (Dean Acheson, Bevin and Schuman). This meeting of Ministers was a somewhat sinister gathering; according to *The Times*, Dean Acheson, the American Secretary of State, brought to it "no new policy, but a conviction, deepened by long experience and profound study, that the 'cold war' must be accepted as a permanent feature of future planning, and that all efforts must therefore be directed to strengthening the political, economic and military forces of the Atlantic Powers".

The Observer reported that "American emphasis will rest on the need for military preparedness even at the cost of economic sacrifice".

At a dinner at the Savoy Hotel on the 10th May, 1950, Acheson said: "Some sacrifice of purely national interest will be unavoidable . . . we must accustom ourselves to the thought."

According to the American columnist Mr. Joseph Alsop, who was known to have the ear of the State Department, Acheson's concrete demand at this time was that the "Atlantic Community" must immediately raise its "defence" expenditure by £5,000,000 *per day;* but Mr. Alsop had not yet learnt—or at any rate did not state—how much of this increase was to fall on Great Britain.

FOREIGN MINISTERS' PRONOUNCEMENTS

The three Foreign Ministers were prodigal of statements. The first, on the 12th May, was a Declaration attacking the U.S.S.R. for its alleged failure to repatriate German prisoners-of-war; the only evidence of any such failure was an assertion by the West German Government that many hundreds of thousands of men reported by the Nazis during the war as captured in the U.S.S.R. had not been returned. There was no doubt that the men so reported had not returned, but there was nothing whatever to suggest that the Nazi reports were reliable or to contradict the statement of the Soviet Government that, apart from certain named men retained as guilty of offences, they had returned every prisoner they had. The truth was almost certainly that during the war the Nazis, in an effort to conceal from their public the appalling casualties suffered on their Eastern front, had reported many hundreds of thousands of men as prisoners when they had in fact been killed in battle, that the semi-fascist West Germans had adopted the story to embitter their people against the U.S.S.R., and that the Foreign Ministers had done the same.

The Times and the *Manchester Guardian*, indeed, both remarked that the main object of making this Declaration was to increase bitterness between Western Germany and the U.S.S.R.; and the *Manchester Guardian* expressed the view that the statement of the Soviet Government was probably correct. But that bit of reason from two of our principal capitalist newspapers did not prevent the Labour Government from joining in a disgraceful and dangerous manœuvre.

On the following day, the 13th May, the three Ministers, having finished their meeting, issued a communiqué, which may be summarised as follows:

1. They had agreed on the main lines of their policy in all parts of the world;

2. The strength of the free world would never be used for aggressive purposes;

3. The free world could achieve social and material well-being in addition to its necessary defence measures, since it commanded by far the greater part of the industrial and technical resources of mankind;

4. They had agreed on a declaration of policy on Germany, which had now been sent to the West German Chancellor, Dr. Adenauer;

5. They envisaged a new joint Western drive to combat "communist imperialism" in both Asia and Africa, including as immediate measures the prevention of arms smuggling, the exposure of communist aims and methods, and co-operation to raise the standard of living of the peoples; and

6. They intended to meet more often in the future.

DECLARATION ON GERMANY

On the following day, the Ministers issued a further Declaration, on the subject of Germany It stated that the German peace treaty could not be concluded so long as Soviet policy remained unchanged; controls, however, would be progressively relinquished and German sovereignty restored to the maximum extent compatible with an occupation régime. As Mr. and Mrs. Coates remark at p. 407 of their book, "the two declarations were tantamount to the tearing up of the Anglo-Soviet Treaty of 1942".

NATO COUNCIL COMMUNIQUÉ

The meeting of the NATO Council itself, already mentioned, followed, on the 15th to 18th May, 1950. Its final communiqué was a long one, from which I need only quote one or two paragraphs, as follows:

"4. The Council, recognising the indispensability of self-help and mutual aid among the treaty powers in making progress towards an integrated defence, and convinced that further mutual assistance is essential to rapid progress towards the strength required for the common security of the North Atlantic area, recommended that each party make its full contribution through mutual assistance in all practicable forms.

"5. The Council . . . urged their governments to concentrate on the creation of balanced collective forces in the progressive build-up of the defence of the North Atlantic area, taking at the same time fully into consideration the requirements for national forces which arise out of commitments external to the North Atlantic area."

It will be noticed that these meetings in London coincided with the "Schuman Plan" put forward by the French Government, to which I will refer in a moment.

The comment of the *Sunday Times*' Washington correspondent on the Conference was pretty correct:

"Mr. Acheson perhaps gained more from the Conference than Mr. Bevin or Mr. Schuman. Britain's decision to join the European Payments Union, the general consent to accept Germany as an ally, stepped-up rearmament, agreement on the principle of the collective defence force, and the new permanent executive committee of the Atlantic Council, all represent an acceptance of Mr. Acheson's policies, some of which Britain or France refused to agree to in the past."

The Political Committee of the Communist Party was surely right when it issued a statement on the 25th May (the day after Bevin made the speech in the House of Commons about the recognition of the Chinese People's Republic and the refusal to let it take its place in the U.N.) to the effect that:

"This Conference was in fact a war council entirely aimed at speeding up the preparations for an aggressive world war. . . .

"Military plans have been drawn up, in accordance with a so-called 'integrated Atlantic strategy' to establish American control over the military expenditure, training and equipment of forces, and strategic role of Britain and the other Western European Powers.

"Decisions have been taken to intensify the wars now in progress against the peoples of S.E. Asia, with American participation. Under United States pressure all the Atlantic countries have agreed to continue their support of the discredited Kuomintang agents on the Security Council, in order to prevent the participation of the Chinese People's Government.

"Special concentration on the Middle East was emphasised by American and British declarations of their intentions to continue military interventionist 'aid' to the puppet reactionary governments of Greece, Turkey and Persia. . . . Preparations for the rearmament of the fascist forces of Western Germany are now being openly discussed.

"Mr. Bevin's speech in the House of Commons on May 24th was the most openly bellicose, anti-Soviet speech yet made by him."

TRYGVE LIE VISITS MOSCOW

This formidable cold-war conference was contemporaneous not only with the birth of the Schuman Plan (to be discussed in a moment) but also with the visit to Moscow of Trygve Lie, Secretary General of the U.N. At a Press Conference in Paris on the 3rd May, 1950, Lie had said:

"It is proposed to split the world permanently into two camps, and to that road there is only one possible end—a third world war sooner or later. The first step to stop the Cold War must be to restore the United Nations as a meeting place for negotiations on differences among the great Powers. The longer the Cold War lasts the more the U.N. becomes incapable of functioning efficiently";

and he announced that he would visit Moscow to discuss the situation with the Soviet leaders. This proposal not only provided a formidable contrast to the line that was plainly going to be taken by the meeting and the Conference in London, which I have just described, but also pointed out to world opinion that all the elaborate NATO scheming was in truth a breach and defiance of the U.N. Charter, for the pretence that NATO was a regional pact within the Charter—the hollowness of which I explained in Chapter 21—was by now long forgotten.

Lie arrived in Moscow on the 11th May, and returned to the U.S.A. on the 25th May. *The Times*, in the same issue in which it described Acheson as bringing to London "no new policy, but a conviction . . . that the cold war" was a permanent feature (quoted above) wrote that Lie represented the "belief that a great effort must be made this year to put an end to the cold war, preferably through the agency of the United Nations".

Lie was well received in Moscow, and returned to the U.S.A. with the feeling, as he reported, that his conversation with the Soviet leaders had been positive, with an undertone of peace, and that he had been satisfied with them. In sections of the U.S. Press he was accused of having become "an agent of the Kremlin".

In a Press Conference which he gave at the headquarters of the U.N. on the 26th May, he repeated his warnings that if the Cold War was not brought to an end the world would be faced by a third world war; but he added:

"My trip has confirmed my belief that no Government wants war. It has been the undertone of all the conversations I had with the Soviet leaders."

THE SCHUMAN PLAN

The Schuman Plan was put forward by the French Government on the 9th May, 1950; the proposal was, in essence, that "an authority should be created which should take over control of the production of all steel and coal in Western Europe; it would not have ownership rights, but it would have controlling power". It was proposed to embrace France, Germany, Britain, Italy, Holland, Belgium and Luxemburg.

The main background on which the plan had been formulated was the approaching end of the post-war shortage of coal, which at one time had been extremely acute. At the end of March, a statement issued by the Press Office of the United Nations said that during the second quarter of 1950 Europe would have a surplus of 3,000,000 tons of gas and steam coal and domestic coke.

Further, the rate of German steel production had risen between January and March from 10,900,000 tons a year to 12,200,000, French production in the same period falling from the rate of 11,200,000 to that of 7,900,000 tons.

This plan was put forward because French big business and heavy industry were becoming greatly alarmed at the resurgence of Germany as an economic competitor; moreover, the French steelmasters wanted to have cheap coking coal from the Ruhr, and a "cartel" arrangement with the Germans, as they had had before the war, to share out markets.

GERMANS WELCOME SCHUMAN PLAN

The Germans—both the government and the Ruhr industrialists—welcomed the plan, which they took to be the end of the limitations imposed on German steel production and the first big step towards throwing off other shackles that had been imposed by the occupying powers to prevent a repetition of German aggression.

The Americans were of course delighted, it helped their aim of complete European economic integration and the creation of a single vast market in Europe.

The substance of the plan was well stated in an article in *World News* on the 24th June, 1950:

"The Schuman Plan is a plan for pooling coal and steel production under an international authority, whose decisions would have to be accepted by the governments of the countries taking part. . . . It is a get-together of the most powerful monopolies of Germany and France . . . the most important thing of all is that it openly restores the monopoly capitalism of Western Germany to full status alongside the other European capitalist powers.

"This must be seen in conjunction with the announcement by Professor Ehrhard, West German Minister of Economics, that the ban on foreign investment in German industries is now definitely to be lifted. To this add American High Commissioner McCloy's statement that 'so long as the allies were in Germany—and they expected to be here for some time—they would do everything to help the Germans on their own way' and the essence of the Schuman Plan becomes clear.

"It is a plan to build up European monopoly capitalism, centred on Germany, and to use its industries as arsenals for war. . ."

POLITICAL AIMS OF SCHUMAN PLAN

The political objects of the Plan were at least as important as the economic. On both sides of the Atlantic, comment emphasised that the main object of the Plan was to achieve "political ends by economic means"—that it was in short a move in the Cold War. The *Economist* wrote of it on the 20th May:

"The strategic priorities must take precedence over everything else. Politically, the Schuman offer stands or falls on the question whether it strengthens or weakens the Atlantic link, and whether it makes easier or more difficult an effective defence for Europe."

In other words, the plan was designed to restore the power of the Ruhr magnates and to harness Ruhr coal and steel to the armed force of the United States.

BRITISH HESITATION

The British Government was hesitant in its attitude. On the 11th May, 1950, in the House of Commons, Attlee said that it "would approach the problem in a sympathetic spirit and a desire ... to welcome this French initiative to end the age-long feud with Germany". But industrial and commercial anxieties gained ground, and by the time a six-power conference on the Plan was held in Paris on the 20th June the British attended as observers only, and in the end they did not accept the Plan. The Foreign Office wanted to do so, but Cripps, still a powerful figure in spite of his illness, prevailed, and swung the Government to reject participation.

He pressed the view that we must avoid any commitment, political or economic, which might damage the sterling area and the network of trading and monetary policies built upon it.

When the matter was debated in the House of Commons on the 27th June, Cripps said:

"In our view, participation in a political federation limited to Western Europe, is not compatible either with our Commonwealth ties or our obligations as a member of the wider Atlantic Community or as a world power."

The Schuman Plan was in a sense a forerunner of the Common Market, and the divisions of British opinion in 1950 as to what should be done were very like those of 1962 relating to the Common Market.

CHAPTER 31

The War in Korea

By far the most important international event of 1950 was the outbreak of the Korean War. It began on the 25th June, 1950. It has, technically speaking, not yet ended, but it came to a standstill in July 1953.

It was one of the most important of wars, pregnant of infinite evil, and in particular of the acute danger of a third world war; for it was built up by the United States into a major item of "proof" that the socialist world was bent on aggression, and thus into a pretext for the long U.S. occupation of Taiwan (Formosa), all American interest in which had been expressly disclaimed by President Truman as recently as the 5th January, when he rejected General MacArthur's programme for aggressive military action there, declaring that "the U.S. Government will not provide military aid or advice to Chinese forces on Formosa"; Acheson at the same time stated that "we are not going to get involved in any way on the island of Formosa".

The war was used, too, both by the U.S.A. and Britain, as an additional pretext for their refusal as to give the Chinese People's Republic its place in the U.N. and indeed it has always served as one of the more important pretexts for the continuation and intensification of the arms race and the Cold War.

WHO BEGAN IT?

It was presented to the world by the U.S.A. and its satellites, including the British government, as a clear and simple case of aggression by the Korean People's Democratic Republic (North Korea) egged on by the U.S.S.R. against the Republic of Korea (South Korea), an aggression which called imperatively for the immediate intervention of the United Nations as an honourable and lawful step in the defence of peace.

Whilst that version was given to the people of the West, what the government and people of North Korea, and the socialist world

X

generally, maintained as the truth was that the aggression came from South Korea, armed, equipped, trained, to some extent actually offic-ered, and instigated by the U.S.A.

It is one of the frightening features of modern propaganda that, at a time when literacy and education are more widely spread than ever before, and the means of diffusion of information infinitely more copious, it is possible for two halves of the world to be largely con-vinced the one of one version and the other of the exact opposite, in relation to events vital to the existence of all of us. The Korean War is not the only example of this evil, but is one of the worst.

Where did the truth lie? It was, and still is, a matter of acute con-troversy. One could write a book about it; indeed, the writer of this book did write what practically amounted to a book* about it; that eminent Conservative ex-civil servant Sir John Pratt wrote another†; and the courageous and well-informed American journalist Mr. I. F. Stone wrote yet another.‡

It is not practicable within the limits of this book to give an account of all the evidence on this controversy, which I myself have marshalled and studied as thoroughly as I ever studied anything; I must content myself with a series of propositions, all of which I and others have demonstrated to be true:

1. That the war was begun by South Korea attacking North Korea, with American aid and equipment, after South Korea had been seeking to attack for years, being always—until this time—held back by the U.S.A. because the latter thought that the time was not ripe, and the South not yet strong enough;

2. That when a decision was purported to be made by the United Nations to intervene in the war, on the ground that the North had attacked the South, the U.N. had no evidence whatever before it that the attack *had* come from the North.

3. That the decision purported to be made by the U.N. to intervene was in fact null and void, since decisions of the Security Council on matters of this sort could only be valid if all the five permanent members of the Council concurred in the decision, and the U.S.S.R. did not concur. (It was absent for the "boycott" reasons discussed above.)

4. That the entry of the U.S.A. into this war did not take place in

* *Light on Korea; Korean Handbook; New Light on Korea.*
† *Korea: the Lie that led to War.*   ‡ *The Hidden History of the Korean War.*

pursuance of any decision or request—even invalid ones—of the U.N., but was decided on by the U.S.A., and in fact actually carried out, before the U.N. had even had time to purport to arrive at any decision or make any request.

PROOF

The proof of these propositions, so far as they are matters of fact, is derived not from North Korean or other socialist sources, but solely from statements of American and South Korean Ministers, including John Foster Dulles and Li Sing Man (Syngman Rhee), from documents captured in South Korea, and from the American Press. Sir John Pratt and I—standing politically as far apart as could be imagined—arrived at substantially identical conclusions on the evidence available; and Mr. Stone, although not going quite the whole way with us, gives us a great deal of support. Evidence that has come to light since we wrote our respective books, particularly from the South Korean Ambassador to the U.S.A., who stated in so many words over the radio in New York that South Korea had in fact started the war—this very remarkable confession, heard by some thousands of listeners, was reprinted in two newspapers only in the whole of the U.S.A.—has strongly reinforced the assertions of myself and Sir John Pratt.

This crime against humanity was in the first instance a United States crime; but the British Government has to share the guilt, for it supported it unreservedly from the start, and sent troops to Korea to fight under U.S.A. command. (The fiction was maintained throughout that the war was a U.N. operation; but the conduct of the war was purported to be entrusted by the U.N. to the U.S.A.)

It is a part of the story of this war which ought not to be passed over in silence that the U.S.A. conducted it with a brutality and a disregard of civilian lives as reckless and as revolting as anything done by Hitler's armies. And the war amounted in the end to a colossal and humiliating military defeat for the U.S.A., which lost in killed alone 33,629 men, apart from numbers who died in captivity.

The Korean War was debated in the House of Commons on the 5th July, 1950, the Government—naturally enough, for a policy which was commended by the leaders of both the Labour and Conservative parties—securing approval without a division. But there was some good opposition. The excellent left-wing Member for Merthyr Tydfil, S. O. Davies, moved: "That this House expresses its deep concern at the alarming situation in Korea, and recognises the possibility of another world conflict arising therefrom. It therefore calls upon the Government to withdraw all British naval forces from the affected area; to give, in accordance with the decisions of the Cairo Conference in 1943 and the Moscow Conference in 1945, full recognition to the claim of the Korean people for the unification and independence of their country; to repudiate all British commitments which involve on our part any obligations to maintain the present division of the world into two powerful and dangerously poised hostile groups, and to declare in conformity with the Government's socialist principles our determination to give every encouragement to all peoples aspiring for freedom and self-government."

In his speech on this Motion, Davies said:

"The Government have allowed themselves to be drawn into this tragic situation by the wholly irregular action of the United States and in direct violation of the letter and the spirit of the United Nations Charter. . . . I should have expected a Socialist Government to be a little more deliberate and cool-headed in such a situation as this and not to have plunged headlong in support of the reckless irresponsibility of the United States. . . ."

REARMAMENT

The next matter that comes up for consideration is the further measures of rearmament taken in July, as a result of the Korean War.

Already in May, 1950, large extensions to service aerodromes were announced, to be carried out by engineer units of the United States Air Force, with a view to making the aerodromes capable of dealing both with the large American B36 bombers and with the fighters that would escort them in operations; also in contemplation was the preparation for a new range of U.S. bombers, requiring runways three miles in length. But in July, after the Korean War had begun, our own military strength was increased; on the 25th July, the Air Minister announced that Air Force policy was to be re-organised; and on the 26th the War Minister stated that land reinforcements were to be sent to Korea, and another £100 million to be made available for defence, which Parliament approved. On the 28th, the release of members of the Regular Army was suspended, and a limited selective recall of reserves was announced.

On that same 28th July, 1950, conveniently enough, Parliament adjourned until the 17th October; the innocent bystander might have assumed that the £100 million increase just approved by Parliament was all that was to be made; but on the 3rd August the Government stated, not to Parliament or to the British people but to the U.S. Ambassador in London, that we would increase our Defence expenditure to £3,400 million over the next three years (which figure was raised to £3,600 million when increases in Forces' pay were given). The British public learnt the news when the memorandum was made public; they were not expressly informed of the fact that the decision was made in response to a peremptory demand made by the U.S.A. on the 26th July.

This expenditure represented an increase of 49 per cent. over that of 1949-50, and was 45 per cent. above the Budget estimate. (The U.S.A. had announced a "new programme" of $10,000 million on the 19th July, following on an earlier increase of $20,000 million, equal together to £11,000 million *increase* for one year).

Attlee, in a memorandum dated the 4th August, 1950, said that it involved cutting exports and depending more on America. "It will entail real and substantial sacrifices by the British people. It will delay the recovery, and postpone the improvement in the circumstances, for which they had hoped as a result of their efforts since the end of the war." We shall see, in the course of this year's story, repeated statements by Ministers that this expenditure would have a grave effect on our non-military policies and activities. It is plain that they knew we were being forced by the U.S.A. to do far more than we reasonably could; but they had not the will or the courage to resist.

CONSCRIPTION LENGTHENED

On the 11th August, it was decided to recall Parliament on the 12th September, to discuss defence, and on the 30th August it was stated that National Service was to be extended from 18 months to two years, and that the U.S. Bomber Force in Britain was to be increased from 180 to 1,000 involving the use of thirty airfields instead of three, with a minimum of 50,000 American troops stationed here. On the 15th August, staff talks were held with the U.S.A. and Canada for the standardisation of navies.

On the 10th September, 1950, the Tory opposition stated that it would support the Government's defence proposals, and on the 12th September, when Parliament met, there was all-party support for them.

Attlee said that the reason for the enlarged arms programme was that

"Britain was approached by the United States and asked what she could undertake".* He said that the effect on living standards "must be great and must cause some degree of hardship". World rearmament was bound to cause a further rise in import prices, which was "bound to have an effect on the cost of living". But the wage freeze policy was to stay. Mr. Gaitskell, the Minister for Economic Affairs, emphasised that the workers would bear the brunt of this: "We ought to shield both our exports and investments from the heaviest burdens of rearmament. As far as we can, we ought to take on the burden ourselves as consumers. Even if it involves, as it almost certainly will, no further advance in our standard of living for the time being, even if it involves some reduction, as it well may, I feel sure that from the point of view of the future military and economic strength of our nation that it is the better course to pursue."

And on the 14th September, 1950, the Bill to increase National Service to two years was presented, receiving the Royal Assent four days later.

ARMING WEST GERMANY

On the 18th September, 1950, it was announced that Bevin, after full consultation with the Government, had accepted in principle the eventual formation of a West Germany Army; only an earthquake or a hint from the U.S.A. could ever lead that stubborn man to change his mind. It is probable that this announcement followed directly on a secret Conference of the three Western Foreign Ministers in New York, which led to the NATO Council session instructing its agencies to work out urgent recommendations for arming the Federal Republic.

On the 19th September, Britain, France and the U.S.A. issued a joint statement that any attack on West Germany or Berlin would be treated as an attack on themselves. And on the same day they announced agreement: To end the state of war with Germany; to help in creating a "mobile armed police force" in West Germany; to remove all restrictions on the production of steel and of merchant shipbuilding for export; and to study further the question of German participation in a European army. They added that a review of the agreement on prohibited and limited industries in Germany was to be undertaken in the light of the developing relationship with the German Federal Republic.

* This was no doubt a reference to the instructions of the 26th July mentioned above.

The response from the socialist world to this last step came on the 20th October, 1950, when Ministers of the East European countries met in Prague, and made a Declaration calling for: A Four-Power Declaration against remilitarisation of Germany and the carrying out of the Potsdam Agreement; the development of Germany's peace economy, while the restoration of its war potential is prevented; a Peace Treaty, the restoration of German unity, and the withdrawal of occupation troops within a year after the conclusion of the Peace Treaty; and an all-German Constituent Council on a party basis, to prepare the way for a provisional democratic peace-loving all-German government.

On the 25th October, Dean Acheson announced the rejection of these proposals; and on the 28th talks on German re-armament began in Washington. This time they broke down without any agreement being reached, owing to French opposition.

It is not unnatural that, on the 12th October, 1950, at the Annual Conservative Conference, Harold Macmillan had boasted that:

"Never in our history has an Opposition been able so effectively to impose its foreign policy upon the Government of the day. During this period, under the same powerful influence, there has proceeded at a slow but steady pace what one might call the painful process of educating Uncle Ernie."

CHAPTER 32

Colonial Policy, 1950

ITS colonial activities in 1950 reflected little credit on the Government. The war in Malaya continued; the nationalist movement in Africa went on growing, if without any particular or immediate achievements; the racialist policy in the Union of South Africa (not strictly a colonial matter) developed; the Seretse Khama affair in Bechuanaland led to much controversy; and the ground-nuts scheme staggered towards its end.

MALAYA

In Malaya the war went on, showing the typical signs of waste, cruelty, failure and profit-seeking of an "old-fashioned" colonial war. It was costing at least £100 millions a year even before 1950, and in 1950 it went from bad to worse. On the 15th March, John Dugdale, Minister of State for the Colonies, said in the House of Commons that an extra brigade and a squadron of Lincoln bombers were being sent to Malaya "to give the jungle troops a rest", and incautiously added: "We are satisfied these additional reinforcements are the final requirements"—a ludicrous statement which led to indignant outbursts in the Press.

On the 20th March, John Strachey, speaking on the Army Estimates, said:

"The gravest problem in the Far East remains the campaign in Malaya, where there can be no likelihood of spectacular success by the Army which might change the situation overnight."

And on the same day, *The Times* published a report from its Singapore correspondent expressing serious concern over the increased activities of the Malayan People's Liberation Army, the success of which he attributed to the "Communist victory in China", the "new leadership of the Malayan Communists", and the reaction to the government-sponsored "Anti-Bandit" campaign.

On the following day, the *Daily Telegraph* printed a report from a special correspondent in Malaya, which said: "I have just returned from a tour of the fighting areas and can say that Mr. Dugdale's opinion"—i.e. his complacency—"is shared neither by those directing the campaign nor by those fighting it. On the contrary, the men directing the campaign said that more troops were urgently needed and that without substantial reinforcements there was no possibility of ending the emergency now or in the foreseeable future." He quoted the *Straits Times* as saying: "The Anti-Bandit campaign has turned out to be a 'boomerang'. Not only has no progress been made for half a year or more in suppression of the Communist revolt, but no progress seems likely with the present methods."

The "anti-bandit" campaign was no more than a decorative and highly colonialist name given by the Government to a much publicised drive to bring the war to an end. No Tory could have thought of a more objectionable label; the clearer it became that the war was a struggle by a colonial people to gain their freedom, the more their patriotic forces were labelled not just "rebels" but "terrorists" and "bandits". The true character of the war was stated in the House of Lords on the 5th April, by Lord Killearn, former British Commissioner-General in South-East Asia:

"I have just returned from Malaya. . . . The situation is very bad. In the past we have talked about these people as bandits. I ask whether their character has not changed; whether it is not really guerrilla warfare . . . they were fully organised . . . in battalions and companies and very ably directed. They were served by a large number of others not in uniform. Their intelligence service is extremely good— personally, I suspect it is better than ours."

On this same 21st March, an attempt was made in Parliament to allay the indignation caused by Dugdale's statement about "final requirements"; the Financial Secretary to the War Office announced that that department was not proposing to close the doors to "reassessment of our requirements".

TRADE UNIONS IN MALAYA

Another typical example of the dishonesty or incompetence of those in the Colonial Office who were "briefing" Dugdale had come up in his speech of the 15th March, already quoted. He was led to add to the stupidity about "final requirements" the shameless statement that "anti-bandit month"—what a light-hearted bit of publicity, treating a bloodthirsty colonial war on the same lines as an advertising campaign for a brand of detergent—was "warmly supported by trade unions". If the truth had been supplied to Dugdale for his speech, he would have said:

"Since we banned the Pan-Malayan Federation of Trade Unions last June, with its 300,000 members—91 per cent. of all those organised in trade unions—and arrested 185 trade union officials, many of whom we have shot, I am happy to be able to tell the House that the government-sponsored (or 'stooge') unions which are allowed to exist, with a membership which we claim to amount to 40,000, or something over one-seventh of the membership of the banned federation, warmly support the 'month'."

The true position to which the Government had brought the trade union movement in highly-industrialised Malaya can be seen from the speech of the Chairman of a mining company at this period, announcing an increase of dividend to 65 per cent. He said:

"No serious difficulties with labour were experienced, and it is significant that this happy state of affairs should have existed when, so far as our labour was concerned, there were no trade unions in existence, many of them having disappeared on the introduction of the Government's emergency regulations."

The former General Secretary of the Transport and General Worker's Union, Ernest Bevin, no more protested against this destruction of trade union power that he had done over the similar treatment of the unions in Greece.

On the 6th and 7th April, Malaya was debated in the House of Commons; James Griffiths, Secretary of State for the colonies, said that a total of 70,000 police and 11,000 ground forces had been operating against the "bandits", and that there was to be a reinforcement of 2,000 Gurkhas. This constituted an official figure of 83,000, in addition to the squadrons of the R.A.F. and naval units. The *Sunday Times* of the 9th April put the total figure at "something like 130,000 armed men". No one could say that the Government was disobeying the demand, made in the debate by Oliver Stanley, former Tory Secretary for the Colonies, "to regard this question of Malaya as Priority No. 1, not only in foreign and defence policy, but in our economic policy, because all will come crashing to the ground if we lose this war in Malaya".

(I knew Stanley well; he was one of the very few Conservatives with whom I was able to remain on good terms. In the Parliament of 1935-45 we had many disputes—mostly by correspondence or interviews—over incidents of colonial oppression; and when the Labour Government came in in 1945 he waited a year or two before asking me quietly: "Do you see any difference in the behaviour of the Colonial Office, now that I have been replaced by a Labour Minister?" What *could* I answer?)

On the 13th May, 1950, the *Manchester Guardian* quoted Malcolm MacDonald, High Commissioner for South-East Asia, as saying:

"The situation has deteriorated. . . . With every month that the Government fails to restore its authority, British military competence is held up to scorn, our prestige sinks, and the danger grows of the Malayan war turning into something as serious as the war in Indo-China."

And on the 25th May *The Times* wrote in an editorial:

"The rebellion must be recognised for what it is—a state of actual war."

On the 8th June, the cost of the "emergency" was reported to be increasing, and more financial aid from Britain was demanded. (Some time later, on the 14th August, the U.S. was asked for aid "to help fight Communism in Malaya". By that time, of course, the British were busy, as explained in the previous chapter, "helping the U.S.A. to fight Communism" in Korea.)

This month of June marked the second anniversary of the Malayan war. As described in *World News* of the 10th June, the position was that over 1,000 Malayan patriots (or "bandits") had been shot, hanged or otherwise executed; over 10,000 had been deported; and over 10,000 were in concentration camps. Villages had been bombed and razed to the ground. Any Malayan giving food or shelter to a Malayan patriot faced the death penalty. Yet the liberation struggle was stronger than ever.

POVERTY AND PROFITS

The terrible contrast of continued poverty for the Malayan population and high profits (in dollars) for the British capitalists continued. Whilst prices rose and living standards remained terribly low, the City correspondent of the *Daily Herald* wrote on the 22nd March that—

"a list of twenty tin-producing companies shows that profits increased £919,609 to £1,444,213 during the past two years' operations.

"Some of the dividend increases are phenomenal—Ayer Hitam 65 per cent. against nil; Kamunting 25 per cent. (15 per cent.); Malayan 50 per cent. (25 per cent.); Penkalen 20 per cent. (5½ per cent.); Southern Tronoh 50 per cent. (15 per cent.); Sungei Besei 60 per cent (10 per cent.); Tronoh 65 per cent. (30 per cent.); Kramat Pulai 200 per cent. and bonus of 100 per cent. (100 per cent.); Renong 20 per cent. (nil)."

And in terms of dollar earnings the tin and rubber of Malaya were greater than all the United Kingdom exports put together.

The *Economist* of the 25th March summed up the contrast neatly enough: "Living standards urgently need improvement, but the country is remarkably prosperous(!) and has maintained—even increased—production of its precious dollar-earning raw materials in difficult and dangerous conditions."

SERETSE KHAMA

The Seretse Khama case was a large act of hypocrisy and bad faith in a small setting. Seretse Khama was the prospective chief of the Bamangwato tribe in Bechuanaland, a British protectorate bordering on the Union of South Africa. The Bamangwato reserve has an area of about 40,000 square miles and a population of about 100,000. Seretse was the grandson of King Khama, who had sought British protection against the Boers in 1900; he was the heir to his father, who had succeeded Khama in 1923 and died two years later, when Seretse was four years old; Tshekedi, Seretse's uncle, being installed as regent. Tshekedi ruled the tribe whilst Seretse grew up and was educated at Oxford and the Middle Temple. Two years before the events of 1950, namely in 1948, Seretse married an Englishwoman, and soon afterwards returned to Bamangwato.

There is a good deal of uncertainty as to the facts at that stage, and as to the degree of pressure exercised by the British Government; but it is certain that, after two "kgotlas" (tribal assemblies) in November and December, 1948, decided that the marriage was against tribal custom, a third kgotla, held in June, 1949, accepted Seretse as King by a vote of 5,000 to 43; Tshekedi, the regent, thereupon went into voluntary exile, accompanied by the 43 minority voters.

Under the "Bechuanaland Protectorate Native Administration Proclamation" of 1943, the choice of a successor to the Kingship lay with the kgotla, subject to recognition by the High Commissioner and confirmation by the Secretary of State; and a judicial enquiry could be held, to report to the High Commissioner. The British Government, which claimed that after such an enquiry the final decision as to who should be the King lay with itself, decided after the June, 1949, decision of the kgotla to hold a judicial enquiry to examine the suitability of Seretse for the position, although no suggestion had hitherto been made against his fitness.

The enquiry was duly held, and the report was made in December, 1949; all that one knows of the report is that it was neither made public nor even shown to Seretse or his advisers, but we were told that the Government had "studied it carefully". It can hardly have been unfavourable to Seretse; but the Government asserted, for those who cared to believe anything it said, that the report advised against the recognition of Seretse.

In January, 1950, Seretse was invited to come to London with his wife, who had joined him in Bechuanaland, for discussions. According to Seretse, he had been orally assured by the Resident Commissioner that he would be allowed to return to Bechuanaland; the Government denied this.

In the discussions, the Government urged him to give up his claim to the succession; according to his statement, he was offered an annuity of £1,000 a year if he would stay out of Bechuanaland, which he refused to do. Ultimately, the Government decided that recognition should be withheld for five years. Seretse was not to be allowed in Bechuanaland during that time, whilst Tshekedi would be required to live outside the Bamangwato reserve, but not outside Bechuanaland.

On the 13th March, 1950, the High Commissioner summoned a meeting of the tribe, in order to give the news of this decision, but not a single person attended, the tribe having determined to boycott the meeting and to refuse to pay taxes.

SERETSE EXCLUDED FROM HIS COUNTRY

On the 31st March, Seretse arrived in Bechuanaland, and was at once served with an "exclusion order".

There can be little doubt that the motive of the British Government in opposing Seretse was to "appease" the South African Government, whose racialist views were horrified by a mixed marriage. The British

Government stated that it was "of course aware that a strong body of European opinion in South Africa would be opposed to recognition", but that "no representations have been received from the South African Government". The pro-Malan Johannesburg newspaper *Die Transvaaler*, however, reported on the 10th March that the Prime Minister, Dr. Malan, had stated as far back as the 27th October, 1949, that the British Government had been informed by telegram of the Union's attitude to the marriage.

SOUTH AFRICAN DISTURBANCES

Whilst the behaviour of the Union of South Africa, either in connection with Seretse Khama or in any other matter, is not strictly a matter of British colonial policy, I may notice briefly that on the 13th March, 1950, Malan proposed the resumption of negotiations with Great Britain on the transfer of Bechuanaland, Swaziland, and Basutoland to the Union; that on the 2nd May eighteen Africans were killed in "May Day rioting" in the Rand townships; that on the 5th May a Bill was introduced into the Union Parliament "to outlaw Communism", followed on the 29th May by a new Bill for racial segregation; and that on the 13th June the "Group Areas (Racial) Bill" was introduced, designed to bring about the complete transplantation of the races in South Africa into separate geographical areas.

GROUND–NUTS

Of the Ground-nuts Scheme in 1950, relatively little needs to be written; it was approaching its ignominious end, which was to come in 1951. On the 24th May, 1950, it was announced that Sir Leslie Plummer was giving up the chairmanship of the Overseas Food Corporation; on the 12th June, that body's Report stated that the original Ground-nuts Scheme was impracticable, and that the advances made up to the preceding 12th April amounted to £34,650,000; on the 14th June, Sir Leslie Plummer received £8,000 compensation; on the 13th July, the ground-nuts harvest report showed big losses at Kongwa; and on the 28th September drastic cuts were announced in the cultivation of ground-nuts and other produce there.

CHAPTER 33

The Economy, 1950

THE course of economic life in Britain had a less regular pattern in 1950 than in previous years. The earlier months were overshadowed by the American slump, which was marked by 3,500,000 unemployed in the U.S.A., with unsaleable goods piling up; and it was even expected that we should have an "over-production" of steel, coal and tin, in sharp contrast to the years of acute shortage.

This pattern was soon changed by the outbreak of the Korean War in June; for, just as capitalism makes wars, wars tend to make capitalism superficially prosperous. The rest of the year was marked by heavy burdens of rearmament, and by the nervous "stock-piling" of vast quantities of raw materials by the rulers of the U.S.A.—those easily frightened men who talked of "containing communism" but plainly seemed unable to contain themselves—with resultant uncertainties, price rises, and shortages.

ECONOMIC SURVEY

The *Economic Survey*, published in April, showed an overall increase of production in 1949 of 6½ per cent., with an increase of only 1 per cent. in the labour force. On consumption, it reported that, "as supplies of other goods increased, consumers offset increased expenditure on these by reducing their expenditure on drink, tobacco and entertainment. This implies that during the course of 1949 the amount which consumers were willing or able to spend did not increase so quickly as supplies available. The increase in the stocks of retail distributors which seems to have occurred during 1949 supplies supporting evidence."

BALANCE OF PAYMENTS

The balance of payments position had not changed greatly. The nett gold and dollar deficit was $1,531 million as compared with $1,710 million twelve months earlier. Exports increased by £236 million, but imports—owing to the rise in prices—rose by £200 million.

The "target" for increased production for 1950 was put at the modest figure of $2\frac{1}{2}$ per cent., which was to be achieved by increased productivity, no increase in manpower being expected. In the field of consumption, £250 million worth of extra goods were envisaged; there were to be fewer houses, no new hospitals, no extension of the school meals service, and a reduction of $12\frac{1}{2}$ per cent. in expenditure on school building.

The prospect of maintenance or improvement of trade and of the balance of payments was said to depend on the U.S.A. maintaining a high level of activity and taking more British goods. The colonial empire was to remain the great source of dollars:

"Exports to dollar markets are not expected to expand sufficiently rapidly in the first half of 1950 to compensate fully for the fall in their dollar prices following devaluation. In the longer run, however, provided that the competitive advantage resulting from devaluation is not dissipated by inflation, that productivity continues to increase at least as rapidly as in competitive countries, and that the U.S. continues to be willing to accept increased imports from the U.K., a substantial increase should be possible in earnings from direct dollar exports to North America and other dollar countries."

(A sad number of provisos.)

The trend of exports, the Survey said, was very difficult to predict, but there might be a small reduction in the deficit. It concluded:

"The Government, therefore, regard it as of vital importance that we should continue the major economic and financial policies by which we have been guided over the last five years. Reasonable restraint in our personal claims on production, increased efficiency and lower costs in industry, the elimination of all waste in private and public sectors of our economy alike, are the necessary price at which to obtain our objective of economic independence and improved standards of living."

This plainly implied that the wage freeze was to continue.

The comment of the *Economist* on this Survey was amply justified. It wrote that it was a "humble document, meek almost to the point of being meaningless. There is nothing here of the notions of 'democratic economic planning' as proclaimed in earlier Surveys, which presented a working pattern for the year's economic effort, and left all men of good will to work for it. Indeed, the perplexing thing about the Survey for 1950 is its lack of plan."

WHITE PAPER ON NATIONAL INCOME

In the same month of April there came the White Paper on National Income. It showed that the total national income of 1949 was 8 per cent. higher than 1948, excluding inventory changes and income from abroad. The rise in output per man-year was 4 per cent. The prices of consumer goods on an average rose by 2 per cent. in 1949 compared with 1948; prices of bread and cereals rose 4 per cent.; of meat and bacon 15 per cent.; of dairy products 3 per cent.; the price of sugar fell 6 per cent.; potatoes and vegetable prices were unaltered. The share going to wages and salaries fell slightly, from nearly 62 per cent. in 1948 to just under 60 per cent. in 1949.

Gross profits rose. "Most of the increase went to provide for larger depreciation, or was added to business reserves. The incomes of farmers, professional men, and small traders rose by £37 million, the dividends and interest received by shareholders hardly at all." Average earnings rose by 4½ per cent., a rise less than half that of 1948.

THE BUDGET

In the same month came the Budget. The estimates showed moderate rises in defence (£780·8 million compared with £759·9 million in the previous year), education, national insurance and health; and reduced expenditure on housing, war pensions, national assistance, and food expenditure (including subsidies).

The changes in taxation were small, consisting mostly in minor income-tax reliefs. The tax on petrol was substantially increased; the purchase tax on expensive cars was reduced, and purchase tax was imposed on commercial vehicles, to encourage manufacturers to export them.

In June, it was announced that the May exports had reached a record figure, and in July Cripps stated that the June figures for both exports and imports were records.

To quote again Mr. Ernest Watkins at pp. 227-8 of *The Cautious Revolution*, the economic story worked out thus:

"In the first half of 1949 the country faced a dollar deficit of $962 millions. In the first half of 1950 the Treasury could report a surplus of $220 millions, a swing over of no less than $1,182 millions. The running leak of gold and dollars seemed to have at last been plugged. . . .

Y

"This return to prosperity had come from two causes. The two events in 1949 that had set the scene for 1950 had been the recovery of the United States from the recession at the start of the year, and devaluation. When the trend of business activity began to move upwards during 1949, it produced its customary consequences, the resumption of importing from overseas by the United States on a more normal scale. In the first half of 1950 imports were 12 per cent. greater in dollar value than they had been during the corresponding period in 1949. . . .

"The effects of devaluation were much sharper. By the act of devaluation, to everyone using pounds sterling, everything originating in the dollar area became immediately 44 per cent. more costly. The long-term effects of that were to be mixed, but the first effects were almost entirely in Britain's favour. Not only did every sale from the sterling area to the dollar area become that much easier or that much more valuable (depending on how close to the former dollar price the seller felt able to keep his new dollar price). Every other country usually buying from the United States found it that much more advantageous to buy from this country, if it could, for again, expressed in its own currency, either dollar prices rose or sterling prices fell. Britain became a most attractive market place. Order books filled and exports flowed out. Equally, the value of invisible exports rose. . . .

"But devaluation, of course, had its reverse. . . . Devaluation meant that everything bought from the dollar area was 44 per cent. dearer and it was impossible for the sterling area to stop buying from the dollar area altogether. The Treasury had hoped that this rising trend of prices, in terms of sterling, would not play too large a part in the national economy during 1950. Its efforts had been directed to the cutting down of precisely these imports (and with considerable success) and to the stimulation of production to offset the effects of the higher prices for those purchases that could not be avoided. But the assumption on which the Treasury experts had based their premise, that the benefits flowing from devaluation would exceed the inevitable burdens that would follow it, was itself based on another assumption, that the prices of raw materials originating within the sterling area would not immediately jump up to the dollar level.

"The invasion of South Korea in June changed that situation radically. It made the United States take rearmament seriously. By so doing it destroyed any hope of low prices in the sterling area's production of raw materials."

By July, 1950, the effect of devaluation on the level of prices had been clearly felt in the field of retail prices, especially food.

The position, taking June 1947, as 100, was as follows:

	Prices generally	Food prices	Wage rates
1949, September . .	112	116·8	109
1949, December . .	113	119·5	109
1950, June . . .	114	123·1	110

DEFENCE EXPENDITURE

On the 3rd August, 1950, as already mentioned, it was announced that Defence expenditure was to be increased to £3,400 million over the next three years, or £1,133 million per annum, as compared to the Budget figure, four months earlier, of £780·8 millions. And on the 30th August, it was announced that service pay was to be increased and national service was to be extended to two years; the additional cost of these two steps added £200 million to the £3,400 million just mentioned (or £1,200 million per annum.)

The *Economist* commented:

"It would be foolish to suppose that Britain can rearm without tears. That was possible in the early stages of the rearmament effort of the thirties, because there was then a large pool of idle resources that could be tapped. Now, however, as the Government memorandum (of 3rd August) points out, Britain's economy is 'fully stretched'. The only way in which the total output can be expanded without measures of special mobilisation of manpower is by increasing the average output of workers already in employment—through increased efficiency and/or by longer hours of work. Unless the additional output obtained in this way is at least equal to the net additional burden of defence, there must inevitably be some contraction in the investment programme or in civil consumption, or a return to an overall deficit in the balance of external payments—and probably a combination of losses under all three heads."

In the Defence debate already mentioned in Chapter 30, on the 13th September, Gaitskell, Minister of State for Economic Affairs, explained the effect of this expenditure on the national economy, forecasting shortages, and arguing for "wage restraint" and against the idea that the pay of workers should be raised because Forces pay had been increased. Attlee, in the same debate, admitted that world rearmament would cause a further rise in import prices, which was bound to have an effect on the cost of living. But the Government stood by its policy of the wage freeze (which in times of rising prices is in reality wage reduction). Wholesale prices at the time were already greatly increased; wool was up 40 per cent., and cotton, butter, coffee, cocoa and leather had also gone up. Much of the increases, as already indicated, were due to "stock piling" by the U.S.A., and to a small extent by other countries.

In October, it was announced that the gold and dollar reserves of the sterling area had increased by $300 million in the third quarter of 1950.

In the same month, Cripps resigned owing to failing health, and Gaitskell was appointed Chancellor of the Exchequer in his place.

PRICES RISING

In October, too, many prices were rising, and the *Financial Times* wrote on the 14th October:

"There can be no mistaking the effects of the post-Korean upsurge in raw material prices on the wholesale price index for September. During the month, by far and away the biggest increases occurred in this group. Wool led the way with a rise of 24 per cent. on the month (now 120 per cent. above September 1949), and non-ferrous metals recorded the heavy increase of 9½ per cent. (which puts them 53 per cent. above the level of a year ago).

"Although less spectacular, there was nevertheless an appreciable rise in other sections of the index. Taken together the total index rose by 3·1 per cent.—a record which puts it almost 18 per cent. above the September 1949 figure. This development is significant; it means that the rise in the prices of imported commodities is spreading to other items; and the whole must in due course be reflected at the retail level."

CHAPTER 34

The Nationalised Industries, 1950

IN June, 1950, the Annual Report of the National Coal Board showed a net profit for 1949 of £9,500,000, compared with £1,700,000 in 1948 and a deficit of £23,200,000 in 1947; the operating profit was £31,100,000, compared with £17,500,000 in 1948 and a loss of £6,200,000 in 1947. The 1948 profit was made in the main out of the "super-charge" of approximately £1 per ton on coal exported, the exports being 19,000,000 tons, or 3,000,000 more than in 1949.

Out of the £31,100,000, £13,200,000 went in compensation to the former owners, £3,500,000 to profits tax, £4,000,000 to additional provision for Workmen's Compensation, £800,000 to compensation for loss of office and £100,000 to interest payments; the resulting net profit of £9,500,000 mentioned above went to reduce the deficit carried forward from 1947.

COAL OUTPUT RISES

The output rose from 197,600,000 tons in 1948 to 202,700,000 tons in 1949; the output per man-shift went up from 22·2 cwt. to 23·2 cwt.; in the first quarter of 1950, it was 24 cwt. (In 1938, it had been 22·8 cwt.) The output per man-year rose from 273 tons in 1948 to 282 tons in 1949, and 294 tons in the first quarter of 1950. (In 1938, 290 tons.)

That the output per man-year did not keep pace with the output per man-shift was put down in the report mainly to absenteeism; but there were a number of other factors that must have accounted for a great deal of it—the five-day week, the holidays with pay, which made it possible for more men to take holidays, the increase of mechanisation, which caused production to depend on fewer key-workers at the coal face, who tend to have a higher rate of absenteeism, and the lack of any reserves of manpower. (Manpower fell from 724,000 in 1948 to 719,000 in 1949, and subsequently to 698,000.)

The average earnings rose from £8 per week in 1948 to £8 15s. per week in 1949; but in that average lay hidden the fact that 400,000 men were getting no more than £5 per week for surfacemen and £5 15s. for underground workers, figures well below the average for industry in general, where the work is in the main less exacting and less dangerous.

There was considerable variation in efficiency and profitability between different types of pits and quantities of coal. The profitable pits earned £50 million.

Capital investment in the pits in 1949 was only about 2½ per cent. of the total for British industry, much below the average for industry.

The Report stated that the aim of the Board to bring output up to 30 cwt. per man-shift could only be achieved by technical improvement, or by cutting out less efficient pits, which would reduce total production. Lord Hyndley, addressing the Annual Conference of the National Union of Mineworkers, said: "The need for more production is as insistent as it ever was. The consumption of coal is continuing to rise. Industry is for ever demanding more electric power or gas. . . . Abroad the demands for those kinds of coal for which the British coalfields have been famous in the past is still unsatisfied. This should be taken as a further assurance about prospects of employment in the industry."

COAL—MINERS DISSATISFIED

The year showed a growing dissatisfaction of mineworkers with the wages policy of the Coal Board. At the Annual Conference of the National Union of Mineworkers it was resolved that the Executive should take immediate steps to secure an increase for lower-paid workers. Although a minority of pieceworkers might earn £10 or £12 per week, more than half the men in the industry were day-wage workers, getting £5 per week on the surface or £5 15s. below ground. They had had no wage increase since 1947, though prices had risen some 13 per cent. and production had increased. The Board's Report planned to use future profits to pay off the rest of the 1947 deficit and to build up a reserve fund, and not to give any wage increases.

A demand by the workers for an increase of 12s. a week to day-wage men was met on the 25th July, 1950, by an offer from the Board of 5s. which was rejected. On the 27th October, after further negotiations, the Union accepted the award of the National Reference Tribunal of £3,500,000, which meant an increase of 5s. a week on the minimum. Some pits in Scotland struck against this award, but on the 2nd November a national delegate conference of the Union accepted it.

TRANSPORT

The Report of the Transport Commission, published in September, 1950, showed a less favourable result for 1949 than the coal industry. The net revenue had fallen from £45,200,000 to £31,300,000 whilst expenditure other than working costs rose from £49,900,000 to £52,100,000 so that the deficit was increased from £4,700,000 to £20,800,000. Interest payments on British Transport Stock (which rose a little from £33,100,000 in 1948) were £33,500,000 and the provision for capital redemption (which also rose a little from £2,500,000 in 1948) were £2,600,000; thus the compensation burden was still considerably greater than the deficit.

One of the items contributing to the deterioration was the decline in gross receipts of British Railways of over £10 million.

The Report showed that considerable economies had been effected, particularly in wage costs; for example, during 1949, the saving on British Railways from reduction of staff (23,151) and economy in the use of overtime was £4,900,000. Other economies included the closing down of a number of marshalling yards, stations and track, and longer and faster runs for locomotives.

The finances of the Commission were still suffering from inherited disadvantages; on the railways, for example "large blocks of old and relatively unserviceable wagons still remain and hamper the efficiency of train operation to a degree disproportionate to their numbers". (Total compensation for the old private owners' wagons was estimated at £42,700,000.) Restrictions on the supply of materials had held up the wagon-building programme; steel requirements for the year had been estimated at 1,000,000 tons but the allocation was only 810,000.

Good progress had been made in 1949 in restoring the track but "in 1950-2 there will be a sharp set-back as a result of the restriction on capital investment. . . . The general outlook for the next year or two is a matter of some concern." The continued growth in the number of C-licence road vehicles must also have affected the Commission's finances. The number increased from 590,516 at the end of 1948 to 672,301 at the end of 1949.

ELECTRICITY

The first Report of the British Electricity Authority showed that the Authority and its Area Boards had a profit of £4,400,000 after paying all interest charges and something towards the redemption of capital.

STEEL

Steel nationalisation was of course in its infancy. The Act, as mentioned in Chapter 23, had provided that the Iron and Steel Corporation of Great Britain was to have a Chairman and not less than six or more than ten other members, to be appointed by the Minister not before the 1st October, 1950. The appointments were in fact made on the 2nd October, in spite of a boycott of steel executives. On the 19th September, 1950, the Minister of Supply told the House of Commons that, when he invited the spokesman of the steel interests to submit the names of "experienced men who would be acceptable to their fellow indusrialists for inclusion in the Corporation", the Executive Committee of the Iron and Steel Federation refused to do so, "on the grounds that in their opinion the Government had no mandate to carry out the Iron and Steel Act". "They warned me at the same time," said the Minister, "that the Corporation, deprived of such people, would be unable successfully to plan the steel industry. Further, I was informed that every effort would be made to dissuade any important man I might approach from serving on the Corporation. . . . In short, these people decided to threaten, and indeed they did carry out, a political strike." There was, in fact, he said, "a gentleman's agreement"—an odd phrase—"throughout firms in the industry not to serve on the Corporation . . . concerted action by a number of people for the specific purpose of sabotaging an Act of Parliament."

Nevertheless, the Government was able to secure the Chairman of the British Oxygen Co. Ltd., who was a member of the Labour Party and a director of some 34 industrial companies, as Chairman of the Corporation; a director of Thos. Firth and John Brown Ltd., as deputy Chairman; three full-time members (including one official of the Amalgamated Engineering Union, and one General); and two part-time members, who were also industrialists.

CHAPTER 35

Industrial Affairs, 1950

THE principal features of the year in the industrial field, apart from the Trades Union Congress itself, were a great struggle against the wage freeze and a number of strikes.

RESISTING THE WAGE FREEZE

The swelling resistance to the wage freeze was seen in full operation in May, 1950, when in a single week six Union Conferences rejected this policy. The main cause of the resistance was to be found in the increase in the cost of living; between September, 1949 when the pound sterling was devalued, and April, 1950, the retail price index rose from 112 to 114, and the food index from 117 to 122. By June, 1950, food prices had risen by 7 per cent.; in the same period, wage rates for men rose by less than 1 per cent. Profits per worker earned by employers ranged from £2. 6s. 0d. per week in transport distribution and one or two other industries to £5 10s. per week in manufacturing and mining; and they were still increasing! The Conference of the Railway Clerks Association, as it was then called, which had previously supported the wage freeze, rejected a resolution of its executive committee endorsing it, and instructed the committee to consider urgently the problem of the salaries of clerical and supervisory staffs. The Electrical Trades Union overwhelmingly supported the recommendation of its executive to vote for strike action in the forthcoming engineers' ballot, and urged its executive to secure wage increases out of profit. The National Association of Theatrical and Kine Employees, which had previously supported the wage freeze, resolved on unanimous opposition to "all forms of wage restraint in the entertainment industry". The National Union of Bank Employees opposed the wage freeze. The Union of Post Office Workers, which had for a time supported the wage freeze, reaffirmed an earlier decision to oppose it, in spite of the opposition of its general secretary. And the Civil Service Clerical Association instructed its executive committee to re-open negotiations for increases for all grades, and censured eleven members of the executive for having supported the wage freeze at the T.U.C. Conference in January, 1950, mentioned in Chapter 24.

At the time of these six declarations of opposition, there were already a number of claims for wage increases pending. The Confederation of Shipbuilding and Engineering Workers had a claim for £1 a week increase; this had been rejected by the shipbuilding employers in March, and strike ballot papers had been issued in April. The National Union of Railwaymen also had a wage claim, and on the 30th May the Amalgamated Society of Locomotive Engineers and Firemen instructed its executive to make a claim; and as already mentioned the National Union of Mineworkers was also claiming.

The crop of trade union conferences that came around Whitsuntide led to new claims from a further number of unions, including the Union of Shop, Distributive and Allied Workers, the Tobacco Workers Union, and the Agricultural Workers Union. And on the 6th June, 1950, the Executive Committee of Bevin's union, the Transport and General Workers, passed a resolution calling on the Government to do everything possible to reduce prices and to give greater consideration to limitation of profits, and on the General Council of the T.U.C. to "deal with and obtain some flexibility in regard to wages paid to people in the lower income group, particularly those on fixed weekly wage rates".

T.U.C. GENERAL COUNCIL'S ATTITUDE

In June, the Trades Union Congress General Council issued a new statement on wages policy, which, whilst obviously showing signs of compromise, nevertheless marked an advance. It was to the effect that the rigid restraint which had been advocated after devaluation had been a substantial factor in the improvement in the country's economic situation, but that the improvement itself had made it impracticable to continue the policy. Restraint was still necessary, but greater flexibility was now desirable, and as no formula as to how that flexibility would operate could be devised the question must be left to the good sense of the unions. The General Council would, however, give facilities for such consultation as affiliated unions might desire.

In July, the claims previously mentioned were still being pressed; the claim of the Shipbuilding and Engineers Union for £1 per week increase had been referred to the Minister of Labour, the strike ballot having decided negatively. Further the Amalgamated Union of Building Trade Workers had reaffirmed its claim for an increase, and the National Federation of Building Trades Operatives had put in a claim. Road haulage workers were demanding an increase of 10s. per week, and the meat drivers at Smithfield had gone on strike owing to the slow progress of negotiations over their pay claim; I will deal with their strike later.

But the right-wing trade union supporters of the wage freeze were not inactive. Sir William Lawther, President of the National Union of Mineworkers, denounced general wage increases, asserting that the country could not afford them; and Sir Luke Fawcett, general secretary of the Amalgamated Union of Building Trade Workers, pleaded without success with his members not to specify a definite increase in their claim. The leaders of the National Union of General and Municipal Workers succeeded in persuading their Annual Conference to continue support of the wage freeze.

SOME WAGE INCREASES

In November, 1950, *Labour Research*, reviewing recent wage movements, recorded that increases had been won between June and October by electrical contracting workers, retail Co-operative employees, Post Office engineers, Smithfield meat drivers, road haulage workers, laundry workers, maintenance gas-workers, agricultural workers and miners; that claims were still pending by the Engineering and Shipbuilding Confederation, civil service unions, Co-operative Wholesale Society employees, bank employees, and the London County Council Staff Association; and that claims were being formulated for dock workers, provincial—and possibly also London—road passenger workers, and for the National Federation of Building Trades Operatives. The number of workers involved was in all 4,380,000. Many of them had had no increase for a long time—in some cases not since 1947, so that much of the post-devaluation and post-rearmament price increases had not yet been reflected in wage increases (or even in wage claims).

T.U.C. CONFERENCE

The Trades Union Congress met in Brighton in the first week of September, 1950. It presented an odd mixture of alternating success and failure in the opposition to the right-wing leadership.

There was an important debate on the Report and Declaration of the General Council on the International Situation, introduced by Sir Vincent Tewson. This declared firm support of the United Nations, regarded the Brussels Pact and the North Atlantic Pact as measures taken purely for defence and as furthering the objects of the United Nations; supported what was done in the name of the U.N. in Korea, and profoundly regretted Russia's failure to co-operate in this; and condemned the Peace Campaign as a disgraceful and hollow sham instigated by the Cominform.

Walter Stevens, of the Electrical Trades Union, moved the reference back of the Report on the grounds that opposition to the Peace Campaign was inspired by Wall Street capitalists, and pointed out that the Stockholm Conference had declared that the first user of an atomic bomb should be branded as a war criminal. The reference back was lost and the Report was adopted by 6,942,000 votes to 595,000.

On the control of atomic energy a composite motion—showing the signs of compromise common to such motions—was moved by Walter Padley, M.P. This, while approving the attachment of the Labour Government to the principles of the U.N., urged the Government to exercise a fresh initiative through that organisation for the reopening of the question of international control and supervision of atomic energy production, the banning of atomic weapons, and the destruction of all atom bomb stocks. The motion was lost by 5,601,000 votes to 1,972,000.

On East-West trade, the Congress rejected a motion from the Foundry Workers calling for unfettered trade with China, the U.S.S.R. and the Eastern Democracies, and declaring hostility to the restraints on trade imposed by Marshall Aid.

On Greece, a resolution calling upon the Government to use its influence to bring an end to internal strife in Greece, the abolition of the terrible concentration camp on the island of Makronisos, and a general amnesty, was accepted by the General Council.

On wages, prices and profits, a composite resolution noted that, since the issue of the White Paper on Personal Incomes, prices and profits had continued to rise and working-class living standards to fall, and protested that no effective steps had been taken to prevent increased profits. It continued:

"Congress is of the opinion that until such time as there is a reasonable limitation of profits, a positive planning of our British economy, and prices are subject to such control as will maintain the purchasing power of wages at a level affording to every worker a reasonable standard of living, there can be no basis for restraint on wage applications. Congress declares that wage increases can be met without resulting in increased prices, for example by reducing profits, and therefore calls on the General Council to abandon any further policy of wage restraint, and at the same time urges the Government to introduce statutory control of profits."

This resolution was carried by 3,949,000 to 3,727,000, and the Report of the General Council on this question, which urged a policy of modified wage restraint, was defeated by 3,898,000 to 3,521,000. This was the main clash at Congress and a major defeat for the right-wing policy of supporting the wage freeze.

On equal pay for women, a resolution declaring that the time was now opportune for operating this policy and urging the Government to give a lead to other employers, was carried by 3,898,000 to 3,521,000 against the opposition of the General Council.

ORDER 1305

On what was generally called "Order 1305"—namely, the Conditions of Employment and National Arbitration Order, S.R. & O., 1940, No. 1305"—an important debate took place on a motion urging the Government to repeal the Order immediately, on the ground that organised labour was being prevented from taking advantage of conditions of full employment to press wage claims—a motion which one would have expected any trade union gathering to endorse unanimously. Order 1305 was a war-time survival, hampering strikes to an extent amounting in effect to total prohibition. Strikes are serious actions and few people want to resort to them unnecessarily; but they are the only substantial weapon the working classes possess, and if they are deprived of them they are as defenceless as an army without weapons. The right to strike must therefore be preserved and defended as something vital to labour, which wins many victories without actual strikes, by its mere existence; and its prohibition constitutes a standing advantage for employers.

Order 1305 was made during the war, on the 18th July, 1940; it did not in simple language prohibit strikes, but achieved the same result in many words, for it provided that it should be a crime, punishable by fine or imprisonment up to six months, for any person to take any part in a strike in connection with a trade dispute, unless two conditions were first fulfilled, firstly that the dispute had been reported to the Ministry of Labour and twenty-one days had elapsed since the report, and secondly that the dispute had not during that period been referred for settlement or arbitration. Thus, any strike is illegal for the first three weeks after a dispute has arisen and been reported, and the Ministry can make the proposed strike indefinitely illegal by simply ordering a reference to arbitration. The Order was made as a war-time measure, and the Minister of Labour who made it, Ernest Bevin, promised that it would be repealed when the war ended. (In the First World War a substantially similar provision had been made, and the same promise given. But then the promise had been kept.) This time, Order 1305 was still in force in 1950, five years after the end of hostilities or of any need for a restriction on strikes; it was maintained in force by the Labour Government, and we shall see in a moment the use made of it by the Government in the London gas strike early in October, 1950. We shall see, too, in Chapter 43, more serious attempts to use it in 1951, followed by its repeal, six years after the end of the war.

But at this moment in September, 1950, the General Council opposed the motion. They put up (Sir) Tom Williamson to bring up the old argument that the Order was a useful one because it provided for arbitration; he added that 80 per cent. of the claims referred to the National Arbitration Tribunal by trade unions were wholly or partially successful (which might be read as showing that the claims were well-founded and would have achieved still greater success if the workers had been able not necessarily to strike but effectively to threaten to do so). Williamson added that, if it were not for Order 1,305, strikes would take place and would "destroy the policy of full employment"; he seemed to ignore the fact that strikes or threats of strikes in a period of full employment are very helpful to the workers and are apt to succeed very quickly. He ignored equally the provisions for prosecution of strikers, of which he was destined to see a glaring example within a month.

This time however the right wing triumphed, and the resolution was lost by 5,166,000 to 2,423,000.

T.U.C. ON NATIONALISED INDUSTRIES

On the nationalised industries, a motion sponsored by the National Union of Mineworkers and the Railway Clerks Association, requesting the General Council to give early attention to the financial structure of the mining industry and of British Transport, with a view to easing the burden placed on those industries by the compensation and redemption funds, was accepted; but a motion that at least one-third of the members of Boards of nationalised industries should be representatives of the trade union movement, of whom half should have worked in the industry concerned, was defeated by 5,613,000 to 1,169,000.

Thus, the right wing carried the day on foreign policy, but was well defeated on the wage freeze; the Congress in effect was endorsing the cold-war policy but rejecting its social consequences.

The wage freeze remained government policy notwithstanding the Congress rejection of it; in the defence debate in this September, referred to in Chapter 31, Attlee repeated his request for wage restraint and expressed his confidence that the unions would show moderation in pressing for increases.

STRIKES

Strikes occurred during the year in the docks, in Smithfield meat market, in the gas industry, and in the printing industry. Their special significance lay in their taking place against the background of the wage freeze and its rejection by the Trades Union Congress; in the right-wing trade union leaders using union discipline against the strikers in the docks and Smithfield; in the Government bringing in troops in the docks, at Smithfield, and in the gas industry; and in the use of Order 1305 against the gas-workers.

The trouble in the docks began on the 14th March, 1950, when the Transport and General Workers Union expelled three docker-members from the union because of the part they had played in the Canadian seamens' strike in 1949, described in Chapter 25. In protest against these expulsions a mass meeting of dockers, called on the 26th March by the Portworkers' Defence Committee, an unofficial rank and file body, decided to place a ban on overtime working. This ban was withdrawn on the 3rd April, but when the appeals of the three expelled men were rejected on the 18th April, a protest strike started on the following day in the "Royal" group of docks. By the 21st April 9,000 men were out, and a mass meeting called for a ballot of portworkers to decide whether the union action should be upheld; and on the 22nd and 23rd a deputation went to the union headquarters with a petition for such a ballot. On the 24th April, troops were moved into the docks, and a further 4,500 men came out, making a total of 12,453. On the 25th April some 1,000 permanent men came out; by the 26th the numbers on strike totalled 14,441, and 4,500 troops were working. On the 27th April the London Dock Labour Board issued a statement that all men who failed to report for work on May 1st would have their registrations cancelled, which would have the effect of expelling them from the industry; and the Port Workers' Committee went to the House of Commons to interview M.P.s. On the 29th April, a mass meeting decided to return to work and to fight the expulsions in the branches. On the 11th May, the Minister of Labour, the late George Isaacs, announced that a Committee of Enquiry would be set up to investigate stoppages in the London Docks over the past three years. On the 18th May, the Committee of Enquiry was appointed: there was a chairman, and four members, of whom one was a former trade union general secretary.

SMITHFIELD STRIKE

The Smithfield strike had its beginnings on the 24th June, when some 1,200 meat drivers based on Smithfield struck in protest against the delay in settling their claim for an increase of 19s. per week. On the 28th June, troops began to transport corned beef from meat storage depots to butchers, and on the 3rd July troops moved into Smithfield market itself. Immediately, 900 porters and marketmen walked out, followed by provision porters, shopmen, poultry pitchers, and porters; and the men at several cold stores refused to work alongside troops. By the 5th July, there were 3,400 men out. Then, on the 7th July, 200 drivers employed by British Road Services at Brentford struck and a meeting of the London Road Haulage Stewards' Association (an unofficial body) decided to call out all general road haulage drivers in two days, this short delay being designed to give time for the delivery of perishable goods already loaded.

Sir Arthur Deakin, always ready to beat the anti-communist drum, declared that the Stewards Association was acting "with the support of active Communists", and that "agitators"—that word so dear to all anti-working-class forces—"had a reckless determination to create the maximum difficulties for the country". No Tory or employer could have done better than that; whilst one can be sure that Communists would resent the introduction of troops as active strike-breakers, one can be equally sure that every class-conscious non-communist worker would resent with equal vigour that extreme manifestation of government hostility to the working class.

On the 10th July, a further meeting of the Road Haulage Stewards' Association heard a report of a deputation to Deakin and agreed to recommend a return to work on the basis that negotiations on the Smithfield claim would be opened in 24 hours, that the union would resist all attempts to worsen conditions, and that the general haulage claim should come before the union executive, which would not delay in dealing with it. On the 11th July there was a general return to work.

On the 21st August, certain leaders of the Smithfield strike were suspended from membership of the Executive Committee of the Transport and General Workers Union. On the 28th August the Industrial Court awarded 8s. a week increase to all the workers concerned.

GAS STRIKE

The gas strike had its start on the 2nd August, when a mass meeting of gas mechanics employed in London threatened to take strike action on the 1st September if no satisfactory reply to their wage claim had been received by then; the claim, for a substantial increase, had been presented as long ago as March. No such reply being forthcoming, the men at nineteen London gas works struck on the 1st September, but returned to work on the 4th, deciding to work no overtime or shift work until the Gas Council's reply to their claim had been considered at a mass meeting. On the 14th September, an increase of $1\frac{1}{2}d.$ an hour was agreed at a meeting of the Gas Council and the Confederation of Shipbuilding and Engineering Unions, but on the 15th the men at the Beckton Gasworks struck, being dissatisfied with this award, and were followed in the next three days by the men in thirteen other gas works. On the 20th the strike spread to fifteen works in the North Thames District and three in the Eastern Area. Some 1,500 men were involved.

PROSECUTIONS

On the 26th September, Sir Robert Gould, the chief conciliation officer of the Ministry of Labour, wrote to the General Secretary of the Confederation of Ship-building and Engineering Unions, stating that the strike was a challenge to the authority of the unions. And on the 3rd October naval ratings left Chatham barracks to take over maintenance work at the gas works, and summonses were issued against ten of the strikers, employees of the North Thames Gas Board, under the Conspiracy and Protection of Property Act, 1875, and Order 1305. "The decision to apply for the summonses was taken . . . at a meeting of the Government", The Times reported. On the 5th October, ten men, who pleaded guilty to a breach of Order 1305, were sentenced to one month's imprisonment, but given leave to appeal; the charges under the 1875 Act were not pressed.

On the 6th October, agreement was reached on the basis of no victimisation, the withdrawal of troops before the men returned to work, and immediate negotiations on a bonus scheme. On this understanding the men returned to work on the 9th October.

On the previous day, a mass meeting in Hyde Park had called for a nation-wide campaign for the repeal of Order 1305.

The ten men who had been sentenced appealed, and had their sentences reduced on the 22nd November from imprisonment to fines of £50 each. It was pretty plain that a mass movement of protest had influenced the appellate Court. A delegate conference, called at very short notice and attended by delegates representing 194,000 trade unionists, nine district committees, 161 trade union branches, five trades councils, and many important shop stewards' committees, had elected a committee to launch a national campaign for the acquittal of the ten gas-workers, the repeal of Order 1305, and the disbanding of all police organisations set up to spy on trade unionists. The appellate Court stated that it felt able to do away with the sentences of imprisonment because the men had not known that they were offending against the criminal law.

PRINTERS' STOPPAGE

The strike in the printing industry was more of a lock-out than a strike; its history is a little complicated. In April, 1950, the London Society of Compositors submitted a claim for an increase of 9s. 9d. per week. The employers offered 2s. 6d. for compositors and an extra 6d. for Linotype and Monotype operators. The Society rejected this and on the 18th May placed a ban on overtime. The employers referred the dispute to the Arbitration Tribunal, who awarded 3s. 6d., on the condition that the overtime ban was withdrawn. Late in August the union instructed members affected by the overtime ban also to work strictly to rule. On the 25th August the London Master Printer's Federation decided that if members of the Society did not withdraw their "restrictive practices" by the 30th, they would be dismissed. On the 29th August, the Minister of Labour asked the Society to withdraw the ban and announced the setting up of a Court of Enquiry. The Society maintained that the employer's action was a lock-out and illegal under Order 1,305. On the 30th August, other unions in the Printing and Kindred Trades Federation announced that unions with provincial members were instructing them not to handle work transferred from London because of the dispute.

On the 1st September, London master printers gave provisional notice to members of other unions in their employment, whose agreements provided for a fortnight's notice. On the 4th September, a meeting of the two sides with Ministry of Labour officials brought no result. On the 11th September, after mediation by officials of the Printing and Kindred Trades Federation, agreement was reached that the 3,500 men dismissed should be reinstated on the 12th September, that the Society should withdraw the overtime ban and "restrictive practices", and that both sides would ask for the adjournment of the Court of Enquiry so that a conference could be held to attempt to settle differences. Accordingly, on the 12th September, the Court was adjourned and the two sides met on the 15th September. On the 20th, a meeting between the Society and the London Master Printers reached deadlock; Mr. Willis, the Secretary of the Society, said that the employers had deliberately misled the Society, and the overtime ban and "restrictive practices" were accordingly reimposed. On the 27th September, a special delegate meeting of the Society instructed their Executive to take steps to abrogate all existing agreements, and the Executive began to prepare an agreement for negotiation with individual master printers. On the 28th September the Court of Enquiry resumed its sittings.

On the 29th September, the Master Printers again discharged their compositors who belonged to the Society, claiming that they were guilty of breach of contract. The union claimed that this amounted to a lock-out.

On the 6th October, Sir Robert Gould wrote to Mr. Willis drawing attention to Order 1,305. On the 23rd October, the Report of the Court of Enquiry was published, ruling that negotiations should be reopened, the dismissed men should be reinstated, and normal working, including overtime, should be resumed. The Report contained detailed suggestions for an agreement. On the 26th October, a Special Delegate Meeting of the Society accepted a proposed wage increase of 15s., but rejected proposals as to adult trainees; it also passed a resolution protesting against the failure of the Government to take action against the employers for dismissing 4,000 compositors. *The Times* reported: "The resolution referred to a letter on October 18th from the Prime Minister, saying that the Attorney-General and the Director of Public Prosecutions believed that both the employers and the union had infringed the order but that prosecutions would not be in the public interest at this stage."

On the 27th October, the London Master Printers announced they had agreed to a resumption of work as recommended, and would negotiate an agreement. Work was in fact resumed on the 1st November.

CHAPTER 36

Social Services and Other Matters, 1950

ON housing, with which I dealt in Chapter 26 in respect of 1948-9, it is useful, even at the cost of a little repetition, to look at the record of the whole four and a half years of Labour Government.

Up to the end of 1949, the total post-war housing provided was:

New Permanent houses:

Built by local authorities, housing associations, and government departments		492,529
Built by private builders		130,818
		623,347
New Temporary houses		157,146
Existing Housing brought into use:		
By conversion and adaptation . . .		125,697
By repair of vacant war-damaged dwellings . .		141,654
By requisition		27,539
Temporary Huts		3,041
Service Camps		25,895
Grand total		1,104,319

As a result of the restriction on the building of new houses, the number of new permanent houses provided in 1949 was 197,627, compared with 227,770 in 1948.

The new houses provided in 1945 to 1949 were more than had been built in 1918 to 1922 by the post-war Tory Government, but the programme set out in *Let Us Face the Future* given in Chapter 2, was not achieved. Of the promises there made to undertake drastic action to ensure an efficient industry; to prevent restrictive price rings; to introduce modern methods and materials; to maintain a due balance between housing, schools and factories; to institute centralised purchasing and price control; and to set up a Ministry of Housing and Planning; not one had been fulfilled. There were still hundreds of thousands of families without a separate home, and thousands still lived in slums. Men and materials which should have gone into housing had been used on non-priority work in hotels, offices, shops, and other buildings. No more than a quarter of the building trade operatives had ever been working on new houses. And building costs had risen so high that the rents of new dwellings were often beyond the means of those who most needed them.

On the 9th March, 1950, a number of M.P.s pressed the Minister of Health, Aneurin Bevan, to state how many applicants for houses were on the lists kept by local authorities. In reply, Bevan produced a statement saying that, in a White Paper produced in 1945 (by the previous Government), it was estimated that some 750,000 houses were needed to "afford a separate dwelling for every family which desires to have one", and that a further 500,000 were needed "to remove houses already condemned as unfit, and to abate overcrowding since 1935". The estimated increase of population in Great Britain since 1945 was about 1,400,000, which on an average of three and a half persons per household would require some 400,000 further houses; statistical information on the increase in the number of families was not available. By the end of 1948, over 800,000 additional houses had been provided, and on the basis of the estimates made in 1945, and with the knowledge that the housing demand was not spread evenly through the country, it would have been expected that in many districts the demand from families without a home of their own would have been substantially met and that these authorities would in the near future be able to turn to the task of abating overcrowding and the removal of unfit houses.

The information published by local authorities as to the number of applicants did not, however, support this view, the statement said. Local authorities had been asked to sift their records, and to inform the Ministry how many still desired accommodation, but it was found that local authorities differed greatly in their arrangements for accepting applicants for waiting lists; the total results received centrally therefore gave an erroneous picture; totals were inflated by duplication and, if published, would therefore be misleading. (The inference is unescapable that, if the figures of the local authorities' lists had been made public, everyone would have been appalled.) It continued:

"Two conclusions emerge, however. . . .

1. After making every allowance for variations in the local arrangements for classifying and reviewing applications, the original estimate which was made during the war has in post-war circumstances turned out to have been a substantial underestimate of the true position. . . .

2. The number of applications which have been accepted by local authorities and are still outstanding from families requiring a new home will call for the continuance of the housing programme at the highest rate that is possible, having regard to the other claims on the national resources, in order to enable a separate home to be offered to each family who desire to have one."

COST OF HOUSING

On the 2nd July, 1950, the second Report of the Girdwood Committee on the cost of housing construction was published. It showed that the average cost of a "traditional" local-authority three-bedroom house had gone up by 8 per cent. since 1947. The average size of such houses was 1,050 sq. ft. in October, 1949, compared with 1,029 sq. ft. in October, 1947; the average number of man-hours required to build a house was 2,575, compared to 3,034 in 1947 (the 1938 figure had been 2,092). The cost of labour had fallen by £9 per house on an average, the increase in wages being more than off-set by greater productivity. But the cost of materials had risen by £86 per house, and contractors' overheads and profit had also gone up.

EDUCATION

On education, the Ministry's Report for 1949, published in August, 1950, showed that 86 new schools—68 primary and 18 secondary—had been completed and brought into use, an improvement on 1948, but far from adequate, as the population was increasing. On improvements to existing schools, the expenditure for the year was £3,276,600; the Report added that "it is a matter of regret that because of the need for economy there must now be some reduction of the rate of expenditure for this kind of work".

On technical education, the Report said that "the year saw a big increase in work started, but the lack of suitable accommodation is so great that it cannot be claimed that the surface of the problem has been more than scratched".

Nearly one thousand canteens had been provided for the school meals service, but there were still 1,938 schools and departments with no meals service at all, and "economy" had banned all expenditure for the further development of the service.

Of other facilities, the Report said:

"During the earlier part of the year a certain amount of building was done, mainly by means of minor works, to extend the provision of youth clubs, village halls and other similar places. In October it unfortunately became necessary to place a ban on any new works of this nature."

Secondary education was still dominated by the system of selection at "11 plus". The Report showed that those children who failed to get to a grammar school had only a negligible chance of getting to a university; in 1949, nine children from secondary modern schools and 25 from secondary technical schools achieved this. The proportion of over-large classes had increased. And, in the face of all these difficulties, a 12½ per cent. cut on building was imposed on 1950 programmes and a further 12½ per cent. cut on 1951 programmes.

NATIONAL ASSISTANCE

The Annual Report of the National Assistance Board for 1949 showed that over 2,000,000 persons, or 4 per cent. of the population, were being dealt with. The Board was paying out 1,150,000 weekly allowances covering, with dependants, about 1,750,000 persons. It was also paying non-contributory pensions to 440,190 old people, of whom 342,206 were not receiving the weekly allowances just mentioned.

During the year, the number of people receiving weekly allowances increased by over 123,000, partly because of the increasing number of old people but also because the existing level of insurance benefits was becoming less adequate. Half the payments made by the Board were to supplement insurance benefits of one kind or another.

On the 3rd May, 1950, new scales to be operated by the Board were approved, to come into operation from 12th June. The rate for married couples was increased from 40s. to 43s. 6d. and that for a person living alone from 24s. to 26s. To these scales allowance for rent has to be added. Usually the rent was met in full, except where it was considered unreasonably high, in which case it was sometimes only partially met.

LOCAL ELECTIONS

The Local elections in England and Wales held in May, 1950, showed net Labour losses of 58 in County Boroughs, and net Labour gains of five in non-County Boroughs; in Urban and Rural District Councils, there were net Labour gains of 158. After these elections, Labour controlled 32 out of 83 County Boroughs, compared with 46 in the peak year of 1946, and about 20 pre-war; it lost control of four County Boroughs.

MAY DAY PROCESSION BANNED

On the 7th May, 1950, the Government having once again prohibited *all* processions in London over a period which covered May Day, on the ground that the fascists had announced their intention to hold a May Day "march", as mentioned in Chapter 26, a workers' May Day procession, held in spite of the ban, was broken up by the police, who arrested seventy of the participants.

CHAPTER 37

Labour Party Policy, 1950

IT was natural that the Labour Party, with its tiny majority in the House of Commons, and with the economy in a state of crisis and some of the war-time scarcities and rationing nearing their end, should devote a good deal of attention to policy in the course of the year. A meeting of Labour Party leaders was held in Dorking in May, 1950, to work out the line for the Labour programme at the next General Election. No publicity was given to the meeting, but it became known that economic policy was the central topic of discussion, in the light of the rising wage movement and of the repudiation by a majority at the Trades Union Congress—and a majority of trade unionists throughout the country—of the wage freeze. (It was immediately after the Dorking talks that the General Council of the T.U.C. made the declaration in favour of the wage freeze, without "excessive rigidity in its application", mentioned in Chapter 35.)

It was decided at Dorking to get rid of as many controls as possible, and the *Economist* remarked on the 3rd June that the progressive elimination of controls showed "how superficial are the differences in economic policy between the two major parties". On the same day, the *New Statesman* remarked that "planning is disappearing along with scarcity".

DROPPING NATIONALISATION

At Dorking it was also decided to drop nationalisation from Labour policy; as John Gollan remarked in the *Labour Monthly*, at p. 307, "Dorking therefore marks a new stage in the efforts of the right-wing leaders to destroy the identity of the Labour movement in complete class collaboration with monopoly capitalism."

Morgan Phillips, general secretary of the Labour Party, went straight from Dorking to the International Socialist Conference at Copenhagen, where he attacked the growing world movement for the banning of the atom bomb. This made it pretty clear that Dorking had declared war on the peace movement. (He said, too, that British Socialism—by which he meant official Labour policy—was not Marxist, a point on which everyone would agree with him.)

"EUROPEAN UNITY"

Soon after the Dorking meeting, the National Executive of the Labour Party issued a statement on foreign policy entitled *European Unity*. Here, unity meant, of course, the unity of capitalist Europe, in hostility to the socialist countries. The statement sought to present the policy of the "third force", i.e. of a third force standing between the U.S.A. and the U.S.S.R.; and the direction in which such a force would face was made clear by the phrase in the statement that "the Third Force must be a world-wide political alliance against totalitarianism wherever it is found". This declaration really proclaimed as Labour Policy the military alliance of the Labour Government and American monopoly capital against socialism. (Any idea of a Third Force in Europe had in truth been destroyed by the Atlantic Pact.)

"LABOUR AND THE NEW SOCIETY"

In August, the Executive Committee issued an important policy statement entitled *Labour and the New Society*, for consideration at the Labour Party Conference in October. With its curious mixture of unsocialist verbiage and of references to capitalism as if it were something that had already been abolished, this document was in essence a defence of the existing capitalist order, an advocacy of preparation for war, and a defence of colonialism and imperialism.

It began with a section on "the moral basis of the new society", although a socialist would have been sorely puzzled to find anything new—certainly anything new and socialist—in the society of 1950. "The true purpose of society," it said, is "to promote and protect the dignity and well-being of the individual. Capitalism"—which the Government had been striving for five years to maintain—"degraded humanity because it rejected this purpose. When the purpose of gain was proclaimed a major virtue, values were lowered and the claims of human brotherhood were sacrificed to the demands of private profit . . . the rights of property came before the rights of man." Here we have capitalism referred to in the past tense, as if all its citadels, which the Government had failed to capture or destroy, had somehow vanished.

Socialism, said the statement, is dedicated to a different end—it appeals to the good in people, and relies on fellowship and friendliness, not fear and greed: "We proclaim the rights of man."

"All peoples have the right to live in peace"—but the Labour Governments had lined us all up in the American war camp.

"All peoples have the right to the full fruits of their industry"—but the Labour Government was leaving 80 per cent. of industry in the hands of private capitalists who retained the fruits for themselves.

"We reject the claims of the few to live on the labour of the many. . . Fair shares should be the national rule"—but the Government had left the few free to live on the labour of the many, had attempted by a wage freeze in a time of rising prices to reduce the share of those in the nation who had less than the few, and left the few free to increase their wealth and profits.

"Everyone should have equal rights and opportunities"—but no advance had been made towards the only system that can give that equality; and education, which can make a reality of opportunities, had been skimped to prepare a war against the socialist world of equal opportunity.

"We proclaim the right to work. Full employment has been achieved, and will be maintained only by asserting control over economic forces"—but what control had been won?

"We proclaim the right to democracy. In the past a small minority held sway over the great majority. The majority should rule. We aim at economic and political democracy in which the people play a continuous and responsible part in running their common affairs"—but had anything happened in the five years to diminish the sway of finance or to widen the operation of any kind of democracy?

The Statement claimed that the Government had started to put these principles into practice over the past five years; production and exports were higher, destitution had been abolished (!), and for most people the standard of living was higher than before the war. But now, it said, "the future calls . . . the immediate task is to clarify the principles and purposes of the Labour Movement. At this critical stage of the world's history, the Labour Party should re-state its principles and review its policy". And it went on to state some principles.

The first was "to live in peace". The Party and the Government, which were crowning their surrender to American aggressive militarism and their acceptance of German rearmament against the socialist world with attacks on the World Peace Movement, opened this section of the statement with a claim to have friends and allies in the diverse progressive movements of the Commonwealth, Europe and the U.S.A.—note the careful exclusion of any idea of friendship with the socialist world, which is classified as "other nations (having) less acceptable systems and ideas"; and they produced a series of smooth platitudes, in which anti-Soviet sentiments were scarcely concealed; large-scale unemployment must be avoided because when it is present "millions turn towards communist or fascist dictatorships"—we are not even spared the political dishonesty (or illiteracy) of treating fascism and communism as falling into the same category. Such a prostitution of thought may be forgiven to Tories, or to Royal Commissions appointed by Tories, but we can surely ask those calling themselves socialists to understand that, however much they dislike communism or fascism, these are wholly different systems and philosophies bearing no resemblance whatever to one another except that some people hate both!

The document goes on to talk of "military preparedness (which) together with economic development are [sic] part of a single plan for defending and developing the whole free world"—"the whole free world" is of course a stock phrase to describe the capitalist world whose "freedom" consists of the right for those who have the means of doing so freely to exploit the labour of others. "Labour," it added, "will seek peace through unity of the democracies, through a strong defensive alliance of democratic nations, and through a world plan for mutual aid to bring economic advance"—"democracies" is a code word meaning "non-socialist countries".

The document went on to say that nations must work together to extend freedom and rid mankind of mass unemployment—did the draftsman have the grace or honesty to put in the word "mass" before unemployment because he knew that a good deal of unemployment is inevitable under the capitalist system which he was working to maintain?

The association with the U.S.A., Canada and the countries of *Western* Europe in the Atlantic Community of free and democratic nations was explicitly affirmed—leaving no doubt that the alignment of the country with the main capitalist and anti-socialist countries was to be integrally maintained.

On "the defence of the *free world*", there was similar bombast about "restraining aggressive nationalism and imperialism", although every informed critic of the U.S.S.R., however hostile, agreed that that country had no intention of starting a war. It added that this policy demands military preparedness: "Britain will not shirk. The cost of defence is high. It is bound to limit the money available for social services or tax reduction. But it is the only safeguard against aggression."

The theme for a "World Plan for Mutual Aid", of co-operation by the *free world*, was also developed. This world plan was to be worked out to take the place of Marshall Aid in 1952.

In a section on "the full fruits of their industry", the aim of Labour was a little more cautiously formulated: "Labour would *seek* to remove extreme inequalities."

HOUSING

On housing, the document contained blithe promises, with no hint that the Government had so far failed. Labour's aim, it said, was to secure a decent separate home for every family, to demolish the slums, to bring up to modern standards older houses which were still habitable but lacked amenities, to cut building costs without impairing the hard-won advances of building workers, and to keep rents within reasonable limits. Many builders were inefficient; the nation must not tolerate any obstacle to greater efficiency. Sound incentive schemes, closer control of production, a steadier supply of raw materials, and better training for management were urgently required. They could have worded all these promises just as accurately, if less attractively, by just saying: "Everything we promised in 1945 and did not fulfil, we promise again."

In a section on "equal responsibility to the community", we are told that "it is wrong to take money for nothing and to take rewards which have not been earned"; but when it comes to practical application we are told that *large unearned* incomes are unjustifiable (but not that they will be taken away) and that *large inherited* incomes are *particularly* unfair, and justify heavy death duties on larger fortunes—a principle established many decades before.

In the section on "control of economic power by the people", we find again one of the odd references to capitalism in the past tense, as if it had all been swept away:

The people should collectively control and direct the economic forces which affect their daily lives and the nation's well-being: "those who take the key decisions in the economy must be answerable to the people".

"Under capitalism these decisions were guided by the expectation of private gain." The theory was this would promote public good, but it did not. "Big business men, aristocratic landowners, bankers and merchants directed the economic life of the nation", and decided whether there would be prosperity and work for all or slumps and unemployment. Powerful trusts closed shipyards and factories on which thousands depended. "Monopolists exploited consumers through high prices. Property owners drew fat rents from ugly tenements in congested streets and obstructed public efforts to wipe out slums. . . .

"The whole nation was imperilled by private control of the economy . . . therefore the public will must be supreme. It can be applied in two ways—by public ownership, and by ensuring that private industry responds to public needs."

When one reads the last sentence one is tempted for a moment to believe that the Party was going back to its advocacy of nationalisation, which seemed to have been dropped at Dorking; but the hope is soon destroyed, for after a few sentences of praise for public ownership we get the following:

"The following three tests should be applied in deciding what industries are suitable for public ownership:

"Public ownership as a means of controlling basic industries and services on which the economic life and welfare of the community depend. Control cannot be safely left in hands of private owners not answerable to the community.

"Public ownership as a way of dealing with industries in which inefficiency persists and where private owners lack either will or capacity to improve.

"Public ownership as a means of ensuring that monopolies do not exploit the public. Where monopoly is inevitable there should be public ownership."

This is followed by the suggestion that public ownership can take many forms other than nationalisation, such as municipal enterprise, competitive public enterprises within industries, voluntary co-operation by consumers through the Co-operative movement, co-operation by producers, agricultural co-operation, and by publicly-owned factories and equipment being leased to private manufacturers. This section is plainly an attempt to conciliate on the one hand the large masses in the Labour Party who resented each and every betrayal of socialism, and on the other the middle-of-the-road non-socialist voters whom the

Labour leaders always hoped could be prevailed upon to vote Labour if Labour didn't frighten them by talking socialism.

The document contained some praise for the industries that had been nationalised, an affirmation of the Government's intention to go ahead with the nationalisation of iron and steel, and some verbiage designed to hide the fact that no more nationalisation was really intended.

PRAISE FOR PRIVATE ENTERPRISE

There follow these words:

"Private enterprise has a proper place in the economy. Indeed we shall aid and encourage its efficiency and enterprise. But the community has a right to see that it works in the interest of the nation. Britain must never again be put in pawn to big business. Private owners must never be allowed to amass great concentrations of power. This imposes the need for a socialist attitude to private enterprise which is sensible, firm and public spirited."

The notion that immensely powerful organisations like Imperial Chemical Industries were not "great concentrations of power" is almost amusing.

These and other optimistic platitudes were followed by the remark that there were four great dangers in the way of maintaining full employment, viz.:

1. that world trade will collapse;
2. that prices of British goods will be too high to sell in competitive export markets;
3. that the purchasing power of the British people will fall; and
4. that there may be local unemployment in certain areas.

All these dangers are inherent in the operation of capitalism which in many passages the document treats as a thing of the past, and it offers no real remedy for them. Trade with the Commonwealth and with the colonies will be developed, we are told; so will trade with Western Europe. Lest anyone should mention the two-fifths of the world that is socialist, it is added that we are "always prepared to trade as much as we can with Eastern Europe"—no mention at all of China, one-fifth of the world—"given the necessary co-operation"—the implication is clear that the blame for the non-development of trade with the socialist world is the fault of "the Russians", and not a matter of policy or of American direction. (But in fact, in June, 1950, an agreement was signed in Moscow for the supply of a large quantity of Soviet timber—which we urgently needed.)

There are many further proposals and promises, such as any electioneering party makes, to wage-earners, consumers, rural workers —"fair rewards for farmers and farm-workers"—and all other sections of the community.

DEMOCRATIC SOCIALISM

In conclusion, we are told that the Statement has set out the object-ives of Democratic Socialism—a new name for Social Democracy: the struggle for peace, for social justice, for full employment and higher production, for a democratic society in which the people will bear responsibility as rulers—all this as part of one effort to build the new society:

> "The brotherhood of man, integrity of spirit, pride in family and pride in the nation—these are the forces which will carry us forward. Our faith and our hope is in the essential goodness of ordinary men and women. We believe that they will respond to the high demands that the new life makes of them. We believe in people."

After that fine rhetoric, which could have been adopted by either the Tories or the Liberals, one had to wait a little over a year to see how far people believed in them.

The only things not mentioned in the statement were the wars in Korea and Malaya, the cuts in housing, health, and education, our complete subservience to the U.S.A.—and, pretty well, any socialist hopes or outlooks.

LABOUR PARTY CONFERENCE

The Labour Party Conference was held at Margate in September. It was marked by a strong anti-Soviet, cold war, attitude from the leadership, and a good deal of opposition from the left wing.

Labour and the New Society was approved unanimously after a day of debate in which there was a certain amount of opposition, particularly to the abandonment of further nationalisation. Morrison sought to appease this by saying that the nationalisation of cement, sugar, and industrial insurance had not been dropped, although not mentioned in the document; these industries were, he said, "within the field of eligibility for consideration".

Foreign policy took a prominent place. The policy of the platform—

and of *Labour and the New Society*—was opposed by a composite resolution covering seven points:

A demand for a conference to resolve "Big Five" differences, renewed efforts for friendship with the U.S.S.R.; the outlawing of the atom bomb; support for the U.N. and avoidance of all commitments contrary to the Charter; the pressing on with measures for improving backward areas and to end trade barriers between East and West; to "take further action" to get the People's Republic of China on the Security Council; and to end dollar dependence by 1952.

This resolution was sponsored by the Electrical Trades Union, the Amalgamated Union of Foundry Workers, and thirty-nine constituency parties.

To meet this challenge, the National Executive Committee made a Supplementary Report on the International Situation, in which it asserted that "the policy of the Soviet Union is the main obstacle to higher standards throughout the world, compelling our own and other governments to direct to armed preparations resources which might have gone directly to improve the life of the ordinary man". The main argument was that "collective security through the United Nations is the keystone of the Labour Government foreign policy. By leaping to the aid of South Korea against unprovoked aggression from the North the United Nations has immensely strengthened its authority and prestige.★ Peace cannot be defended without arms—or by arms alone." The burden would be heavy, but would be justly borne.

The necessity for increasing the wealth of the world's undeveloped areas was also emphasised.

In spite of opposition from the platform the composite resolution was pressed to the vote, being defeated by 4,861,000 to 881,000. Of these 881,000 votes, 430,000 came from Constituency Labour Parties, i.e. almost half the local Labour Parties voted for this resolution despite opposition from the platform.

On the topic of wages, prices, and profits—the wage freeze and its contrasts—a composite resolution, which was accepted by the platform, ran:

"This Conference, taking note of the improved economic position of the country and in particular of the increased and increasing

★ Compare the facts as to the origins of the Korean War stated in Chapter 31.

AI

productivity of industry and the high profits received by employers, calls upon the Government to facilitate, in conjunction with the T.U.C., improvement in the real wages of the workers by taking the most energetic action

"1. to stem the upward trend of prices and bring about a reduction; and

"2. to control and reduce profits.

"Further, this Conference calls the particular attention of the Government to those industries and sections of industries in which the workers are still paid wages too low to enable them fully to benefit by the Government's policy of fair shares."

The feelings expressed in the debate were so strong that *The Times* reported that "the mood of the party is now such that it will now look for some action".

On the nationalised industries, a very critical resolution, supported by the National Union of Railwaymen and the Amalgamated Engineering Union, complained that nationalised industries had been left in the hands of those who had mismanaged them in the past, and claimed that interest should be halved; it also pointed out that earnings on the railways were deplorably low. The resolution was defeated, but only by 2,878,000 to 1,891,000.

"The outstanding characteristic of the Conference", wrote John Gollan in *Labour Monthly*, at p. 511, "was the evidence in practically every debate of the unbridgeable gulf and essential conflict between the right-wing leadership and the Labour rank and file."

CHAPTER 38

The 1950-1 Session

WHAT proved to be the last session of the second Parliament, and the last year of a Labour Government for a good many years, began on the 31st October, 1950, and lasted until the 4th October, 1951. As in the previous year, the tiny majority which the Government possessed did not encourage any ambitious legislation.

THE KING'S SPEECH

The King's Speech started by referring to the world being once more troubled with the menace of war (arising in particular from the developments in Korea with which I will deal in the next chapter). The avoidance of war was, it said, the supreme desire of the Government, which would seek by all means to ensure the success of measures of rearmament (!); the necessary increases in production for defence would call for further efforts and sacrifices.

In Korea, the Speech ran, the forces under the flag of the United Nations were overcoming the invaders (a reference to temporary advances which I will discuss later). The success of this historic action marked, it said, a decisive moment in world affairs, and was arousing fresh hopes of achieving a united, free, and democratic Korea, thus giving proof of the ability of the United Nations to meet a threat to world peace.

The Government also supported strongly the efforts of the specialised agencies of the U.N. to improve the standard of living in impoverished or backward countries.

It promised to maintain the closest relations with other governments of the Commonwealth to safeguard freedom and peace.

In respect to NATO the Government would work with the other governments signatory to the North Atlantic and the Brussels Treaties to strengthen NATO to improve the defences of the North Atlantic area, and thus to achieve security against attack.

In consultation with other governments, it was to give further study to plans for promoting the economic development of South and South-East Asia.

The development of the colonial territories and the welfare of their peoples was to receive attention, and there was to be legislation to supplement the sums made available by the Colonial Development and Welfare Act, 1945.

Preparations were going forward for holding the Festival of Britain, 1951.

With reference to social policy, the Government promised to continue, although rearmament would make heavy demands upon our resources, the high priority (!) given to housing, and to maintain the essentials of its social policy. It would do its utmost to ensure stability of costs and prices, and to maintain the export drive.

In order to defend full employment, to ensure the full use of our resources to the best advantage, and to avoid inflation, legislation was proposed to give Ministers, on a permanent basis and subject to appropriate parliamentary safeguards, powers to regulate production, distribution, and consumption, and to control prices.

Civil Defence was to be further developed.

Legislation was to be introduced for a number of minor—and useful —reforms, including the hearing of appeals from convictions by Courts martial; rights of reinstatement in civilian employment for reservists recalled to the Forces and for certain National Service men; the restoration of land devastated by the extraction of ironstone; and the transfer to public ownership of the shares in the British Sugar Beet Corporation not already held by the Exchequer.

The whole speech could have been delivered with very few alterations, on behalf of a Tory government.

In the debate on the address, Attlee delivered an attack on the World Peace Congress (with which I shall deal at a little length in the next chapter), and denounced the demand for the control of atomic energy on the ground that "it would operate only in free countries but there would be no restraint on totalitarian states"—as always, in his dictionary, "free" meant capitalist and "totalitarian" meant socialist.

TORY FOREIGN POLICY

Churchill "rubbed in" the criticisms of the left by declaring that the Government had carried out his Fulton policy, and said that there was such agreement on foreign policy that for all practical purposes there was a coalition on foreign affairs, so that the Labour leaders had to "hunt round" to find some domestic issue to differentiate themselves from the Tories.

The Tories in general, in this debate, made housing the principal issue against the Government, demanding a "target" of 300,000 houses a year; (they did not of course suggest cutting the armament policy to make this possible, but advocated reducing the standards of house building). On other social services, they called for cuts; Oliver Lyttelton, for example, said: "We may have to do with fewer technical colleges; we may have to postpone the educational programme."

A good deal of concern was shown on the Labour benches; Emrys Hughes made a strong protest on Korea, and denounced the plans for the re-armament of West Germany.

None of the legislation passed during the Session calls for more description than can be read in the King's Speech itself or in the course of later chapters.

GOVERNMENT CHANGES

There were some changes in the Government during the Session. On the 17th January, 1951, Bevan became Minister of Labour, and Hilary Marquand took his place as Minister of Health. On the 9th March, 1951, Bevin, who had in fact only a few more weeks to live, gave up the Foreign Ministry and became Lord Privy Seal; he was succeeded by Herbert Morrison.

Some more important changes—the resignations of Bevan, Harold Wilson (President of the Board of Trade), and a junior Minister John Freeman, on the 21st April, 1951—will be dealt with in Chapter 41.

I should write a few words on the departure of Bevin and the selection of Morrison to take his place. Bevin, in very bad health, but extremely tenacious and always hopeful of recovery, held on and on. There are stories that Attlee, when he finally determined that Bevin's health was really too bad for him to remain, was very abrupt and tactless in the manner of asking him to resign; it can matter little whether they are correct or not. But it does matter that for little less than six years this obstinate, opinionated, forceful, and pretty ignorant bigot, blindly anti-communist and anti-Soviet, should have been in charge of the foreign policy of what was meant to be a socialist government, at one of the greatest moments in history—and not only in charge of foreign policy but also exercising a great deal of influence on policy generally.

I agree fully with the summing up of Bevin by Palme Dutt, in the

Notes of the Month for April, 1951, at pp. 147-8 of *Labour Monthly* written after Bevin's resignation but before his death.

He wrote:

"Mr Bevin's six years at the Foreign Office have brought Britain to a lower point even than the degradation of Munich and Neville Chamberlain. When he took over, all the cards were in his hands. Britain, united with the Soviet Union in the British-Soviet treaty, could have led Europe along the paths of anti-fascist progressive development, curbed American reaction, ensured the banning of the atom bomb and the reduction of armaments, and made the United Nations a reality. Potsdam, with Britain's signature, laid down the lines for a demilitarised denazified peaceful Germany—the very policy which the Western Powers now denounce as a 'power vacuum'. It is only necessary to recall the speeches, articles and broadcasts from Moscow then to realise what a fund of goodwill there was in the Soviet Union towards Britain, which Mr. Bevin proceeded to squander. Mr. Bevin had only one principle as Foreign Minister: a pathological anti-communist anti-Soviet hatred, which blinded him to Britain's true interests and made him the tool of American reaction. From his very first speech as Foreign Minister he launched out into a violent anti-Soviet diatribe, whose intemperance of language startled the diplomatic world, with the memories of the anti-fascist alliance still recent, and led the way in the anti-Soviet warmongering crusade, before any American politician, and before Mr. Churchill. . . .

"Through all the muddled inconsistencies and confusion of his policy, the blustering boasts followed by invariable fiascos, the only consistent principle was this blind anti-communist anti-Soviet hatred, which led him to dissipate Britain's resources in overseas adventures and military interventions on the side of reaction all over the world, from Indonesia to Greece, and from Palestine to Malaya.

"This same anti-Soviet hatred led him to sell out Britain to its principal imperialist rival and antagonist, the American financial-militarist oligarchy. . . . A close co-operation with France and the Soviet Union could have saved the balance against the crushing weight and openly insolent expansionist aims of American imperialism, which was following up its colossal war profits by seizing military and strategic bases all over the world and proclaiming the advent of the 'American century'."

The question who should succeed Bevin caused some trouble. Herbert Morrison, who had little experience of foreign affairs, wanted the position, and Attlee, after hesitating a little, finally appointed him. It was not an easy post, and Morrison had quite a few problems in the less than seven months of his tenure.

CHAPTER 39

Foreign Policy, 1950-1

THE main features of the year were mainly intensifications of the earlier features rather than the emergence of new ones. Capitulation to the U.S.A. was more complete; rearmament was heavier than ever; attacks on the U.S.S.R. were also worse. The drive for the rearmament of Western Germany was a new feature—entirely consistent, of course with the old ones, if not with many statements made by Bevin and other ministers in the past.

KOREAN WAR

Developments in the Korean War were sensational and dangerous in the latter part of 1950. In the early months of the war, the American and South Korean forces had been pinned down in the south, but the fire-eating and uncontrollable U.S. General MacArthur, who was in command of all the U.S. and satellite forces (nominally on behalf of the United Nations), secured one remarkable if fleeting success (the subject of the reference in the King's Speech, quoted above) by landing troops from the sea behind the North Korean forces far to the North of the 38th Parallel (the frontier artificially fixed after the defeat of Japan in the Second World War between North and South Korea). Logically, if the Americans had wished to act consistently with their story that they had intervened in Korea only to defend South Korea against "invasion" from the North, MacArthur should have been content to restore to South Korea secure possession of the territory south of the 38th Parallel; but in fact—by this successful landing—he carried the war far into the North and up to the Chinese Korean frontier.

The North Koreans were compelled to retreat northwards towards the Chinese-Korean frontier, pursued by MacArthur.

The Chinese People's Republic had given clear warnings that if MacArthur advanced beyond the 38th Parallel, they would intervene for their own protection. MacArthur had ignored these warnings, and continued his advance. As a result, numbers of Chinese volunteers came to the aid of the North Koreans, and in the end these two armies drove the

"United Nations" forces back in headlong retreat to the 38th Parallel. MacArthur, flushed with his temporary victory, and lavishing promises to the American forces that they would be "home by Christmas", wanted to carry the war into China, thus creating a danger—approaching certainty—of a third world war, and exciting an instantaneous and vigorous hostile reaction from British public opinion.

ATTLEE VISITS WASHINGTON

Francis Williams, in *A Prime Minister Remembers* at pp. 232 *et seq.*, describes the British reaction to this proposal:

"By November . . . Attlee's fears . . . that the Korean campaign might become the springboard for a third world war were greatly increased by a turn in American policy which seemed to ignore the principle accepted as essential during the global strategy review in Washington, that an extension of the Korean War must be avoided.

"After a brilliant initial advance towards the Manchurian frontier the United Nations forces under General MacArthur had suffered a reverse as a result of the intervention of Chinese Communist 'volunteers' and there were widespread demands throughout America for a widening of the war. A request by General MacArthur for authority to retaliate against air attacks on his forces from Manchurian bases was passed to the British and other Governments with forces in Korea, and was strongly opposed by all. But it was clear that there was a strong group in the Pentagon which was anxious for a showdown with Russia and that it was gaining in force. It also seemed to Attlee that the control exercised over MacArthur by the U.S. Administration was dangerously slight. Finally a statement by Truman himself, at a White House Press Conference, to the effect that the U.S. Government was determined to meet the military situation in Korea by whatever steps were necessary, and that this covered consideration of all weapons, including the atom bomb, convinced Attlee that it was time to make quite clear once more that Britain was absolutely opposed to any avoidable extension of the Korean War and would not countenance use of the atom bomb. He instructed the Foreign Office to send a telegram . . . for transmission to the President informing him of his intention to fly to Washington. The telegram, dated 30th November, 1950, read:

" 'They (the Cabinet) feel that nothing less than a personal discussion with the President will meet the situation. The President's statement this afternoon has caused the most serious difficulties here . . . the Prime Minister will come in no sense in a mood of criticism, but we feel that it will allay public anxiety, at all events in this country, if a meeting is arranged.

" 'The Prime Minister would wish to discuss in addition to the Far Eastern situation

" '(a) the raw materials position

" '(b) Western European defence'."

Attlee flew to Washington on the 3rd December, 1950: Francis Williams quotes him as saying:

"It had always been our view that the war should be confined to Korea, and that it would be a most dangerous mistake to have large forces committed to a major campaign in Asia which would give the Russians exactly the opportunity they wanted for large-scale mischief elsewhere—an open invitation to commit aggression in other parts of the world while we were bogged down. I wasn't satisfied with the control over MacArthur. . . . Finally, there was the report of Truman's remark on the atom bomb. I was much perturbed by that."

Attlee gave this account of his talks with Truman:

"I pointed out that we were engaged in a global struggle against Communism and it would be suicidal to allow our forces to be bogged down in China, fighting the wrong people in the wrong place at the wrong time"—it would be interesting to know whom he had in mind as the right people to fight, and the right places and times . . . "to start bombing in Manchuria was bound to be taken as a form of aggression. Of course there were the so-called volunteers infiltrating, but we had been warned by the Chinese earlier that if we went beyond the 38th Parallel they would intervene. It was Mac-Arthur who insisted on going beyond. . . . Now he was keen on bombing Chinese industrial installations on the other side of the border. I was quite sure this was the wrong policy. . . .

"The Americans raised the question of the threat of the Chinese Communists' claim to Formosa. I said 'You must understand that this is purely an American opinion. You consider it an offence to American interests. But it has nothing to do with what we are doing under U.N.O! . . . It seemed to me absurd not to face the fact that the Communist Government was head of the real China and get them into the U.N.O. However it was very difficult to persuade the Americans on that."

In his autobiography, *As it Happened*, at p. 201, Attlee had written of this same meeting:

"I found a general understanding of the British position, and agreement on the need for preventing the extension of the war. . . . On the question of the recognition of the Chinese Government and the position of Formosa we agreed to differ. . . . We then turned to the difficult question of the allocation and procurement of raw materials for rearmament by the Allies. . . . We agreed to set up a number of commodity committees. Unfortunately, in my view, the urgency of the matter was not sufficiently realised on that side, with the result that prices were forced up before the committees could get to work."

I agree with what George Matthews wrote in *World News* on the 16th December, 1950:

"Last week they (the British imperialists) expressed concern about American policy, not because they disagree with the general line of war against Communism and the progressive forces, but because differences in the war camp about *where to fight* were sharply emerging. . . .

"Attlee flew to Washington with four main aims. . . .

"1. To discuss how to retrieve the position in the Far East and in Korea, while at the same time carrying forward the war preparations in Europe.

"2. To discuss the speeding-up of rearmament in Western Europe and especially the remilitarisation of West Germany.

"3. To try to get agreement on economic questions, especially those arising from the American stock-piling policy, which is leading to difficulties for the European countries through shortages and high prices of raw materials.

"4. To try to damp down the powerful upsurge against war with China and the use of the atom bomb by pretending that the visit was to save peace.

". . . The communiqué on the Truman-Attlee talks . . . cannot conceal the fact that it puts forward a policy for continued war in Korea and the Far East and intensified preparations for war in Europe.

"On the question of the atom bomb . . . the statement makes it absolutely clear that American imperialism reserves to itself the sole right to decide when this terrible weapon shall be used. . . . All it says is that Truman will 'keep the Prime Minister informed of developments which might bring about a change in the situation'.

"On Korea, the communiqué . . . says 'the forces of our two countries will continue to discharge their responsibilities'. . . . The aim is clear—to stay in Korea, continue the war. . . .

"Truman and Attlee put in phrases about 'negotiations'. But they make no approach to a position which could lead to successful negotiations. Instead they attempt to put the entire blame for the position in Korea on the Chinese People's Government, and in the U.N. the British and American representatives continue to call for the withdrawal of Chinese volunteers as the prerequisite to a settlement. . . .

"In Europe Truman and Attlee agreed to strengthen the war drive. . . to speed up rearmament and expand arms production as speedily as possible and appoint the Supreme Commander for Europe at the earliest possible date.

"The key to their plans in Europe is the rearmament of Western Germany. While Truman and Attlee were talking in Washington the French Government gave way to American pressure. . . . and announced its agreement with the proposals to establish German 'combat units' each having 6,000 men, in the proportion of one German unit to five supplied by the Atlantic Pact countries."

MORE TROOPS TO KOREA

The British Government might seem to deserve some credit for having—under strong pressure from a greatly aroused public opinion—contributed something to stop the war spreading into a third world war, and to prevent the use of the atom bomb. But at the same time Attlee agreed to send further troops to Korea, accepted American command over "integrated" British and German troops in Europe, and agreed both to Truman making use of the atom bomb when he should see fit, so long as he "informed" the British of his decision, and to the continued exclusion of the Chinese People's Republic from the United Nations. And in the following May, as is disclosed by Mr. Miliband, in *Parliamentary Socialism* at pp. 312-13, the Americans were told that "His Majesty's Government had decided that in the event of heavy air attacks from bases in China upon United Nations forces in Korea they would associate themselves with action not confined to Korea".

Negotiations for a cease-fire in Korea began in this very December, 1950, but dragged on without real success until after the Labour Government had gone out.

PROPOSED SHEFFIELD PEACE CONGRESS

In the latter part of 1950, there were revealing and shameful developments in the attitude of the Government to the World Peace Movement. Following on the great Congress in Paris and Prague in April of 1949, mentioned in Chapter 21, there had been on the one hand the various manifestations of British Government hostility to the Movement which I have already noticed, and on the other the sensational success of the Movement's "Stockholm Appeal" against the use of atomic weapons, which had received a tremendous welcome all over the world. The Movement had by now established itself in the eyes of virtually everybody not deeply infected with the virus of anti-communism—so well described by Thomas Mann as the "main idiocy of our time"—as an organisation genuinely seeking peace.

The Movement was anxious to hold a similar Congress in Britain in November, 1950, and had concluded—to some extent, I must confess, on my advice—that the British Government would not be either malevolent enough, or bold enough, to stop the Congress being held. (This was not the first, nor the last, occasion on which I underestimated the malevolence of the Labour Government and of the "Establishment" generally.)

Arrangements were accordingly put in train, Sheffield being selected as the venue. A tremendous response was received from this country as well as from many others; and the organisers began to think that their anxieties lest the freedom of expression so long boasted of in Britain had no longer any reality had been unnecessary.

For a time, all seemed well. When the Government was pressed by the Americans and by some of our own reactionaries to ban the Congress, it used some good words—making mention of "our ancient traditions of freedom"—and cited some correct law, to the effect that it had no power to ban the Congress (since Peace could hardly, yet awhile, be regarded as treasonable or subversive). These statements were taken to mean that the ban which could not be imposed *de jure* would not be effected *de facto* by wholesale refusal of visas or of admission. The Government in effect confirmed this by announcing that there would be no quantitative restrictions, and that individual delegates would be excluded only if they were *personae non gratae*—a technical diplomatic term used to label those who for some personal reason can definitely not be admitted. And it was further implicitly confirmed by the consent given by the Ministry of Civil Aviation to charter flights from Prague to London (nine by B.E.A. and nine by Czechoslovak Airlines) to bring hundreds of delegates from Eastern Europe and Asia.

The organisers waited with not too much anxiety; the Government refused to make any statement as to whether any particular person would or would not be admitted; those who needed visas had to wait until the last moment to see whether they received them or not, and those whose nationality permitted them to come without visas, having failed to get any indication whatever as to what would happen when they landed, had to incur the expense of travelling here, in order to discover at the seaports or airports whether they would get in or not. (Some of the more innocent of us were quite shocked to discover that one motive of this government reticence was to provide an opportunity for the immigration officers to interview the arrivals, look at their documents, copy out the names and addresses of every British resident that they had in their notebooks or other documents, and *then* send them away on the next ship or plane.)

WHOLESALE EXCLUSIONS

In the last few days before the date of opening, the true picture became clear, and clearly black. The Government, either on American pressure or of its own inherent malice, interpreting its promise to exclude only *personae non gratae* as meaning that any prominent peace-lover was *non gratus*, had carefully sifted through all the people seeking to come from abroad, and picked out for exclusion all those of the slightest importance, whatever country they came from, leaving the organisers with the choice of holding a meeting, as it were, of the privates without the officers, or of changing the venue. The organisers waited as long as they could, in the hope of being reasonably able to hold the Congress; but in the end, on the 12th November, they had to change the venue to Warsaw, where all delegates from all countries were admitted without delay or difficulty, and an invaluable Congress was held.

A good deal of indignation found expression in the House of Commons, where the Home Secretary admitted that, up to the evening of the 10th November, 561 applications for visas had been received, 300 granted, and 215 refused; some arriving *with* visas were actually refused admission.

The Home Secretary said in defence of his conduct:

"It is not part of my duty to allow persons like the President of the World Peace Committee and the members of his committee, whose first allegiance is not even to their own countries, but to Russia, to come here and use this country as a sounding board."

Thus did the Home Secretary of a Labour Government, in a country which makes a boast of its freedom of speech, insult as a *persona non grata* one of the most eminent and honourable men and scientists of the century, the late Professor Joliot-Curie.

I repeat the comments of this performance which I wrote in an article in the *Labour Monthly* for 1950, at pp. 554 *et seq.*

"In the end, the Government's behaviour was almost the exact antithesis of its professions and statements. It was heralded by a tirade from Attlee himself at a dinner of the Foreign Press Association. . . .

"The Government rejected delegates wholesale—priests, writers, playwrights, artists, scientists, medical women, wounded air-pilots, and a host of other people whom any decent person would be honoured to welcome on our soil. It even cancelled, without explanation, the consent to the aeroplane flights. It acted in such a way and on such a scale as to make it impossible to hold the Congress at Sheffield, and the venue had accordingly to be altered to the other side of Goebbels' Iron Curtain, where in conditions of freedom it went on to even greater successes than it would have achieved at Sheffield.

"What is the political essence of all this? It is easy, of course, on the surface, to point out that this is how Tory-Social-Democrat politicians behave, that you can expect nothing better from frightened little men intoxicated with power, and that in any case they were largely under the control of other frightened little men further West, drunk with far greater power and insolently disregarding our traditions, our laws, and our reputation for common decency.

"But that is no more than the surface. We must probe more deeply, and examine the eipisode as part of the whole development of 'our' foreign policy, the policy of 'our' Tory Party, 'our' Foreign Office, and 'our' Labour Government.

"This policy is no longer just one of general anti-Soviet activity and propaganda; it now goes further and rules out even the idea of negotiation or discussion with the U.S.S.R. in the search for peace or good relations. The attitude can be stated thus:

"'We say that the U.S.S.R. intends aggressive war in the relatively near future, and it is therefore useless to talk to it unless we are 'strong'.

"'We are not strong at present, and so must set out to build up strength as fast as possible, and not even think of talking to the U.S.S.R. until we are strong enough.'

"One answer to this, of course, is that it is wholly wrong, both because the U.S.S.R. hasn't the slightest intention of starting a war, and because attempts to 'get strong' whilst the supposed enemy is also able to 'get strong' are always worse than futile; they constitute a form of lunacy known as 'armament-racism'; they are in fact contradictory of every principle of the United Nations Charter; and they have never led to 'strength' but practically always to economic misery and bankruptcy, the degeneration of civil liberties, and war.

"One could answer further that it is criminally irresponsible to parrot the cry of 'Arm! Arm! Arm!' and 'Don't talk!' at a time when the supposed enemy, the U.S.S.R., is repeatedly proposing, both inside the United Nations Organisation and outside, that there should be discussions about peace, about reduction of armaments, about banning the bomb—in short about everything that could be done to relieve tension and make war less likely. And one could add that the responsibility is not lessened by the fact that our densely populated country, studded with atom-bomber bases but not equipped with atom bombs, will in any case be virtually exterminated in any war into which we are thrown.

"Perhaps the most significant point is the 'Thou shalt not even talk'. One would naturally expect, in a 'democracy', that we should argue out the questions whether the U.S.S.R. wants war and whether it would do any harm to talk to it to see if we can't reach some *modus vivendi*. If it were really true that the £5,000,000 or so we are now asked to spend on military preparations every 24 hours represented our only choice between survival and extinction, the British people are great enough to examine the facts, make up their minds to accept the position, and act accordingly. If, on the other hand, it is not true, but is just nonsense—and imported nonsense at that—then we should get into discussions with the U.S.S.R., reach some agreement, cut our arms expenditure to a tenth of its latest figure, and develop our future and our children's future in friendship, prosperity, and tranquillity. There never was a position in which the price of not even talking was so awful, or the possible rewards of successful talks so magnificent.

"But it is just at this point that the Government's position seems to become not just wrong but almost childishly demented; for it goes one step further and insists that the citizens of this democracy must not even talk about talking to Moscow! To speak of negotiation is, it suggests, treasonable, because it 'weakens the public will'— the will I suppose to shoulder the burden of the armaments race, which in the end amounts to a will to war.

"It is clearly this attitude which lay at the root of the Government's behaviour over the Sheffield Congress, which was far worse than just silly, or reactionary, or cowardly. The attitude is in effect that no one should talk about peace, because if they once do so they will be captured by its tremendous appeal and will insist on having it. At Sheffield, they were going to talk about it for a week, and the result would have been 'fatal', i.e. an immense encouragement to the peace movement. Hence the Government's action, and hence the stream of Press abuse, presenting talk of peace as an 'evil thing' designed to weaken us."

ATTLEE'S ABUSE

It may be useful, in order to see what the Government's attitude really was, to examine what Attlee said in his tirade, just mentioned, at the dinner of the Foreign Press Association (on the 2nd November), which was plainly selected as the platform for his preliminary announcement of the Government plot to sabotage the Congress. He began by describing the obviously genuine Congress for Peace, called by a well-established and by no means one-sided Peace Movement, as "bogus", without giving any grounds for so describing it except that he attributed the Peace Movement to that infinitely "evil" phenomenon, the U.S.S.R. (Indeed, he displayed what he no doubt thought to be his own superior wisdom—which in all statesmen and politicians nowadays simply means the "wisdom" of those first-rate, second-rate, or ninth-rate "experts" on whom they rely for information—by solemnly asserting that the World Peace Movement was "an instrument of the Politbureau"; it would have been nice to cross-examine him, and more fruitful to cross-examine his "experts", as to what he or they knew of the Politbureau, and how they knew if *it* had created this "instrument".)

Attlee said that there were "limits to the toleration of free countries" (meaning thereby Britain, whose Government was making up its mind "freely" to destroy the opportunity for free discussion about peace) "for those who attempt to undermine our liberties". This is an argument which, when used in the right circumstances, could have great merit; but the Government had persistently refused to listen to it from the left wing, when it protested against the protection of provocative fascist marches by vast bodies of police. But it is a little difficult to classify agitation for peace as an undermining of our liberties. (To be fair to Attlee, I think that the rest of his speech did not show for certain that he thought that to preach peace amounted in itself to an undermining of our liberties, although he could hardly complain if one read his words as meaning that; the probability is that he was so deeply obsessed with hatred of the U.S.S.R. that he regarded anything whatever which originated from that country—as he thought the World Peace Movement did—as designed to "undermine our liberties".)

Having thus explained how fatal it would be—in his view—to let anyone into this country to attend the Congress, he went on to say that, in spite of the "limits" he had mentioned, he "would not deny admission to people who in good faith may wish to attend this conference"—a statement which in the light of events can only be reconciled with the truth by assuming that all those people, from many countries and of the most varied political affiliations whom he was to select for exclusion were not seeking "in good faith" to discuss peace.

Attlee claimed to know that the aim of the World Peace Movement was "to paralyse the efforts of the democracies"—meaning thereby, no doubt, the Western capitalist states—"to arm themselves"; he went so far as to compare its members with Hitler and Goebbels, and referred to some of the delegates, or would-be delegates, as "those who seek to come here to subvert our institutions, (and) to seduce our fellow-citizens from their natural allegiance and their daily duties".

Those whom the gods seek to destroy, they first make anti-communist.

SPAIN

Spain comes briefly into our story in this month of November, 1950. On the 5th November, the United Nations voted in favour of freedom to send ambassadors to Spain, and the British Government immediately announced that it would send one. The struggle of the Spanish people had always been very dear to the left wing of the Labour movement in Britain, and this step seemed like one more sad departure from our socialist outlook.

REARMING WEST GERMANY

The evil business of rearming West Germany took many steps forward in this period. It will be remembered that, as mentioned in Chapter 31, Bevin had at last—and pretty quickly—swung round on the 18th September, 1950, to support this wicked and dangerous policy, and that the decision to adopt it had been foreshadowed in an announcement made in New York on the following day. On the 19th October, the U.S.S.R., in a note to the three Powers, sent primarily to rebut allegations that the People's Police of East Germany had the character of an army, asserted that these allegations must have been made to cover up the steps taken to establish an army in West Germany, and stated that the U.S.S.R. "will not acquiesce" in such measures, "aimed at reviving the German Regular Army in Western Germany".

The U.S.S.R. followed this up on the 3rd November by another Note, proposing a meeting of the Council of Foreign Ministers, "to consider the question of implementing the Potsdam Agreement on the militarisation of Germany", and asked for an early reply. This proposal had a good reception in Britain, and the view was expressed in the House of Lords that the chance should be seized.

DODGING AN ANSWER

The American and British Governments were not however of this mind. Not merely did they delay answering the Soviet Note, but they arranged to achieve a definite decision for the rearmament of Germany before answering. On the 7th December, under heavy American pressure, the French Government agreed to the formation of German "combat teams". On the 15th December, the U.S.S.R. delivered a further Note, in which it drew attention to the fact that "a direct military alliance is being prepared by the Government of Great Britain" with the West German Government, which constituted "a serious threat to peace", and was not only contrary to the Potsdam Agreement but also in manifest contradiction to the Anglo-Soviet Treaty of 1942. This note was "answered" in effect but not in form on the 19th December, the day after Eisenhower was appointed as Commander of all the NATO forces, at a meeting of the Atlantic Powers in Brussels, at which re-militarisation of West Germany was agreed to; and only then, on the 22nd, the British Government replied to the Soviet Note of the 15th, blaming the Soviet Government for the existing international tension, and answering the Soviet proposal of the 3rd November for a meeting of the Council of Foreign Ministers by insisting that any such meeting would have to take up wider questions, to be discussed by a preliminary agenda committee. It was disconcerting for the West when the Soviet Union, on the 30th December, accepted this, for it then had to busy itself finding pretexts for maintaining its position in favour of the rearmament of Germany. On the 3rd January, 1951, Acheson called for "further clarification of the Soviet position in relation to the Four Power Conference"; and on the 9th January an article in the *New York Herald Tribune* betrayed the true position of the U.S.A., which obviously regarded the rearmament of West Germany as an essential part of its war strategy. The article ran:

"In exchange for non-militarisation of Western Germany, both France and Britain believe the Russians may offer the Western Powers genuine demilitarisation of Eastern Germany, which would be open to inspection. . . .

"But what if the Russians did this? Who would gain? Those who support the American position, which is shared by many both in and out of the British Government, believe that the Russians would be the winners and the Western Powers the losers of a limited deal on the neutralisation of Germany.

"If the West renounces . . . German troops, then it follows there can be no effective military force in Western Europe."

The presence of such a force was regarded by the U.S. as essential, although just at that moment Admiral Kirk, U.S. Ambassador in Moscow, was adding his voice to that of many Americans and others (see for example, Chapter 10) who were making it plain to the world that the Soviet Union had no intention of making any attack which an "effective military force in Western Europe" would be needed to resist. The *U.S. News and World Report*, in its issue of the 15th December, 1950, reported the Admiral in Frankfurt:

"Currently, Admiral Kirk detects none of the signs of war that experts watch for.

"For example: Soviet army units are remaining at peace-time strength. No over-age classes are being called up. No extraordinary movements of troops or supplies have been detected.

"There is no drive in Russia to build bomb shelters, or restrict civilian consumption of critical materials. There is no shifting of labour away from peace-time to war-time industries. . . .

"As U.S. and British military experts in Frankfurt see it, there is no sign of any build-up of Soviet forces in East Germany."

NON-MILITARY "AGGRESSION"

To keep alive the fear of Soviet "aggression", when there were no grounds for such fear, the story was revived and re-circulated that "communist aggression" takes other forms than military, for example, propaganda—a plain confession that the German and other forces which NATO was determined to maintain in Western Europe were designed to "resist" propaganda, i.e. to be used not in military defence but in attack, commonly called aggression.

KRUPP BACK IN GOLDEN HARNESS

In January, 1951, whilst the Soviet Union sent further Notes to the Western Powers, the U.S.A. showed its true face by commuting the death sentences of twenty-one Nazi war criminals and reducing the sentences of seventy others, and—much more serious and significant—cancelling the decree that had confiscated the many millions gained by Alfred Krupp out of the Second World War and Hitler's rearmament for it, leaving him free to apply those millions to the rearmament of Western Germany for a third world war. This outrage may have been committed under some bargain with Adenauer (on the lines: "If you want us for the next war, you must drop this business of blaming us for the last"). But it must be confessed that the U.S.A. was quite capable of committing it "all on its own", and the British Government was equally capable of acquiescing in it.

On the 24th February, the U.S.S.R. addressed a further Note to the Western Powers on German rearmament, describing it—with full justification—as a violation of the Anglo-Soviet Treaty and of the Potsdam Agreement, and calling NATO—with equal justification—an aggressive alliance. It added that, in the face of all this, it could not "regard with full confidence" the statement of the British Government that it was willing to negotiate for improved relations. Nevertheless, it said, the U.S.S.R. was still ready to negotiate.

The full infamy of this rearmament of Germany, for the second time in a little over twenty years, and with the same aim of destroying the Soviet State, was dealt with in a scholarly article by R. Page Arnot in the *Labour Monthly* of February, 1951, at pp. 65 *et seq.* He pointed out that, after the First World War, the governments of the time—reactionary enough, in all conscience—had taken seven years to bring Germany into a war alliance with Britain and France against the Soviet State, and seven years more to instal Hitler in power, with the Anglo-German Naval Treaty two years later, "allowing Germany to build submarines, with the tacit understanding that these would be available in the Baltic Sea for use against the U.S.S.R.".

"This time", wrote Arnot, "the process has been speedier"; and he might have added: "under a Labour Government". He continued:

"The second world war ended . . . with the three chief allies (Britain, U.S.A. and U.S.S.R.) in full agreement upon 'our inflexible purpose to destroy German militarism and Nazism, and to ensure that Germany will never again be able to disturb the peace of the world'. For this purpose they were determined to 'disarm and disband all German armed forces' and to 'remove all Nazi and militarist influences from public offices and from the cultural and economic life of the German people' . . .

"This time it took only a matter of months before the process was visible. It took less than eighteen months to the open declaration of hostility in the announcement of the Truman doctrine against Communism and the U.S.S.R. It has taken only a few years this time till Britain and U.S.A. are bringing in West Germans re-militarised, which means the Nazis back again. Six years! Nay, not so much, not six!

"This is the grand outcome of the Marshall 'Plan', the Western Union, the Atlantic War Pact, and all the other fetters by which the Labour Government, operating a Tory foreign policy, tied this country hand and foot to Yankee imperialism.

"With the Yankees hustling them on to war, they have broken their own pledged words, the declared policy of the Labour movement, and the treaty obligations of this country. As late as mid-September, the Foreign Secretary's utterances were still against rearming Germany. . . .

"All that has been thrown overboard. In less than sixteen weeks, the swing-round of the satellite British Government was completed. When Dean Acheson met Bevin and the French Foreign Minister at New York in September it did not take him long—as far as Bevin was concerned. Acheson by this time knew his bull-frog. Just as the previous month the British Government, having got House of Commons sanction for £100,000,000 addition to armaments, then on receipt of a 'request' from the U.S.A. announced a three-year armament expenditure of £3,600,000,000 without any reference to parliament, so now Acheson easily got what he wanted. On September 19 at New York, re-militarisation of West Germany was tentatively announced. (It was some weeks later before the French would agree, under what had become *joint pressure* from Acheson and his tame bull-frog.)"

FOREIGN MINISTERS' DEPUTIES MEET

On the 5th March, 1951, the deputies of the Foreign Ministers of the Four Powers met in Paris to discuss the agenda of the proposed Conference. The U.S.S.R. suggested three points: the demilitarisation of Germany; a Peace Treaty with Germany and the withdrawal of all occupation forces; and reductions in the armed forces of the Four Powers. Discussion of the agenda went on through the month of March; the attitude of the West can be judged from the report of *The Times* Washington Correspondent on the 29th March, that "the United States went into the meeting in a half-hearted mood, convinced that a Conference of Foreign Ministers, even if it could be arranged, would achieve nothing"—a correct conviction, on the assumption that the U.S.A. had no intention of abandoning the rearmament of West Germany.

The attitude of the West can also be illustrated from a comment of Mr. Gromyko, on the 21st March: "When the Soviet delegation accepts one or other provision contained in the Three Powers proposals, then the authors of these proposals themselves lose the taste for their own proposals."

On the 3rd April, it was announced that Britain was ordering a quantity of armaments in West Germany, "to help British rearmament".

On the 18th April, West Germany was brought into the "European Coal and Steel Community" (the Schumann Plan, discussed in Chapter 30).

The Foreign Ministers' Deputies' Conference came to an end on the 21st June; the U.S.S.R. wanted it to continue until it reached some agreement, but the three Western Powers, saying that "continuance of the talks could have no practical utility", insisted on closing them.

By September the three Foreign Ministers of the Western Powers, meeting at Washington, declared their intention of:

1. Permitting the creation of a West German Army, to be included in a European Army under the Atlantic Pact Command.

2. Giving virtual independence to the West German Government in foreign and domestic affairs; bringing West Germany into NATO on basis of equality; and ending the Occupation Statute. The occupation troops were to remain in Germany as long as the division of Germany continued.

"TERMINATION OF THE WAR"

On the 9th July, 1951, the three Western Powers issued unilaterally a declaration of the termination of the war with Germany.

And well before September the German Re-armament Plan, prepared by the Adenauer government, was before the American authorities. According to the *New York Nation* of the 21st July:

"Some of the German proposals are startling. They include: (1) a German tactical air force of at least 2,000 planes, with a minimum air force personnel of 40,000; (2) German armed forces to total about 250,000; (3) eventual re-introduction of conscription and a two year period of compulsory military service. . . .

"The proposed armada of 2,000 German war planes is almost exactly equal numerically to the tactical air force at Hitler's disposal just before World War II."

IRANIAN OIL

The next matter to be dealt with is the crisis over Iranian oil. This arose from Iranian demands, at first for a more favourable division of the vast profits extracted by the Anglo-Iranian Oil Company (owned as to 56 per cent. by the British Government) from the oilfields of Iran and the refinery at Abadan, and later for the nationalisation of all the properties. It came to a head in the Spring of 1951, having been brewing since 1949, when discussions had begun between the Iran Government and the Oil Company over the proportions of profit-sharing.

The picture was familiar to those who have studied that department of colonialism, oil politics. Much of the oil produced in the world comes from colonial-type countries, largely in the Middle East; oil can be produced in those countries at a tiny fraction of the cost of production in the U.S.A.; and much of it was at the time still being produced under agreements negotiated many years earlier, when the oil-countries were even weaker and more dependent than they were in, say, 1950, and the colonialist exploiters even more ruthless and confident. The latter were very rich and powerful, and were playing for enormous stakes; in some of the Middle East countries it was not always easy to determine whether the country was really ruled by the official government, the embassy of the country holding the major interest in the oil, or the offices of the company actually exploiting the oil. And in the home countries of the exploiters the companies were often so powerful that they had a large part in deciding what their governments should do. For oil was and is perhaps the most important raw material in the world, for war and for peace. The principal oil-exploiters were American, British, Dutch and French; in most producing countries they had masked their inter-necine conflicts under agreements to share in exploitation, but in Iran the British had succeeded in keeping the field to themselves, much to the annoyance of the Americans.

Oil naturally produced a number of cross-conflicts. On the exploiting side there were the conflicts between the great capitalist groupings of the four countries I have just mentioned, with the Americans growing steadily stronger than the others. In the producing countries, there was growing indignation, both in the ruling classes and the masses, over the vast profits being taken out of their poor countries, and over the domination of their economies and governments by foreign oil concerns; this led to demands at first for better profit-sharing terms and later for nationalisation. These demands were resisted by the companies; and, even when they felt that prudence called for some concessions, they feared—rightly—that any concession in one country would lead to greater demands from the others. Lastly, there was a potential conflict arising from the mere presence of the socialist world, to which the resentful exploited countries felt they could turn, if they nationalised their oil production, for technical aid, for loans, and perhaps also for markets for their oil if the capitalist world refused to buy it. The position on this point was particularly clear in Iran, which had a common frontier with the U.S.S.R.

Against a background of that sort, the Anglo-Iranian Oil Company and its largest shareholder, the British Government, had to face the growing demands from Iran. They had enormous investments both in the actual oilfields and the refineries and port at Abadan; the profits of their Iran operations were about £70,000,000 a year (on a capital investment roughly indicated by the fact that the British Government had paid only £11,000,000 for its 56 per cent. holding) and they knew or feared that they would have to face not only growing nationalist feeling in Iran but also the dangerous "help" in any emergency of an "honest broker", the U.S.A., which would lift them up when they fell, put its arms round them, and pick their pockets.

By December, 1950, discussions between the Iranian Government and the company had reached the point where the former rejected the existing agreements and demanded increased payment. American influence was already growing in Iran, millions of dollars being provided to build roads and aerodromes and to re-equip the army, and many Americans coming in as military and economic advisers. The "National Front", led by Mossadeq, was already calling for nationalisation, and in February, 1951, the British Ambassador formally warned the Iran Government that, whilst the oil company and the British Government were prepared to discuss the raising of the Iran Government's share of the oil profits to 50 per cent., they would not hold discussions under the threat of nationalisation. "It can scarcely be expected that the British Government can countenance a campaign in favour of nationalisation of the oil industry in defiance of the country's contractual obligations", he said, in a pious and old-fashioned appeal to legality which failed to take into account the fact that obligations under contracts negotiated many years before between strong colonialist powers and weak or corrupt governments had little moral value. But events, driven by popular pressure in Iran, moved rapidly; and by the 6th March the Oil Committee of the National Assembly accepted a proposal for nation-alisation of the oil industry. On the following day, the Premier, Razmara, who was held to be dangerous to the U.S.A., was assassinated, and Hussein Ala, who had been Iranian Ambassador to the U.S.A., was appointed in his place.

The Anglo-Iranian Oil Company's workers then struck against a cut in their bonus payments, and the strike spread. When nine of the strikers in the oilfields were shot down, a crowd of 30,000 marched to the Imperial Palace, and the Shah thereupon dismissed Hussein Ala. Demonstrations calling for nationalisation grew; on the 14th March, a British Government Note to Iran asserted that the operations of the Company could not be legally terminated by nationalisation—which as a matter of law was nonsense—and on the following day, the 15th March, the National Assembly passed a law to nationalise the oil industry. This stung the Company into making an immediate offer of a 50 per cent. share of the profits, but this came much too late in the then state of public opinion.

Herbert Morrison, who had become Foreign Minister on the 9th March, less than a week before, was thus very early confronted with a major crisis, which one can now think of as a sort of rehearsal for the Suez crisis of 1956.

WAR FOR OIL?

The Labour Government behaved as any Tory government would have done, both in its typically capitalist reaction to this interference by a colonial country and in its difficulty in making up its mind how to act. Morrison himself and several other members of the Cabinet wanted to resort to war. He wrote in his autobiography, at p. 281:

"My own view was that there was much to be said for sharp and forceful action. The Cabinet, was however, left in little doubt that mounting an effective attacking force would take a lot of time and might therefore be a failure. In the end we had to abandon any military project, with the exception that we would have used force if British nationals had been attacked."

Attlee was against warlike measures. In *A Prime Minister Remembers* (p. 254), Francis Williams writes:

"There were in the Cabinet, as well as in the country, a number of strong voices in favour of immediate military action against Iran— the new Foreign Secretary's among them. Attlee however took a different view. Not only did he believe . . . that quick and decisive military action on the scale required was in any event impracticable, but also that it would put Britain wrong in the eyes of world opinion, including American opinion, and might thus prove both militarily and politically disastrous."

There seems no doubt that there was strong American pressure against military action; and the fear of Soviet intervention, called for under the Soviet-Persian Treaty of 1921, must also have had some weight. At any rate, nothing more warlike was attempted than the despatch of a cruiser and two frigates to the Persian Gulf, announced on the 28th March; and then, on the 4th April, Morrison informed the House of Commons that the matter was to be discussed, not between Britain and Iran but between Britain and the U.S.A.

TALKS IN WASHINGTON

Officials were sent out to Washington to evolve a "common policy" towards Iran—"common", if you please, to two rivals whose conflicts of interests and ambitions in Iran could no longer be concealed. Morrison said that the negotiations had three objects: to restore stability and avoid the diminution of Western influence; to preserve British access to Iranian oil; and to avoid the blow that oil nationalisation would mean for British economy.

Success in such negotiations was hardly likely, for the Americans wanted the exact opposite of "preserving British access to Iranian oil".

Discussions lasted from the 9th to the 19th April, and the conference ended with the statement that the "conversations were satisfactory to both sides"—a formula often used for hiding failure to agree. According to reliable reports, the Americans insisted on Britain accepting nationalisation, expecting no doubt to come in and "help" Iran to operate the installations, and to help themselves to a good share of them; and the British were unwilling to go further than the payment of a larger share of the profits.

Meanwhile, production of oil at Abadan was stopped by the strikes. On the 1st May, Morrison said in the House of Commons that we could not negotiate under duress, nor could we accept that the position of the Anglo-Iranian Oil Company should be radically altered by unilateral action—an assertion with no reality behind it, but what else could he say? On the 14th May, a Parachute Brigade group was "brought to a state of readiness", and left for Cyprus on the 25th. On the 19th May, in a Note, the Government informed Iran that a refusal to negotiate "would have the most serious consequences".

On the 26th May, Britain took the issue to the International Court at the Hague. By now, however, American pressure on our government to come to terms with Iran was growing stronger, and on the 29th May Morrison told the House of Commons that we had offered a settlement "which would involve some form of nationalisation provided . . . it were satisfactory in other respects".

Following on this, a Mission went to Iran for negotiations, which began on the 14th June and broke down on the 19th. Morrison was, naturally enough, attacked in the Commons by the Tories for weakness, and by his own left wing for giving way to the Americans.

On the 21st June, the British Government applied to the President of the International Court of Justice for an interim injunction restraining the Iranian Government from proceeding any further with its plans for nationalisation until the Court had given its decision on the main application made—as already mentioned—on the 26th May. The Iran Government resisted this application on the ground that the Court had no competence to deal with the matter, and no injunction was granted; the new Iranian Oil Board started taking over the installations, and the Iranian staff in the Company's employment sent in resignations wholesale, whilst those who remained at their posts slowed down operations. On the 26th June, another British cruiser went in to the Persian Gulf, without any resulting advantage.

TRUMAN AS "HONEST BROKER"

On the 9th July, President Truman offered to send Mr. Harriman to Iran to "help to find a solution", and Mossadeq, by now Premier of Iran, accepted the offer. Harriman duly went to Iran; he seemed—with the usual American anti-Soviet obsession—to be more concerned about the possible "loss" of Iran from the Western sphere than about the oil itself. He went from Iran to London, where he got Attlee and Morrison to agree to send another Mission to Iran, to be headed this time by the late Richard Stokes, who was then Lord Privy Seal. This mission went out early in August, and negotiated for some three weeks, without success; the Company then ordered its British staff in the Southern oilfields to be evacuated.

The quarrel dragged on, and on the 10th September the Government used economic pressure against Iran by withdrawing certain trade and financial facilities; on the 25th September, Iran expelled the remaining British employees of the Anglo-Iranian Oil Company.

On the 3rd October, 1951, not long before the General Election, Abadan was finally abandoned. As it happened, it was on that very day that Morrison, addressing the Labour Party Conference, challenged Churchill—who had been attacking the Labour Government for evacuating Abadan—to say whether Britain should have gone to war with Iran, a challenge which had an ironical twist in the light of Morrison's desire to have taken just that step. "If the country wants peace," said Morrison, "it had better vote for the people (i.e. the Labour Government) who can most surely be relied upon to preserve peace."

"PEACE TREATY" WITH JAPAN

A "Peace Treaty" as it was called, was negotiated by the U.S.A. with Japan in the course of the Summer of 1961. The U.S.A., which had at all stages of the occupation of Japan behaved as if it were the sole occupying Power, ignoring its allies, had come to the conclusion that it would be useful to have a Peace Treaty with Japan—in itself of course a good step if a proper Treaty were properly negotiated—and set about the work without any co-operation or communication whatever with the U.S.S.R. On the 4th June, discussions began in London between the U.S.A. and Britain on a draft peace treaty; on the 10th June, the U.S.S.R. sent a Note to the U.S.A., insisting that all the countries who took part in the war against Japan should be brought in; that the Treaty should be based on the Cairo and Potsdam declarations

and the Yalta Agreement; and that a peace conference should be called
—say in July or August—to discuss the draft. The U.S.A. ignored this
and on the 14th June announced that full Anglo-American agreement had been reached on the proposed Japanese Peace Treaty. The
draft on which they were agreed was thus criticised in the *New Statesman and Nation* of the 21st July:

> "The Japanese are offered almost complete freedom from restrictions,
> military, political or economic. . . . As a concomitant of the treaty,
> Washington is to conclude a bi-lateral defence agreement with
> Tokyo, which will certainly have the effect of perpetuating the
> American military bases in Japan. . . . If Britain had stood firm in
> refusing to admit a treaty which leaves Japan free to choose whether
> she will recognise Peking or Formosa, Asia as a whole would have
> stood with us."

But in this instance, too, the British meekly and anti-Sovietically
followed the American lead, and in breach of every obligation of
international law the so-called Treaty was signed in September by
forty-nine nations, including Britain. The U.S.S.R., Czechoslovakia,
and Poland refused to sign; the People's Republic of China was excluded;
India and Burma were not present, and did not support the treaty. The
U.S.S.R. denounced the Treaty "as a draft for a new war"; it did,
among other things, expressly permit Japan, with its black military
history, to rearm freely in direct contradiction to the terms imposed
upon it on its surrender six years before; and the occasion was taken
by President Truman to proclaim in effect the rearmament of Japan,
and its establishment as an American war base.

"DEFENCE EXPENDITURE"

Finally, I should deal in this chapter with "defence expenditure",
armament, rearmament, or whatever it may be called, which under
American pressure was still being increased. I have made several
references already in this and the preceding chapter to the burdens
involved.

On the 29th January, Attlee stated that "defence expenditure", apart
from stock-piling, would be about £1,300 million in the financial
year 1951-2, and that for the next three years the total defence budget,
again excluding stock-piling, "may be as much as £4,700 million"
(£100 per head of the population of England and Wales). This figure
of £4,700 million had already been decided by the U.S.A., and

imposed upon Britain; and the Government had accepted the imposition. He added that "expenditure on production for the Services in 1951-2 will be more than double the rate for the current year, and by 1953-4 it should be more than four times as great. By then we should have quadrupled our annual output of tanks and combat aircraft." In the main, he said, existing factories would be used, and the increase in production would come from turning over "progressively to defence production sections of the engineering industry, especially those producing aircraft, vehicles, radio and radar equipment, and machine tools". Allocation of raw materials would be necessary, and "some less essential production, especially for the home market, will have to be reduced or stopped, by limitation of supply orders and the prohibition of certain end-uses. Factory and storage space will be requisitioned where necessary."

As *World News* put it on the 10th February, this "gigantic new rearmament programme . . . is based on the pretence that there is a tremendous military menace to the people of Britain from the Soviet Union". The lack of any basis for such a pretence has been demonstrated already both in this chapter and earlier in the book; it is remarkable that all these increases coincided with drastic reductions of defence expenditure on the part of the U.S.S.R. and the People's Democracies.

Dalton, at pp. 363-4 of *High Tide and After* writes that "the cause of this (very heavy defence and rearmament programme) was the war in Korea, which we feared might widen into a new world war, with Russia and China both taking part". But the direct cause was quite simply the order of the U.S.A.

On the 29th January, it was announced that 235,000 Army reservists would be called up for fifteen days. And on the 22nd February, nearly 900 notices of recall were sent to the Fleet Reserve.

TURKEY AND GREECE IN NATO

On the 18th July, the British Government agreed to the admission of Turkey and Greece to NATO. It was not easy to believe that these countries were anywhere near the North Atlantic, that they were shining examples of "Western democracy", or that they could contribute to the defence of Western Europe against a Soviet invasion. Their value to anyone planning aggression on the U.S.S.R. was on the other hand obvious.

On the 2nd August it was stated that a U.S. Air Wing of 75 jet fighters was to arrive shortly in Britain, and on the 24th August the

Chief of the U.S. Air Force informed our government that more air-fields were required quickly in Britain by his Air Force.

MORE INCREASES IN DEFENCE EXPENDITURE

There was something even worse to come. In September, 1951, there was a meeting at Ottawa of the Atlantic Pact Powers, preceded by discussions in Washington between Acheson, Morrison, and Schuman on speeding German rearmament, by the proceedings in San Francisco, on the occasion of the signature of the "Peace Treaty" with Japan which I have discussed above, and by conversations in Washington between Gaitskell and the American Secretary Snyder on financial and economic questions, not to mention the decision to bring Greece and Turkey into NATO. At the Ottawa meeting the Americans demanded—and the British and French accepted—a 33 per cent. increase in the rearmament programmes of Britain and other NATO Powers by 1952; i.e. the figure previously agreed of £4,700 millions for three years—the onerous effects of which I have already described—was to go up to approximately £6,260 million. The figure of £4,700 million, imposed by American insistence before the British Parliament ever heard of it, and regarded by all British economists as the extreme limit of what Britain could possibly bear in armament expenditure, was declared to be obsolete and inadequate. The American decision to make this fantastic increase was freely reported in the U.S. Press, but the British public, on the eve of a General Election, was told nothing clear about it. Gaitskell went no further than to say on his return on the 25th September that increases in arms expenditure were "under consideration", and went on:

> "I am bound to say that I cannot see how we in the United Kingdom can do more than we have promised and are carrying out—the £4,700 million programme—unless there were to be a radical change in the economic policies of all the members of NATO, involving something much more like a war economy, both internally in each case and in their relations with each other."

It is often interesting, when one finally learns what politicians were doing at the time of their speeches, to see how their actions and knowledge are partly reflected and partly concealed in what they actually say. Here, Gaitskell was in effect saying, partly to himself and partly to the public whose servant he was:

"I have just committed you all to a ruinous 33 per cent. increase in war expenditure, on the orders of the U.S.A. Of *this*, I tell you no more than that increases of an unspecified amount are 'under consideration'.

"I now do tell you that it is impossible for us to bear these increases, or any increases over the present figure of £4,700 million (as to which you know only that they are being considered, and certainly don't know that they are anything like 33 per cent., whilst I know that they *have* been decided and *are* 33 per cent.), unless all the countries concerned go over to a war economy, with all its economic hardships, cuts in social services, restrictions on this that and the other, and more debts to the U.S.A. if they will lend us enough to keep us out of absolute bankruptcy.

"That's what I tell you, and what I don't tell you. Don't fail to vote for us at the General Election, for we are the party of peace."

No wonder the *Economist*, on the 13th October, recorded "a dangerous state of alarm and despondency among the American satellites in Europe" adding:

"Behaviour in Washington has been of a kind that could be expected to disillusion and repel the allies whose willing co-operation the United States needs and should be able to rely on."

This complaint was partly due to the line taken by the Americans, to the effect that the European countries could easily respond to American demands for greater and ever greater arms expenditure by cutting such "unnecessary" items as housing and social services. As the *New York Times* put it on the 23rd September, Snyder believed that "much of the trouble has stemmed from a 'business as usual' attitude by most countries taking part in the rearmament effort. He has not directly mentioned welfare programmes in Britain or housing programmes in most European countries except in talks with the U.S. delegation. What he has said to the Finance Ministers is that ... there is room for retrenchment in most European budgets and that the time has come to face a few politically unpopular decisions."

CHAPTER 40

Colonial Policy, 1950–1

THE pattern of colonial affairs was much the same as in previous years. The only events that need reporting are the war in Malaya, Egyptian demands for evacuation of British troops, the last stages of the Tanganyika ground-nuts fiasco, and the developments towards independence in the Gold Coast.

MALAYA

In Malaya, new "security" measures were introduced in November 1950, giving powers to conscript labour; and a decree was passed enabling mine and plantation owners to group their workers into "resettlement camps", which were in reality concentration camps. These grouped the workers into large villages surrounded by barbed wire, so that they could be locked in at night and thus prevented from helping the liberation forces with food or money. The total number of persons in these areas was 120,000; Tom Driberg, M.P., after visiting them, described them bluntly as "a disgrace to the Labour Government, the Federation and the Commonwealth". It was planned to put into such re-settlements 500,000 people, ten per cent of the population.*

In December, 1950, rewards were offered for the capture *dead or alive*, of Communists, ranging from £7,000 for the Secretary-General of the Communist Party to £233 for an ordinary Party member.

In January 1951, two villages were collectively fined £5,000 and £3,000 for refusing to give information about the killing of a planter,

* Two or three years later, I had a brief glimpse of one of these re-settlement areas, and learnt of the bitter hatred that they had created. I had just won a case for some students in Singapore who were accused of sedition, and two well-known progressive Singapore Chinese suggested that I should go with them to see one of the "re-settlements" on the mainland. When we arrived, every Chinese we approached turned his back on us and refused to speak, notwithstanding that the Chinese with me were well-known to them. The mere fact that they had a European with them sufficed to render them untouchable! (The trouble was cured when we found a village headman, showed him a newspaper report of the case I had won, which included a recognisable photograph of myself, and got him to explain to the inhabitants that this particular European was not so bad as to make even the Chinese with him untouchable!)

and in February a battalion of Gurkhas went to a village which had refused to give information as to the whereabouts of liberation forces, removed the entire population of 1,500 Malay, Chinese, and Indian inhabitants to a camp 100 miles away, auctioned the belongings of the villagers, and burnt down all the houses.

In March, 1951, it was announced that 11,630 persons were detained without trial in concentration (not re-settlement) camps.

By October, 1951, the war had been raging for two years, with many changes in British commands but no success, and no sign of an end; 133,000 men of the armed forces had been put into action, together with 380,000 conscripted special constabulary.

EGYPT

The demand of Egypt for evacuation of British troops, whose occupation of the country had begun in 1882, was an old one which flared into life in 1951. The then existing basis of the right to occupy was a Treaty made between Britain and Egypt in 1936, which permitted the installation of British defences in the Canal Zone, where British troops were to be allowed to remain until the Egyptian Army could "assure by its own means the freedom and entire security of the Canal". The treaty provided for the stationing of up to 10,000 troops and 400 aircraft, with ancillary personnel, in the Canal Zone, but in fact these figures were exceeded.

After the end of the Second World War, there were many demands, backed by popular demonstrations, for the renunciation of the 1936 Treaty, and the complete evacuation of British troops, of which at least 70,000 were stationed in various parts of the country, By March, 1946, troops had to be withdrawn from Cairo and Alexandria, and negotiations began for revision of the Treaty. Attlee said at that time that we had decided "freely and unconditionally to evacuate the troops from Egypt"; but they remained. In 1947, Egypt appealed to the Security Council of the U.N. to direct the immediate removal of British troops; this move was unsuccessful, and the agitation continued. Meantime, the British established a huge base at Fayid, in the Canal Zone, and—as *The Times* put it on the 20th December, 1949:

"The whole of the Suez Canal Zone is virtually a building area dotted with army camps and airfields which are linked by good roads. Altogether there are more than a dozen R.A.F. establishments in the Canal Zone. . . ."

The negotiations for revision of the Treaty were deadlocked, partly because of the claims of Egypt to end the Anglo-Egyptian "condominium" in the Sudan.

In January, 1950, a new government of the Wafd Party came to power in Egypt, pledged to secure the abolition of the Treaty, and in the following November the "speech from the throne" at the opening of the Egyptian Parliament included an insistence on ending the Treaty. This brought from Bevin the remark in Parliament, on the 20th November, that "the British Government has no intention of leaving the Middle East defenceless".

Nothing very much developed until the 8th October, 1951, three days after writs had been issued for the General Election in Britain, when the Egyptian government denounced the Treaty and proclaimed Farouk as King of the Sudan. No doubt this move developed from the Iranian defiance of Britain described in the previous chapter. Morrison, as Foreign Secretary, showed a good Tory attitude; as he wrote in his autobiography:

"It could have been that another surrender to a minor and irresponsible power was imminent. I strongly advocated a stiff line with Egypt, and Attlee agreed."

On the 16th October, British reinforcements were sent to Egypt; on the 18th, a British army convoy was attacked, and British troops took over vital points on the canal, the Egyptians then organised passive resistance in the Canal Zone.

The Labour Government went out, as we shall see; it was defeated at the polls on the 28th October, and its Egyptian troubles passed, with all its others, to the Tories.

GROUND-NUTS

On the ground-nuts scheme, there was by now little to attend but the funeral. On the 9th January, 1951, the Minister of Food, Maurice Webb, announced the abandonment of the scheme and the writing-off of the advances made up to that date.

Ernest Watkins, in the *The Cautious Revolution*, at p. 190, summarised the position thus:

"£36,500,000, the amount advanced to the Overseas Food Corporation . . . was to be written off. The proportion of the cleared areas devoted to agriculture was to be drastically reduced; about three-quarters of the Kongwa clearings were to become pasture.

Further clearings were to be limited to the Southern Province. The large-scale farming units came to an end; units were to be cut from 80,000 acres each to units of between 1,500 and 6,000 acres. Even mechanisation itself had lost all face. Future bush clearings were to be carried out by hand. The function of Kongwa was to 'conduct fully costed full-scale trials on a limited acreage for three years'. And, finally, the Food Ministry abandoned its interest in the whole plan in favour of the Colonial Office. All East Africa retained, besides the memories, were an uncompleted port and an uncompleted railway, a number of experienced and cynical immigrants, the remains of a mass of mechanical equipment, and the benefit of some massive auction sales of the imported stocks of whisky and spirits."

THE GOLD COAST

The story of the Gold Coast during this period is interesting. In September, 1949, the Coussey Committee Report had recommended a legislature of two chambers in both of which there should be a majority of elected Africans, but did not recommend complete self-government. In December, 1950, a new Constitution was granted, with a Legislative Assembly and an Executive Council, presided over by the Governor, who retained some powers of veto.

The composition of the Legislative Assembly—the one body in which African opinion could find expression—was pretty elaborate, as usually happens when the British Government is trying to retain some power in the face of demands for independence. It was to consist of 84 members; nine of these were to be nominated, three of them being members of the Administration ex-officio, three were to represent the Chamber of Mines, and three the Chamber of Commerce.

Of the remaining 75, the Councils of Chiefs were to elect 37. This left 38 out of 84 to be elected by methods which gave the general mass of the African people a fair chance of showing their wishes, for five of them, representing municipalities, were to be directly elected, and the remaining 33, representing rural constituencies, were to be elected by electoral colleges whose members were themselves to be elected by the votes of all over 21 years of age.

There was no mistake about the wishes of the electors in relation to these 38 seats. The Convention People's Party, which stood for "self-government *now*", and whose leader Kwame Nkrumah was serving a sentence in prison for "sedition" and for inciting an illegal strike, won all the five municipal seats, and 29 of the 33 rural seats (and one of the four other rural seats was won by an independent who supported it). Moreover, three of the 37 chiefs declared that they would support the Party. Nkrumah, who had headed the poll at Accra with 20,780 votes, was released from prison.

The Convention People's Party thus had 5 plus 29 plus 1 plus 3 supporters, or 38, and other Africans held 3 plus 34, or 37. The 9 nominated members were in a position to vote down the Party; but independence was obviously many steps nearer.

Under the Constitution, the Executive Council was to consist of eleven members, of whom eight were to be Africans; and six of those eight were to have responsibility for a specific government department. The three non-African members were officials, responsible between them for external affairs, defence, finance, justice, and the civil service. The African members were to be responsible for education, agriculture, commerce and industry, health, labour, communications, local government, and works.

Today, in the 'sixties, this Constitution does not look like a long step forward; but in 1950-1 it was the most forward constititional step taken by any African colony. In the light of the election results, it was bound to lead, as it relatively soon did, to an independent Ghana.

CHAPTER 41

The Economy, 1950-1

MOST of the problems of the year in the economic field, acute enough and familiar enough, resulted to an even greater degree than usual from over-expenditure on armaments.

American stock-piling and a general increase in demand led to a steady increase in raw material prices, which were reflected in due course in retail prices. Shortage of supplies of many raw materials disrupted production to some extent. Rearmament diverted both men and plant from export production, and exports fell in volume; the terms of trade worsened, and the balance of payments problem became acute once again. The Government sought to keep consumption down by freezing wages in the face of rising prices, and the social services were cut to help in meeting the cost of armaments.

In short, it was a year of typical capitalist embarrassment and crisis, due mainly to overwhelming armament expenditure, and sought to be met by typically capitalist—and typically ineffectual—remedies.

In November, 1950, the balance of payments position had improved somewhat, and the trouble at this period turned mainly on rising prices and shortages of materials, due to rearmament and stock-piling.

COAL SHORTAGE

Earlier in 1950, there had been signs of over-production of coal, especially in France and Belgium; but the extra rearmament drive reversed the position, and in November it was announced that the Coal Board would have to buy coal overseas to keep up its stocks; there was not merely an additional demand but a rapid fall in manpower. An average of 2,000 men a month were leaving the pits and going to better paid work. As the miners' leader Abe Moffat pointed out, the Coal Board was likely to spend £9,000,000 more on imports of coal, and had granted increased wages amounting only to £3,500,000.

The prices of basic materials in this November, 1950, were 80 per cent. higher than they had been twelve months earlier. Professor Allen wrote in the *London and Cambridge Economic Survey* for that month that "both wholesale and retail prices must be expected to rise during the coming months. . . . From the middle of 1950 the effects of devaluation have merged with those of the upswing of American business and of the mounting defence expenditure and programmes of the Atlantic Powers."

The writer added however, that: "There is an extraordinarily long time-lag between changes in prices of materials and the corresponding . . . change in retail prices."

PRICES STILL RISING

By December, 1950, the index of retail prices had risen by two points since June, 1950; but the most essential items, food, clothing, fuel and light, had risen by two points from September to November, and Mr. Gaitskell stated that "the prospect for our standard of living is disappointingly gloomy". Like any Tory Chancellor, he went on to say that "the continual pressure and demand for a higher standard of living (was) completely unrealistic. Instead of counting our blessings we must count our weapons. We now turn from dealing with the dollar gap to dealing with the all-too-evident gap in Europe's defences."

PROFITS STILL RISING

Profits, however, had risen steadily in 1950; the *Financial Times* total of profits for the year went up by 10 per cent. and dividends paid out went up by $3\frac{1}{2}$ per cent.

In December, it was announced that sulphur would be rationed as from the 8th January because of the reduction in supplies from the U.S.A.; and in the same month the use of zinc and copper for certain purposes was prohibited. And as a result of the talks in Washington described in a previous chapter, the U.S.A., Britain and France decided to establish "standing international commodity groups to develop 'free world' co-operation to increase the production of essential materials in short supply". The central organisation covering them was to have wide powers "to stop the flow of critical materials to communist-dominated areas; to step up production; and to deal with stock-piling materials going into production, with essential civilian needs, and with requesting some governments to reduce the consumption of certain materials".

In this same December, the weekly meat ration was cut by 6d. as from the 31st December, making it 1s. per head, of which 2d. had to be taken in corned beef. At the same time the foreign travel allowance, then a middle-class luxury, was raised from £50 to £100.

SHORTAGES

In January, 1951, the Ministry of Supply reported an acute shortage of metals and other materials. In the coal industry, both the shortage of coal and the loss of manpower continued, and some small wage increases were negotiated. The Executive of the National Union of Mineworkers undertook to try to get agreement from the miners for the use of foreign labour, hitherto hotly opposed, to campaign against unofficial strikes, and to get as many Saturday shifts worked as possible, and also overtime. Thus was the shortage used to speed up miners' work and worsen their conditions.

In the same January, train services were twice cut to save coal; some tinned-food factories closed down for shortage of tins; and 11,000 car and body workers went on to a four-day week owing to the shortage of steel.

But the balance of payments position improved for a time; gold and dollar reserves were up by $544 million, and it was learnt that 1950 had an overall surplus in balance of payments.

Late in January, another 2d. was cut off the tiny meat ration. The shortage was mainly due to a dispute with the Argentine over prices; the Argentine was demanding a 40 per cent. increase in the sterling price owing to the devaluation of the pound, and the British were refusing.

At the end of January there came the announcement of the armament expenditure for 1951-2, mentioned in the previous chapter.

By March, the official cost of living index was up another three points on December, being now 119 (June, 1947, 100).

THE ECONOMIC SURVEY

In April there came the usual Economic Survey. It anticipated a rise in consumer-goods prices of $7\frac{1}{2}$ per cent.; a reduction in consumption of 1 per cent.; no increase in total real investment; and a "fall in investment for civil purposes". It gave these estimates on the (optimistic) assumption that the necessary raw materials would be available, and stated that if this proved not to be the case the position would be worse. It assumed also that it would be possible to increase textile exports in order to make good the drop in engineering exports involved in the demands of rearmament on engineering capacity. It emphasised the need for a new wage-freeze in spite of price increases. It said bluntly that:

> "Expenditure on works and buildings for defence purposes will rise very sharply. . . . There will be a reduction this year in the amount of building resources available for ordinary civil purposes. There is also a serious shortage of architects, quantity surveyors, draughtsmen and other works staff, and defence building is likely to interfere by making claims on these particular skills."

THE BUDGET

In the same month came the Budget. All the social services, including education, were to cost slightly more in terms of actual cash than in the previous year, but their rise in cost was less than the price rises that had already taken place, and their share of the total expenditure had dropped from 9s. 3d. in the pound to 7s. 7d., whilst Defence was nearly doubled, rising from 4s. 7d. to 7s. in the pound. Food subsidies were to be "pegged" at £400 millions, the increases thus rendered inevitable being passed on to the consumers. There was to be a "ceiling" of £400 million on the cost of the health services, and half the cost of spectacles and dentures were to be paid by the receivers. Income tax, profits tax on distributed profits, and the petrol tax, were all increased.

The basic approach of the Budget was that the consequences of world-rearmament (shortages, higher prices, etc.) were to be met by price rises which were not to be compensated by higher wages or dividends, and that the social services were to be cut to help pay for rearmament.

MINISTERIAL RESIGNATIONS

The Tory Press reacted favourably to this Budget; but its main immediate result was the resignation of Bevan, Harold Wilson, and a junior minister, John Freeman.

Much has been written in the autobiographies of various of the Ministers concerned as to the reasons for Bevan's resignation. What they write is unfortunately more important as a revelation of the personal quarrels and ambitions that make up too much of Labour Party life than as a serious contribution to the political history of the Labour Government; and the best reasons for Bevan's resignation are probably to be found in his letter to Attlee of the 21st April, 1951:

> "The Budget, in my view, is wrongly conceived in that it fails to apportion fairly the burdens of expenditure as between different

social classes. It is wrong because it is based upon a scale of military expenditure, in the coming year, which is physically unattainable, without grave extravagance in its spending.

"It is wrong because it envisages rising prices as a means of reducing civilian consumption, with all the consequences of industrial disturbance involved.

"It is wrong because it is the beginning of the destruction of those social services in which Labour has taken a special pride and which has given to Britain the moral leadership of the world."

Those were good enough reasons for resignation, even from a Minister who had publicly and unreservedly accepted the fatal figure of £4,700 million armament expenditure which I have already fully discussed; and they commanded enough sympathy among back-bench members for fifty-five of them, on the 3rd May, to refuse to vote for the clause imposing charges for spectacles and dentures. But they did not, unfortunately, mean that Bevan would go forward to denounce the policy of subservience to the U.S.A., hostility to the Soviet Union, and fantastic rearmament, to which his colleagues were committed. Still less did they mean that there was any hope of a new policy, or a new leadership, or even a new sectional leader, in Labour Party politics. And Bevan's speech in Parliament explaining his resignation, in which he referred to the figure of £4,700 million as "already dead", and as not possible of achievement "without irreparable damage to the economy of Great Britain and the world", gave no real encouragement or opportunity to the left-wing Labour M.P.s who were looking for a leader to rally and lead them against the fatal policies of the Government. As Palme Dutt put it in his Notes of the Month for June, 1951, at p. 250 of *Labour Monthly*:

"There is no indication here yet of either a new policy or a new leadership; but there is a very indubitable indication of the bankruptcy and crisis of the old policy and the old leadership. If Mr. Bevan, who only in January of this year appeared as the main protagonist of the £4,700 million Rearmament Programme in the parliamentary debate, by April proclaims the same Programme 'already dead' and denounces the Rearmament Budget based upon it, then this is evidence of a considerable speed of political development. . . . If Mr. Bevan claims to voice the sentiment of a considerable section of left opinion or critics in the Labour Party, then it is legitimate for the Labour Party membership to ask what is the political platform of Mr. Bevan on the main question of the day—on rearmament, on the war policy, on the Atlantic Pact, on the anti-Soviet alignment with world reaction, on rearming Germany and Japan, on the wages fight, etc.

"On all these questions, there is very little sign so far of any alternative policy offered by the Bevan group. In his letter of resignation to Mr. Attlee, Mr. Bevan confined his attention to the attack on the health services and living standards in the Budget. But the merciless logic of the real situation did not leave it so easy to sidetrack the decisive issues of the rearmament programme and American war policy which underlie the attack on the social services. By the time of his speech in parliament" (explaining his resignation) "he delivered a resounding onslaught on the physical impossibility of the rearmament programme and on the American economic menace to Britain. Did this mean that he was opposed to the policy of the rearmament programme or the American war alliance? No such conclusion could be drawn. A masterly ambiguity was maintained, by which the dramatic appearance of criticism was combined with the practical reality of support."

It was perhaps for the very reason that Bevan's opposition was so narrow and limited that the resignations did the Government relatively little harm. It replaced the departing Ministers and carried on.

WHY SO FEW RESIGNATIONS?

Looking back on the six years of the life of the Labour Government, and on what must surely be clearly seen now as a long series of betrayals of all the principles and nearly all the policies it was chosen by the electorate to serve, the real cause for wonder is not that three Ministers resigned in April, 1951, but rather that there had not been at any time up to then even one resignation by any Minister on a point of principle.

The month of April also saw increases in the prices of bread, butter and fats, and petrol, in addition to shortages of steel—which led to a decision to reduce exports and restrict deliveries to the home market—and of nickel, tungsten, and molybdenum.

In May a steel works in Wales closed owing to shortage of raw materials, and steel firms in Jarrow cut working hours because of a 20 per cent. cut in supplies.

STEEL SHORTAGE

In June, the steel shortage was more acute; one of the reasons for this was that exports of scrap from West Germany to Britain, which had previously been running at the rate of 1,880,000 tons per annum, had dropped in the first four months of the year to a rate of about 450,000, owing to increased production of steel in the Ruhr. We were also failing to get enough Swedish ore, since that too was by then going to the Ruhr. Six hundred men went on short time in Sheffield strip mills on the 23rd June, and on the 28th the Government announced that all steel would thenceforth be allocated.

PRICES AND PROFITS STILL RISE

The retail price index had now reached 125, nine points above the previous December. The profits of 1,620 companies reporting in the first five months of the year, however, showed 22 per cent. increase in profits over the previous year, and dividend payments were up by 10 per cent. (It was not until the 26th July that the Government decided to limit dividends for the next three years to the 1947 level.)

By June, too, the excess of imports over exports in 1951 was already greater than that of the whole of 1950; in the first six months, the excess was £554 million.

GLOOMY PROSPECT

On the 26th July, Gaitskell reviewed in the House of Commons the financial and economic situation. He gave a prospect of further rises in prices, no increase in subsidies, a worsening trade deficit, shortages of steel and metals, cuts in imports, and fewer goods in the shops. "We are rearming," he said, "at the same time as a world inflation is occurring and the high prices caused by this inflation are not being off-set by increased subsidies." He promised, as I have just mentioned, to limit dividends by legislation to be introduced in the autumn.

He complained that wages had been rising faster than in the previous years, but did not mention that prices had been rising faster than wages. The index of wage rates in August was 120, and that of retail prices 127. He uttered the old old Tory warning of "further serious consequences to the balance of payments if rising wages increase export costs".

Nevertheless, he found it possible to say that the deterioration in the third quarter of the year was "largely on account of seasonal factors", and that "so far as I can see at present the fourth quarter's results will not be unfavourable, though again I think it unlikely they will show a surplus". In fact, in the last three months of the year, our gold and dollar reserves were to fall by $934 million. Mr. Miliband's comment, at p. 313 of his book, was that "within a few months [of the Budget] Britain was again in the throes of a major balance of payments crisis, which the Government had entirely failed to foresee".

In the debate, Harold Wilson, now free to criticise, quoted with some effect the *Financial Times* of the 17th July:

> "The Chancellor took a major decision . . . to use the weapon of taxation as sparingly as possible, and with deliberate cold intent to rely upon the cost of living to price the consumer out of the market to a sufficient extent to release resources for the rearmament programme."

Wilson argued that the arms programme meant economic crisis, and attacked in particular the American ban on Britain's trade with Eastern Europe, saying: "Our American friends must be asked to realise that we are not prepared to cut ourselves off from great and important sources of raw materials in Eastern Europe which are necessary to our economy. . . . American pressure all the time is more and more for a complete blockade."

The sorry story continued in August. Coke supplies to domestic consumers were limited to two tons a year, power supplies were in a worse condition than at any time since 1947, heavy cuts being forecast for the coming winter, and the butter ration was cut from 4 oz. a week to 3 oz. with effect from the 9th September. On the 14th August, it was announced that the trade deficit for the first seven months of the year was £679 million; June alone had shown a deficit of £151 million, twice as bad as the worst figure of the 1947 crisis. The volume of exports was falling because of raw material shortages, diversion of the engineering industry from exports to armaments, and increasing competition from abroad, especially Germany and Japan. The prices of imports were rising faster than those of exports, and the ban on trade with Eastern Europe was helping to increase the dollar gap.

ECONOMIC COMMISSION FOR EUROPE REPORTS

The Economic Commission for Europe reported on Britain:

> "The economy is showing every sign of suffering from severe strain. Inflation is rampant, exports are wavering, and this, combined with the high costs of imports, has created a new balance of payments

problem which will have to be countered by a new export drive or cuts in imports."

For September, the *Financial Times* reported that 2,322 companies reporting in the first nine months of 1951 showed a rise over 1950 of 23 per cent. in profits and 10 per cent. in dividends paid (after tax). In the same month, the Ministry of Fuel warned that there would be a serious fuel shortage in the coming winter. On the 5th September, cuts in milk supplies were announced, to amount to perhaps 50 per cent. and on the 10th a 10 per cent. cut was announced for the London area.

Some members of the Government must have been relieved to have the economic problems taken off their shoulders by the result of the General Election in the following month.

CHAPTER 42

The Nationalised Industries, 1950-1

THE National Coal Board's Report for 1950 showed that production was higher than in 1949; output per man-shift, nearly 24 cwts., was the highest ever recorded.

Production would have been higher still had it not been for the reduction in manpower; at the end of 1950 there were 20,500 fewer in the industry than a year before. In the early part of the year, the fall in manpower had not been alarming, as the coal shortage in Europe was coming to an end, and surpluses were even appearing; but the effects of the Korean War created a new shortage, and coal had to be imported to Britain from the U.S.A. at a high cost.

At the close of 1950, the National Plan, published by the Board, envisaged the investment of about £520 milllion, the closing down of uneconomic pits, extensive modernisation, and the sinking of new pits.

The operating profit for 1950 was £24·2 million, (1949, £29·4 million). Income and interim interest (compensation) took £14·5 million (1949, £13·2 million; the increase was due to a rise in the interest rate). The surplus was £8·3 million (1949, £9·5 million).

Wages rose somewhat in the year, but less than the cost of living, or than productivity. The two rises granted amounted to an increase of 10 per cent. to 12 per cent. for those on minimum rates, whilst the price index rose by 20 per cent.

TRANSPORT

The Transport Report for 1950 showed an improved financial position, due largely to the railways. The operating profit was £40 million, an increase of £8·7 million, and the deficit after paying central charges was £14·1 million, £6·7 million less than in the previous year. Compensation interest took £35·2 million.

Evidence was accumulating that the compensation being paid to the former owners was too heavy. The Transport Commission was still increasing its depreciation provision "in order to take care of assets

which do not in practice stay in service for the full life assumed".
(This was particularly true of the old "private owners' wagons"
for which £41·6 millions was paid; 28 per cent. of them had been
scrapped in the first three years.)

The Commission complained that restrictions on capital expenditure
were holding up re-equipment and modernisation: "much necessary
work had to be held in abeyance".

ELECTRICITY

Electricity's Annual Report for the year ending the 31st March,
1950, showed an overall surplus of £7,163,236, compared to
£4,391,684 in the previous year.

The main problem was that of the shortage of electricity expected
for the following winter. Demand greatly exceeded supply, largely
because the increase in the volume of industrial production was
greater than the increase in electricity supply. The Authority expressed
serious concern at the Government's proposals for limiting capital
investment, and at the shortage of raw materials. The chairman, Lord
Citrine, stated publicly in June 1951 that he suspected that steel intended
for the Authority was being diverted to other purposes.

The Authority had shown a niggardly attitude to the wage claims
of power-station workers. Negotiations over an application for an
increase made in April, 1951, were dragged out for months, and as a
result a ban was placed on overtime which affected some 6,000 men
at 40 stations. The real value of earnings was of course falling all the
time.

With regard to most of the nationalised industries, the low level of
wages and the long-drawn-out negotiations for improvements were
probably one of the main factors in damping the enthusiasm of the
working class for nationalisation on principle.

STEEL

The Iron and Steel Corporation actually "took over" on the 15th
February, 1951.

DI

CHAPTER 43

Industrial Affairs, 1950–1

THE matters calling for attention in this chapter are the wage freeze; the Trades Union Congress; the dock strikes; and the prosecution of dockers in London, with the resulting repeal of Order 1,305.

THE WAGE FREEZE

The wage freeze has been almost sufficiently dealt with in the previous chapter. I need only add a few points.

One is a statement of government policy on wages, in the best Tory tradition, on the 2nd November, 1950, when Gaitskell said:

"The increase in wages should not go beyond what is justified by increases in production, after allowing for other claims, especially the claims of exports and defence."

Apart from its fundamentally unsocialist basis, the sentence deserves a little study, in the hope of determining what it means. That increases in wages should march with increases in production (so that capitalist inefficiency may command the underpayment of workers) has at any rate a definite meaning; but what is the effect of "after allowing"? If it has any meaning, it must involve the proposition that, even if workers can show that production has increased, they can still only have an increase in wages after x per cent. has been "allowed" to pay for armaments or keep down the price of exports. Thus, we have the "socialist" Chancellor of the Exchequer of a "socialist" government saying to the workers who elected him:

"If prices go up against you, and you want an increase in your wages to meet that, and thus to prevent your real wages falling, I must warn you that the policy of the Government is as follows:

"1. You can't have a rise at all unless production, in spite of raw material shortages, plain incompetence on the part of your employers, or other obstacles beyond your control, has shown an actual rise;

"2. You can't have it even then if in the opinion of the Government, or of your employers, competent or incompetent, they cannot get export orders at prices which seem good enough to them, unless they continue to underpay you (but I shall do very little to limit their profits).

"3. And you still can't have it if the Government considers that, if it is to produce the colossal amount of armaments which the Americans order it to produce, it must ensure that you continue to be underpaid."

If that was the Government attitude, one can understand all the wage troubles we have seen in previous chapters; and one can understand, too, how by August, 1951, nearly eight million workers had wage claims pending.

T.U.C.

The Trades Union Congress, held at Blackpool from the 31st August to the 2nd September, 1951, can be thought of as a triumph for reaction or as something of an advance for the left wing, according to taste; for reaction triumphed in most of the votes but at the same time the progressive forces showed a steady maintenance of about two million votes, a definite improvement on earlier positions.

The Report of the General Council, which endorsed the Government's policy, was carried. It was highly critical, not to say abusive, of the U.S.S.R.

The main resolution on Peace and Rearmament—a composite one, as always happens—urged action to help to repair the ravages of war in Korea, consultations with a view to holding free elections for a democratic government there, and negotiation on other Far Eastern problems. It urged the Government to take a new initiative in world peace efforts by formulating a policy to end the cold war, to make possible general disarmament, to control atomic energy for solely peaceful purposes, and to tackle the world food scarcity. It was defeated on a show of hands.

A resolution welcoming the end of Marshall Aid and calling for an end of interference with British trade policy and for the equal exchange of products between nations of East and West, without political discrimination against Russian or China, was defeated by 5,213,000 to 1,795,000, after Sir Arthur Deakin had asserted that the Government had maintained a "sturdy independence" of the U.S.A., and that to trade with the U.S.S.R. meant "a loss of freedom". He even said that the U.S.S.R. would only co-operate on the basis of other countries' acceptance of "International Communism".

A resolution calling on the Government to abandon the policy of supporting the rearmament of Germany and Japan was defeated by 4,482,000 to 2,608,000, after Sir Vincent Tewson had asserted that there was no suggestion that the Nazi and Japanese war lords would be reinstated.

WAGES, PRICES AND PROFITS

On wages, prices and profits, there were two composite resolutions. The first, coming from the right wing, called for a wider and more effective control of the price of home-produced goods, reconsideration of the Government's attitude on limitation of subsidies, investigation of costs and methods of distribution, more effective control of profits with limitation of bonus issues, and removal of purchase tax from household necessities. It was passed unanimously.

The second of these resolutions demanded higher wages, to come out of profits. This was defeated by 5,284,000 to 2,199,000, after the spokesman for the "platform" had attacked the notion of linking wages with profits. Some influence may have been exercised by Gaitskell who had addressed the Conference earlier, justifying rearmament, declaring that prices would rise still further and that living standards must be cut, and appealing for wage restraint. His speech, which received no applause beyond a little mild clapping at the end, deserves a little attention. He adopted what can fairly be called a banker's attitude, expressing anxiety lest too pressing demands by workers might cause inflation, and thus "be fatal to our position as a centre of world trade and finance". As was pointed out in *Labour Monthly*, at p. 468, he did not mention "that British capitalism under American dictation has already abandoned its position in *world trade*—accepting the Wall Street ban on nearly all trade with socialist countries—and that as a centre of *world finance* (i.e. of imperialist monopoly capital) it was recognised by the Scarborough T.U.C. 25 years ago to be a menace to the British and all other workers".

On the issue of payment for dentures and spectacles, a resolution demanding its abolition was defeated by 3,775,000 to 3,272,000; the vote of the National Union of Railwaymen, amounting to 392,000, was not brought in by a mistake. Had it been cast as the delegation of the union had decided, the majority against the resolution would have been reduced to 111,000.

As Peter Kerrigan wrote in an article in *World News* on the Conference, on the 15th September:

"The main decisions on Peace, German and Japanese Rearmament, and East-West Trade ... represent a reactionary policy farther to the right than ever previously.

"The speeches of the President, Mr. A. Roberts, Sir Vincent Tewson, Mr. Arthur Deakin ... Sir William Lawther ... and other members of the General Council reached new untouched depths in attacks on those who supported peace, in deliberate misrepresentation of the policy of the Soviet Union and People's China, and in vulgar abuse of certain of the delegates. ... (But) the debates, the votes, and the general atmosphere ... reflect the growth of the left forces and those struggling for peace."

DOCK STRIKE

The Dock Strike began in Birkenhead on the 2nd February, 1951, when 2,000 port workers struck in protest against the acceptance of an increase of 11s. a week by a delegate conference. It spread to Liverpool at once, and within a day or two to Manchester. At the same time, in London, which was scarcely affected by the dispute at all, 250 men came out in sympathy; and by the 7th February, according to the National Dock Labour Board, there were 9,589 out in Merseyside, and 6,501 working; 2,377 out in Manchester and 128 working; and 450 out in London.

The Government acted with a vigour—and, as it proved in the result, a stupidity—which would have done credit to the most intolerant of Tories. On the 8th February, it arrested seven of the dockers' leaders, four in London, and three in Liverpool (and thereby perhaps relieved the London men from a difficult decision, whether to call all the London men out and meet with an unsatisfactory response since London's only concern with the dispute was one of sympathy, or to appear to be sacrificing the Merseyside men by adopting the more prudent course of not calling London out!).

PROSECUTION

On the following day, the leaders were charged with conspiracy "between the 8th October and the 6th February to incite dock workers to strike in connection with trade disputes, contrary to the provisions of Order 1305", (with which anti-strike legislation I have dealt in Chapter 35). The immediate and inevitable result was that on the same evening 6,700 London dock workers came out on strike.

The case took a curious course. The Government, acting in haste, ignorance, or plain stupidity, had not taken the trouble to notice that Order 1305 dealt only with strikes in connection with trade disputes, and that the strike in question did not turn on a "trade dispute", but on a dispute between members of the Transport and General Workers Union and officials of that union.

The solicitor acting for the dockers' leaders took this point in the police court, but on the 16th March they were committed for trial at the Central Criminal Court. The Government, faced with this point, did not drop the case but sought to get round it by adding two additional charges; the first of these (the second charge in the indictment) accused the men of "conspiracy otherwise than in contemplation or furtherance of a trade dispute to induce dock workers employed under the Dock Labour Scheme to absent themselves from employment without their employers' consent and before completion of their contracts"; and the second (third in the indictment) was "conspiracy to obstruct dock employers in the conduct of their business by inducing dock workers to absent themselves."*

When the case came on for trial on the 9th April, with nearly 10,000 dockers on strike in protest, and demonstrations outside the Court, the jury found the accused guilty on the second charge; they did not consider the third charge because the judge had instructed them not to do so if they were agreed on the second charge; and they failed to agree on the first charge (the charge originally made, based on Order 1305). This was taken to be an illogical verdict, because it was to be assumed that the jury were not agreed on the question whether there was a trade dispute, and if they were not agreed on that they could not logically convict on the second charge, which must rest on a finding that there was no trade dispute.

The Government, having thus got itself into a thorough mess, had to drop the prosecution, mouthing threats against the men as it did so. The strike then stopped.

REPEAL OF ORDER 1305

As I have said, this prosecution led pretty directly to the long overdue repeal of Order 1305, which came on the 14th August, 1951.

* The legal position was a little complicated. If there was a trade dispute, Order 1305 applied; if there was no trade dispute, it did not apply, but then the protection given to workers by the Trade Disputes Act, 1906, and certain older Acts, also did not apply, and the accused might well be held guilty under the common law of conspiracy, which the working class had spent over a century trying to remove from the arsenal of weapons of the ruling class. See the matter more fully dealt with in *The Law Versus the Trade Unions*, Lawrence and Wishart, 1958, pp. 105-5.

CHAPTER 44

Social Affairs, 1950-1

HOUSING suffered, of course, gravely towards the end of the year; but there was something to be said to the credit of the Government.

The total housing efforts for the period of the Labour Government, up to the end of 1950, was:

Permanent dwellings provided by local authorities, housing associations, and government departments .	663,342
Permanent dwellings provided by private builders .	158,176
Temporary houses	157,146
Conversions and adaptations of existing premises . .	135,010
Repair of unoccupied war-damaged dwellings . .	144,421
Requisitioned properties	24,298
Temporary huts	2,852
Service camps	27,415
Total	1,312,660

Of these 821,518 were new permanent dwellings. A little over four-fifths of the permanent dwellings were built by local authorities to rent. During 1950, the proportion built by private enterprise dropped still lower, to 27,358 out of 198,171—or 13 per cent. This aroused much indignation among the Tories (and has been reversed by them since) but in fact was one of the good achievements of the Labour Government. Local authorities in that period built far more dwellings annually than in any year before the war. This meant fewer houses for sale and more to rent at rents within working-class means.

Nevertheless, the new housing provided fell far short of needs. While the number of new dwellings provided in 1950 was just under 200,000—about 1,000 more than in 1949—the actual number of families rehoused each year was dropping, due to the fact that other re-housing measures—conversion, requisitioning, war-damage repairs, etc.—were coming to an end.

In his statement on the rearmament programme on the 29th January, Attlee said "there must also be some reduction in the civil building programme, though we shall do our utmost to avoid large or widespread interference with it".

In the first half of 1951, 6,000 fewer new dwellings were built than in the corresponding period of 1950, a reduction of one-fifth compared with 1948. By September, 1951, the total of new permanent dwellings built in Great Britain since the war was 961,484, of which 787,940 were built by local authorities.

One of the achievements of the Labour Government, though perhaps a negative one, was that it maintained rent control in the face of all Tory attacks.

The effect of rearmament on housing was felt mainly through the shortage of steel which held up progress on numbers of flats in 1951.

EDUCATION

The Annual Report of the Ministry of Education for 1950 showed that the building effort had been devoted to the provision of basic accommodation for school entrants rather than to the development of educational opportunities. In January, 1951, there were still 33,176 classes with over 40 pupils, and 28,234 classes in secondary schools with over 30.

The shortage of teachers was still a problem; the total number increased by about 8,000 in 1950, an increase insufficient to improve staffing standards. The implementation of the provisions of the Education Act for nursery schools for all who wanted them and county colleges for further education were still in abeyance.

On the 28th June, 1951, the Minister of Education, in answer to a Parliamentary question, said that the effect of reductions in the national investment programme on education was that while "the programme to meet the increase in the school roll and for the movement of population to new housing estates and new towns will continue as planned, it will however not be possible to increase certain other parts of the programme at the rate previously contemplated". Further questioned, he said: "The effect of the defence programme will be delay in increased provision for technical education, but as far as the projects approved for 1951-2 are concerned it should not affect the present programme." He said that those parts of the programme which were to be limited were "technical education. . . ; school meals service; special schools; minor improvements to existing schools".

The Ministry's Report for 1951 showed that 444 new schools came into use during the year and another 1,130 were under construction, the highest in any post-war year. The shortage of teachers continued during 1951—the net increase over 1950 was just over 5,000, not enough even to meet the needs of additional children entering school. Thus the reduction in over-large classes achieved in 1950 was not maintained in 1951. The school meals service ceased to expand, and in October 1951 dropped to below the 1947 level. The reasons were two: the increase in price of school meals and, according to the Report, "the demands of the defence programme on raw materials began to have some adverse effect".

HEALTH SERVICES

The Health Services also suffered. The "ceiling" of £400 million imposed by the Budget, at a time when prices were rising, represented a substantial cut.

As a result of the limitations imposed on capital investment, and the diversion of resources to the armaments programme, no new hospitals at all were built in this period; this meant that the whole six years of the Labour Government passed without any at all. And all that remained of the promised health centres was that in April, 1951, one large centre was under construction and tenders for two smaller ones had been invited.

PENSIONS

Rising prices made old age pensions and other benefits increasingly inadequate, and pressure for increases developed. The Minister, replying to Parliamentary Questions, said in February, 1951, that to increase the pension for a single person from 26s. to 30s., with proportionate increases for married couples, would cost about £43 million a year, rising in future years as the number of pensioners increased. The National Association of Old Age Pensioners was asking for 40s. a week. The Minister said she had received a deputation and told them "that their claims would have to be looked at as part of the country's economic position as a whole".

The Chancellor of the Exchequer, asked what was the current value of 26s. and 42s. respectively as compared with October 1946, replied that in January 1951 the purchasing power of 26s. was 22s. 6d. and that of 42s. was 35s. 9d. compared with October 1946. In the Budget the retirement pension was increased from 26s. to 30s. for a single person and from 42s. to 50s. for a married couple, but these increases were only to be paid where the man was over 70 or woman over 65. The amount of earnings permitted without affecting the pension was increased from 20s. to 40s. a week. This was not enough to keep pace with the rise of the cost of living to date—still less with the rise which took place later in the year.

NATIONAL ASSISTANCE

The growing inadequacy of the statutory benefits led to increasing numbers going on to National Assistance. By the end of 1950 the National Assistance Board was assisting to maintain over 2,250,000 people, or 1 in 22 of the population. During the year there had been a net increase of 156,392 in the number catered for by the Board. In September, 1951, new scales of Assistance were introduced, the possible payment to a single person being increased from 26s. to 30s., and that to husband and wife from 43s. 6d. to 50s.; allowance for rent was payable in addition.

LOCAL ELECTIONS

The Local Elections in the year had no very remarkable results. *The Times* of the 12th May, 1951, gave the totals from 392 Boroughs as follows:

	Gains	Losses
Labour	129	132
Tory	188	85
Communist	Nil	Nil
Independent	47	132

A large proportion of the Tory gains were from "Independents", a number of Labour gains were from Liberals. As for the County Boroughs, these elections gave control to Labour of 27 County Boroughs, compared with 32 in 1950 and 52 in 1946. Labour had a net gain in the number of seats in 32 councils and net loss in 28.

In non-county boroughs, Labour did better; in those with a population of over 30,000, it had a net gain in 39 and a net loss in 32.

CHAPTER 45

Labour Party Policy, 1950-1

As it was plain that a General Election might come in the near future, it is not surprising that a number of statements or pamphlets were put out in 1951. On the 27th August—less than two months, as it turned out, before polling-day brought the Labour Government to an end—the Labour Party published a Policy Statement called *Our First Duty Peace*. Shortly before, in July, *One Way Only* was published, with a Foreword by Bevan Harold Wilson, and John Freeman. And on the 21st September, *Tribune* published *Going Our Way*, written by Bevan, Wilson, Freeman, and others.

"OUR FIRST DUTY PEACE"

The official pamphlet, *Our First Duty Peace*, was primarily a defence of the armaments policy of the government against the growing opposition to it within the Labour movement.

I adopt the comments made upon it by John Gollan in *World News* of the 8th September, 1951:

"It is a manifesto for war.

"Despite the deceitful anti-Tory phrases with which each section concludes, its main purpose is the defence of the criminal right-wing policy and its disastrous consequences, against the growing opposition to that policy in the Labour Movement.

"The Agenda for the Labour Party Conference was unprecedented for the number and scope of the critical resolutions tabled. They covered every aspect of policy, but the main target of criticism was the arms programme . . . some of the largest unions and Labour Parties were sponsors for the resolutions. It is against this powerful force, even more than the Bevan group, that the new Executive policy is directed. . . . .

"Tied to the fatal American alliance and preparation for war, the

Executive had nothing to offer the rank and file except reduced standards and rising living costs. With preparation for war as the central issue for the right wing, even the pretence of an 'onslaught' on capitalism goes by the board. . . . Under the pressure of rank and file opposition, the Executive has been compelled to try and present its war policy as a peace policy, to try and argue that rearmament means sacrifice and no sacrifice at the same time.

"It is this which gives the Statement its imprint of patent political dishonesty, fraud and deceit, with windy meaningless platitudes serving to emphasise the complete bankruptcy of right-wing policy.

"The capitalist Press has treated the declaration with open scorn and derision. 'A flat and spiritless document', said the *Express*. The *News Chronicle* found it 'the product of tired minds'. 'It is a tepid document', declared the *Manchester Guardian*, while *The Times* condemned its 'complete absence of a coherent policy to meet the problems of the next few years'.

"Alarm at the growing danger of war is the outstanding feature in the trade unions and Labour Parties. There is no popular support for the American alliance, but on the contrary, the growing fear that the alliance will drag us into war. There is widespread opposition to the rearming of Germany and Japan, and the virtual alliance with Franco. They want a cease fire in Korea. There is concern about the developing tension in Persia.

"The Statement avoids these central issues of discussion in the movement and the country. . . . To attempt to discuss them, to attempt to justify Government policy, would be an exposure of the lie which forms the heart of this document . . . that Soviet policy is the menace and that 'The only aim of our rearmament is to prevent war. This cannot be stated too often.' The arms programme, it continues, is 'the minimum required to deter aggression and to prevent a third world war'.

"But what is the origin of the arms programme? Its roots are to be found not in Korea or Soviet policy, but in the Truman doctrine of 1947, the Marshall Plan and the signing of the Atlantic War Pact in 1949, which disrupted the United Nations.

"From that date the war preparations have been speeded up and the American bases established. The armies were expanded and co-ordinated under Eisenhower, the arms programme worked out, the decisions taken to grab the whole of Korea as a base, rearm the

Germans and Japanese and bring Franco and Tito into the war alliance.

"The Statement then argues: 'Once there is clear proof of a change of heart in the countries which now threaten aggression, negotiations can and must be taken to reduce the weight of armaments in every country . . .' But what clear proof? What change of heart? The very fact that the Executive in its Statement refuses to mention, far less discuss, the Soviet propositions for negotiation, while at the same time it does not advance any itself, is the clearest indication that war, not peace, is the aim.

" 'In diverting a part of our industrial effort towards rearmament', continues the Statement, 'it is vital that we do not endanger the economic and social structure. . . . The burden of rearmament . . . can be carried by our economy without too great a strain.'

"This ludicrous assertion had already been laughed out of court by events. Rearmament has already produced disruption and crisis. . . . The balance of payments . . . has been destroyed. . . .

"Above all the rapidly rising costs of living, one of the main signs of strain in the economy, has produced nation-wide revolt. All the unions are demanding wage increases.

"What measures does the programme propose to halt rising living costs? Some more price controls, a few trifling measures against monopoly practices such as retail price maintenance . . . and windy platitudes which mean nothing. . . . As for the bold claim that the greatest sacrifice 'should be made by those who have large unearned incomes', the proposal boils down to the Gaitskell swindle of dividend 'limitation'.

"All this does not stop the Statement claiming that 'Labour believes that the maintenance of the social services is the first charge on the community. The weak and the sick, the young and the old, must not be made to carry the cost of rearmament.' . . .

"Rearmament is daily reducing the value of the social services and effectively cutting them. It is precisely the sick and the aged who feel the pinch of rising prices most. . . .

"With not a single new proposition for new social advance or attack upon capitalism, with the Statement itself declaring that the essence of socialism is a balance of priorities within present limits, 'Our First Duty—Peace' ends up with the declaration that labour's task has only begun.

" 'There is the high adventure of further socialist advance before us. This is the challenge of today' it concludes.

"This empty windy rhetoric does not terrify the capitalists. The . . . *Daily Telegraph* replies with the taunt: 'When we search the pamphlet to discover in what "the great challenge" consists, we find extraordinary little to justify any such claim.' "

"ONE WAY ONLY"

One Way Only, in its turn, had a hostile reception from the capitalist Press. It contained positive proposals for: negotiations for a general settlement with Russia, reduction of the arms programme, less dependence on the U.S.A., and the use of controls and taxation to bring down prices.

The writers argued that the extreme anti-communist forces in the U.S.A. were now dictating both American and British policy and that "in the past few weeks British resistance to American pressure has been growing weaker instead of stronger". They added that "if today the anti-communist hysteria is able to resurrect Chiang as the champion of Chinese freedom, if today the idea of German rearmament with all its perils is so lightly accepted, what restraints will there be when American power is vastly enhanced? The time has come to call a halt."

This was at once more positive and better than official Labour Party policy, but it suffered from the fatal weakness of all "Bevanite" moves in that, having seen the evils of government policy, and seen, too, what was the correct course to follow, they seemed to be trying to find a half-way house between what was right and what was wrong, in order perhaps to avoid being expelled from the Labour Party by the right-wing leadership, and thus to preserve the opportunity of taking the leadership themselves if mass opinion within the Party should reject the existing policies. Thus, they wanted to negotiate with the U.S.S.R. but they still remained fundamentally anti-Soviet, repeating, for example, the baseless slander that Soviet "aggressiveness" was only restrained by the greater strength of the capitalist powers; they wanted to reduce armaments, but still to maintain them at a high level. They wanted less—somewhat less—dependence on the U.S.A., but still did not oppose NATO, or the American bases in Britain. They were silent on agreed disarmament, on the abolition of atomic weapons, on the proposals for a Five-power Peace Pact, and on all the Soviet proposals on such points.

"GOING OUR WAY"

The *Tribune* pamphlet, *Going Our Way*, set out to show how the criticisms voiced by Bevan and his colleagues on their resignation and in *One Way Only* had been justified by events. It aroused little interest because all attention and efforts were concentrated on the Election by the time it came out.

CHAPTER 46

The General Election, 1951

THE end was approaching. On the 19th September, 1951, it was announced that the election would be held on the 25th October, and Parliament was dissolved on the 4th October.

One of the peculiarly undemocratic features of parliamentary democracy in Britain is the practice that the government in power has the right to choose the date of an election (so long only as the five-year period of a Parliament's life is not exceeded), and thus to try to pick a moment at which it may get a verdict from the electorate which it would not give if the date were fixed by law, and it thus had more time to reflect.

It was hardly to be expected that the Labour Party and Government, which had accepted the whole framework of parliamentary democracy and of capitalism, would give up that advantage; and in fact they sought to make full use of it. There was at the time a good deal of dispute as to whether Attlee had chosen wisely or unwisely, with which it is hardly necessary to concern ourselves, for the choice was made.

LABOUR PARTY CONFERENCE

One result of the choice of date was that the Labour Party Conference held at Scarborough on the 1st October, 1951, and following days, was almost obliterated by the election—something which had happened curiously often before. The Conference was cut short, lasting two and a half days instead of four and a half; there was no debate on specific resolutions, but only a general discussion of the election manifesto; and it was really little more than a large-scale "briefing" meeting.

"BEVANITE" SUCCESSES

The most significant development was the triumph of the "Bevanite" point of view in the election of the seven constituency party members of the National Executive. Four of the successful seven were Bevanites. Bevan was top of the poll, followed by Barbara Castle and Tom

Driberg, both of whom had more votes than either the ever-popular James Griffiths or Herbert Morrison. Dalton was only just elected, getting fewer votes than the fourth Bevanite, Ian Mikardo. Shinwell was defeated.

ELECTION MANIFESTO

The Labour Party Election Manifesto was issued on the eve of the Conference. It was drafted by a Committee consisting of Dalton, Sam Watson (a right-wing miners' leader from Durham) Bevan, and Morgan Phillips (the general secretary of the party), accepted by the Executive with a few minor changes, and adopted by the Conference. Dalton writes at p. 375 of *High Tide and After* that serious divisions in the Executive had been expected, and that he was very proud of having "helped to maintain party unity on a critical issue" by getting it agreed.

The Manifesto paid more attention to praising past achievements than to putting forward any bold or constructive future policy. It set out a platform under four heads:

1. Peace: War was not inevitable and Labour accepted her full part in arming to save the peace by the strengthening of collective defence. But peace cannot be preserved by arms alone, and the development of backward areas was as important as rearmament. Only a Labour Government could be trusted to pursue this. "The Tory still thinks in terms of Victorian imperialism and colonial exploitation. His reaction to a crisis is to threaten force." (Not, perhaps, a very honest criticism, in the light of the Labour Government's attitude in the Anglo-Iranian oil dispute, discussed in Chapter 39.) "He would have denied freedom to India, Pakistan, Ceylon and Burma." The election was critical because if the Tories won there would be no major power in the councils of the Western nations represented by Labour.

2. Employment and Production: Full employment was Labour's greatest achievement. Largely because of it, production had risen twice as fast each year as it had under the Tories. Output was 50 per cent. above pre-war and a higher proportion of the national income than ever before was devoted to investment. World shortages had raised prices and reopened the dollar gap. New sources of raw materials in the Commonwealth must be developed. Restrictionist monopolies and combines must be attacked; concerns which failed the nation must be taken over; and new enterprises must be started wherever this will serve the national interest. (To this tiny scope had the great policy

of nationalisation been reduced, with once again the curious line that only unhealthy or badly run industries should be nationalised.)

Development councils for industry would be established, by compulsion if necessary. Workers would be more closely associated with administration in public industries. The policies which had brought prosperity to the countryside would be continued. Rural amenities would be extended and the tied cottage system checked.

3. Cost of Living: This had increased less in Britain than in most other countries, and the people had been sheltered by price control, rent control, and food subsidies. Despite the improvement in miners' wages, coal was still cheaper than in any other European country. International discussion had stabilised raw material prices and brought about a reduction in textile prices. It was hoped that other prices would fall. To that end, price controls would be extended and improvements made in vegetable and other marketing. The Tories on the other hand were against controls and bulk purchase, utility schemes and the present limit on rents.

4. Social Justice: An elaborate "then and now" contrast was made between pre-war misery and present prosperity. Full employment, social security, and the increased share of the national income falling to the wage earner were stressed, but the ownership of wealth was still concentrated in too few hands. "Labour", it said, "will press forward towards greater social equality and the establishment of equal opportunities for all."

When tax reductions became possible they would be made to benefit earners of moderate incomes; taxes on great fortunes and large unearned incomes would be increased. Steps towards equal pay would be taken. The Conservatives were opposed to a more equal society; they had proposed cuts in taxes on large incomes and opposed the profits tax and dividend freeze, and they would cut the social services in order to reduce taxes. They had voted against the Health Service, and complained that Labour was too hasty in introducing family allowances and raising old age pensions.

Labour had built 1,300,000 new dwellings since the war, would continue to build houses at the rate of 200,000 a year, and would increase the rate as soon as possible. They would give security to householders by leasehold enfranchisement. In conclusion, the choice was put: "Forward with Labour or Backward with the Tories." A look at past records should show how to vote. Under Labour the standard of living, in spite of difficulties, had been far higher than under the Conservatives. Scotland and Wales had a new vitality and the depressed areas were gone.

"Welfare at home, peace abroad, with a constant striving for international co-operation—this is Labour's aim. The Tories . . . promise no light for the future. They would take us backward into poverty and insecurity at home and grave perils abroad."

The aim of socialism seemed to be simply forgotten—or laid aside, perhaps, in the craven belief that more people would vote Labour if they no longer believed that the Party had any socialist aims.

THE TORY MANIFESTO

The Tory Manifesto emphasised the need for a stable government, which would hold the nation above party tactics. The pre-eminent position held by Britain at the end of the war had been impaired, it said, by nationalisation and by government extravagance, which had led to devaluation! A Conservative Government would cut out all "unnecessary" expenditure. The national output must be increased, and hard work, good management, and thrift must receive their due incentive and reward.

In foreign affairs, the "safety, progress, and cohesion of the British Empire and Commonwealth must be put first; to this end Imperial Preference would be maintained. Second came the need for a United Europe, including in the end the countries now behind the Iron Curtain".

The Tories supported the Labour Party's rearmament programme, but believed that better value could be got for the money. Whilst rearmament continued, an Excess Profits Tax would be imposed to deal with any "fortuitous" rise in profits; but a revision of industrial taxation was needed to give relief when profits were "ploughed back".

Restrictive practices on both sides of industry should be subject to investigation by a strengthened Monopolies Commission. All further nationalisation would be stopped. The Iron and Steel Act would be repealed, and the old Iron and Steel Board revived to supervise prices and development.

Publicly owned transport would be reorganised under regional groups. Private road hauliers would be allowed to return to business, and the 25-mile limit on private lorries would be ended. There would be more decentralisation of the coal industry. Housing would be given priority second only to defence; the target remained 300,000 houses a year. Greater freedom must be given to the private builder, and the more people who owned their homes the better. The Conservatives would provide better education and health services for the money now being spent. Town and Country Planning needed drastic overhaul. Pensions would be sympathetically reviewed, and old people encouraged to stay at work. Business must be allowed to comb world markets for food. Agriculture was promised guaranteed prices, better housing and amenities for rural areas. Food subsidies could not be radically changed at present, but later the sytem would be simplified so that only those who needed help were subsidised.

THE ELECTION CAMPAIGN

It was bound to be a curious election in a good many ways. The Labour leadership and the Tories were agreed on every major issue: support of the rearmament programme, which governed the whole field; hostility to the socialist world; the American alliance and the military occupation of Britain as a base for offensive atomic warfare; the rearming of Germany and Japan; the wars in Korea and Malaya; the crippling strategic bans on British trade; and the resulting economic burdens and cuts in the social services. They had to search for matters of serious dispute in what was left of the political and economic field.

The Labour leaders may well have been willing to lose the election in the face of the many problems that would confront the next government. The Tories were obviously hoping, in an election coming after a year of economic hardship and only a few months after a major split in the Labour leadership, for a victory with an ample working majority; and this was freely and confidently prophesied in the early stages of the election.

As for the mass of the electorate, the less politically active and conscious of them were puzzled and unhappy; they were mainly, and increasingly, concerned with the danger of war, and the Labour campaigners seized on this to accuse the Tories of war-mongering—a charge almost as plausible against themselves as it was against the Tories.

The more politically conscious working-class voters, angry as they were with the Labour leadership, were quite clear that the only way to fight their class enemies, the Tories, was to support Labour.

The Communist Party in particular saw this so clearly that it decided to run only 10 candidates instead of 100 as in 1950, in order to avoid split votes and to concentrate its efforts on defeating the Tories, while presenting through its ten candidates its alternative policy for the Labour movement.

All this led to a swing towards Labour in the later part of the campaign, and in the end the total of Labour votes actually exceeded that of the Tories.

THE RESULT

The result was curious. The figures of voting were as follows:

Electorate	.	.	34,645,573 (1950: 34,269,770)
Percentage voting	.		82·5 per cent. (1950: 84 per cent.)
Conservative vote	.		13,717,538 (1950: 12,502,567—43·5 per cent.) (48 per cent.)
Labour vote	.	.	13,948,605 (1950: 13,266,592—46·1 per cent.) (48·8 per cent.)
Liberal vote	.	.	750,556 (1950: 2,621,548—9·1 per cent.) (2·5 per cent.)
Communist vote	.		21,640 (1950: 91,746—0·3 per cent.) (0·1 per cent.)
Others	.	.	177,329 (1950: 290,218—1 per cent.) (0·6 per cent.)

The votes were distributed, under our imperfect electoral system, in such a way that the Tories, with fewer votes than Labour, and with less than half the votes cast, won an over-all majority. They had 321 seats, whilst Labour had 295, Liberals six, and others three.

So ended the election, and the rather over six years of Labour Government. I agree with the statement of the Communist Party Executive that:

"The Tory policy of the right-wing labour leaders has been the principal cause of the Tory victory. . . .

"If the Labour leaders had put forward in this election a real policy of peace, the Tories would have been overwhelmingly defeated. . . ."

I agree too with S. O. Davies, M.P., who wrote in *Labour Monthly* of December 1951, at p. 559:

"The campaign within the Labour movement lacked its traditional *élan* and enthusiasm; lacked distinctive and irreconcilable contrast . . . with immediate Tory policy. . . .

"The Tory Party were not only in agreement with our foreign

policy: in fact they proudly claimed to have been the authors of it, and that they had succeeded in forcing its adoption on the Labour Government. Many Labour candidates, I know, agree with me when I say that, had Labour gone to the country with a socialist foreign policy, that is, a policy for peace, the Tories would have suffered a defeat more severe than that of 1945. But we were hamstrung on immediate fundamentals. . . . We socialists were bedevilled by the threat of war; the appalling cost of preparations for war; its utter senseless futility; the dreadful and sickening feeling that we were hurtling headlong into disaster. . . ."

CHAPTER 47

Conclusions

THAT is the end of the story. What conclusions and lessons must be drawn?

What went wrong? Why were our great hopes and opportunities frustrated and lost? Why was so little achieved, so little changed, so much left intact? Why was there no real advance towards socialism? And why, in the face of all that, did the right-wing leaders keep pretty firm control of the Labour Party and of policy all through the years of betrayal, and for two more General Elections after the defeat of 1951?

And what of the future? How are we to put it right? How are we to find the remedy—not just to get rid of Tory mis-rule but to put in power a socialist-minded government which will really begin the work of transformation that the government of 1945 was elected to carry out?

THE MOMENT OF HOPE AND OPPORTUNITY

The hopes and opportunities of 1945 were very great indeed. The electorate, far in advance of its leaders and inspired by an upsurge of revolutionary or at least semi-revolutionary feeling, had won a great victory, and was ready and eager, if only it were given leadership, to march forward triumphantly to a socialist future, in friendship with the great socialist state of the U.S.S.R. and with all other progressive peoples.

The failure lay with the leadership; it was certainly not due to the strength of the forces of monopoly capitalism, who at the moment had neither morale nor confidence, and knew little of how the post-war world might shape or how long they might hope to last. A few shrewd blows at the start would have meant an end to their power, and the Labour Party could not merely have carried the building of a socialist Britain a very long way, but could have given moral leadership to the whole of Europe.

STARTING WRONG

What went wrong from the start? The Government, overwhelmingly right-wing in composition and outlook, far more conscious of the supposed "enemy on the left" than of the real enemy that the electorate had sent them to power to conquer, accepted the capitalist *status quo*, political and economical, as if it were a law of nature, and never really sought to alter the class-structure of the nation, to attack the seats and sources of power, or even to weaken the ruling class. It was in reality, as Emile Burns puts it at p. 12 of *Right-wing Labour*, "no instrument of social change, but a valuable instrument of the monopoly capitalists in damping down the post-war unease and in helping the monopoly capitalists to solve the contradictions that faced them". It is not surprising that the ruling class soon recovered from its panic and managed to hold a very large measure of its old power.

HOSTILITY TO THE SOVIET UNION

It was natural—if fatal—that such leaders should display hostility to the socialist State from the very moment of taking office. (How deep and important this hostility was can be judged from the answer given to me in the Autumn of 1945 by a Cabinet Minister who had hitherto seemed to be not unfriendly to the U.S.S.R., when I reproached him for joining in the anti-Soviet chorus of his colleagues. He said: "It did not take me long to learn that you cannot get ahead in this government unless you are anti-Soviet.")

It was natural, too, that a leadership which had followed that course should accept the Cold War; to do so was, alas!, a complete ideological surrender, a destruction of any hope of socialism and a guarantee of economic near-disaster.

A LESSON

One lesson to be drawn is, I think, that right-wing Social Democracy can never do more than govern a "welfare" capitalist state with moderate efficiency; certainly, no such government ever has done. It may be that one ought to add one more question to those grouped at the beginning of this chapter: "Had we ever any reason for expecting anything much better?"

What in truth the story of this Labour Government teaches us is that, in this country above all, with its wily and deeply-entrenched ruling class, we can only win socialism through a determined party of the working class, fully understanding and accepting the class struggle, and resolved to carry that struggle through to victory.

WHY ARE THEY STILL THERE?

A more important question today is: how has it been possible that the leadership maintained its position right through the six and a half years, without even any ministerial defection until very near the end? And, even more, that it has since kept that position for so long?

Certainly it is not because the left wing of the Labour Party, or the Communist Party, or any other opponent of the right-wing policy, gave up fighting even for a moment, either in Parliament, or in Labour Party or Trade Union Conferences, or in the country generally; and their success in averting any worse betrayals and in forcing the right wing to some measure of restraint was greater than appeared on the surface. But it was never great enough to dislodge the leadership or to change fundamentally the policy.

Why was it not great enough? There was more than one cause. Probably the most powerful and enduring was the loyalty of the rank and file. The working class, through their trade union movement, had created the Labour Party; it was their political weapon; they were proud of it, and were unwilling lightly to condemn it, or to conclude that the leaders were wrong. When they were betrayed by MacDonald, Snowden, and Thomas, to whom they had given their loyalty, they thought of that treason as a sad aberration, a matter of personal weaknesses, and not as an essential feature of right-wing outlooks and policies; and they gradually fogot the warning it carried. And now, they had put the new leadership in power; they rejoiced, and were willing to support it, to accept its explanations and arguments, and to think that actions or inactions that seemed difficult to understand were due to the economic situation. And very many of them were affected by the incessant anti-communist and anti-Soviet propaganda, developed not only by their leaders but by the delighted capitalists in every newspaper they read (except the *Daily Worker*), and on the radio and television.

There were other causes. In Parliament, and among those who hoped to get into Parliament, a contributory cause was the "stick and carrot" technique of the management—perhaps I should call it "sweets and blackmail"—of which many left-wing Members complained bitterly to me in private. It was easy to tell Members that if they opposed the Government they could give up all hope of promotion to office;

that, if they went a little further, steps would be taken to see that they were not nominated by their constituencies to stand at the next General Election; and that, if they went a little further still, they would be expelled from the Party. And aspirants for parliamentary seats could be given similar lessons; moreover, left-wing aspirants, even after constituency parties had adopted them, might find themselves rejected by Transport House.

At conferences, the great experience and skill of the management could be brought to bear to work directly and indirectly for favourable votes, and if necessarily the leadership could resort to the powerful appeal "not to rock the boat in a rough sea" lest you help the Tories.

One way and another, all these causes combined to keep the leadership in the driving seat from 1945 until the present time; but one of the results was the sad elections of 1950, 1951, 1955, and 1959.

WHAT IS TO BE DONE?

How is all this to be remedied? One cannot march towards socialism under the present leadership of the Labour Party. Nor can the battle be fought otherwise than by the strength of the organised working class, whose mass trade union organisations are marshalled within the Labour Party, which thereby continues to hold the loyalty of the majority of the workers despite disappointments, betrayals and defeats. The tactics of the dominant leadership in the Labour Party are to maintain its hold by dividing the ranks of those truly fighting for socialism, by disciplining the left as "disrupters", and by banning association with the Marxist section of socialist workers organised in the Communist Party. Victory for socialism will require the unity of the progressive forces in the country, the Labour Party, the working class, the youth, the intelligentsia, and the Communist Party, a body, if I may paraphrase what R.H. Tawney wrote as far back as 1932, "at once dynamic and antiseptic ... possessing not merely opinions but convictions, and acting as it believes". And, as Tawney added: "Till something analogous to it develops in England, Labour will be plaintive, not formidable, and its business will not march."

When all these elements are united, they will find it easy to rally the mass of the people, already militant, profoundly disgusted with the Tories, and longing for the chance to express itself through a mass working-class party. The prospects for relatively swift changes are favourable; the increased militancy of the trade union movement, the enthusiastic contribution of youth in the various developments of the peace movement, and the recent growth of the Communist Party, all bring great promise and encouragement.

We shall then have a struggle not just to end the series of electoral defeats which the right-wing leadership has earned, but to transform the Labour movement and the whole political atmosphere of the country.

The struggle will succeed; we shall be on our way; we shall once more be proud of our country and its people, once more worthy successors of the workers who built the trade union movement and created Chartism.

Index